European Commission

CWITHDRAWN

European Union
Public Finance
Fourth edition

**Europe Direct is a service to help you find answers
to your questions about the European Union**

Freephone number (*):
00 800 6 7 8 9 10 11

(*) Certain mobile telephone operators do not allow access to 00 800 numbers or these calls may be billed.

More information on the European Union is available on the Internet (http://europa.eu).

Cataloguing data can be found at the end of this publication.

Luxembourg: Office for Official Publications of the European Communities, 2008

ISBN 978-92-79-06937-6

Photo credits:
Cover, © Corbis

Printed in Belgium

PRINTED ON WHITE CHLORINE-FREE PAPER

Foreword

Welcome to the fourth edition of *European Union public finance,* which provides a comprehensive update on EU budgetary and financial developments. Over the past 20 years, the EU has carried out significant reforms to the way money is made available for the EU budget as well as to its financial and budgetary procedures. These changes have accompanied and helped to deepen European integration. In today's Union of 27 countries, this edition comes at a time when effective financial and budgetary management is more important than ever before.

The first and second editions of this book covered budgetary and financial developments in the 1990s. The 1993-99 financial framework saw the adoption of the Treaty on European Union as well as the arrival of three new Member States when Austria, Finland and Sweden joined the EU in 1995. The third edition covered the financial framework negotiated under Agenda 2000, which brought us through the programming period 2000-06. EU financing in this period played a key role in paving the way for the Union's largest and most dramatic wave of enlargement to 25 Member States in 2004.

In addition to a fresh look at these important past developments, this latest edition presents the new financial framework 2007-13 and its impact on the EU budget. The accession of Bulgaria and Romania in 2007 is duly accounted for, as well as recent institutional changes. These major political and budgetary developments have been carried out in tandem with the European Commission's far-reaching reforms of its internal workings and procedures. Modernising and simplifying budgetary and financial management has led to more efficient and effective financial procedures and, crucially, faster payments. Administrative reforms are also helping to ensure a closer match between activities performed and resources allocated.

I am confident that this publication can provide a useful and accurate insight into Community public finances. It is also my hope that it will serve as a solid reference work for all those interested in EU budgetary matters.

The European Union's finances are in constant development. The system they represent is both a legacy of the past – which explains in part the complexity – and an ongoing effort to improve and adapt. Further changes will be required in the years ahead.

The budget is the EU's financial lever in developing its policies and goals. It is my wish that this publication provide readers with the information they need to gain a better understanding of the financial aspects in building a competitive and more prosperous Europe.

Dalia Grybauskaitė

Member of the Commission
EU Commissioner for Financial
Programming and Budget

Contents

Part 2 – The characteristics of the present financial system

Introduction

This document is divided into six parts dealing with the various aspects of the European Union's system of public finance.

Part 1: The development of the Community's financial system looks back at the series of reforms throughout the history of the European venture, which together has produced the present system. Starting from the entirely novel system first established (Chapter 1), it reviews the crisis in the Community's finances (Chapter 2), followed by the thorough overhaul at the end of the 1980s (Chapter 3). The following three chapters look at the subsequent multiannual financial frameworks (Chapters 4 to 6).

Part 2: The characteristics of the present financial system sketches out the legal basis for the Community financial system (Chapter 7), the Community financing system (Chapter 8) and the arrangements adopted since 1988 to provide a multiannual financial framework (Chapter 9).

Part 3: Establishment of the general budget describes the general principles governing the Community budget (Chapter 10) which, in order to maintain a balance between the prerogatives of the institutions, underlie the annual budgetary procedure (Chapter 11).

Part 4: Structure of the Community budget gives details of the major types of European Union revenue and expenditure. While the financing system is based on a simple basket of resources (four main categories) its operation is highly complex, as a result of the arrangements which have been made to correct certain imbalances in the net positions of the Member States (Chapter 12). Expenditure is presented by heading in the multiannual financial framework (Chapter 13).

Once the budget has been voted, the amount entered must be spent in accordance with the rules and in a cost-effective manner. The mechanisms for achieving this are set out in **Part 5: Implementation and external control.** Chapter 14 presents the rules governing budget implementation. This is followed by a broad description of the Union's accounting system (Chapter 15), internal control in the Commission and the arrangements for external scrutiny of Community spending by the Court of Auditors and the European Parliament (Chapter 16).

Finally, **Part 6: Operations outside the general budget** presents the ancillary financial mechanisms: borrowing and lending operations (Chapter 17) and the European Development Fund (Chapter 18).

This fourth edition includes two new chapters (Chapters 6 and 13 on the 2007-13 financial framework). Many chapters have undergone in-depth revision compared to the previous editions. In particular, Chapter 5 includes an analysis of the budgetary impact of the 2004 enlargement. The new (2007) own resources decision is dealt with in Chapters 8 and 12. Chapter 15, on consolidated accounts, and Chapter 16, on internal and external control, have been almost entirely rewritten.

Part 1

THE DEVELOPMENT OF THE COMMUNITY'S FINANCIAL SYSTEM

Chapter 1

The development of an original financial system (1951-75)

A number of major developments marked the Community's financial system during its first 20 years of existence:

— the move towards the unification of the budgetary instruments;

— progress towards the financial autonomy of the Community;

— the development of common policies;

— the search for a balance between the institutions in the exercise of powers over the budget;

— the first enlargement of the European Communities.

These are examined in turn.

1. The move towards unification of the budgetary instruments

The creation, in a few years, of the European Coal and Steel Community, the European Economic Community and the European Atomic Energy Community led to the co-existence of a number of separate budgets for European policies.

— The 1951 ECSC Treaty [1] provided for an administrative budget and an operating budget.

— The 1957 EEC Treaty [2] established a single budget.

— The 1957 Euratom Treaty set up an administrative budget and a research and investment budget.

Subsequently, an important effort was undertaken to unify and simplify the European institutions and, notably, their budgets.

— The 1965 Merger Treaty incorporated the ECSC and Euratom administrative budgets into the EEC budget. This Treaty replaced the three Councils of Ministers (EEC, ECSC and Euratom) and the two Commissions (EEC, Euratom) and the High Authority (ECSC) with a single Council and a single Commission, respectively. This administrative merger was supplemented by the institution of a single operative budget.

— The 1970 Luxembourg Treaty incorporated the Euratom research and investment budget into the general budget. This Treaty replaced the system whereby the Communities were funded by contributions from Member States with that of own resources. It also put in place a single budget for the Communities.

— The expiry of the ECSC Treaty in 2002 further simplified the budget of Community institutions. Between 1970 and 2002 two budgets co-existed: the general budget and the ECSC operating budget. The rules of the Treaty establishing the European Community have applied to the coal and steel trade since the expiry of the ECSC Treaty. A protocol on the financial consequences of the expiry of the ECSC Treaty and on the research fund for coal and steel is annexed to the Treaty of

---

[1]   The Treaty establishing the European Coal and Steel Community was signed in Paris on 18 April 1951 and entered into force on 24 July 1952, with a validity period limited to 50 years. The Treaty expired on 23 July 2002 after being amended on various occasions.

[2]   The 'Treaties of Rome' were signed in Rome in March 1957. The first Treaty established the European Economic Community (EEC) and the second the European Atomic Energy Community, better known as Euratom. These two Treaties entered into force on 1 January 1958.

Nice (2001). This protocol provides for the transfer of all assets and liabilities of the ECSC to the European Community and for the use of the net worth of these assets and liabilities for research in the sectors related to the coal and steel industry.

2. Progress towards financial autonomy

2.1. ECSC

The original 1951 Paris Treaty gave the ECSC financial autonomy. Article 49 of the Treaty stated that 'the High Authority is empowered to procure the funds it requires to carry out its tasks:

— by imposing levies on the production of coal and steel;

— by contracting loans.'

Further provisions of the ECSC Treaty defined which expenditure could be undertaken with the levies. The Treaty stipulated that the levies should be assessed annually on the various products according to their average value and that the rate thereof should 'not exceed 1 % unless previously authorised by the Council, acting by a two-thirds majority'. The Treaty also stated that 'the mode of assessment and collection shall be determined by a general decision of the High Authority taken after consulting the Council' [1].

In other words, the High Authority was granted extensive autonomy as to decisions regarding levies, within the limits laid out by the Treaty.

Since the 1965 Merger Treaty, the ECSC administrative budget has been incorporated in the general budget. The operating budget alone continued being treated separately until the Treaty expired in 2002, but in practical terms this became less and less significant as the levy yield diminished.

---

[1]   See Article 50, ECSC Treaty.

2.2. General budget

From 1958 to 1970 the EEC budget and the Euratom budget (and, from 1965 onwards, the ECSC administrative budget) were financed by a system of Member States' contributions.

In addition to imposing an obligation to balance budgets, the EEC Treaty established a 'scale' applicable to the financial contributions of Member States (28 % for Germany, France and Italy, 7.9 % for Belgium and the Netherlands and 0.2 % for Luxembourg), irrespective of any other revenue. At the same time, a different scale was applied for financing the European Social Fund (set up in 1957 by the Treaty of Rome and later reformed in 1971). Unanimity was required to modify these scales.

The Treaty further indicated that the Commission should submit proposals to the Council to replace the contributions of Member States by the Community's own resources, 'in particular by revenue accruing from the common customs tariff' [1].

The Decision of 21 April 1970 [2] introduced the system of own resources for the general budget, as a progressive 'replacement of financial contributions from Member States', with effect from 1971. Own resources included:

— customs duties, which, in a gradual process lasting from 1971 to 1975, were transferred to the Community;

— agricultural levies, which have been paid in full to the Community since 1971;

— VAT-based revenue (initially limited to a 1 % rate): the Community VAT arrangements were applied gradually as progress was made in harmonising the VAT base (sixth directive in 1977 and ninth directive in 1979).

During the progressive implementation of this new system, financial contributions from the Member States were required to ensure that the budget of the Communities was in balance. However, Article 4 of the

[1]   See Articles 200-201 *et seq.* of the EEC Treaty (1957).
[2]   OJ L 94, 28.10.1970, p. 19.

decision provided that, 'from 1 January 1975 the budget of the Communities [should], irrespective of other revenue, be financed entirely from the Communities' own resources'.

This would notably entail setting the rate applicable to value added tax 'within the framework of the budgetary procedure', that is, on a yearly basis with potentially frequent changes. In case the rate had not been adopted at the beginning of the financial year, the decision further stated that the rate previously fixed should remain applicable until the entry into force of a new rate.

This own resources decision, which could not be changed unless unanimity was reached in the Council, thus created a stable basis for financing the Union. The general budget would henceforth not depend on Member States' contributions, which could have placed the Community in a state of budgetary as well as political dependence towards the Member States.

The Decision of 21 April 1970 started applying in 1971 and has been applied in full since 1979. Member States paid transitional contributions to balance the general budget over the period 1971-78, then very small residual contributions from 1979 to 1981 and exceptionally reimbursable and non-reimbursable advances in 1984 and 1985 before the 'balancing' GNP/GNI-based own resource was introduced in 1988 (see Chapter 3).

3. The development of common policies

The early achievements were:

— the creation of the European Agricultural Guidance and Guarantee Fund (EAGGF) in April 1962;

— the research policy, initially based on the Euratom Treaty (and therefore confined at the outset to the nuclear field), but since extended to many other fields;

— the reform of the European Social Fund (ESF), set up by the Treaty of Rome, in 1971;

— the establishment of the European Regional Development Fund (ERDF) in March 1975.

It is striking to note that the successors to these early programmes still constitute a significant part of the current EU budget.

4. Search for a balance between the institutions

4.1. ECSC budget

The 1951 Treaty of Paris provided that decision-making powers on budgetary matters were all exercised by the High Authority and an auditor was appointed for the purposes of budget control.

The 1975 Treaty of Brussels assigned budget control powers to the Court of Auditors.

4.2. General budget

Under the 1957 Treaties of Rome EEC and Euratom budget decisions were the exclusive prerogative of the Council, the sole budgetary authority. In practice, the institutions were responsible for the various stages of the budgetary procedure as follows:

— establishment of the preliminary draft budget: Commission;

— adoption of budget: Council, after consulting Parliament;

— implementation of budget: Commission;

— discharge: Council.

Budget control was exercised by an autonomous body: the Audit Board.

The 1970 Luxembourg Treaty made the following changes to budgetary decision-making powers:

— introduction of the distinction between compulsory expenditure and non-compulsory expenditure;

— power to adopt the budget attributed to Parliament, but not the power to decide (the last word) on non-compulsory expenditure;

— budgetary discharge given by joint Council/Parliament decision.

The next stage was the 1975 Brussels Treaty, which laid down the main rules still in force today [1]:

— Decision-making powers on budgetary matters are shared between the Council and Parliament, which henceforth form the two arms of the budgetary authority. In this new legal set-up, Parliament has the last word on non-compulsory expenditure, can reject the budget, and acts alone in granting discharge.

— Budget control is exercised by the Court of Auditors, which replaced the Audit Board from 1976 onwards.

5. First enlargement of the European Communities

The first enlargement occurred on 1 January 1973 when three new Member States – the United Kingdom, Denmark and Ireland – joined the Communities. Accession negotiations were also held with Norway, which even signed the Accession Treaty [2] but eventually refused to accede, for the first time [3].

The enlargement coincided with gradual implementation of the first own resources decision and the new Member States had to respect its provisions. But their payments were phased in (45 % in 1973, 56 % in 1974, 67.5 % in 1976 and 92 % in 1977) to reach the total amounts due in 1978. For the United Kingdom a first correction was agreed in 1975 and was gradually introduced from 1976 (see Chapter 2).

The payments in these years consisted only of traditional own resources and financial contributions from the Member States needed to balance

---

[1]   Possible changes which could be introduced by a reformed treaty are discussed in Chapter 7.

[2]   OJ L 73, 27.3.1972.

[3]   The same situation occurred during the 1995 enlargement.

the budget and other specific contributions to finance some supplementary programmes. The VAT-based resource was paid for the first time in 1979 as described in Section 2.2 above.

Chapter 2

The crisis in the Community's finances (1975-87)

The legal, political and institutional balance in the Community's financial arrangements established in the early 1970s was gradually upset over the next 10 years.

Relations among Member States and between the European institutions became increasingly strained during this period and the situation gradually degenerated into open conflict. As a result, the operation of the budgetary decision-making process became extremely difficult between 1980 and 1988 and the series of incidents was unending: numerous actions or counter-actions before the Court of Justice brought by the Council, the Commission or some Member States; delays in the adoption of the budget; rejection of the budget by Parliament; application of makeshift solutions, such as advances or special contributions, in order to finance expenditure. The budgets for 1980, 1985, 1986 and 1988 were not adopted until the financial year was well under way, so that the provisional-twelfths arrangements had to be applied for periods of five to six months.

There were three reasons for this state of affairs:

— the climate of conflict in relations between the institutions;

— the question of budgetary imbalances;

— the inadequacy of resources to cover the Community's growing needs.

1. The climate of conflict in relations between the institutions

The institutional arrangements for power-sharing between the Council and Parliament established from 1975 onwards proved difficult to implement, for two main reasons: first, some of the criteria applied were not defined in enough detail, were open to different interpretations or were difficult to adapt to changing developments in the Community budget – this was for instance the case for provisions related to compulsory vs. non-compulsory expenditure; second, no specific procedures were laid down for resolving any conflicts that might arise by applying conciliation mechanisms or imposing solutions in the absence of agreement.

Moreover, the increased legitimacy and influence enjoyed by Parliament following the direct elections in June 1979 (Act signed in Brussels in September 1976) placed a constant strain on its relations with the Council in budgetary matters.

Nevertheless, the institutions concerned did establish a dialogue to try to overcome these difficulties, leading among other things to the joint declaration by the European Parliament, the Council and the Commission of 30 June 1982 on various measures to improve the budgetary procedure[1]. But these attempts, which prefigured the first Interinstitutional Agreement concluded in 1988[2], proved to be somewhat makeshift.

1.1. The distinction between compulsory and non-compulsory expenditure

Compulsory expenditure is defined in Article 272(4) of the EC Treaty as 'expenditure necessarily resulting from this Treaty or from acts adopted in accordance therewith', other expenditure being considered by contrast as non-compulsory. Such a distinction, which is in fact used in a number of national budget systems, can be useful when drawing up a budget in order to assess whether, in the light of the legislation, different categories of expenditure are more or less indispensable or, on the contrary, discretionary.

---

[1]   OJ C 194, 28.7.1982, p. 1.
[2]   See Chapter 3.

In terms of the Community budget, the problem is that, while technical and vaguely defined, this criterion has major institutional implications, since it determines the breakdown of budgetary responsibilities between the Council and Parliament and the basic framework for Parliament's own budgetary powers (¹).

1) The breakdown of budgetary responsibilities

Under the budgetary procedure laid down in Article 272, the Commission draws up its preliminary draft budget, which then passes back and forth between the two arms of the budgetary authority: first, the Council establishes the draft budget, which is then given two alternate readings by each of the institutions(²). The Council has the final say over compulsory expenditure, the amount of which is fixed at its second reading, while Parliament has the last word on the volume of non-compulsory expenditure at its final reading of the draft budget.

The Treaty does not provide for any mechanisms to overcome disagreement between the two institutions on applying the distinction between the two types of expenditure, which is nevertheless crucial for the demarcation of their respective budgetary powers.

2) The framework for Parliament's budgetary powers

However, there are limits on Parliament's power to set the final total of non-compulsory expenditure. Without prejudice to the constraints imposed by the volume of own resources available and the need to maintain strict budgetary balance, Article 272(9) lays down a maximum rate of increase for such expenditure in relation to expenditure of the same type to be incurred during the current year(³). The Commission determines this maximum rate on the basis of objective economic parameters.

There are two cases where the maximum rate of increase may be relaxed. If the rate of increase resulting from the draft budget established by the Council is over half the maximum rate, Parliament may further increase

---

(¹)   At the time of preparing this new edition (end of 2007), Article 272 is still applicable. Proposed modifications to Treaty rules, including eliminating the distinction between compulsory and non-compulsory expenditure, are discussed in Chapter 7.

(²)   For a more detailed description of the budgetary procedure, see Chapter 11.

(³)   For a full analysis of the rule on maximum rates of increase, see Chapter 11.

the volume of non-compulsory expenditure up to half of the maximum rate. The maximum rate may also be exceeded by agreement between the Council and Parliament. However, there are three potential problems with this mechanism with regard to the exercise of budgetary powers.

— The classification of expenditure for a given financial year determines not only the extent of Parliament's power in establishing the budget for that year, but also the actual margin for manoeuvre enjoyed by Parliament in the next financial year or even subsequent years, since it serves as a basis for applying the maximum rate of increase.

— The method of calculating the maximum rate of increase is not directly or immediately tied to changes in actual budgetary requirements arising, for example, from the introduction of new policies or, more drastically, from enlargement of the Community.

— There are no Treaty provisions laying down at exactly which stage of the budgetary procedure agreement should be reached on exceeding the maximum rate of increase, or how that agreement is to be reached.

3) The 1982 joint declaration

In order to improve the budgetary procedure, the European Parliament, the Council and the Commission made a joint declaration on 30 June 1982 [1].

The declaration defined compulsory expenditure as such expenditure as the budgetary authority is obliged to enter in the budget to enable the Community to meet its obligations, both internally and externally, under the Treaties and acts adopted in accordance with the Treaties.

Annexed to the declaration was a list of all the then existing budget lines, classified as compulsory or non-compulsory. A new procedure (the trialogue between the Presidents of the three institutions) was introduced to determine the classification of new budget lines or existing lines for which the legal basis had changed.

---

[1]   Joint declaration by the European Parliament, the Council and the Commission of 30 June 1982 on various measures to improve the budgetary procedure (OJ C 194, 28.7.1982, p. 1).

The declaration also specified that the Commission should propose a classification of expenditure in its preliminary draft. If either arm of the budgetary authority could not agree with this classification, the Presidents would hold a trialogue meeting and endeavour to resolve the matter before the draft budget was established.

The declaration also laid down some rules for applying the maximum rate of increase: the basis for calculating Parliament's margin of manoeuvre would be the draft budget established by the Council at its first reading, including any letters of amendment; the maximum rate of increase should be observed not only in the initial budget but also in supplementary or amending budgets for the same financial year; the rules on exceeding the maximum rate may be applied differently to appropriations for payments and appropriations for commitments.

In these respects, the 1982 declaration proved effective in the first few years following its adoption. However, disputes over the classification of expenditure and the maximum-rate-of-increase mechanism resurfaced in 1986, when the Community had to meet requirements arising from the accession of Spain and Portugal. In the absence of agreement between the two arms of the budgetary authority, the Council brought an action before the Court of Justice, which subsequently annulled the budget for the 1986 financial year.

1.2. The clash between legislative power and budgetary power

The EEC and Euratom Treaties themselves contained the seeds of the dispute between the Council and Parliament from 1975 to 1982; while legislative power was vested exclusively in the Council, budgetary power was shared between the Council and Parliament.

Prior to this, when the Council – the legislative body – was the sole authority (up to and including the 1974 budget), powers over both fields were vested in a single institution, and so in practice no significant conflicts could arise.

After acquiring its budgetary powers, the Parliament took the view that the budget by itself was a sufficient legal basis for using the appropriations entered. So from the 1975 budget onwards, it inserted many new budget lines and entered appropriations which could sometimes be used to start up new actions; the amounts increased over the years.

For its part, the Council developed a practice of setting maximum amounts for relevant expenditure in the legislative instruments it adopted. Parliament argued that this had the effect of encroaching on its own budgetary powers over non-compulsory expenditure.

The joint declaration of 30 June 1982 also set out to find a compromise solution to this dispute.

The declaration laid down the principle that 'in order that the full importance of the budget procedure may be preserved, the fixing of maximum amounts by regulation must be avoided'.

On the other hand, in this joint declaration, Parliament, the Council and the Commission acknowledged that a legal basis separate from the budget was required for the utilisation of appropriations for any 'significant action': if such appropriations were entered in the budget before a proposal for a regulation had been presented, the Commission would present this proposal, and the Council and Parliament would then endeavour to adopt it as quickly as possible.

Implementation of these aspects of the declaration proved rather disappointing in practice.

— The 'maximum amounts' were, in practice, replaced by 'amounts deemed necessary', which the Council entered systematically in multi-annual programmes. This new concept might appear legitimate if construed as representing purely indicative estimates of the budgetary implications of the action carried out. In reality it was interpreted differently by the two institutions. The Council saw these amounts as ceilings on expenditure set by the legislator, whereas Parliament tended to consider them as minimum levels, which it could top up with additional allocations in line with its own priorities.

— As regards the need to have a legal base in order to utilise appropriations, the agreement implied that there was a consensus between the institutions on what was meant by 'significant action'. In reality, there was a tendency in a number of fields to prolong artificially the preparatory measures that required no legal base, even though the projects in question had moved on to the operational stage.

2. The question of budget imbalances

Debates on budgetary imbalances in the 1970s and 1980s mainly evolved around the contributions of two net contributors, namely the United Kingdom and Germany.

2.1. The British issue

1) The origin of the budgetary imbalance

At the time of its accession, the UK had a small agricultural sector with a large proportion of farm produce imported from outside the Community. As a result, very little of the Community's agricultural spending benefited the UK.

On the other hand, the UK contributed a relatively large amount to the financing of the Community budget mainly because its VAT base represented a higher percentage of GNP compared to other Member States.

This structural imbalance in the UK's financial links with the Community became a major political headache for the Community as early as 1974. It was the issue underlying the 1975 referendum on the question of the UK's continued membership of the Community.

2) Various arrangements introduced to resolve this matter

A first correcting mechanism was agreed at the European Council meeting in Dublin in March 1975. It was formally enforced from 1976 to 1980. This mechanism was to provide compensation (in the form of a partial repayment of the VAT-based contribution) from the Community budget to any country bearing an unacceptable financial burden. It was to be triggered if three indicators coincided: per capita GDP below 85 % of the Community average; rate of growth less than 120 % of the Community average and share of own resources payments exceeding by 10 % the share of total Community GDP. The mechanism was never triggered.

A second correcting mechanism was agreed at the Dublin European Council in November 1979 [1]. It provided for a complex compensation mechanism limiting the UK contribution to the Community budget.

---

[1] Council conclusions of 30 May 1980 on the United Kingdom contribution to the financing of the Community budget, Bulletin EC 5-1980.

Finally, a third compensation mechanism, applied to the UK contribution to Community revenue, was agreed at the Fontainebleau European Council in June 1984 and given effect by the Decision of 7 May 1985 (¹).

This decision covered two distinct arrangements:

— For 1985, compensation was provided through an ECU 1 billion reduction of the UK VAT-based contribution.

— From 1986 onwards, two-thirds (66 %) of the difference between the UK share in VAT bases and its share of total allocated expenditure, applied to total allocated expenditure, was refunded to the UK by way of a reduction in the UK VAT-based payments. This was financed by all the other Member States, in accordance with their respective percentage share of VAT payments (with the exception of Germany, which paid only two-thirds of its normal share, the balance being divided between the other Member States on the same scale).

2.2. The German issue

From 1981 onwards, Germany highlighted its position as the main contributor to the Community budget and demanded a reduction in its share of financing the rebate to the United Kingdom. The Fontainebleau Arrangement catered for this demand by making a one-third reduction in Germany's share of financing the rebate.

3. The inadequacy of resources to cover the Community's growing needs

3.1. The sources of the problem

1) The erosion of own resources

The erosion of own resources was an initial cause of the inadequacy of revenue. It was produced by the combination of two developments:

(¹)   OJ L 128, 14.5.1985.

— the diminishing yield of traditional own resources (customs duties and agricultural levies) as a result of the progress made in dismantling tariffs (GATT negotiations) and the Community's increasing self-sufficiency in food and its impact on imports of agricultural products;

— relative stagnation of VAT-based revenue, limited by a maximum rate of call, in relation to economic activity because of the declining share of GNP accounted for by consumer expenditure in the economies of the Community countries.

2) The rise in expenditure

The rise in expenditure, triggered by four different factors, was the main reason why resources were increasingly unable to keep pace with the Community's needs.

— A number of existing policies were strengthened. This was in particular the case with the revision of the European Social Fund in October 1983 and the European Regional Development Fund in June 1984.

— New policies were being launched. These included a common fisheries policy, with a common organisation of the market in that sector, in December 1981, and the establishment in 1983 of a Community system of authorised quota (total allowable catches); the establishment of the first framework programme (1984-87) for Community research; the decision taken in February 1984 on new programmes and new arrangements for Community aid to research (Esprit); the introduction of the Integrated Mediterranean Programmes in July 1985.

— Inability to contain Community agricultural expenditure. Between 1982 and 1986 actual expenditure under the EAGGF Guarantee Section grew by an average of 16 % per year and systematically exceeded the estimates made in drawing up the preliminary draft budget.

— The financial impact of the accession of new members to the Community. Greece (member since 1981) and Spain and Portugal (members since 1986) were net beneficiaries from the Community budget.

3.2. The initial attempts at a solution and their limitations

1) Moves to raise additional Community resources (1984-86)

The period after 1984 was one of insecurity for the financing of the Community. The action taken to adjust the level of revenue to expenditure requirements tended to be passive, late and makeshift (e.g. the intergovernmental advances).

From the start of the 1984 budgetary procedure it was clear that the VAT-based resources available within the 1 % limit would not be sufficient to cover the real needs during the year.

Political agreement was reached at the Fontainebleau European Council in June 1984 on the principle of raising the VAT ceiling to 1.4 %. This agreement was given practical shape in the Decision of 7 May 1985 and took effect on 1 January 1986.

In the meantime, transitional financing solutions were applied for the budgets in 1984 (repayable intergovernmental advances outside the VAT ceiling) and 1985 (non-repayable advances).

The final outturn of the 1986 budget was virtually at the 1.4 % VAT limit. The balance was only maintained because certain items of agricultural expenditure were deferred to 1987.

The problem of the exhaustion of VAT resources under the 1.4 % ceiling became acute in 1987. To cover ECU 4 billion in excess agricultural requirements, two months' payments of EAGGF advances had to be deferred.

2) The outlines of budgetary discipline and the first disappointing results

Budgetary discipline was the second type of response to the various constraints affecting the Community's finances.

The first move came on 22 March 1979 when the Council agreed on an internal code of conduct[1] to guide its decisions so that it would unilaterally restrict the growth of non-compulsory expenditure: the draft budget

---

[1]   Bulletin EC 3-1979, point 2.3.2.

was to be established on its first reading within half of the maximum rate of increase, in order to limit the impact of Parliament's margin of manoeuvre during the subsequent stages of the budgetary procedure.

The Fontainebleau European Council in June 1984 extended the scope of budgetary discipline. The Decision of 4 December 1984[1], the first reference instrument on budgetary discipline, transformed the Fontainebleau guidelines into rules, the main ones being that EAGGF Guarantee expenditure should not increase faster than the own resources base and the increase in non-compulsory expenditure should be kept below the maximum rate provided for by the Treaty (confirmation of the 1979 code of conduct).

These rules, however, turned out to have hardly any practical effect because of the growing disputes between the Council and Parliament (Parliament refused to recognise the decision on budgetary discipline, which it considered a unilateral act binding solely on the Council) and the fragmentation of the decision-making process in the Council in its various compositions (particularly the reluctance of the agriculture ministers to accept the budgetary discipline arrangements for agricultural expenditure laid down by the finance ministers).

4. Enlargements of the European Communities

In the period described in this chapter two successive enlargements took place. Greece joined the Communities on 1 January 1981, Portugal and Spain on 1 January 1986.

All three Member States benefited from transitional measures in relation to the own resources based on VAT or GNP payments (applied for the Member States that did not have the VAT bases in compliance with the Sixth Council Directive). Although they were obliged to pay these own resources in full from the first day of accession, they were immediately refunded by the percentages agreed in relevant articles of the Accession Treaties[2]. In practice this meant reducing their payments.

---

[1]   Bulletin EC 12-1984, point 1.3.3.
[2]   For Greece OJ L 291, 19.11.1979, p. 47. For Spain and Portugal OJ L 302, 15.11.1985, pp. 80 and 134.

The scenarios for the two enlargements were slightly different. In practice, Greece paid 30 % of its contributions in 1981, 50 % in 1982, 70 % in 1983, 80 % in 1984, 90 % in 1985 and 100 % from 1986 onwards. The scenario for the other two acceding Member States was more favourable to the new acceding countries, requiring Spain and Portugal to pay 13 % in 1986, 30 % in 1987, 45 % in 1988, 60 % in 1989, 75 % in 1990, 95 % in 1991 and 100 % from 1992. However, these reductions in payments for Spain and Portugal did not apply to their contribution to the financing of the UK rebate introduced by the own resources decision of 7 May 1985.

The accession of Spain and Portugal had a significant impact for the expenditure side of the Community budget. This aspect of the third enlargement is developed in the following chapter.

Chapter 3

Reform of the Community's finances: the Delors I package (1988-92)

1. From the Delors I package proposals (February 1987) to the decisions in June 1988

The third enlargement in 1986 and the conclusion of the Single Act provided the Community with a new political stimulus. The accession of Spain and Portugal and a treaty which defined fresh ambitions for the enlarged Community (single market, economic and social cohesion, research framework programme) both provided a political base for a thorough reform of the Community's financial system.

In February 1987, the Commission presented comprehensive reform proposals, the Delors package, in two communications:

— the Single Act: A new frontier for Europe (COM(87) 100);

— report on the financing of the Community budget (COM(87) 101).

In the second half of 1987, the Commission produced a series of specific proposals on agricultural policy and the Structural Funds, as well as the general budgetary and financial framework (new own resources, amendment of the Financial Regulation, budgetary discipline and the correction of budgetary imbalances).

The Brussels European Council on 11 and 12 February 1988 adopted the broad lines of the financial reform of the Community. This reform covered three main political points. First of all, it was agreed that the Community should be given additional resources to enable it to operate properly during the period 1988-92. In return, undertakings were given at the highest level concerning the overall distribution of the expenditure to be financed by these new resources: priority would be given to the cohesion policies, and budgetary discipline arrangements would be introduced to place an effective brake on agricultural expenditure. Lastly, a more equitable system of financing the Community would be introduced, linking Member States' budget contributions more closely to their level of relative prosperity.

Most of the decisions giving practical effect to the conclusions of the Brussels European Council were formally adopted on 24 June 1988.

2. The broad lines of the Community's financial reform

2.1. Own resources

The February 1988 Brussels European Council agreed that the Community should be given suitable resources that would be sufficient, stable and guaranteed, and enable it to operate correctly throughout the period from 1988 to 1992.

The practical details for achieving this were contained in Council Decision 88/376/EEC, Euratom of 24 June 1988 [1].

1) A new concept: the global own resources ceiling

The total amount of available own resources was no longer determined by the yield of traditional own resources combined with the ceiling of the VAT-based resource, but was expressed as a percentage of the Community's total GNP, increasing from 1.15 % for 1988 to 1.20 % for 1992.

A further overall ceiling of 1.30 % of total Community GNP was set for 1992 in terms of appropriations for commitments.

---

[1]   OJ L 185, 15.7.1988, p. 24.

2) The new own resources

The range of own resources was extended and the rules altered.

— The system of 'traditional' own resources was rationalised: customs duties on products covered by the ECSC Treaty were added to the common customs tariff duties; the 10 % collection costs were now to be deducted at source and no longer reimbursed separately and charged to the expenditure side.

— The arrangement for the VAT-based own resource was adjusted to better take into account the regressive nature of VAT (differences in the proportion of Member States' GNP accounted for by consumption). The VAT-based resource continued to be established by applying for all Member States a 1.4 % rate to the uniform VAT base, as determined by the Community rules. In addition, a 'capping' mechanism was introduced whereby a Member State's VAT base was not to exceed 55 % of its GNP at market prices.

— A new category of revenue – the fourth resource – was introduced, based on Member States' GNP, the most representative indicator of their economic activity, in order to match each Member State's payments more closely to its ability to pay. From now on, this 'balancing item' automatically provided the necessary financing for the Community budget, within the limit of the own resources ceiling. It was calculated by applying to a base, made up of the sum of the Member States' gross national product at market prices, a rate to be determined during the budgetary procedure in the light of the yield of all the other categories of own resources.

3) Correction of budgetary imbalances

The UK correction was adjusted to neutralise the impact of the new elements in the system of own resources (VAT base capped at 55 % of GNP and introduction of a fourth resource based on GNP). Indeed, the very objective of the June 1988 Decision was that the position of the United Kingdom should be exactly the same as it would have been if the Decision of 7 May 1985 had continued to apply (with VAT call-in rates above 1.4 %).

In technical terms, the amount of compensation was calculated as follows[1]:

— The amount was calculated in accordance with the Decision of 7 May 1985 on the assumption that the budget was to be financed in full by non-capped VAT;

— From this result was subtracted the saving which the United Kingdom enjoyed because of the capping of the VAT base at 55 % of GNP and the introduction of the fourth resource;

— The United Kingdom received the correction calculated in this way in the form of a reduction in its VAT payments.

The other 11 countries no longer financed this compensation in proportion to their VAT bases, but in proportion to their GNP. Germany was still allowed a one-third reduction of the amount it was supposed to pay.

2.2. Budgetary discipline

The European Council laid down the principles for tighter budgetary discipline in order to produce a better balance between the different categories of Community budget expenditure and to control their growth. Two documents, with different legal status, implemented these principles:

— Council Decision 88/377/EEC of 24 June 1988 concerning budgetary discipline[2];

— the Interinstitutional Agreement on budgetary discipline and improvement of the budgetary procedure, signed by Parliament, the Council and the Commission on 29 June 1988[3].

The new discipline arrangements covered all categories of expenditure and were binding on all the institutions associated in their operation: the Interinstitutional Agreement made budgetary discipline the shared responsibility of the three institutions party to it, without encroaching on the powers vested in them by the Treaties.

---

[1]   A more detailed description is provided in Chapter 12.
[2]   OJ L 185, 15.7.1988, p. 29.
[3]   OJ L 185, 15.7.1988, p. 33.

1) The financial perspective 1988-92

The financial perspective 1988-92 (see Table 3.1), an integral part of the Interinstitutional Agreement, was the key to the new budgetary discipline arrangements. It was designed to produce harmonious and controlled growth in the broad sectors of budget expenditure, while at the same time establishing a new balance in the allocation of expenditure by means of the guarantees for the development of policies connected with the Single Act and in particular the structural policies.

TABLE 3.1

Financial perspective 1988-92 (Interinstitutional Agreement of 29 June 1993 on budgetary discipline and improvement of the budgetary procedure)

Appropriations for commitments

(million ECU at 1988 prices)

	1988	1989	1990	1991	1992
1. EAGGF Guarantee	27 500	27 700	28 400	29 000	29 600
2. Structural operations	7 790	9 200	10 600	12 100	13 450
3. Policies with multiannual allocations (IMPs, research)	1 210	1 650	1 900	2 150	2 400
4. Other policies	2 103	2 385	2 500	2 700	2 800
of which: non-compulsory	1 646	1 801	1 860	1 910	1 970
5. Repayments and administration	5 700	4 950	4 500	4 000	3 550
(including financing of stock disposal)	1 240	1 400	1 400	1 400	1 400
6. Monetary reserve	1 000	1 000	1 000	1 000	1 000
Total	45 303	46 885	48 900	50 950	52 800
of which: compulsory	33 698	32 607	32 810	32 980	33 400
of which: non-compulsory	11 605	14 278	16 090	17 970	19 400
Payment appropriations required	43 779	45 300	46 900	48 600	50 100
of which: compulsory	33 640	32 604	32 740	32 910	33 110
of which: non-compulsory	10 139	12 696	14 160	15 690	16 990
Payment appropriations as % of GNP	1.12	1.14	1.15	1.16	1.17
Margin for unforeseen expenditure	0.03	0.03	0.03	0.03	0.03
Own resources required as % of GNP	1.15	1.17	1.18	1.19	1.20

Subject to the technical adjustment and revision procedures provided for in the Interinstitutional Agreement, Parliament, the Council and the Commission accepted that the financial amounts set in this perspective were to be regarded as binding expenditure ceilings for the Community.

So for the first time in the Community's history, a reference framework existed within which the various institutions would have to manoeuvre during each of the annual budgetary procedures.

This reduced the risk of clashes between legislative power and budgetary power, by requiring overall consistency between the budgetary implications of legislative decisions and the financial framework laid down.

2) Containment of agricultural expenditure

The Council laid down the principle of a guideline for controlling agricultural expenditure, setting out the practical arrangements for calculating and applying it in its decision on budgetary discipline. The agricultural guideline applied to expenditure under the EAGGF, Guarantee Section. It formed the ceiling for heading 1 in the 1988-92 financial perspective.

(a) Annual rate of growth

The annual rate of growth in expenditure was not to exceed 74 % of the annual rate of growth of Community GNP. The 1988 expenditure figure, ECU 27 500 million, was taken as the base from which to calculate the agricultural guideline in later years. This led to a relative decrease of agricultural expenditure in relation to GNP.

(b) Agricultural stocks

Mechanisms were adopted for the systematic depreciation of existing and future agricultural stocks, so that the stock situation would return to normal by 1992.

(c) Stabilisers

The stabilisation mechanisms were reinforced and extended to other production sectors. Further measures were introduced aimed at limiting supply directly by encouraging the temporary abandonment of land (set-aside) with the possibility of direct income support.

(d) Early warning system

An early warning system on the development of EAGGF Guarantee Section expenditure was introduced. It monitored expenditure chapter by chapter (and not simply as an aggregate as in the past). If the Commission were to see that expenditure was exceeding the forecast profile, or seemed likely to do so, it would make use of the management powers at its disposal. If these measures were inadequate, the Commission would examine the functioning of the agricultural stabilisers and, if necessary, present proposals to the Council to enhance their action. The Council had two months within which to act to remedy the situation.

(e) Monetary reserve

In order to contend with developments caused by significant and unforeseen movements in the dollar/ecu market rate compared with the rate used in the budget, a monetary reserve of ECU 1 000 million would be entered in the budget each year as provisional appropriations. The appropriations for the monetary reserve were not included in the amount of the agricultural guideline.

3) Discipline arrangements for non-compulsory expenditure

Parliament and the Council agreed to accept, for the financial years 1988 to 1992, the maximum rates of increase for non-compulsory expenditure deriving from the budgets established within the ceilings set by the financial perspective. In practice, this meant that Parliament could each year increase the non-compulsory expenditure up to the limit compatible with the ceilings in the financial perspective. This joint commitment on the part of the institutions therefore radically altered the scope of the Treaty provisions relating to the application of the maximum rate of increase, and eliminated the problems of reaching an agreement on exceeding this rate [1] during the annual budgetary procedure.

The institutions also gave an undertaking that any revision of the compulsory expenditure in the financial perspective would not lead to a reduction in non-compulsory expenditure. This clause to 'protect' non-

---

[1] See Chapter 2.

compulsory expenditure ensured that the application of budgetary discipline would not put compulsory expenditure in a priority category.

Certain other undertakings were also given in the Interinstitutional Agreement by the two arms of the budgetary authority. These included:

— the undertaking to bear in mind the assessment of the possibilities for implementing the budget made by the Commission in its preliminary draft;

— the undertaking to respect the allocations of commitment appropriations for the Structural Funds, the specific industrial development programme for Portugal, the integrated Mediterranean programmes and the research framework programme. These amounts were therefore not only expenditure ceilings but should also be regarded as expenditure targets. This expenditure therefore enjoyed preferential treatment, particularly as, under another provision, any part of these allocations which had not been used in the course of a given year would be carried over to subsequent years.

4) Improvement of budget management and reform of the Financial Regulation

The February 1988 European Council decided to improve the Community's budget management so as to strengthen the principle of annuality. This was done by Regulation (ECSC, EEC, Euratom) No 2049/88 of 24 June 1988 [1], which amended a number of important provisions of the Financial Regulation:

— Differentiated appropriations would no longer be carried over automatically; the Commission could authorise certain carryovers provided they were duly substantiated on the basis of specific criteria spelled out in the Financial Regulation;

— Appropriations corresponding to commitments cancelled could, exceptionally, be made available again by Commission decision on the basis of specific criteria.

---

[1]   OJ L 185, 15.7.1988, p. 3.

2.3. The reform of the Structural Funds

The Single Act provided for close coordination between the three existing Structural Funds (EAGGF Guidance Section, Social Fund and Regional Fund) with a view to clarifying and rationalising their tasks and enhancing their effectiveness. This coordination, the arrangements for which would be laid down in a single instrument covering all three Funds, was intended to promote the harmonious development of the entire Community, by reducing the gap between regions and helping the less-favoured regions to catch up.

The Brussels European Council decided that the growth of the Structural Funds had to be guaranteed in the medium term: the commitment appropriations in 1993 would be twice as high in real terms as in 1987.

For the purposes of rationalisation, the European Council also decided that Community action through the Funds would be targeted at the following five general objectives:

— objective 1: promoting development and structural adjustment in less-developed regions;

— objective 2: converting the regions, frontier regions or parts of regions (including employment areas and urban communities) seriously affected by industrial decline;

— objective 3: combating long-term unemployment;

— objective 4: facilitating the occupational integration of young people;

— objectives 5a and 5b: with a view to reform of the common agricultural policy, speeding up the adjustment of agricultural structures and promoting the development of rural areas.

The detailed arrangements for giving effect to this decision were adopted by the Council on 24 June 1988 [1].

---

[1] Council Regulation (EEC) No 2052/88 of 24 June 1988 on the tasks of the Structural Funds and their effectiveness and on coordination of their activities between themselves and with the operations of the European Investment Bank and the other existing financial instruments (OJ L 185, 15.7.1988, p. 9).

To coordinate the operations of the Funds, it was specified that they would contribute as follows to the attainment of the five objectives set by the European Council:

— objective 1: ERDF, ESF and EAGGF Guidance Section;

— objective 2: ERDF and ESF;

— objective 3: ESF;

— objective 4: ESF;

— objective 5a: EAGGF Guidance Section;

— objective 5b: EAGGF Guidance Section, ESF and ERDF.

On the basis of the principles and general provisions laid down in the framework regulation, the Commission presented proposals on 30 August 1988 for implementing regulations for the individual policies. These proposals were adopted by the Council on 19 December 1988 to take effect on 1 January 1989.

3. First assessment of the reform: 1988-92

Two reports on the implementation of the 1988 reform were presented on 10 March 1992 by the Commission to Parliament and the Council:

— a report on the application of the Interinstitutional Agreement (COM(92) 82);

— a report on the system of own resources (COM(92) 81).

Their conclusions were largely positive as regards the main objectives pursued: orderly progression of expenditure, improvement in the budgetary procedure and budget management, and adequate own resources.

Favourable economic conditions undoubtedly helped to achieve these results. It is true that some difficulties were encountered in the application of the agreement, particularly as regards the revision of the financial framework. The Community budget was nevertheless able to cope with new tasks, deriving mainly from the considerable upheavals on the international scene during this period. There is little doubt that the problems encountered would have been far more acute in the absence of the financial framework imposed in 1988, which enabled the debate to be confined within agreed limits and rules.

3.1. Orderly progression of expenditure

1) The successive revisions of the financial perspective

Pursuant to the Interinstitutional Agreement, the financial perspective was revised or adjusted no less than seven times during the period, to accommodate new activities or to strengthen existing policies.

These revisions mainly concerned the introduction of new operations linked to changes in the international environment: cooperation with the countries of central and eastern Europe then technical assistance to the republics of the former USSR, German unification, the Gulf crisis, financial aid to Israel and the Occupied Territories, humanitarian aid to the Kurdish refugees and to the former Yugoslavia, combating famine in Africa, etc.

Some existing Community policies were strengthened half-way through the period, for example: internal policies and cooperation activities in favour of developing countries in the Mediterranean, Asia and Latin America.

The other revisions were of a more technical nature: adjustments to allow a more regular progression in the budget available for administrative expenditure, *ex post* adjustments to the appropriations for the Structural Funds in line with actual inflation, revaluation of the repayments to be made to Spain and Portugal following accession and to the Member States in respect of expenditure incurred on disposal of agricultural stocks, allowance for the change in the rate of clearance of commitments under certain programmes (e.g. structural aid to the new German *Länder*, research).

2) The actual shape of the financial framework

Table 3.2 shows the changes (after adjustment and revision) in the financial perspective over the period 1988-92 in relation to the original table agreed.

TABLE 3.2

Actual application of the financial perspective 1988-92

	Rate of increase (%) in real terms 1992/88		Distribution (%) of the total appropriations for commitments		
	Original financial perspective	Actual financial perspective	Original financial perspective		Actual financial perspective
			1988	1992	1992
EAGGF Guarantee Section	7.6	6.8	60.7	56.1	52.5
Structural operations	72.7	94.8	17.2	25.5	27.1
Multiannual policies	98.3	101.1	2.7	4.5	4.3
Other policies	33.1	136.5	4.6	5.3	8.9
Repayments and administration	-37.8	-42.8	12.6	6.7	5.8
Monetary reserve	–	-16.2	2.2	1.9	1.5
Total appropriations for commitments	16.5	23.7	100	100	100
Total appropriations for payments	14.4	22.6	96.6	94.9	95.8

In all, the ceiling on expenditure was raised in real terms by 5.5 % per year on average for appropriations for commitments, as opposed to the 3.9 % originally planned.

This overall trend covered changes in the structure of expenditure in accordance with the priorities adopted, but which were more pronounced than was envisaged in 1988.

As foreseen, the ceiling for the EAGGF Guarantee Section (agricultural guideline) rose by far less than that for total expenditure. Actual agricultural expenditure remained well within this ceiling. The additional cost in this field, resulting from German unification, could thus be covered without the guideline having to be raised.

However, this result was due as much to a favourable economic climate as it was to a reform of agricultural market mechanisms. Even though the guideline was respected, agricultural expenditure remained very sensitive to external parameters and the economic effects of the stabilisers proved to be limited. Under these circumstances, and in view of the commitments to be entered into at international level under GATT, reform of the common agricultural policy was essential. This reform was to be oriented towards direct aid reflecting production capacity, rather than being based almost exclusively on a system of guaranteed prices.

The rise in the ceiling for the heading 'Other policies' (see Table 3.2) was much higher than planned, mainly as a result of the increase in the Community's external action over that period. The ceiling for the 'Structural operations' heading (see Table 3.2) also rose by more than expected. This was mainly due to the transfer of allocations which could not be used in earlier years to the end of the period, rather than to an increase in the total amounts originally planned.

3.2. Improvement in the budgetary procedure and budget management

1) Compliance with the basic principles of the Interinstitutional Agreement

The budget for each of the years covered by the agreement was adopted on time without any major conflicts between the institutions during the budgetary procedure. There was full compliance with the financial perspective in terms of both authorisation and implementation of the budget. The annual adjustments in line with movements in prices and GNP and with outturn, as well as the revisions of the financial perspective, were all made in accordance with the agreement. A solution acceptable to the parties was found whenever problems of interpretation arose in this respect.

However, these revision or adjustment procedures proved to be cumbersome in practice (taking an average of three months) and often coincided with the actual annual budgetary procedure, thereby diminishing the instrument's characteristics of containment and medium-term guidance. The two arms of the budgetary authority had differing views on how to finance the new needs which arose, with Parliament advocating using the margin available under the own resources ceiling, and the Council giving priority to redeployment of the expenditure budgeted under each heading.

2) More rigorous budget management

In line with the objectives adopted and by means of the new provisions in the Financial Regulation, there were significant improvements in budget management from the point of view of implementation, especially concerning:

— the principle of annuality, with a sharp reduction, in absolute amounts and in relative terms, of carry-overs from one financial year to the next and appropriations made available again;

— the principle of specification, with a substantial reduction in transfers between chapters during the financial year.

In addition, the average utilisation rate of appropriations was appreciably higher than it had been during the years preceding the reform. The clearance of commitments was also speeded up, in terms of both forecasts and actual outturn.

Finally, the Commission took a range of measures to make a cost-effectiveness approach more systematic in devising proposals for action and in organising its management.

3.3. Sufficient financial resources

Despite the successive upward revisions of the financial perspective, the total expenditure ceiling, and hence the actual amount of budget expenditure, remained beneath the ceiling of available own resources.

TABLE 3.3

Use of the own resources ceiling

(% of GNP)

	1988	1989	1990	1991	1992
Own resources ceiling	1.15	1.17	1.18	1.19	1.20
Ceiling on appropriations for payments (actual financial perspective)	1.12	1.06	1.08	1.13	1.19
Total appropriations for payments entered in the budget and actually used	1.12	1.02	0.99	1.09	1.13

This result was, however, achieved through the combination of two favourable factors:

— a moderate increase in requirements for agricultural expenditure;

— more rapid economic growth than initially forecast, leading to a considerably larger volume of available own resources.

3.4. Structure of own resources

As far as the structure of own resources was concerned (see Figure 3.1), the proportion of traditional own resources continued to decline. The VAT-based resource remained by far the largest. The GNP-based resource was negligible in 1988 and 1989 and was not called in at all in 1990. However, it exceeded 20 % of the budget in 1992.

FIGURE 3.1

Structure of own resources (1980-92)

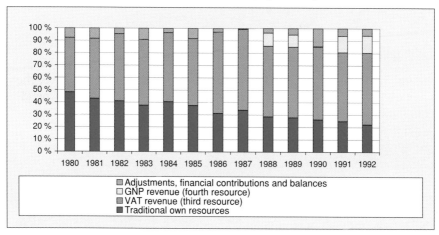

Despite the 1988 reform, regressive elements remained in the system of own resources, principally because VAT bases were high in relation to GNP in the least prosperous Member States. Despite capping at 55 % of GNP, the VAT bases of Greece, Ireland and Portugal remained above the Community average, which in 1992 amounted to 49.3 % of GNP.

Chapter 4

Consolidation of the 1988 reform: the Delors II package (1993-99)

1. The Commission's proposals

1.1. The objectives of the Delors II package

1) Consolidating the achievements of the 1988 reform

The 1988-92 financial perspective and the Interinstitutional Agreement concluded in 1988 were due to expire at the end of 1992. Likewise, in the absence of a new decision on own resources, 1992 marked the end of the gradual rise in the own resources ceiling, which would have been frozen at 1.20 % of GNP.

As the Commission's assessment of the system introduced in 1988 had been positive, it came to the conclusion that the financial perspective and the Interinstitutional Agreement should be renewed for a further period, even though certain improvements could be made in the light of experience.

2) Updating the financial framework

Several decisions with major implications for the budget had been made or were expected, making review of the Community's financial framework inevitable. In particular, there was a need:

— to take account of the financial impact of the reform of the common agricultural policy which started in 1992;

— to take stock of the reform of the Structural Funds and to adopt a new regulation, since the framework established in 1988 would be expiring at the end of 1993;

— to guarantee the development of the policies needed for the internal market to run smoothly and to provide the Community with sufficient resources to meet its new international responsibilities.

3) Applying the Maastricht Treaty

The Delors II package flanked the Maastricht Treaty during its first years in the same way as the Delors I package contributed to the implementation of the Single Act. Nevertheless, the direct budgetary implications of the new Treaty were quite modest and left the institutions a power of political appraisal regarding their implementation.

The main budgetary impact of the Maastricht Treaty was the establishment of the Cohesion Fund to finance infrastructure, transport and environment projects in countries with a per capita GNP below 90 % of the Community average (Greece, Spain, Ireland and Portugal) in order to support their efforts towards economic convergence in the context of the economic and monetary union.

The other budgetary implications of the Treaty included:

— the Protocol on economic and social cohesion annexed to the Treaty, which was a strong political signal in favour of strengthening all the regional policies of the Community;

— the new powers allocated explicitly to the Community in a large number of sectors, such as trans-European networks, education, industry, and culture, which in certain cases implied stepping up Community action in these sectors;

— the provisions of the common foreign and security policy and of cooperation in the field of justice and home affairs, which stipulated that the administrative expenditure incurred by the institutions through the implementation of these policies was to be charged to the Community budget and that operating expenses might also be financed by the Community budget provided there was a unanimous decision by the Council.

1.2. The Commission proposals

In February 1992 the Commission presented its proposals in two communications:

— 'From the Single Act to Maastricht and beyond: The means to match our ambitions', better known as the 'Delors II package', COM(92) 2000 of 11 February 1992;

— 'The Community's finances between now and 1997', COM(92) 2001 of 10 March 1992.

The Commission proposed raising the annual ceiling on appropriations for payments by ECU 20 billion (1992 prices) over five years, which would mean raising the own resources ceiling gradually from 1.20 % of GNP in 1992 to 1.37 % in 1997. Three major political priorities were adopted:

— economic and social cohesion, through the development of new structural operations;

— external action to take account of changes in the international environment;

— strengthening the competitiveness of European industry, notably by boosting research and participating in the financing of trans-European networks.

The first debate at the Lisbon European Council in June 1992 ended in deadlock, so the Commission proposed that achievement of these objectives be spread over seven years up to 1999 instead of 1997. The Commission's amended proposal required setting the own resources ceiling at 1.32 % of GNP in 1999, giving a ceiling on appropriations for payments of 1.29 % of GNP, with a margin for unforeseen expenditure of 0.03 % of GNP.

2. The Edinburgh European Council and the conclusion of the 1993-99 financial package

2.1. The conclusions of the Edinburgh European Council

The Edinburgh European Council of 11 and 12 December 1992 finally opted for a gradual rise in the own resources ceiling from 1.20 to 1.27 % of GNP in 1999, allowing a margin for unforeseen expenditure of 0.01 % of GNP. The overall ceiling on appropriations for commitments was fixed at 1.335 % of GNP.

1) Own resources

Apart from fixing new ceilings for the period, the European Council decided to alter the structure of own resources in order to reduce certain regressive aspects of the existing system by increasing the significance of the GNP-based 'fourth resource'.

— The maximum rate applicable to the uniform VAT base was reduced from 1.4 to 1 % in equal steps over the period 1995-99.

— For the least prosperous Member States (Greece, Spain, Ireland and Portugal), the threshold for the cap on the VAT base was reduced from 55 to 50 % of GNP from 1995 and, for the other Member States, in equal steps over the period 1995-99.

The mechanism for correcting budget imbalances in favour of the United Kingdom was retained.

2) Expenditure

The European Council selected two major priorities, structural operations and external action, and adopted the following main policies, whilst calling on the institutions to conclude a new Interinstitutional Agreement:

(a) Agriculture

As the Commission had proposed, the trend in agricultural expenditure continued to be governed by the agricultural guideline, with arrangements unchanged, i.e. an increase limited to 74 % of growth in GNP. The expenditure covered by the guideline was amended slightly, in particular to include all the expenditure under the reformed CAP, including the accompanying measures, and the Guarantee Fund for fisheries. The monetary reserve was cut to ECU 500 million from 1995, reflecting the lesser dependence of the reformed CAP on world farm prices.

(b) Structural operations

The European Council agreed with the Commission's priorities. The total amount of expenditure earmarked for economic and social cohesion increased by 75 % in real terms from just over ECU 17 billion in 1992 to ECU 30 billion in 1999. Community actions now focused on the Structural Funds and Cohesion Fund. The budgetary resources of the Structural Funds were concentrated more on the least favoured regions (objective 1 regions) and in 1999 the four beneficiary countries of the Cohesion Fund were to receive, under the Cohesion Fund and objective 1 of the Structural Funds together, twice the amount they received in 1992 under objective 1 of the Structural Funds.

(c) Internal policies

The amounts available under this heading increased by some 30 % over seven years, which was less than the Commission and the European Parliament would have wished. According to the conclusions of the European Council, research continued to represent the main item of expenditure and, as was already the case, accounted for between half and two thirds of the total for the heading. Growth in expenditure to finance trans-European networks had to be particularly strong, reflecting the new priority given to this sector.

(d) External action

Apart from the allocations provided for under this heading, which now grouped together all external action, including the external aspects of internal policies (fisheries, environment, etc), two new reserves were established. Including these two reserves, intended for emergency aid in non-member countries and to cover possible calls on the guarantee granted by the Community for loans to non-member countries, the Edinburgh decisions entailed an ambitious increase of some 55 % in the resources for external action.

(e) Administrative expenditure

There was a strict budgetary constraint on administrative expenditure as most of the planned increase was earmarked for pensions.

3) Adoption of the financial framework for 1993-99

The European Council agreed on a new financial perspective for 1993-99 on the basis of these guidelines (see Table 4.1) ([1]).

TABLE 4.1
Financial perspective 1993-99
Appropriations for commitments

(million ECU at 1992 prices)

	1993	1994	1995	1996	1997	1998	1999
1. Agricultural guideline	35 230	35 095	35 722	36 364	37 023	37 697	38 389
2. Structural operations	21 277	21 885	23 480	24 990	26 526	28 240	30 000
— Cohesion Fund	1 500	1 750	2 000	2 250	2 500	2 550	2 600
— Structural Funds and other operations	19 777	20 135	21 480	22 740	24 026	25 690	27 400
3. Internal policies	3 940	4 084	4 323	4 520	4 710	4 910	5 100
4. External action	3 950	4 000	4 280	4 560	4 830	5 180	5 600
5. Administrative expenditure	3 280	3 380	3 580	3 690	3 800	3 850	3 900
6. Reserves	1 500	1 500	1 100	1 100	1 100	1 100	1 100
— Monetary reserve	1 000	1 000	500	500	500	500	500
— External action							
• emergency aid	200	200	300	300	300	300	300
• loan guarantees	300	300	300	300	300	300	300
Total appropriations for commitments	69 177	69 944	72 485	75 224	77 989	80 977	84 089
Appropriations for payments required	65 908	67 036	69 150	71 290	74 491	77 249	80 114
Appropriations for payments (% GNP)	1.20	1.19	1.20	1.21	1.23	1.25	1.26
Margin for unforeseen expenditure (% GNP)		0.01	0.01	0.01	0.01	0.01	0.01
Own resources ceiling (% GNP)	1.20	1.20	1.21	1.22	1.24	1.26	1.27
Pro memoria: total external expenditure	4 450	4 500	4 880	5 160	5 430	5 780	6 200
Pro memoria: the inflation rate applicable for the 1993 budget is 4.3 %.							

[1]   This table incorporates minor changes made for 1994 following negotiations with Parliament after the Edinburgh European Council, which led in October 1993 to the conclusion of a new Interinstitutional Agreement (see point 2.2 of this chapter).

2.2. Renewal of the Interinstitutional Agreement on budgetary discipline and improvement of the budgetary procedure

The European Council's agreement on a new financial framework for 1993-99 was not the end of the negotiations. Nearly a year of tough negotiations was needed before the European Parliament, the Council and the Commission were able to conclude a new Interinstitutional Agreement on 29 October 1993 (¹), thereby bringing into force the financial perspective, which formed an integral part of this agreement.

Judging the financial framework agreed in Edinburgh to be disappointing in the sense of being too restrictive, the European Parliament gave its agreement to the figures subject to significant progress at institutional level.

1) Rules for the application of the financial perspective

The Commission had proposed renewing most of the provisions of the 1988 agreement, which was accepted by both the European Parliament and the Council. In particular, several undertakings entered into by the institutions in 1988 were reiterated.

— The rule on the maximum rate of increase for non-compulsory expenditure remained neutralised, since the two arms of the budgetary authority confirmed that for the period 1993-99 they would accept the maximum rates imposed by the ceilings of the financial perspective.

— Protection of non-compulsory expenditure continued to be assured: a revision of compulsory expenditure may not lead to a reduction in the amount available for non-compulsory expenditure.

— Preferential treatment of expenditure for structural operations, including the new Cohesion Fund, was continued. The allocations for heading 2 of the financial perspective consequently represented both a ceiling and an expenditure target, with the two arms of the budgetary authority undertaking, for these operations, to transfer the appropriations not used during a financial year to subsequent years. It should be noted that the expenditure for research and technological development no longer fell into the category of privileged expenditure.

(¹)   OJ C 331, 7.12.1993.

The provisions relating to the procedures for the technical adjustment, the adjustment in line with the conditions of implementation and the revision of the financial perspective remained largely unchanged. However, when drawing up the budget, the institutions had to ensure that there was a margin beneath the ceilings for the various headings (except for heading 2, which was an expenditure target) so that additional appropriations could be entered where necessary without first revising the financial perspective.

2) Provisions concerning the budgetary procedure

As a result of the institutional demands of the European Parliament, the new Interinstitutional Agreement's major innovations were to be found in this field.

— The institutions agreed that all expenditure under headings 2 (structural action) and 3 (internal policies) of the financial perspective was non-compulsory expenditure. In a statement appended to the agreement, it was also agreed that expenditure on financial protocols with non-member countries which were concluded or renewed would be considered non-compulsory. The ongoing financial protocols, EAGGF Guarantee expenditure, some external expenditure (fisheries agreements, subscription to the capital of international financial organisations, etc) and expenditure on the pensions of former officials or other staff of the institutions were classified as compulsory expenditure.

— A new procedure for interinstitutional collaboration in budgetary matters was introduced, with an exchange of views on budget priorities and conciliation on compulsory expenditure, allowing Parliament to initiate a dialogue with the Council on the amount of compulsory expenditure to be entered in the budget, even though the Council had the last word on the matter.

— A 'negative co-decision' procedure was introduced to mobilise the reserves (the monetary reserve, the reserve for loan guarantees and the reserve for emergency aid). If the Commission's proposal failed to secure the agreement of the two arms of the budgetary authority, and if the budgetary authority was unable to agree on a common position, the proposal would be deemed to have been approved.

2.3. The legislative provisions of the Delors II package

The Commission submitted a series of proposals for legislation to the Council to implement the conclusions of the Edinburgh European Council and to put into legal form the commitments entered into by the institutions under the Institutional Agreement.

After lengthy discussions, these proposals led on 31 October 1994 to the Council adopting new texts and amending existing texts [1].

— A new own resources decision (Decision 94/728/EC, Euratom), incorporating the adjustments made to the system of own resources and the revised ceilings, was adopted after ratification by all Member States according to their respective constitutional requirements.

— The Council Decision of 24 June 1988 concerning budgetary discipline was replaced by Council Decision 94/729/EC.

— The entry in the budget of the two new reserves associated with external action required an appropriate legislative framework. The Council therefore amended both the Financial Regulation (Council Regulation (ECSC, EC, Euratom) No 2730/94 amending the Financial Regulation of 21 December 1977 applicable to the general budget of the European Communities), and Regulation 1552/89 on the system of own resources (Regulation (EC, Euratom) No 2729/94). It also adopted Regulation (EC, Euratom) No 2728/94 creating a guarantee fund to cover the risks incurred as a result of guarantees granted under the general budget.

— In the field of structural operations, the five 1988 regulations on the Structural Funds were revised and a sixth regulation on the financial instrument for fisheries guidance (FIFG) was adopted on 20 July 1993 [2].

In accordance with the Treaty on European Union, a Cohesion Fund was established by Council Regulation (EC) No 1164/94 of 16 May 1994 [3],

---

[1] OJ L 293, 12.11.1994.
[2] Council Regulations (EEC) Nos 2080/93, 2081/93, 2082/93, 2083/93, 2084/93 and 2085/93 (OJ L 193, 31.7.1993).
[3] OJ L 130, 25.5.1994.

after the temporary application of a cohesion financial instrument established on 30 March 1993.

3. Application of the financial framework, 1993-99

3.1. The impact of the economic recession on the early years of this period

1) The deterioration in the economic situation over the period 1992-94

The management of the financial perspective 1988-92 was greatly facilitated by a favourable economic climate. Growth was stronger than originally expected, thus generating an increased volume of overall available own resources and providing cover for new costs arising in particular from the development of international activities [1].

The first years of application of the financial framework 1993-99 were characterised by the reverse economic climate. The successive downward revisions of forecast growth for 1992 to 1994 led to a big reduction in real GNP and, consequently, of overall available own resources. It was only during the second half of 1994 that signs of economic recovery appeared.

Despite this unfavourable situation, the principles of budgetary discipline underlying the Interinstitutional Agreement were not called into question.

2) Increased constraints for the application of the financial framework

(a) The constraint on agricultural expenditure

Lower economic growth resulted in a reduction of the agricultural guideline, and Community currency realignments (occurring since the end of 1992) resulted in additional costs for the common agricultural policy. Nevertheless, actual agricultural expenditure remained well within the reduced limits.

---

[1]   See Chapter 3.

(b) The ceiling on own resources

The economic recession led to the disappearance of the small margin of 0.01 % of GNP (as opposed to 0.03 % in the financial perspective 1988-92), which had been left available between the total ceiling on appropriations for payments and the ceiling on own resources.

To forestall any overshooting of the own resources ceiling in the implementation of the 1994 budget, the Commission took various measures during the year for economical management of the appropriations available.

During the technical adjustment of the financial perspective ahead of the budgetary procedure for 1995, it even emerged that the ceiling on own resources was liable to be insufficient to cover the level of expenditure provided for in the financial framework. The preliminary draft budget presented by the Commission took account of this constraint. Had this situation persisted, it would have led to a downward revision of the financial perspective for the following years of the framework, as provided in the Interinstitutional Agreement.

(c) The shortfall in own resources

The economic recession brought about a reduction in the yield of traditional own resources and in the bases for the VAT and GNP resources compared with the levels forecast when the budget was established. This resulted in particularly large revenue shortfalls in 1992 (ECU 2 billion) and 1993 (about ECU 6.5 billion).

Even though the budgets for 1992 and 1993 were implemented within the own resources ceiling, these shortfalls created negative balances in outturn which, in accordance with the Financial Regulation, had to be entered in the following year's budget as expenditure, thus reducing in principle the expenditure capacity defined in the financial perspective.

Parliament made its acceptance of the new Interinstitutional Agreement subject to the condition that the treatment of negative balances arising from revenue shortfalls would not reduce the amounts available under the expenditure ceilings. The Council undertook to find a suitable solution to this problem.

The Commission presented a proposal to amend the financial rules but thanks to very prudent management of available resources, sufficient margins could in fact be found to cover the revenue shortfalls. The budgetary authority therefore preferred not to amend the Financial Regulation.

3.2. Enlargement of the European Union

During the enlargement negotiations with Norway, Austria, Finland and Sweden, the budget was a decisive factor. In view of their relative prosperity, the applicant countries would contribute more to the Community budget than they might expect to receive by way of expenditure.

1) The stated positions

(a) **The applicant countries had expressed two major concerns:**

— They were worried about the 'shock' to their own finances of their contribution to the Community budget and therefore wished to obtain a gradual 'phasing-in' of the own resources mechanism;

— They were worried about the consequences of the agriculture aspects of the negotiations for their national public finances. The Union had proposed an immediate alignment of their agricultural prices with the generally lower Community prices, accompanied by degressive aid financed exclusively by national budgets and designed to cushion the impact of this fall in prices on farmers' incomes. The applicant countries had expressed their preference for a system of 'accession compensatory amounts' (ACAs) which would have allowed gradual adjustment of prices and made this budget aid unnecessary.

(b) **For its part, the Union had three major concerns:**

— Firstly, envisaging a permanent exemption from the system of own resources was out of the question;

— Secondly, if a transitional system were to be considered, its justification should lie in 'loss of income' for the acceding countries resulting from the fact that Community action in their favour would be implemented only gradually;

— Finally, care had to be taken not to cover the entire cost of adjustment of the agricultural sector of the applicant countries. In addition, the introduction of ACAs would have run counter to a single market without internal frontiers.

In any event, following enlargement, the Community should not find itself in a more difficult financial situation than previously.

2) The results of the negotiations

At the end of the negotiations, the applicant countries were offered budgetary compensation, commonly known as the 'agri-budgetary' package. These amounts, which are recorded in the Act of Accession, are made up of two components.

— Compensation for loss of earnings during the first year in the agriculture sector on account of the non-payment to the applicant countries of direct per hectare aid for major crops and beef and veal premiums. This payment should have been based on the statements to be made at the beginning of 1994, which was obviously impossible since these countries were not members of the Community at that time.

— Degressive compensation over four years, with the overall aim of supporting the budgetary efforts of the applicant countries in favour of their agricultural sectors following the fall in prices (direct compensatory aid and depreciation of stocks). All the applicant countries were allowed this compensation, which avoided penalising Sweden for having already adjusted its agricultural sector.

Furthermore, it was agreed that the Community budget would cover the financial commitments entered into by the applicant countries under the agreement establishing the European Economic Area (EEA).

The Act of Accession also provided for appropriations which the new Member States could claim under the Structural Funds.

— Only the Burgenland region of Austria was considered eligible for objective 1 of the Structural Funds.

— A new objective 6 was introduced in favour of regions with a population density not exceeding eight inhabitants per km², which boiled down to restricting its geographical cover to a few regions in the north of Scandinavia and Finland. Objective 6 was subject to rules similar to those of objective 1 and received an allocation per inhabitant which was slightly lower.

— The applicant countries were obviously eligible for the other objectives of the Structural Funds on the same footing as the other Member States for a total amount also laid down in the Act of Accession.

3) The adjustment of the financial perspective

As provided for in the 1993 Interinstitutional Agreement, an adjustment of the financial perspective was necessary to take account of the new requirements and resources of the enlarged Community. Following the proposals put forward by the Commission in early October 1994, the institutions agreed on an adjusted financial perspective for 1995-99 on 29 November. The matter had been expedited so quickly that the 1995 budget could then immediately be adopted for a Community of 15 Member States (the Norwegians had voted against entry in their referendum).

The ceilings for the headings were raised to cover the requirements resulting from the enlargement of the Union and the outcome of the accession negotiations.

— Common agricultural policy: the agricultural guideline was raised by 74 % of the percentage increase in GNP generated by enlargement.

— Structural operations: the allocations for the Structural Funds were increased for the acceding countries in accordance with the Act of Accession. Simultaneously, the budget covered the contribution of the three acceding countries to the EEA financial mechanism and a new subheading was created specifically for this purpose under heading 2.

— Internal policies: the ceiling for the heading was raised by 7 %, corresponding to the relative size of the GNP of the acceding countries.

— External action: the ceiling for the heading was raised by 6.3 %, allowing the development of external action in line with the increase in the European Union's ability to contribute.

— Administrative expenditure: heading 5 was increased by an average 4.66 % over the period from 1995 to 1999.

A new heading 7 was also added to accommodate the compensation to be received by the new Member States from 1995 to 1998 in accordance with the Act of Accession.

The institutions also availed themselves of this adjustment of the financial perspective and the new resources available to the Union to amend the ceilings for headings 2 and 3, in order to meet specific requirements which had emerged more recently.

— Heading 2 was increased by ECU 200 million (1995 prices), divided into three equal annual instalments from 1995 to 1997. This lump-sum increase for Community initiatives was to finance the Northern Ireland peace programme as stipulated by the Essen European Council.

— Heading 3 was increased by ECU 400 million (1994 prices), divided into equal instalments over the next five years to finance the programme to modernise the textiles and clothing industry in Portugal, the principle of which had been adopted when the Uruguay Round was concluded.

As shown in Table 4.2 (1995 prices), the new framework for the financial perspective of the enlarged Community left a margin between the ceiling on appropriations for payments and the own resources ceiling which was distinctly larger than that provided for in Edinburgh; it now amounted to 0.03 % of GNP at the end of the period.

TABLE 4.2

Financial perspective for the enlarged Community 1995-99

Appropriations for commitment

(million ECU at 1995 prices)

	1995	1996	1997	1998	1999
1. Common agricultural policy	37 944	39 546	40 267	41 006	41 764
2. Structural operations	26 329	27 710	29 375	31 164	32 956
Structural Funds (¹)	24 069	25 206	26 604	28 340	30 187
Cohesion Fund	2 152	2 396	2 663	2 716	2 769
EEA financial mechanism (²) (³)	108	108	108	108	0
3. Internal policies	5 060	5 233	5 449	5 677	5 894
4. External action	4 895	5 162	5 468	5 865	6 340
5. Administrative expenditure	4 022	4 110	4 232	4 295	4 359
6. Reserves	1 146	1 140	1 140	1 140	1 140
Monetary reserve (²)	500	500	500	500	500
Guarantee reserve	323	320	320	320	320
Emergency aid reserve	323	320	320	320	320
7. Compensation (²)	1 547	701	212	99	0
8. Total appropriations for commitments	80 943	83 602	86 143	89 246	92 453
9. Total appropriations for payments	77 229	79 248	82 227	85 073	88 007
Appropriations for payments as % of GNP	1.20	1.21	1.22	1.23	1.24
Margin as % of GNP	0.01	0.01	0.02	0.03	0.03
Own resources ceiling as % of GNP	1.21	1.22	1.24	1.26	1.27

(¹) Between 1996 and 1999 the annual technical adjustment for the amounts intended for the new Member States, fixed at 1995 prices in the Act of Accession, were based on 1995 prices.

(²) Current prices.

(³) The ceiling for this subheading could be changed, if necessary, under the technical adjustment procedure provided for in paragraph 9 of the Interinstitutional Agreement in line with the actual payments in the course of each financial year.

3.3. Results in terms of budgetary discipline and improvement of the budgetary procedure

1) Changes in the budget and in the financial framework

Apart from the adjustment which had to be made from 1995 onwards to take account of the enlargement of the European Union, the financial framework remained unchanged throughout its whole period of application. The proposal which the Commission presented in 1996 for redeploying and reclassifying expenditure in individual headings in order to strengthen certain internal policies which could promote growth and employment was not endorsed by the Council.

(a) Expenditure

Two distinct sub-periods may be noted in the application of the financial framework (see Figure 4.1).

— Between 1993 and 1996 the annual budgets adopted were close to the ceilings in the financial perspective but underspending was significant in 1994 and 1995. This under-utilisation of appropriations was largely accounted for by agriculture and structural operations. In the case of agriculture, this demonstrated the need for improved expenditure forecasts and the monitoring of implementation. The underspending on structural operations was due to the delays in introducing the new programmes from 1994 onwards, particularly those relating to Community initiatives and objectives 2, 5a and 5b. The transfer of unused appropriations provided for in the Interinstitutional Agreement was concentrated at the end of the period and came to almost EUR 3.3 billion in 1999, artificially inflating the level of expenditure for that financial year.

— However, from 1997 onwards, the annual budgets were adopted leaving substantial margins beneath the ceilings of the financial perspective and improved budget implementation reduced underspending.

FIGURE 4.1

Financial perspective ceilings, expenditure entered in budget and outturn
Total appropriations for commitments (million ECU at current prices)

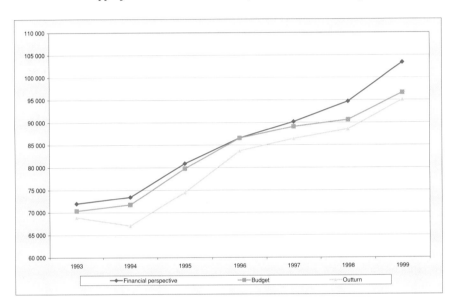

(b) Own resources

Since the level of GNP had to be revised downwards several times due to unfavourable economic conditions, total appropriations for payments entered in the budget were close to the own resources ceiling until 1996 and turned out to be even slightly higher in the first year of the period [1]. A growing margin was then left available during the rest of the period. The trend in the implementation of appropriations for payments was similar to that for commitments: after a marked deterioration in 1994 and 1995, the rates of implementation picked up, but were still far below the own resources ceiling.

---

[1]   The amount of own resources actually called in during that year was still consistent with the ceiling laid down, as other revenue was used for the financing.

TABLE 4.3

Own resources ceilings, appropriations for payments entered in the budget and outturn

(% of GNP)

	1993	1994	1995	1996	1997	1998	1999
	EU-12				EU-15		
Own resources ceiling	1.20	1.20	1.21	1.22	1.24	1.26	1.27
Budget	1.21	1.18	1.17	1.21	1.16	1.12	1.10
Outturn	1.17	1.03	1.03	1.14	1.12	1.09	1.07

As regards the structure of own resources, the yield from traditional own resources remained largely constant over the period, although the proportion of total revenue they accounted for continued to decline. The net drop in the proportion accounted for by the VAT-based resource (from 52.5 % in 1993 to 35.5 % in 1999) was in line with the objective pursued when the own resources decision was amended. The proportion accounted for by the resource based on the GNP of the Member States thus came to slightly more than 48 % of receipts at the end of the period.

FIGURE 4.2

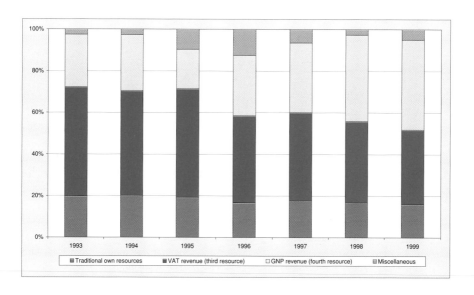

| Traditional own resources | VAT revenue (third resource) | GNP revenue (fourth resource) | Miscellaneous |

Structure of own resources, 1993-99

2) Improvement of the budgetary debate

At first, the procedure of interinstitutional collaboration introduced by the 1993 agreement encountered difficulties which were again related to the problem of the classification of expenditure. Parliament took the opportunity of conciliation on compulsory expenditure not only to discuss the amounts, but also to call the classification into question. Parliament's unilateral reclassification of certain lines of expenditure in the 1995 budget was annulled by the Court of Justice after an action was brought by the Council. The situation was then regularised, albeit without any basic agreement on this issue.

After this difficult start, the procedure did gradually generate a conciliation mentality which tended to spread to all expenditure and continued throughout the budgetary procedure. Several agreements were subsequently reached to smooth the course of the budgetary procedure.

In March 1995 the institutions signed a joint declaration on the entry of financial provisions in legislative instruments to improve the 1982 declaration. Through this declaration, the institutions rejected the practice of 'amounts deemed necessary' and made allowance for the new legal situation resulting from the extension of Parliament's legislative powers with the introduction, in certain areas, of the legislative co-decision procedure for basic instruments.

— Multiannual programmes adopted under the co-decision procedure include reference amounts which are binding on the institutions during the annual budgetary procedure.

— Multiannual programmes based on instruments not covered by the co-decision procedure do not include such amounts. Should the Council still wish to enter a financial reference in such an instrument, it will be taken as illustrative of the will of the legislative authority and is not, therefore, binding on the institutions during the budgetary procedure.

— In December 1996 a joint declaration was adopted on improving information to the budgetary authority on the negotiation and conclusion of fisheries agreements.

— In April 1997 the institutions agreed in principle that a letter of amendment should be presented towards the end of the budgetary procedure (October) to update expenditure forecasts for the agricultural sector.

— In July 1997 an Interinstitutional Agreement was concluded on the financing of the common foreign and security policy.

— In October 1998 agreement was reached on the question of legal bases and implementation of the budget, another point which had only partly been settled in the 1982 declaration. This agreement confirmed the principle that the utilisation of appropriations entered in the budget requires prior adoption of a basic instrument. Exceptions to this principle were spelt out and may apply to three types of action: pilot projects, preparatory measures and one-off actions. In the first two cases, there are strict limits to these exceptions as regards both time and amounts.

Chapter 5

Establishment of a stable budgetary base for enlargement of the European Union: the Agenda 2000 package (2000-06)

In December 1995 the Madrid European Council decided that a start should be made on preparing for the post-1999 period and called on the Commission to present a communication on the future financial framework for the Union with a view to enlargement.

In response, the Commission produced its 'Agenda 2000' [1] communication in July 1997. It followed this up in March 1998 with a detailed set of proposals for the reform of a number of Community policies, preparations for the accession of new Member States and the financial framework for the period ahead [2], and then in October 1998 a report on the own resources system [3].

---

[1]   Agenda 2000: for a stronger and wider Union, COM(97) 2000; Bulletin EU, Supplement 5/97.

[2]   On these financial aspects:
       Communication from the Commission to the Council and the European Parliament on the establishment of a new financial perspective for the period 2000-2006, COM(98) 164, 18.3.1998.
       Report on the implementation of the Interinstitutional Agreement of 29 October 1993 on budgetary discipline and improvement of the budgetary procedure. Proposals for renewal, COM(98) 165, 18.3.1998.
       Commission working document. Draft Interinstitutional Agreement on budgetary discipline and improvement of the budgetary procedure, SEC(1998) 698, 29.4.1998.

[3]   The financing of the European Union. Commission report on the operation of the own resources system, COM(98) 560, 7.10.1998; Bulletin EU, Supplement 10/98.

The context for the negotiations on these proposals was, in a number of respects, more difficult than at the time of the discussion of the Delors II package in 1992.

— Apart from establishing a new financial framework (taking into account the financial impact of the forthcoming enlargement), major decisions had to be taken on the reform of the CAP and structural operations. In contrast, at the time of the 1992 negotiations, the CAP had already undergone an initial reform prior to the establishment of the financial framework. In respect of structural operations, the primary concern had been the size of the allocations, with no substantial changes having been proposed in the basic rules. Enlargement to take in the Nordic countries and Austria was on the horizon, but these were relatively prosperous countries whose accession did not entail any additional net costs for the Union budget.

— There was far greater concern about imposing tight budget management, in connection with the establishment of monetary union, whereas in 1992 the principle of raising the own resources ceiling had been fairly broadly accepted from the outset.

— A number of Member States were very insistent on the issue of their net contribution to the Union budget, whereas in 1992 such demands had been more moderate.

This was why the negotiations on Agenda 2000 lasted nearly two years. The broad lines were agreed at the Berlin European Council in March 1999. A new Interinstitutional Agreement, containing the financial framework for 2000-06, was concluded on 6 May that year([1]). The regulations on the reform of the CAP, on the new guidelines for structural operations and on the pre-accession financial instruments to be introduced were adopted in May and June. But it was not until September 2000 that the Council adopted the new regulation on budgetary discipline([2]) and the new decision on the own resources system([3]).

([1]) Interinstitutional Agreement of 6 May 1999 between the European Parliament, the Council and the Commission on budgetary discipline and improvement of the budgetary procedure (OJ C 172, 18.6.1999, p. 1).

([2]) Council Regulation (EC) No 2040/2000 of 26 September 2000 on budgetary discipline (OJ L 244, 29.9.2000, p. 27).

([3]) Council Decision 2000/597/EC, Euratom of 29 September 2000 (OJ L 253, 7.10.2000, p. 42).

1. The Commission's proposals

1.1. The financial framework

The Commission's proposals maintained the own resources ceiling at its 1999 level, i.e. 1.27 % of GNP, beneath which would be financed the reform of the common agricultural policy and structural operations, the continuation of the other internal policies and external action and an initial round of enlargement of the Union, while still leaving an adequate safety margin.

1) Common agricultural policy

The aim was to prevent any return to expensive surpluses, for which in future no export possibilities would exist under the new international rules, and so to be in the best possible position for the next round of WTO negotiations. The general guideline was to continue the path of the 1992 reform. Reductions in intervention prices were therefore proposed for arable crops (down by 20 % from the 2000/01 marketing year onwards), milk (down by 15 % over four years) and beef (down by 30 % over three years). These reductions would be largely offset by an increase in direct aid to producers. It was proposed that such aid should be degressive when it exceeded EUR 100 000 per holding. Reforms were also proposed for tobacco, olive oil and wine. Under these proposals, expenditure would initially have increased, before levelling off after 2003.

Another objective of the proposed reform was to back up the market organisation measures (intervention and compensatory aid) with a stronger and more uniform set of measures to promote rural development. The EAGGF Guarantee Section would have financed not only the rural accompanying measures brought in by the 1992 reform (forestry, early retirement and agri-environmental measures) but also operations which hitherto had come under objectives 5a and 5b of the Structural Funds and structural measures for fisheries.

2) Structural operations

After the very sharp rise in allocations over the previous decade, the Commission's approach was to maintain the financial effort for cohesion at the relative level reached in 1999 (0.46 % of GNP), but to include in this overall amount the structural component of pre-accession aid and the cost of structural measures arising from the first round of enlargement of the Union. In the light of experience a three-fold approach was proposed.

— Concentration of resources, with the objectives assigned to the Structural Funds being reduced from seven to three: objective 1 for the least well-off regions (per capita GDP less than 75 % of the Community average); a revised objective 2 to cover areas undergoing change (in industry, services or fisheries), rural areas in decline and urban areas in difficulty; and a new objective 3 to support the adaptation and modernisation of education, training and employment systems. It was also proposed that the number of Community initiatives be reduced from 14 to 3.

— Geographical concentration, achieved by strict application of the threshold of eligibility for objective 1 and a reduction in the population numbers eligible for the new objective 2. A phasing-out scheme was proposed for regions which would no longer be eligible.

— Simplification of the management rules.

3) The other areas of expenditure

The Commission's proposals tended to flatten distinctly the slope of the increases in ceilings which had been agreed over the previous period.

For internal policies the Commission proposed that priority be given to programmes which, at Community level, contributed most to growth and employment: research framework programme, trans-European networks, education and training, environment, promotion of small businesses. The ceiling for this category of expenditure was to rise in line with EU GNP.

On the other hand, the expenditure ceiling for external action would rise more slowly, following the sharp increase over the previous period. Apart from the candidate countries, the regions closest to the European Union would be given priority.

Administrative expenditure was set at levels which assumed there would be no increase in staff numbers, while allowance was made for building programmes already underway and an appreciable increase in foreseeable expenditure on pensions.

4) The impact of enlargement

The Commission proposed putting in place pre-accession aid for the 10 candidate countries of central and eastern Europe(¹) with three components.

— For these countries the Phare programme would be boosted and would focus on support for the development of administrative capacity and the investment required to take over the *acquis communautaire*.

— A second instrument (Sapard) would serve to modernise the agri-food chain and rural development projects.

— Lastly a structural instrument (ISPA) would contribute to financing projects on transport and the environment.

A constant annual allocation over the period 2000-06 was proposed for these three instruments. This amount would remain unchanged after the first accessions so that the remaining countries would then receive larger shares.

On the question of enlargement proper, the technical assumption made was that six countries would join no earlier than 2002: Poland, Hungary, the Czech Republic, Slovenia, Estonia and Cyprus. The Commission proposed that an overall amount be left available within the financial framework from that year on to cover the cost of this first round of enlargement.

— The assumptions concerning expenditure on agriculture were relatively limited. This is because the Commission proposed that no direct compensatory aid should be granted to farmers in these countries, as accession should not, in principle, result in a lowering of internal agricultural prices for them. On the other hand, too sharp an increase in agricultural income in relation to other sectors of production would have a harmful distorting effect on the economy. In addition to market support measures, the bulk of spending would be on aid for rural development, which would take over from, and increase, the pre-accession aid granted for this.

(¹)   Cyprus and Malta qualified for the programmes for Mediterranean non-member countries.

— The largest amounts to be set aside for enlargement were on structural operations. The aim was to strike a balance between the enormous potential requirements of these countries and their ability to absorb and co-finance such aid, which would have to go to economically viable programmes.

— The other additional expenditure concerns the participation of the new Member States in internal Community policies and the administrative costs of the institutions.

1.2. The financing system

When the Delors II package was adopted, the Commission undertook to present a report on the own resources system before the period ended in 1999. Given the importance of the budget financing aspects for the discussion of Agenda 2000 and the question of the distribution of the burden of financing raised by Germany, the Netherlands, Austria and Sweden, the Commission presented this report earlier than planned (October 1998). The report did not make specific proposals for reforming the existing system but analysed its operation and reviewed possible amendments.

1) Operation of the system

The Commission found that the existing system had provided the necessary resources and had become fairer, in that the costs borne by individual Member States were distributed more or less in line with their ability to contribute as measured by GNP. Two types of reform were considered:

— introduction of new own resources, closer in their nature to genuine tax resources;

— simplification of the system, which would involve replacing the VAT resource, and even traditional own resources, by the GNP resource alone.

2) The UK correction mechanism

The report noted that the context had changed since this mechanism was set up. The United Kingdom's relative prosperity had improved. And the United Kingdom was not the only country to experience a budgetary imbalance in relation to the EU budget. Originally the UK's budgetary imbalance had stemmed mainly from agricultural expenditure. However, the correction mechanism applied indistinctly to other categories of expenditure. Since these had come to account for a significantly larger proportion of the Community budget (in particular cohesion expenditure), the UK correction had departed from its original purpose. Similarly, upon enlargement, pre-accession expenditure, which benefited non-member countries and did not therefore enter into the calculation of the correction, would be replaced (and the amounts increased) by internal EU expenditure, which would count towards the United Kingdom's correction.

3) The issue of net contributions to the Community budget

The report acknowledged the existence of a problem with the net contributions of Germany, the Netherlands, Austria and Sweden, and pointed to three possible ways, should a consensus be achieved, of dealing with this matter.

— One option would be to move towards a more straightforward and transparent own resources system, stripped of all regressive aspects. This would include phasing out the UK correction, which imposes an additional burden on all the other Member States, and the full or partial replacement of the other resources by the GNP own resource.

— A second approach would be to introduce corrections on the expenditure side. The report considered, for instance, the possibility of only partial reimbursement of CAP direct aid to producers. The remainder, under regulations which would still be common to all Member States, would be paid from national budgets.

— A third possibility would be to introduce a generalised correction mechanism for negative balances with thresholds and parameters to be determined.

1.3. Renewal of the Interinstitutional Agreement

On the basis of the satisfactory application of the earlier agreement concluded in 1993, the Commission proposed that the instrument be renewed in its dual function of recording the agreement of the institutions on the financial framework and the arrangements for implementing it over the period covered and continuing with the improvement of the annual budgetary procedure.

The Commission took the view that the essential parts of the existing agreement should be retained. There were, however, proposals for other more technical adjustments of two types.

— The financial framework envisaged for 2000-06 offered less latitude than its predecessor. In particular it gave Parliament a margin of manoeuvre over non-compulsory expenditure which, in overall terms over the period, was probably smaller than what Parliament would have enjoyed under the terms of the Treaty. The Commission therefore proposed inserting flexibility mechanisms which would allow transfers between certain headings or allow amounts not used in one year to be spent the following year in excess of the ceilings. These procedures were less cumbersome than a revision of the financial framework but involved only limited amounts.

— The Commission also proposed consolidating and updating in the new agreement all the other arrangements for improving the budgetary procedure which the institutions had concluded in specific agreements or joint declarations. The conciliation procedure between Parliament and the Council introduced in 1993 would be extended to all expenditure and would go on throughout the budget discussions, thereby confirming the practice which had been established *de facto*. In addition rural development expenditure integrated in the reformed CAP would, under the Commission's proposal, be treated as non-compulsory expenditure.

2. The outcome of the negotiations

2.1. Stabilisation of Community expenditure

Stabilisation of expenditure was the main concern of the Member States during the negotiations, even beyond what was required to keep the own resources ceiling at 1.27 % of GNP and to accommodate the first new Member States. Consolidation of expenditure was seen by all Member States as an essential contribution to the tight budgeting they had started to impose at national level. Stabilisation was also the means for net contributors to ensure that their deficit did not increase in absolute terms, especially as discussions revealed the difficulties in securing agreement on a substantial reform of the own resources system.

TABLE 5.1 A

Financial perspective (EU-15)

(million EUR at 1999 prices)

Appropriations for commitments	2000	2001	2002	2003	2004	2005	2006
1. Agriculture	**40 920**	**42 800**	**43 900**	**43 770**	**42 760**	**41 930**	**41 660**
CAP (not including rural development)	36 620	38 480	39 570	39 430	38 410	37 570	37 290
Rural development and accompanying measures	4 300	4 320	4 330	4 340	4 350	4 360	4 370
2. Structural operations	**32 045**	**31 455**	**30 865**	**30 285**	**29 595**	**29 595**	**29 170**
Structural Funds	29 430	28 840	28 250	27 670	27 080	27 080	26 660
Cohesion Fund	2 615	2 615	2 615	2 615	2 515	2 515	2 510
3. Internal policies ([1])	**5 930**	**6 040**	**6 150**	**6 260**	**6 370**	**6 480**	**6 600**
4. External action	**4 550**	**4 560**	**4 570**	**4 580**	**4 590**	**4 600**	**4 610**
5. Administration ([2])	**4 560**	**4 600**	**4 700**	**4 800**	**4 900**	**5 000**	**5 100**
6. Reserves	**900**	**900**	**650**	**400**	**400**	**400**	**400**
Monetary reserve	500	500	250				
Emergency aid reserve	200	200	200	200	200	200	200
Guarantee reserve	200	200	200	200	200	200	200
7. Pre-accession aid	**3 120**	**3 120**	**3 120**	**3 120**	**3 120**	**3 120**	**3 120**
Agriculture	520	520	520	520	520	520	520
Pre-accession structural instrument	1 040	1 040	1 040	1 040	1 040	1 040	1 040
Phare (applicant countries)	1 560	1 560	1 560	1 560	1 560	1 560	1 560
Total appropriations for commitments	**92 025**	**93 475**	**93 955**	**93 215**	**91 735**	**91 125**	**90 660**
Total appropriations for payments	**89 600**	**91 110**	**94 220**	**94 880**	**91 910**	**90 160**	**89 620**
Appropriations for payments as % of GNP	**1.13 %**	**1.12 %**	**1.13 %**	**1.11 %**	**1.05 %**	**1.01 %**	**0.97 %**
Available for accession (appropriations for payments)			**4 140**	**6 710**	**8 890**	**11 440**	**14 220**
Agriculture			1 600	2 030	2 450	2 930	3 400
Other expenditure			2 540	4 680	6 440	8 510	10 820
Ceiling, appropriations for payments	**89 600**	**91 110**	**98 360**	**101 590**	**100 800**	**101 600**	**103 840**
Ceiling, payments as % of GNP	**1.13 %**	**1.12 %**	**1.18 %**	**1.19 %**	**1.15 %**	**1.13 %**	**1.13 %**
Margin for unforeseen expenditure	**0.14 %**	**0.15 %**	**0.09 %**	**0.08 %**	**0.12 %**	**0.14 %**	**0.14 %**
Own resources ceiling	**1.27 %**	**1.27 %**	**1.27 %**	**1.27 %**	**1.27 %**	**1.27 %**	**1.27 %**

([1]) In accordance with Article 2 of Decision No 182/1999/EC of the European Parliament and of the Council and Article 2 of Council Decision 1999/64/Euratom (OJ L 26, 1.2.1999, p. 1 and p. 34), EUR 11 510 million at current prices is available for research over the period 2000-02.

([2]) The expenditure on pensions included under the ceiling for this heading is calculated net of staff contributions to the pension scheme, up to a maximum of EUR 1 100 million at 1999 prices for the period 2000-06.

TABLE 5.1 B

Financial framework (EU-21)

(million EUR at 1999 prices)

Appropriations for commitments	2000	2001	2002	2003	2004	2005	2006
1. Agriculture	40 920	42 800	43 900	43 770	42 760	41 930	41 660
CAP (not including rural development)	36 620	38 480	39 570	39 430	38 410	37 570	37 290
Rural development and accompanying measures	4 300	4 320	4 330	4 340	4 350	4 360	4 370
2. Structural operations	32 045	31 455	30 865	30 285	29 595	29 595	29 170
Structural Funds	29 430	28 840	28 250	27 670	27 080	27 080	26 660
Cohesion Fund	2 615	2 615	2 615	2 615	2 515	2 515	2 510
3. Internal policies (¹)	5 930	6 040	6 150	6 260	6 370	6 480	6 600
4. External action	4 550	4 560	4 570	4 580	4 590	4 600	4 610
5. Administration (²)	4 560	4 600	4 700	4 800	4 900	5 000	5 100
6. Reserves	900	900	650	400	400	400	400
Monetary reserve	500	500	250				
Emergency aid reserve	200	200	200	200	200	200	200
Guarantee reserve	200	200	200	200	200	200	200
7. Pre-accession aid	3 120	3 120	3 120	3 120	3 120	3 120	3 120
Agriculture	520	520	520	520	520	520	520
Pre-accession structural instrument	1 040	1 040	1 040	1 040	1 040	1 040	1 040
Phare (applicant countries)	1 560	1 560	1 560	1 560	1 560	1 560	1 560
8. Enlargement			6 450	9 030	11 610	14 200	16 780
Agriculture			1 600	2 030	2 450	2 930	3 400
Structural operations			3 750	5 830	7 920	10 000	12 080
Internal policies			730	760	790	820	850
Administration			370	410	450	450	450
Total approps for commitments	92 025	93 475	100 405	102 245	103 345	105 325	107 440
Total appropriations for payments	89 600	91 110	98 360	101 590	100 800	101 600	103 840
of which: enlargement			4 140	6 710	8 890	11 440	14 220
Appropriations for payments as % of GNP	1.13 %	1.12 %	1.14 %	1.15 %	1.11 %	1.09 %	1.09 %
Margin for unforeseen expenditure	0.14 %	0.15 %	0.13 %	0.12 %	0.16 %	0.18 %	0.18 %
Own resources ceiling	1.27 %	1.27 %	1.27 %	1.27 %	1.27 %	1.27 %	1.27 %

(¹) In accordance with Article 2 of Decision No 182/1999/EC of the European Parliament and of the Council and Article 2 of Council Decision 1999/64/Euratom (OJ L 26, 1.2.1999, p. 1 and p. 34), EUR 11 510 million at current prices is available for research over the period 2000-02.

(²) The expenditure on pensions included under the ceiling for this heading is calculated net of staff contributions to the pension scheme, up to a maximum of EUR 1 100 million at 1999 prices for the period 2000-06.

1) Total expenditure

In the financial framework finally adopted, the overall ceiling on payments for the 15-member EU dropped appreciably, as a percentage of foreseeable GNP, from 2003 onwards to 0.97 % in 2006 as against 1.10 % in the 1999 budget. Including the amounts left available for an initial round of enlargement which was supposed to take place in 2002, there was still an unused margin beneath the own resources ceiling ranging from 0.09 to 0.14 % of the GNP of the EU-15.

These payment ceilings took account of the need to cover the clearance of commitments entered into over the previous period. This meant that the constraints on the ceilings for new commitments were even tighter. These ceilings were, each year, lower than the amount in the 1999 budget, and of course lower than the ceilings set for that year in the previous financial framework.

2) Agricultural expenditure (heading 1)

The definition of this heading was amended. It was agreed that the ceiling would no longer be the agricultural guideline but that it would correspond to the expenditure actually resulting from the reformed CAP. The guideline, a higher figure, continued to be calculated but it no longer appeared as such in the financial framework. Its scope was broadened to cover not only heading 1 expenditure but also the agricultural components of pre-accession aid and the amount planned in this field for the forthcoming enlargement. Heading 1 also had two subheadings: one applied to expenditure on common market organisations (intervention, direct aid for producers, veterinary and plant-health measures) and the other to rural development measures (measures accompanying the 1992 reform and structural measures previously coming under the Structural Funds).

The line taken during the negotiations was to set a level of expenditure for the reformed CAP of more or less the same amount as was entered in the 1999 budget. The necessary savings were first found by reducing intervention prices by less than proposed, hence the compensation in the form of aid to producers was less: the reduction in prices was 15 % in two stages for arable crops (instead of a single 25 % reduction) and 20 % (instead of 30 %) for beef. The reform of the milk sector was also postponed to the end of the period.

Other formulas were considered but not adopted:

— the possibility of reimbursing Member States only part of the expenditure they advance as direct aid to producers (formula known as 'cofinancing' of expenditure);

— direct aid granted on a declining scale over time (known as 'degressivity') and/or above a certain threshold per farm (known as 'capping').

3) Structural operations (heading 2)

The amounts set were lower than those proposed by the Commission. However, the proposals concerning the concentration of operations, the distribution criteria and the simplification of management methods were adopted without any major changes.

4) Other categories of expenditure

The ceilings for the internal policies, external action and administrative expenditure headings were appreciably lower than those proposed by the Commission. The reductions were imposed very much across the board, with no real discussion about the future content of these categories of expenditure. The starting point for this approach was not the existing 1999 ceilings but the lower figures of appropriations actually entered in the 1999 budget.

On the other hand, the amounts proposed by the Commission for pre-accession aid and for the estimated cost of the first round of enlargement were accepted without change.

2.2. Limited adjustment of the own resources system

In the end the Berlin European Council did not adopt any of the three options for rebalancing budget positions that the Commission examined in its report. The solution to this problem was found instead in measures to contain expenditure growth and redirect flows. The results obtained were enhanced by relatively slight adjustments to the financing system.

The European Council decided:

— to lower the maximum call-in rate for the VAT resource to 0.75 % in 2002 and 0.50 % in 2004;

— to increase the percentage of traditional own resources that the Member States retain to cover collection costs from 10 to 25 %;

— to retain the United Kingdom compensation mechanism, with some small adjustments, to offset for instance the benefit that would arise upon enlargement from the replacement of pre-accession aid by internal EU expenditure;

— to reduce the share paid by Germany, the Netherlands, Austria and Sweden in the financing of the UK correction to a quarter of their normal share.

2.3. Conclusion of a new Interinstitutional Agreement

1) The rules for applying the financial framework

These rules remained essentially unchanged. But some new provisions were added.

— Some restrictions were placed on the 'privileged' nature of expenditure on structural operations, in conjunction with the new basic regulations in this area. The allocations made in the financial framework continue to be expenditure targets, which must be entered in the budget each year. But the possibility of transferring to subsequent years the part of the allocations which could not be committed in a given year was confined to the first year of the period (2000) and then only if non-implementation was the result of a delay in the adoption of programmes.

— In the event of a revision of the financial framework, the 'pre-accession' heading and the amount left available for future enlargement were to be treated as 'water-tight compartments': in other words there could be no transfers between these two amounts nor between either of them and the ceilings for the other headings set for the EU-15.

— A 'flexibility instrument' was introduced. It is intended to allow financing, for a given financial year, of clearly identified expenditure which could not be financed beneath the ceilings available. As a rule the instrument should not be used for the same requirements two years running. This instrument was allocated EUR 200 million a year. The portion not used in a given year may be carried over for the following two years. Decisions to make use of the instrument are taken, during the budgetary procedure or in the course of the budget year, by joint agreement between the two arms of the budgetary authority, acting by qualified majority on a proposal from the Commission.

2) Budgetary procedure aspects

As proposed by the Commission the new agreement consolidated a number of arrangements agreed by the institutions to improve the operation of the budgetary procedure. Two additions were made.

— The conciliation procedure for the establishment of the budget was extended to cover all expenditure (compulsory and non-compulsory) and continued throughout the budgetary procedure.

— Guidelines were laid down, by broad categories, for the classification of expenditure.

3. Application of the financial framework, 2000-06

In general, the financial framework 2000-06 was applied following the implementing provisions as set out in the Interinstitutional Agreement (see point 2.3. above). However, two issues deserve to be looked at more closely: the annual budget debates and the enlargement of the European Union.

3.1. The budget debates for 2000-06

The budget procedures for the years 2000-06 were undoubtedly smoothed by the existence of the new Interinstitutional Agreement (IIA). A series of challenges had to be faced, in particular in the field of external actions. The new flexibility instrument allowed for a financial response, which would not otherwise have been possible.

The limitations of the ceilings set by the European Council already became clear in 1999, with the impact on the budget of the conflict beginning in Kosovo at that time. Very quickly the Commission was forced to present two proposals (in November 1999 and May 2000) for the revision of the heading 4 ceiling to accommodate the financing of a multi-annual programme of assistance for the Balkans region. These proposals, which were supported by Parliament, met with Council opposition. For the 2000 and 2001 budgets, the solution found in each case was to apply the new flexibility instrument, the decision coming at the end of the budgetary procedure after difficult discussions on the necessary redeployment of expenditure on the other programmes covered by the heading.

In the budgetary procedures for 2002 and 2003 the Commission once again proposed using this instrument to finance under heading 2 a programme for the conversion of fishing vessels which, following the failure to renew the agreement with Morocco, could no longer operate in Moroccan waters.

The flexibility instrument was mobilised in each subsequent year of the financial framework. Part of the support for reconstruction in Iraq was financed through flexibility in 2004, 2005 and 2006. Rehabilitation and reconstruction needs in the countries affected by the Tsunami were funded in 2005 and 2006. Also under heading 4 in 2006 compensation for the ACP sugar producers affected by the reform of the common market organisation for sugar, as well as part of the CFSP budget, was financed through flexibility.

Outside of heading 4, in 2005, some of the financing for the PEACE II programme[1] (subheading 2a) and part of the budget for the decentralised agencies (heading 3) came from mobilisation of the flexibility instrument.

3.2. Enlargement of the European Union

1) Determining the general budgetary framework

The overall Berlin framework envisaged annual amounts for 2002 to 2006, taking account of an enlargement in 2002 with a first group of six new Member States[2]. A second group, lagging in progress, was not expected to join before 2007.

---

[1] The EU Programme for Peace and Reconciliation in Northern Ireland and the Border Region of Ireland.

[2] Cyprus, the Czech Republic, Hungary, Poland, Estonia and Slovenia, also known as the 'Luxembourg group'.

The Helsinki European Council in December 1999 abolished the distinction between the two groups of accession countries, which opened up the possibility of more than six countries acceding during the period 2000-06.

While the assumption, made in Berlin, that the first round of enlargement would take place in 2002 was a justified precaution from the budgetary point of view, it turned out not to be realistic. Consequently, the accession date was moved back and the Laeken European Council of 14 and 15 December 2001 decided that 10 candidate countries (¹) could be ready to join the EU in 2004. Negotiations with the remaining two (Bulgaria and Romania) would be opened on all chapters in 2002.

The delay created additional room under the ceilings because of the phasing-in of expenditure related to structural actions. Since the first accessions would take place later than 2002, the amounts scheduled in principle for enlargement in 2002 and 2003 were not available (²). Nevertheless, the annual amounts reserved for the period 2004-06, initially intended to cover the needs related to the third, fourth and fifth year of the accession of six new Member States, would now be available for the first three years of the accession of 10 new Member States.

On the other hand, the Berlin sub-ceiling for agriculture did not include any amounts for direct payments to farmers in the new Member States. In their position papers, however, all candidate countries demanded to be fully integrated into this aspect of the common agricultural policy upon accession. The Berlin ceiling did not provide for any transitional budgetary arrangements either, although such arrangements had been part of all accession agreements in the past.

As planned in Laeken, the Commission presented at the beginning of 2002 its global approach for the draft common positions in the fields of agriculture, regional policy and the budget (³). The Communication introduced the necessary adjustment of the Berlin scenario to take into

---

(¹)   The Luxembourg group plus Latvia, Lithuania, Malta and Slovakia became from then on the 'Laeken group'.
(²)   The annuality of the financial perspective ceilings did not allow transfer to later years.
(³)   Communication from the Commission – Information note – Common Financial Framework 2004-2006 for the Accession Negotiations, SEC(2002) 102 final.

account the later accession date and the increased number of acceding countries. It also presented the following new elements:

— Given that immediate introduction of 100 % direct payments would have served to freeze existing structures and to hamper modernisation in agriculture, it was proposed to phase in direct aids over a period of 10 years, thus going well beyond the 2000-06 financial framework. Thus, the new Member States obtained assurance about the moment when they would be fully integrated into the CAP.

— Certain measures were proposed to make the transition to the EU rural development policy better adapted to the needs of the new Member States, such as increasing the EU co-financing rate up to 80 % for the rural development measures financed by the EAGGF Guarantee Section.

— In order to find a middle ground between the limits on absorption capacity and a faster profile than envisaged in Berlin for the first three years after accession, it was proposed that the phasing-in for structural actions be increased, with Cohesion Fund expenditure boosted to 33 % of total structural actions, compared to 18 % for the other beneficiary Member States.

— Additional allocations would be made for nuclear safety, to support the effort to decommission nuclear plants, and for institution building, to enhance the building up of adequate administrative structures and administrative capacity.

— Transitional budgetary arrangements were proposed based on the principle that no new Member State should find itself in a net budgetary position vis-à-vis the EU budget which was worse than the year before enlargement.

2) Agreement on the EU common position

The Commission Communication was accepted as a general basis for discussion and most delegations found the overall approach to be balanced and realistic. There was general agreement that budgetary compensation, if any were to be granted, should be fully financed below the Berlin ceilings.

In October 2002 ([1]), the Commission declared that, in line with the conclusions from the 2002 Regular Reports, the 10 countries of the Laeken group fulfilled the Copenhagen criteria and would be ready for membership from the beginning of 2004.

The Brussels European Council on 24-25 October endorsed these Commission findings and recommendations and took the final decisions with respect to the EU negotiating position. EU leaders agreed in Brussels on the following:

— Direct agricultural payments were to be introduced following a 10-year phasing-in schedule, expressed as a percentage of the level of such payments in the Union ([2]).

— A ceiling for heading 1a (common agricultural policy) for the EU-25 covering the entire period up to 2013 was established on the basis of the 2006 ceiling, increased by 1 % per year in nominal terms. The overall expenditure for market-related expenditure and direct payments for each year in the period 2007-13 was to be kept below this ceiling.

— For reasons of absorption capacity, the total allocation for structural operations was reduced from EUR 25.5 billion to EUR 23 billion.

— The own resources *acquis* was to apply to the new Member States as from accession.

— Temporary budgetary compensation, offsetting any deterioration of the *ex ante* estimated net budgetary position of the new Member States in comparison with their situation in the year before accession, would be offered in the form of lump-sum, temporary payments on the expenditure side of the EU budget. The compensations had to remain within the annual margins left under the Berlin ceilings for enlargement.

---

[1] 'Towards the enlarged Union — Strategy paper and report of the European Commission on the progress towards accession by each of the candidate countries', COM(2002) 700 final.

[2] Twenty five per cent of the full EU rate in 2004, 30 % in 2005, 35 % in 2006, 40 % in 2007. Thereafter, in 10 % increments so as to ensure that the new Member States reach in 2013 the support level then applicable.

After the Brussels Council the EU was now ready to negotiate the final terms of the accession with the candidate countries.

3) Agreement with the candidate countries in Copenhagen

After seven weeks of negotiations, on 13 December 2002, Heads of State or Government from the EU and 10 candidate countries reached agreement on the terms for enlarging the EU. Following the decision of the Copenhagen Summit, Cyprus, the Czech Republic, Estonia, Hungary, Latvia, Lithuania, Malta, Poland, Slovakia and Slovenia would join the EU on 1 May 2004.

The Copenhagen agreement acknowledged the financial needs of new Member States, since they were all expected to enjoy the status of net beneficiary with regard to the EU budget from the very beginning, while respecting the ceilings established in the financial framework for enlargement.

Under the terms of the final agreement, the following elements had been added compared to the EU common position determined in Brussels:

— a lump-sum cash-flow facility in the year 2004 to help all countries improve their net budgetary position during the first year and to further reduce the risk of any country seeing its net position worsen in the first year of enlargement [1];

— an extra package consisting of the Schengen facility, an increase in the rural development allocation and an increase in the transitional nuclear safety package;

— the cost of agricultural market measures had been recalculated to include the cost associated with some further concessions in this field.

All these measures, while increasing the expenditure, also automatically reduced the temporary budgetary compensation, which was calculated as the difference between each new Member State's estimated receipts from and payments to the EU budget (in comparison with the situation in the

[1] This was justified by the fact that direct agricultural payments related to the year 2004 would only be reimbursed by the EU budget to Member States in 2005.

year before accession). To offset this mechanism, a further allocation was made available as additional budgetary compensation for the disadvantaged countries.

Finally, budgetary compensation was further increased for certain Member States, offset by an equivalent reduction of their cohesion expenditure.

4) The adjustment of the financial framework

As provided for by the 1999 Interinstitutional Agreement, the European Parliament and Council needed to adjust the financial framework to take account of the expenditure requirements resulting from enlargement. Following the proposals put forward by the Commission in February 2003 ([1]), the budgetary authority agreed on 19 May 2003 on the adjustment of the financial framework in order to reconcile the EU-15 financial framework for the period 2004-06, at 1999 prices, with the situation of an enlarged Union of 25 members ([2]).

— The crucial modification was mainly technical and consisted in transferring appropriations for the 10 new Member States which had been earmarked in heading 8 (enlargement) to the regular headings. Consequently, for agriculture, structural operations, internal policies and administration (headings 1, 2, 3 and 5), the annual ceilings for commitments were raised in total by EUR 9 927 million for 2004, EUR 12 640 million for 2005 and EUR 14 901 million for 2006.

— As for pre-accession aid (heading 7, renamed 'pre-accession strategy'), the ceiling remained unchanged but it was set to cover also appropriations for pre-accession assistance concerning Turkey (previously included in heading 4). For Bulgaria and Romania the amounts earmarked for pre-accession instruments (Phare, Sapard and ISPA) were increased for the remaining years of the period by 20 %, 30 % and 40 % respectively compared to the average of the preceding years.

— A new heading 8 (compensation) was introduced, including the amounts envisaged for the so-called 'temporary budgetary compen-

([1])   Proposal for a Decision of the European Parliament and the Council on the adjustment of the financial perspective for enlargement, COM(2003) 70.

([2])   Decision 2003/429/EC of the European Parliament and of the Council of 19 May 2003 on the adjustment of the financial perspective for enlargement (OJ L 147, 14.6.2003, p. 25).

sation' and 'special lump-sum cash-flow facility' in favour of the 10 acceding countries. The amounts were EUR 1 273 million in 2004, EUR 1 173 million in 2005 and EUR 940 million in 2006.

— A provision was included in the adjusted financial framework whereby, in the event of a political settlement leading to the reunification of the island of Cyprus, supplementary amounts would be automatically added to each of the headings concerned. The budgetary implications resulting from the implementation of such a political settlement were estimated for the period at EUR 273 million at 1999 prices.

Compared to the situation envisaged in the Interinstitutional Agreement, the overall ceiling for commitment appropriations, at 1999 prices, was reduced by EUR 410 million for 2004, EUR 387 million for 2005 and EUR 939 million for 2006. In accordance with the Copenhagen European Council conclusions, the corresponding overall ceiling in payments (EU-25) for the years 2004-06 remained unchanged compared to the corresponding ceiling set out in Annex I of the Interinstitutional Agreement. The own resources ceiling for EU-25 remained unchanged in percentage terms and was established at 1.24 % of GNI-25.

Once the adjustment of the financial framework for enlargement was made in 1999 prices, it was necessary to establish the financial framework in 2004 prices, in line with the changes in gross national income (GNI) and prices. This adjustment was calculated by applying the same deflators used in the exercise of the technical adjustment of the financial framework for EU-15 at 2004 prices [1].

Furthermore, following the joint decision of the European Parliament and Council on the adjustment of the financial framework for enlargement, both arms of the budgetary authority agreed to revise the financial framework, increasing the annual ceilings for commitments in heading 3 (internal policies) by EUR 50 million for 2004, EUR 190 million for 2005 and EUR 240 million for 2006.

The resulting financial framework for an enlarged European Union with 25 members, at 1999 prices, is presented in Table 5.2.

---

[1]   COM(2002) 756 final, 23.12.2002.

The corresponding financial framework resulting from the technical adjustment for 2004, in line with movements in gross national income and prices, is presented in Table 5.3.

5) The accession of Bulgaria and Romania

After the long and difficult negotiations on the budgetary aspects of the accession of the 10 new Member States, it was clear from the outset that the budgetary negotiation with Bulgaria and Romania would be very much predetermined by the outcome of the 2004 accession.

On the one hand, it would be hard to imagine that the 25 Member States (including the 10 that had recently acceded) would be willing to offer a different (i.e. more generous) package to Bulgaria and Romania. On the other hand, it would be inconceivable that both candidate countries, being less affluent than the 10 new Member States in terms of GDP per capita, would settle for anything less. In view of these particular circumstances, the negotiations on the budgetary package went quite smoothly and the final agreement was almost identical to the Commission proposal (which was in line with the outcome of the accession of the 10).

The main lines of the budgetary package for Bulgaria and Romania were:

— phasing-in of direct agricultural payments over a 10-year period;

— phasing-in of structural actions over a three-year period;

— a three-year lump-sum cash-flow facility, which included the Schengen facility;

— no temporary budgetary compensation, since it was clear that neither Bulgaria nor Romania were at risk of seeing their budgetary situation vis-à-vis the EU budget deteriorate after accession in comparison with the situation in 2006.

Finally, there was no need for an adjustment of the financial framework since the accession negotiations coincided with the negotiations on the new financial framework and all the amounts scheduled for both new Member States were already incorporated.

TABLE 5.2
Financial framework (EU-25)
adjusted for enlargement

(million EUR at 1999 prices)

Commitment appropriations	2000	2001	2002	2003	2004	2005	2006
1. Agriculture	40 920	42 800	43 900	43 770	44 657	45 677	45 807
1a Common agricultural policy	36 620	38 480	39 570	39 430	38 737	39 602	39 612
1b Rural development	4 300	4 320	4 330	4 340	5 920	6 075	6 195
2. Structural actions	32 045	31 455	30 865	30 285	35 665	36 502	37 940
Structural Funds	29 430	28 840	28 250	27 670	30 533	31 835	32 608
Cohesion Fund	2 615	2 615	2 615	2 615	5 132	4 667	5 332
3. Internal policies	5 930	6 040	6 150	6 260	7 877	8 098	8 212
4. External actions	4 550	4 560	4 570	4 580	4 590	4 600	4 610
5. Administration (¹)	4 560	4 600	4 700	4 800	5 403	5 558	5 712
6. Reserves	900	900	650	400	400	400	400
Monetary reserve	500	500	250	0	0	0	0
Emergency aid reserve	200	200	200	200	200	200	200
Guarantee reserve	200	200	200	200	200	200	200
7. Pre-accession strategy	3 120	3 120	3 120	3 120	3 120	3 120	3 120
Agriculture	520	520	520	520			
Pre-accession structural instrument	1 040	1 040	1 040	1 040			
Phare (applicant countries)	1 560	1 560	1 560	1 560			
8. Compensation					1 273	1 173	940
Total appropriations for commitments	92 025	93 475	93 955	93 215	102 985	105 128	106 741
Total appropriations for payments	89 600	91 110	94 220	94 880	100 800	101 600	103 840
Ceiling, approps for payments as % of GNI (ESA 95)	1.07 %	1.08 %	1.11 %	1.10 %	1.08 %	1.06 %	1.06 %
Margin for unforeseen expenditure	0.17 %	0.16 %	0.13 %	0.14 %	0.16 %	0.18 %	0.18 %
Own resources ceiling	1.24 %	1.24 %	1.24 %	1.24 %	1.24 %	1.24 %	1.24 %

(¹) The expenditure on pensions included under the ceiling for this heading is calculated net of staff contributions to the pension scheme, up to a maximum of EUR 1 100 million euros at 1999 prices for the period 2000-06.

TABLE 5.3

Financial framework (EU-25)
adjusted for enlargement

(million EUR at 2004 prices)

Commitment appropriations	Current prices					2004 prices	
	2000	2001	2002	2003	2004	2005	2006
1. Agriculture	41 738	44 530	46 587	47 378	49 305	50 431	50 575
1a Common agricultural policy	37 352	40 035	41 992	42 680	42 769	43 724	43 735
1b Rural development	4 386	4 495	4 595	4 698	6 536	6 707	6 840
2. Structural actions	32 678	32 720	33 638	33 968	41 035	41 685	42 932
Structural Funds	30 019	30 005	30 849	31 129	35 353	36 517	37 028
Cohesion Fund	2 659	2 715	2 789	2 839	5 682	5 168	5 904
3. Internal policies	6 031	6 272	6 558	6 796	8 722	8 967	9 093
4. External actions	4 627	4 735	4 873	4 972	5 082	5 093	5 104
5. Administration ([1])	4 638	4 776	5 012	5 211	5 983	6 154	6 325
6. Reserves	906	916	676	434	442	442	442
Monetary reserve	500	500	250	0	0	0	0
Emergency aid reserve	203	208	213	217	221	221	221
Guarantee reserve	203	208	213	217	221	221	221
7. Pre-accession strategy	3 174	3 240	3 328	3 386	3 455	3 455	3 455
Agriculture	529	540	555	564			
Pre-accession structural instrument	1 058	1 080	1 109	1 129			
Phare (applicant countries)	1 587	1 620	1 664	1 693			
8. Compensation					1 410	1 299	1 041
Total appropriations for commitments	93 792	97 189	100 672	102 145	115 434	117 526	118 967
Total appropriations for payments	91 322	94 730	100 078	102 767	111 380	112 260	114 740
Ceiling, approps for payments as % of GNI (ESA 95)	1.07 %	1.08 %	1.11 %	1.09 %	1.08 %	1.06 %	1.06 %
Margin for unforeseen expenditure	0.17 %	0.16 %	0.13 %	0.15 %	0.16 %	0.18 %	0.18 %
Own resources ceiling	1.24 %	1.24 %	1.24 %	1.24 %	1.24 %	1.24 %	1.24 %

([1]) The expenditure on pensions included under the ceiling for this heading is calculated net of staff contributions to the pension scheme, up to a maximum of EUR 1 100 million at 1999 prices for the period 2000-06.

Chapter 6

Policy challenges and budgetary means of the enlarged Union: the multiannual financial framework 2007-13

In February 2004, the Commission presented its approach (¹) for the multiannual financial framework 2007-13. The document included the proposed breakdown of expenditure by broad category for the period 2007-13. In July 2004, the Commission confirmed and detailed its original stance (²) and proposed a new text for the related Interinstitutional Agreement (IIA) (³); it also presented a first 'legislative package' covering a number of legal bases for spending programmes and for the 2007-13 period. Following technically adjusted proposals from the Commission (⁴) and intense negotiations at European Council level in June 2005, agree-

---

(¹) Communication from the Commission to the Council and the European Parliament 'Building our common future. Policy challenges and budgetary means of the enlarged Union 2007-2013', COM(2004) 101 final/2, 26.2.2004.

(²) Communication from the Commission to the Council and the European Parliament 'Financial perspective 2007-2013', COM(2004) 487 final/2, 14.7.2004 and 'Financing the European Union. Commission report on the operation of the own resources system', COM(2004) 505 final, vol. I and II, 14.7.2004.

(³) Proposal for renewal of the Interinstitutional Agreement on budgetary discipline and improvement of the budgetary procedure, COM(2004) 498, 14.7.2004.

(⁴) Commission working document 'Technical adjustments to the Commission proposals for the multiannual financial framework 2007-2013', SEC(2005) 494 final, 12.4.2005.

ment on a multiannual financial framework for 2007-13 was reached among Heads of State or Government at the Brussels European Council on 15-16 December 2005. Following negotiations with the European Parliament, the new IIA was then adopted on 17 May 2006 [1]. Finally, a new decision on the own resources of the Communities was adopted on 7 June 2007 [2].

The Commission proposal stressed the necessity to turn the opportunities offered by the enlargement to 10 new Member States on 1 May 2004 and to Bulgaria and Romania on 1 January 2007 into reality, by developing 'a Europe of solidarity and partnership, which gives people the opportunity to build a lasting prosperity in common'. Three main objectives were highlighted for the new financial framework:

— Europe should work together for higher growth with more and better jobs. Robust, coordinated and coherent action was needed to avoid economic decline and improve Europe's economic performance;

— European citizenship should serve to guarantee concrete rights and duties, in particular freedom, justice and security;

— Europe should be a strong global player. It should in particular play an important role vis-à-vis its neighbours.

The discussions were held 'against the background of a troubled world and internal uncertainty'. Two influential factors shaping the negotiation context should be stressed in particular:

— The Treaty establishing a Constitution for Europe had been adopted by the European Council on 17 July 2003 but the ratification process in the Member States did not succeed. The rejection of the draft Constitution by France on 29 May 2005 and by the Netherlands on 1 June 2005 led to a prolonged period of institutional and political uncertainty in the EU.

---

[1] Interinstitutional Agreement between the European Parliament, the Council and the Commission on budgetary discipline and sound financial management (OJ C 139, 14.6.2006).

[2] Council Decision 2007/436/EC, Euratom of 7 June 2007 on the system of the European Communities' own resources (OJ L 163, 23.6.2007). It is expected that the decision will be ratified by the Member States no later than the beginning of 2009.

— The discussions occurred in a context of disagreements among a number of Member States on key international issues, in particular the war in Iraq.

The negotiation was further influenced by three very important considerations:

— The enlargement to new Member States would add only 5 % to the Union's GDP – and to its revenues – but the increase in population would amount to 30 %. It followed that EU budget expenditure would increase more than revenue, particularly in view of the fact that – as stressed by the Commission – enlargement would mean four million additional farmers, an increase of 50 %, and a doubling of income disparities between rich and poor.

— During the final stage of the negotiation opening the way for enlargement, in October 2002, the European Council reached a compromise on CAP spending in a Union of 25 until 2013 at the instigation of France and Germany. This decision predetermined a large share of the EU budget even before the Commission made its proposals (see Chapter 5 for more details on the budgetary impact of enlargement).

— Again prior to the Commission proposals, six Member States (Germany, France, the Netherlands, Austria, Sweden and the United Kingdom) – all net contributors to the EU budget – informed the Commission that they did not see room for an EU budget near the current ceiling for own resources. The 'letter of the six', sent to the President of the Commission on 15 December 2003 [1], stressed that average expenditure during the next financial framework should not exceed 1.0 % of EU GNI, including agriculture spending within the ceiling set by the European Council in October 2002. This letter did not specify whether the 1.0 % limit applied to payments or to commitment appropriations.

In such a context, obtaining an agreement proved particularly lengthy and difficult. The negotiations on the multiannual financial framework and the new own resources decision stretched over almost three and a

---

[1]   See Information to the Press – IP/03/173 from the Commission:
       http://europa.eu/rapid/pressReleasesAction.do?reference=IP/03/1731&format=HTML
       &aged=1&language=EN&guiLanguage=en.

half years. The negotiations were once again largely shaped by the issue of Member States' net contributions.

1. The Commission's proposals

1.1. The financial framework

The Commission's proposals maintained the ceilings of the own resources decision at their 1999 level, i.e. 1.24 % of GNI (1.27 % of GNP) for appropriations for payments and 1.31 % of GNI (1.335 % of GNP) for appropriations for commitments, beneath which would be financed the common agricultural and cohesion policies (both areas of marked interest for most of the new Member States), the renewed Lisbon agenda focusing on competitiveness policies (in particular research), and external action of the EU as a global player, while still leaving an adequate flexibility margin.

The Commission's proposal, published in February 2004, reflected an ambitious approach taking into account the various constraints imposed by the circumstances. With average yearly appropriations for payments of 1.14 % of GNI, the proposal seemed to anticipate Member States' reluctance to increase the budget in an environment of sluggish economic growth. In doing so, it also took notice of the constraints imposed on national budgets by EMU rules. Furthermore, the Commission integrated the spending levels for the common agricultural policy agreed upon in October 2002 into its own proposal.

Nevertheless, as can be seen in Table 6.1, the initial Commission proposal contained a marked shift in the allocation of resources between the different budget headings, and, in particular, a 'shift towards growth and employment with a focus on knowledge based activities such as research and innovation' (¹).

(¹)   Cf. European Commission: New proposals for growth and jobs under the next Financial Framework 2007-2013, Brussels, 6 April 2005 (IP/05/389).

TABLE 6.1

Shift in the allocation of resources between budget headings 2006-13 according to the Commission's original proposal from February 2004

(million EUR at constant 2004 prices)

Commitment appropriations	2006 (¹)	2007	2013	Difference 2006-2013
1. Sustainable growth	47 582	59 675	76 785	+ 61.4 %
1a Competitiveness for growth and employment	8 791	12 105	25 825	+ 193.8 %
1b Cohesion for growth and employment (²)	38 791	47 570	50 960	+ 31.4 %
2. Preservation and management of natural resources	56 015	57 180	57 805	+ 3.2 %
of which market related expenditure and direct payments	43 735	43 500	42 293	- 3.3 %
3. Citizenship, freedom, security and justice	1 381	1 630	3 620	+ 162.1 %
4. The EU as a global partner (³)	11 232	11 400	15 740	+ 40.1 %
5. Administration (⁴)	3 436	3 675	4 500	+ 31.0 %
6. Compensations	1 041			
Total appropriations for commitments	120 688	133 560	158 450	+ 31.3 %
Total appropriations for payments (ᵇ) (ᶜ)	114 740	124 600	143 100	+ 24.7 %
% of GNI	*1.09 %*	*1.15 %*	*1.15 %*	
Margin	*0.15 %*	*0.09 %*	*0.09 %*	
Own resources ceiling	*1.24 %*	*1.24 %*	*1.24 %*	

(¹) 2006 expenditure under the MAFF 2000-06 has been broken down according to the proposed new nomenclature to facilitate comparisons.

(²) Includes expenditure for the Solidarity Fund (EUR 1 billion in 2004 at current prices) as from 2006. However, corresponding payments are calculated only as from 2007.

(³) Integration of the EDF into the EU budget is assumed to take effect in 2008. EDF commitments for 2006 and 2007 are included only for comparison purposes. Payments on commitments before 2008 are not taken into account in the payment figures.

(⁴) Includes administrative expenditure for salaries, pensions, European Schools, and institutions other than the Commission. Other administrative expenditures are included in the first four expenditure headings.

Source: Figures based on COM(2004) 101 final, 10.2.2004, p. 29.

In particular, subheading 1a 'Competitiveness for growth and employment', heading 3 'Citizenship, freedom, security and justice', and heading 4 'The EU as a global partner' were to benefit from large increases in spending (see Table 6.1). These came in stark contrast with almost stagnating spending proposed under heading 2, which included the common agricultural policy expenditures.

However, these trends must be considered bearing in mind that the figures cover a seven-year timespan. In practice, the proposals made by the Commission entailed a very limited increase in spending as a percentage of EU GNI, i.e. from 1.09 % of GNI for payment appropriations foreseen in 2006 to 1.15 % thereafter, despite enlargement and the requirements related to both competitiveness, e.g. the renewed Lisbon agenda, and external objectives, e.g. in the context of the European Neighbourhood Policy. Right from the start, it was quite clear that the final result would lie somewhere between the Commission's proposal and the 1.0 % limit set by six of the net contributors.

The agreement already reached in the context of the CAP (heading 2), the critical importance of cohesion policy for a number of Member States – and in particular the increased needs related to enlargement (subheading 1b), and the relatively small amounts in absolute terms envisaged for headings 1a, 3, 4 and 5, *de facto* limited the room for manoeuvre for subsequent negotiations. As shown in the next section, the Commission's ambitions, most notably regarding the Lisbon agenda, had to be significantly downsized by the time of a final agreement.

However, examining the Commission proposals in greater detail, it is useful to highlight the following innovative elements pointing towards the realisation of the Lisbon goals. The Commission made budgetary but also qualitative proposals aimed at achieving these goals [1].

1a) Competitiveness for growth and employment

The Commission made very ambitious proposals to strengthen the European effort in research and technological development. The proposals, for instance, included the idea of creating a European research area, to act as an internal market for research and technology, and a very significant increase in direct financial support for research and student mobility.

Additional efforts were envisaged in the area of trans-European networks. The need for further efforts in developing infrastructures and improving connections between the Member States was underlined, with projects such as high-speed rail lines, 'motorways of the sea' or Galileo. The overall level of investment required to realise the 26 priority trans-

---

[1] All quotes in this subsection refer to COM(2004) 101 final, *op. cit.*

port projects would amount to EUR 220 billion up to 2020, with funding to peak between 2007 and 2013.

Another innovative element was a Growth Adjustment Fund of up to EUR 1 billion per year, available within the competitiveness for growth and employment heading. This new fund was intended to optimise the delivery of the growth and cohesion objectives by introducing flexibility margins in the budget to make the EU able to react swiftly to changing economic circumstances.

1b) Cohesion for growth and employment

The Commission pushed for the Lisbon goals to be integrated into the national or regional development plans to be negotiated as part of the cohesion policy. Resources would be concentrated on investment in order to increase and improve the stock of physical and human capital and thus exert maximum impact on competitiveness and growth. Emphasis would thus be placed on job creation in new activities. Particularly for the second objective of the cohesion policy, the 'regional competitiveness and employment' goal, the Commission made it clear that 'interventions would need to concentrate on a limited number of policy priorities linked to the Lisbon and Göteborg agenda'.

2) Sustainable management and protection of natural resources

The reform of the common agricultural policy (CAP), decided in the wake of the agreement of October 2002, was 'aimed at meeting the objectives of competitiveness, solidarity and better integration of environmental concerns thus becoming a key step in the Lisbon and Göteborg development strategy' and involved three key elements. First, a substantial simplification, by decoupling direct payments to farmers from production. Second, further strengthening rural development by transferring funds from market support to rural development through reductions in direct payments to bigger farms (modulation). Third, a financial discipline mechanism would set a ceiling on expenditure on market support and direct aid between 2007 and 2013.

In the environment area, priorities would include implementing the EC Climate Change Programme, a number of thematic strategies addressing specific environmental priorities and the Environmental Technology

Action Plan (ETAP), and developing and implementing the Natura 2000 network in the area of biodiversity.

The other areas of EU action were not so much focused on the Lisbon and Göteborg agenda, but rather responded to specific concerns and object-ives. In general, these policies involved more limited funding in absolute terms, in particular for heading 3, as detailed hereafter.

3) Citizenship, freedom, security and justice

A starting point for the Commission proposals was the recognition that 'the challenges posed by immigration, asylum, and the fight against crime and terrorism can no longer be met adequately by measures taken only at the national level'. Besides, enlargement would bring particular chal-lenges, for example in terms of the security of 'our external borders'. Specific importance was thus given to a common asylum policy and a common policy on immigration, as well as an effective area of justice and preventing and fighting crime and terrorism.

4) The EU as a global player

The Commission stressed that the Union has developed a broad, though incomplete, spectrum of external relations tools and that enlargement would entrust the EU with even greater responsibilities, as a regional leader and as a global partner. Therefore, the expanded EU would stabil-ise its wider neighbourhood and support its development through close cooperation. It would create a 'stability circle' meaning a common space, a community of 'everything but the institutions'.

Cooperation with developing countries would focus on the eradication of poverty, making a 'strong and coherent contribution to progress towards reaching the Millennium development goals, set at the 2000 United Nations General Assembly'.

All in all, the Commission's scope to set the agenda for the upcoming budget debates was limited. After this initial phase of agenda-setting, the Commission tabled a number of working documents on specific details of its proposals and their financial implications. The Commission also pre-pared a package of legislative proposals for the spending programmes – more than 30 pieces of legislation – in order to table them immediately after a political compromise on the multiannual financial framework had been reached.

1.2. The financing system

According to own resources decision 2000/597/EC, Euratom, the Commission was to undertake a general review of the own resources system before 1 January 2006. In response to a request from the European Parliament, the Commission had furthermore undertaken (in a statement annexed to the Council minutes when Decision 2000/597/EC, Euratom was adopted) to submit this review before the end of 2004.

When the Commission subsequently adopted its first Communication on the post-2006 financial framework on 10 February 2004 [1], it set out the basic principles for the reform of the financing system. A communication, a detailed report [2] and a proposal for a new own resources decision and related implementing regulation on a generalised correction mechanism [3] were adopted by the Commission on 14 July 2004, together with more detailed proposals on spending.

The 2004 own resources report included two major features that could transform the own resources system:

— The report proposed replacing the specific correction mechanism used for one country only (the United Kingdom) by a general correction mechanism applying to any country that fulfilled relevant pre-determined criteria. The new mechanism should be effective as from 2007, with phasing-in provisions to facilitate the transition for the UK.

---

[1]   See COM(2004) 101 final, *op. cit.*

[2]   See 'Financing the European Union. Commission report on the operation of the own resources system', COM(2004) 505 final, vols I and II, 14.7.2004.

[3]   See Proposal for a Council Decision on the system of the European Communities' own resources and Proposal for a Council Regulation on the implementing measures for the correction of budgetary imbalances in accordance with Articles 4 and 5 of the Council Decision of (...) on the system of the European Communities' own resources, COM(2004) 501 final/2, 2004/0170 (CNS), 2004/0171 (CNS), 3.8.2004. NB: This is the reference of the proposals *cum corrigendum* only in English. COM(2004) 501 final was adopted on 14 July 2004.

— The report also presented 'three main candidates as possible future fiscal own resources: a resource based on 1. energy consumption, 2. national VAT bases, and 3. corporate income'. It called on the Council 'to take note of the Commission's intention to prepare a roadmap in view of replacing, on the basis of a Commission proposal, the current VAT resource by a genuine tax-based own resource by 2014' [1].

The Commission thus formally proposed a thorough reform of the system of correcting budgetary imbalances by progressively replacing the UK correction with a generalised correction mechanism with the same rules applying to all Member States without exception. For the first time since the introduction of the UK correction in 1984, there was consequently a concrete proposal on the Council's table which placed the correction on the political agenda as an item for discussion.

This proposal was justified on two grounds:

— The necessity to treat equally Member States that are in comparable positions. The Commission stressed that the UK benefited from a special rebate mechanism, which did not benefit a number of net contributors with broadly similar levels of GNI. This was contrary to the principle adopted at the 1984 Fontainebleau European Council that 'any Member State sustaining a budgetary burden which is excessive in relation to its relative prosperity may benefit from a correction at the appropriate time'. The solution would be to either eliminate the correction mechanism or to propose a mechanism applying equally to all the Member States.

— The analysis of the evolution of the UK correction following enlargement highlighted that the correction would increase over time to such an extent that the UK would become the smallest net contributor. In fact, it could be argued that the UK would not be contributing its fair share to the cost of enlargement, despite being one of the main advocates of such enlargement. This last argument proved instrumental in leading to a modification of the UK correction (see Chapter 12).

Furthermore, an important conclusion of the Commission regarding possible new own resources was the recognition that 'the implementation

---

[1]   See COM(2004) 505 final, vol. I, *op. cit.*

of an energy- or VAT-based resource would be feasible over the medium term, whereas a fiscal resource based on corporate income [would be] a much longer-term option'. A few years would be sufficient to reform in depth the financing system, provided the political will existed.

Under the Luxembourg and UK presidencies (first and second halves of 2005) the focus of the negotiations among Member States shifted away from the Commission's proposals. The 'negotiating boxes' of these Presidencies instead sought ad hoc changes to the current own resources system in order to accommodate specific interests of the Member States in the context of a global agreement on the expenditure and revenue side of the post-2006 financial framework.

Consequently, following broad political agreement achieved during the European Council on 15-16 December 2005, a new own resources decision was adopted, more than a year later, in June 2007 (¹). This long delay, necessary to reach a final consensus on the fine-tuned technical decision, was symptomatic of the difficulties and complexity of the broad political agreement achieved.

1.3. Renewal of the Interinstitutional Agreement (IIA)

The preparation of a new Interinstitutional Agreement (IIA) extended over two years. On 14 July 2004 the Commission presented a proposal (²) for the renewal of the IIA on budgetary discipline and improvement of the budgetary procedure for the period 2007-13.

This proposal was followed, on 8 June 2005, by a European Parliament resolution on 'Policy challenges and budgetary means of the enlarged Union 2007-13' (³), then a resolution on the Interinstitutional Agreement on budgetary discipline and improvement of the budgetary procedure (⁴) adopted on 1 December 2005.

(¹)   See Council Decision 2007/436/EC, Euratom, *op. cit.*

(²)   See Commission Working Document 'Proposal for renewal of the Interinstitutional Agreement on budgetary discipline and improvement of the budgetary procedure', COM(2004) 498 final, 14.7.2004.

(³)   See European Parliament document P6_TA(2005)0224.

(⁴)   See European Parliament document P6_TA PROV(2005)0453.

Following the political agreement on the financial framework 2007-13 reached by the European Council on 15-16 December 2005 ([1]), the European Parliament adopted a new resolution on the European Council's position on the financial framework and the renewal of the Interinstitutional Agreement 2007-13 ([2]).

A revised proposal ([3]) was therefore tabled by the Commission in February 2006. After further negotiation between the three institutions, the IIA was adopted on 17 May 2006.

The proposals made by the Commission for a new IIA suggested maintaining unchanged the main features of the financial framework. Agenda 2000 had successfully fulfilled its main purposes as regards financial discipline, the orderly evolution of expenditure and interinstitutional collaboration during the budgetary procedure. The budget of the European Union had been adopted on time each year, and the two arms of the budgetary authority had jointly adjusted Agenda 2000 to face supplementary financial requirements linked to the enlargement to 10 new Member States on 1 May 2004.

On the other hand, the Commission stressed the importance of flexibility as 'the essential corollary to financial discipline. If properly designed, it contributes to enhancing effective resources allocation while allowing responding to unforeseen needs or new priorities. Several parameters influence the degree of flexibility of the financial framework: the length of the period covered by the financial framework; the number of expenditure headings; the margins available within each expenditure ceiling; the margin below the own resources ceiling; the share of EU spending pre-determined by 'amounts of reference' in co-decided legislation; pre-allocated multiannual programmes; the general attitude towards using the revision procedure. The degree of flexibility has evolved over time with the changing mix of those parameters'. As shown below, several

---

([1])   See Document 15915/05 Cadrefin 268, 19.12.2005.

([2])   See PE 368.274, B6-0049/2006.

([3])   See Commission Working Document 'Revised proposal for renewal of the Interinstitutional Agreement on budgetary discipline and improvement of the budgetary procedure', COM(2006) 36 final, 1.2.2006, and Commission Working Document 'Contribution to the interinstitutional negotiations on the proposal for renewal of the Interinstitutional Agreement on budgetary discipline and improvement of the budgetary procedure', COM(2006) 75 final, 15.2.2006.

modifications and new instruments, as well as a reduction in the number of headings, brought additional flexibility to the system.

The Commission further considered that experience with the 2000-06 financial framework had shown that there was no longer any need for maintaining the agricultural guideline provided for in Council Regulation (EC) No 2040/2000 on budgetary discipline, since agriculture expenditure was already constrained by ceilings agreed until 2013.

2. The outcome of the negotiations

2.1. Slight decrease in Community expenditure

Stabilisation or even reduction of contributions to the EU budget was a priority for a number of net contributors, as is for instance reflected in the 'letter of the six' (cf. *supra*), which argued that average expenditure during the next financial framework should not exceed 1.0 % of EU GNI. The letter did not specify whether the 1.0 % related to commitment or to payment appropriations, which opened up a useful margin for negotiation. Indeed, during the negotiations this norm related first to commitment appropriations, then, at a later stage in the negotiation, to payment appropriations – an objective easier to comply with. Nevertheless, the constraint imposed by the letter weighed heavily in the negotiation, in particular as the new Member States were very keen on securing an agreement which would grant them access to substantial additional expenditure from the EU budget.

Table 6.2 below illustrates the dynamics of negotiation. The process started with a Commission proposal which intended to create a strong impetus for, notably, Lisbon-related expenditures. The European Parliament suggested limited shifts across headings, in particular an increase in heading 3. The subsequent Council discussions led to markedly reduced overall levels of commitment appropriations under the Luxembourg and UK presidencies. The conclusion of the Interinstitutional Agreement allowed for a very limited upward adjustment.

Detailed figures on the yearly commitments from 2007 to 2013 illustrate another facet of the multiannual financial framework. As detailed in Annex 1 to the Interinstitutional Agreement 2007-13, the global ceiling for commitment appropriations will fall from 1.10 % of EU GNI in 2007 to 1.01 % in 2013 (from 1.06 % to 0.94 % for payment appropriations). This includes the (increasing) cost of enlargement, considering the phasing-in of various policies, in particular the CAP, in the new Member States. In practice, if a future financial framework (beyond 2013) was stabilised at the level of 2013, i.e. 1.01 % of EU GNI for commitment appropriations, global multiannual commitments would decrease compared to the average level of 1.05 % of EU GNI foreseen for 2007-13.

TABLE 6.2

Total 2007-13 commitments – from Commission proposal to agreement

(million EUR at 2004 constant prices)

	Commission proposal *(14 July 2004)*	EP resolution *(8 June 2005)*	European Council *(15-16 Dec. 2006)*	Final agreement *(17 May 2006)*	*Change vs. Commission proposal*	
1. Sustainable growth	457 995	446 930	379 739	382 139	-75 856	-17 %
1a. Competitiveness	121 687	110 600	72 120	74 098	-47 589	-39 %
1b. Cohesion	336 308	336 330	307 619	308 041	-28 267	-8 %
2. Natural resources	400 294	392 306	371 244	371 344	-28 950	-7 %
of which CAP	301 074	293 105	293 105	293 105	-7 969	-3 %
3. Citizen, freedom, security, justice	14 724	16 053	10 270	10 770	-3 954	-27 %
3a. Freedom, security and justice	9 210	9 321	6 630	6 630	-2 580	-28 %
3b. Citizenship	5 514	6 732	3 640	4 140	-1 374	-25 %
4. The EU as a global player	61 223	62 436	48 463	49 463	-11 760	-19 %
5. Administration	57 670	54 765	50 300	49 800	-7 870	-14 %
6. Compensations (BG and RO)	800	800	800	800	—	—
Total commitments	992 706	973 290	860 816	864 316	-128 390	-13 %
% of EU-27 GNI	1.20 %	1.18 %	1.05 %	1.05 %		

NB: Original figures have been adjusted to ensure comparability with the final outcome. Heading 4 excludes the European Development Fund (EDF) as well as the Emergency Aid Reserve. The exclusion in the final agreement of EUR 500 million staff pension contributions under heading 5 and of the Emergency Aid Reserve (EUR 1 547 million) allowed the actual increase of EUR 4 billion obtained by the European Parliament to be presented in the financial framework table as an increase of only EUR 2 billion. The original documents referred to in this chapter contain the unadjusted figures.

2.2. A moderate shift in the budget structure

In the context of strict budgetary discipline, involving a decrease in commitments as a percentage of GNI over the period 2007-13, and considering the agreement reached for agriculture before the negotiation of the financial framework, the bulk of adjustment in relative terms during the negotiation was mainly borne by headings 1a and 3. The December 2005 agreement involved a cut of 39 % and 27 % for these headings respectively, compared to the initial Commission proposal.

Although the Council and the Member States agreed on the importance of an ambitious Lisbon and Göteborg agenda, and the related need to increase efforts in areas such as research or the environment, this proved difficult to translate into budgetary terms. For many Member States cohesion policy, agriculture, and specific rebates on their contributions came as priorities.

2.3. Limited adjustment of the own resources system

In the agreement it reached on 15-16 December 2005, the European Council took the following main decisions on the future own resources system:

— The ceilings laid down in the decision on own resources should be maintained at their current level of 1.24 % of EU GNI for appropriations for payments and of 1.31 % EU GNI for appropriations for commitments;

— The distinction between agricultural duties and customs duties would be abolished;

— 'In the interests of transparency and simplicity', in particular the elimination of the complex frozen rate mechanism, the uniform rate of call of the VAT-based resource would be fixed at 0.30 % (see Chapter 12).

— For the period 2007-13 only, the rate of call of the VAT-based resource would be fixed at 0.225 % for Austria, 0.15 % for Germany and 0.10 % for the Netherlands and Sweden.

— For the period 2007-13 only, the Netherlands would benefit from a gross reduction in its annual GNI contribution of EUR 605 million and Sweden from a gross reduction in its annual GNI contribution of EUR 150 million, measured in 2004 prices.

— The correction mechanism in favour of the United Kingdom should remain, along with the reduced financing of the correction benefiting Germany, Austria, Sweden and the Netherlands. However, after a phasing-in period between 2009 and 2011, the United Kingdom should participate fully in the financing of the costs of enlargement, except for direct agricultural payments and market-related expenditure, and that part of rural development expenditure originating from the European Agricultural Guidance and Guarantee Fund (EAGGF), Guarantee Section. The corresponding reduction of the UK correction should not exceed EUR 10.5 billion in constant 2004 prices during the period 2007-13.

The European Council of 15 and 16 December 2005 concluded that the above changes should take effect on 1 January 2007. In practice, the entry into force of the changes would be retroactive, following the ratification of own resources decision 2007/436/EC, Euratom[1], a process which the Council expected to be completed no later than the beginning of 2009[2].

Overall, the own resources system remains largely unchanged. However, with the notable exception of the fixing of the rate of call of the VAT-based resource, the changes introduced render the system even more complex and less transparent than before.

2.4. Conclusion of a new Interinstitutional Agreement

The Interinstitutional Agreement of 17 May 2006 was largely based on the agreement adopted for the previous multiannual financial framework. This was in particular the case for the structure by headings and the use of ceilings.

---

[1] Pursuant to Article 11 of this Decision (in accordance with Article 269 of the Treaty): 'Member States shall notify the ... Council without delay of the completion of the procedures for the adoption of this Decision in accordance with their respective constitutional requirements. This Decision shall enter into force on the first day of the month following receipt of the last of the notifications ... It shall take effect on 1 January 2007'.

[2] See point 78 of Council document No 15915/05, *op. cit.*

Nevertheless, a number of useful changes, making for further simplification and flexibility, were introduced.

(a) Simplification, consolidation

— The agreement incorporated the Interinstitutional Agreement of 7 November 2002 on the creation of the European Union Solidarity Fund (EUSF), agreed on during the period of the 2000-06 financial framework as a separate supplementary Interinstitutional Agreement. The current rules for mobilisation of the EUSF are maintained. When the Fund is mobilised, corresponding expenditure is 'entered in the budget over and above the relevant headings' in the financial framework.

— Simplification of the method for the technical adjustment, by extending the predetermined 2 % annual inflation rate used for structural funds and agriculture to the rest of expenditure. The table of the multiannual financial framework included in the IIA is expressed in constant 2004 prices. However, in view of the fixed annual inflation rate the ceilings are already fixed in current prices for the entire period covered by the multiannual financial framework.

— The provisioning of the guarantee fund for loans to third countries is rationalised so that there is no longer any need for a 'reserve' to this end. The related (reduced) expenditure to be budgeted becomes part of the instruments available for the Union's external policy.

(b) Flexibility: taking stock of the experience of Agenda 2000

On 15 and 16 December 2005, the European Council reached a political agreement which entailed expenditure ceilings significantly lower than those proposed by the Commission. Tighter expenditure ceilings would in turn entail more rigidity in the financial framework and risked undermining the Union's ability to address future challenges, hindering rather than encouraging effective resource allocation.

In order to find the proper balance between budgetary discipline and efficient resource allocation, new flexibility instruments were introduced to facilitate the deployment or redeployment of financial resources within the expenditure ceilings:

— a new European Globalisation Adjustment Fund intended to provide additional support for workers who suffer the consequences of major structural changes in world trade patterns, to assist them with their reintegration into the labour market. The Fund could not exceed a maximum annual amount of EUR 500 million (current prices);

— the possibility for the budgetary authority, on the basis of a Commission proposal in the framework of the annual budgetary procedure, to depart by up to 5 % from the so-called 'reference amounts' concerning multiannual programmes adopted under the co-decision procedure (except for cohesion programmes).

Some other instruments could be mobilised above the agreed expenditure ceilings within certain limits. These instruments, to be used in the framework of the annual budget procedure according to the relevant provisions set out in the IIA, included:

— the European Union Solidarity Fund, with unchanged amount (EUR 1 billion at current prices) and mobilisation procedure;

— the Flexibility Instrument, with an annual ceiling of EUR 200 million, with the new possibility to cover requirements of a multiannual nature. The mobilisation procedure remains unchanged;

— the Emergency Aid Reserve of EUR 221 million in constant prices was moved outside the multiannual financial framework. Its purpose is to respond to emergency situations in third countries. Both the amount and the mobilisation procedure remain unchanged.

3. Initial years of application: the budget debate for 2007 and 2008

The Commission presented the first preliminary draft budget (PDB) under the new multiannual financial framework on 3 May 2006. The PDB already took into account the increases to the ceilings agreed, which remained to be formalised in the Interinstitutional Agreement of 17 May (IIA).

As had been the case in the final years of the 2000-06 financial frame-work, one of the key issues in the negotiation process was the level of payment appropriations, with Council seeking to cut the Commission's PDB, and Parliament seeking to increase it. Other important aspects for discussion were a proposal by Parliament to reduce the level of the CFSP below the figure agreed in the IIA, as well as moves by the Council to seek reductions in the Commission's staffing levels.

It proved impossible to achieve a final agreement on the budget for 2007 at the November conciliation. However, only one week afterwards, a trialogue procedure resulted in the successful conclusion of the negotia-tions, within the newly agreed financial framework, and for the first time since 2000, without recourse to the flexibility instrument. The level of the CFSP budget was restored to that proposed in the PDB, and no adjust-ments were made to the Commission's human resources.

In parallel to the negotiations on the budget, discussion took place on the review of the Financial Regulation. This process was successfully con-cluded at the November conciliation.

The 2008 budget procedure saw a return to the issue of the margin under heading 4, which had been so dominant in the 2000-06 procedures. Just as in the 2000 and 2001 procedures, developments in Kosovo were a catalyst in launching the debate on the need for the flexibility instru-ment.

An initial amount of EUR 200.25 million was entered in the PDB for CFSP actions. During the course of the procedure, the Council proposed that this amount be increased to EUR 285.25 million, to cover greater financing needs for Kosovo. However, this increase, in combination with Parliament's wish to increase appropriations for other programmes in the field of external actions, could not be accommodated under the ceiling of heading 4. A compromise was reached at the conciliation meeting of 23 November, resulting in the mobilisation of the flexibility instrument for EUR 70 million in respect of heading 4.

Furthermore, the failure in early 2007 of the negotiations with a private consortium on the financing of the European Navigation Satellite Sys-tem programme 'Galileo' through a public-private partnership resulted in an additional financing requirement from the EU budget of EUR 2.4

billion. Given that the possibilities for redeployment of funds within sub-heading 1a were extremely limited, the Commission made a proposal, on 19 September 2007, to revise the financial framework in accordance with points 21 to 23 of the Interinstitutional Agreement(¹). This proposal was also intended to cover an additional financing need (EUR 309 million) for the European Institute of Technology (EIT), whose establishment had been proposed by the Commission as part of the mid-term review of the Lisbon strategy(²).

On the basis of the Commission proposal, the European Parliament, the Council and the Commission agreed, at the conciliation meeting of 23 November 2007, to provide this financing by, *inter alia*, revising the multiannual financial framework 2007-13 so as to raise the ceilings for commitment appropriations under subheading 1a for the years 2008 to 2013 by an amount of EUR 1 600 million in current prices. This increase was offset by lowering the ceiling for commitment appropriations under heading 2 for the year 2007 by the same amount. The reduction of the ceiling for heading 2 in 2007 was made possible by the combined effect of favourable market conditions in the agricultural sector and assigned revenue carried over from 2007 to 2008, which led to an increase in the global margin available under heading 2 in 2007. The programmes and payments to be financed under heading 2 thus remained totally unaf-fected by the revision of the financial framework.

The three institutions also agreed that, in order to keep an appropri-ate relationship between commitments and payments, the annual ceilings for payment appropriations would be adjusted. The global amount of the ceilings for commitment appropriations and payment appropriations expressed in current prices remained unchanged compared to the initial 2007-13 financial framework.

The remaining financing requirements of Galileo and the EIT were made available from different sources: EUR 400 million were reprofiled within

---

(¹) See Communication from the Commission concerning the revision of the multiannual financial framework (2007-2013), Proposal for a Decision of the European Parliament and of the Council amending the Interinstitutional Agreement of 17 May 2006 on budget-ary discipline and sound financial management as regards the multiannual financial framework, COM(2007) 549 final/2.

(²) See Proposal for a Regulation of the European Parliament and the Council establishing the European Institute of Technology, COM(2006) 604 final/2.

the transport-related activities of the seventh research framework programme, EUR 200 million were redeployed from other programmes within subheading 1a, and the flexibility instrument was mobilised for an amount of EUR 200 million. The remaining amount (EUR 309 million) was to be covered from the margin available under the ceiling of subheading 1a for the years 2008-13 (¹)(²).

4. The budget review of 2008-09

The December 2005 European Council agreed that, as a component of the overall negotiation package for 2007-13, a review of EU expenditure and revenue should take place: 'the European Council … invites the Commission to undertake a full, wide ranging review covering all aspects of EU spending, including CAP, and of resources, including the UK rebate, to report in 2008/9. On the basis of such a review, the European Council can take decisions on all subjects covered by the review. The review will also be taken into account in the preparatory work of the following Financial Framework' (³).

The Interinstitutional Agreement of May 2006 provides for certain arrangements associating the European Parliament in the process: 'during the examination phase following the presentation of the review by the Commission, it will be ensured that appropriate discussions take place with the European Parliament on the basis of the normal political dialogue between the institutions and that the positions of the European Parliament are duly taken into account'.

Finally, Article 9 of the new decision on own resources adopted on 7 June 2007 stipulates that, in the framework of the budget review, the Commission must undertake a general review of the own resources system.

A roadmap leading to the review has been described in an information note from the President of the Commission (⁴). The review started in Sep-

---

(¹)   The multiannual financial framework was again amended in 2008 in accordance with Article 48 of the Interinstitutional Agreement (see Section 2.3 of Chapter 9).
(²)   The revised ceilings for the multiannual financial framework can be found in Chapter 13.
(³)   See paragraphs 79 and 80 of Council document 15915/05 CADREFIN 268, *op. cit.*
(⁴)   See Information Note from the President 'The review of the internal market, the social stocktaking and the budgetary review', SEC(2007) 42/2 of 15 January 2007.

tember 2007 with a broad consultation process launched by an issues paper ([1]).

In the information note, it was made clear that 'the review is not to be perceived as the preparation of a new multiannual financial framework and should not anticipate on it. The task of proposing the next multiannual financial framework will be for the new Commission, which will be able to draw on the review as input to its work'.

Unlike past discussions on the future of the budget, this review aims to allow for a visionary approach, not so much focused on short-run negotiations, but rather on preparing long-term initiatives.

In this context, parallel to the work undertaken by the Commission, the European Parliament proceeded with its own reflexion on the future financing system of the Union. In a resolution of 29 March 2007([2]), Parliament stressed the importance of examining 'the creation of a new system of own resources based on a tax already levied in the Member States, the idea being that this tax, partly or in full, would be fed directly into the EU budget as a genuine own resource, thus establishing a direct link between the Union and European taxpayers'.

Parliament also expressed its wish to pursue the examination of options for the future financing of the EU budget in close cooperation with the national parliaments before taking a final position. At the same time, it intended 'to discuss and adopt its final position on a new system of own resources for the European Union in time for it to be taken into account in the deliberations concerning the comprehensive review of EU revenue and expenditure as agreed in the Interinstitutional Agreement of 17 May 2006'.

---

[1] See Communication from the Commission 'Reforming the budget, changing Europe. A public consultation paper in view of the 2008/2009 Budget review', SEC(2007) 1188 final, 12.9.2007.

[2] European Parliament resolution of 29 March 2007 on the future of the European Union's own resources (2006/2205(INI)), P6_TA-(2007)0098.

Part 2

THE CHARACTERISTICS
OF THE PRESENT FINANCIAL SYSTEM

Chapter 7

The legal instruments

The European Union's financial system is based on three types of legal instrument:

— the provisions of the Treaties ([1]);

— secondary legislation;

— provisions adopted by agreement between the institutions.

The last type of instrument is specific to the budget sector and has no real equivalent in the other fields of Community law.

1. The financial provisions of the Treaties

Most of these provisions are contained in the Treaty establishing the European Community. Some provisions of the Treaty on European Union also relate to the budget sector. The EC Treaty was amended by the Maastricht Treaty, which entered into force on 1 November 1993, and the EC Treaty and EU Treaty were last amended by the Nice Treaty, which entered into force on 1 February 2003. The Lisbon Treaty is discussed in section 4 of this chapter.

([1])   See Annex 1.

In an opinion of 21 October 1990 concerning the planned revision of the then Treaty establishing the European Economic Community (now 'Treaty establishing the European Community'), the Commission suggested taking this opportunity to consider the status of public finance. The contributions it presented to the intergovernmental conference proposed a substantial revision of the financial provisions of the Treaty, in particular to incorporate certain aspects agreed in the 1988 Interinstitutional Agreement and to establish a better balance between the institutions in the budgetary procedure [1].

The financial aspects were not really discussed and the Maastricht Treaty made no fundamental changes to the Community's financial system. The same is true of the Amsterdam Treaty. The Nice Treaty involved no changes to the financial provisions, except a number of amendments to Article 279 of the EC Treaty.

1.1. The Treaty establishing the European Community

The financial provisions of the Treaty are contained in Title II (Articles 268 to 280) of Part Five, which deals with the Community institutions, and they cover five main aspects.

1) The general rules governing the budgetary procedure

— Article 268 establishes the principles of unity, universality and equilibrium. It also contains the main terms for including in the budget expenditure relating to common foreign and security policy and to cooperation in the fields of justice and home affairs, which are set out in greater detail in the Treaty on European Union.

— Article 270 incorporates the concept of budgetary discipline into the Treaty.

— Article 271 establishes the principles of annuality and specification.

— Article 277 establishes the principle that the budget must be established in a unit of account.

---

[1] Intergovernmental Conferences: contributions by the Commission. Bulletin EU. Supplement 2/91.

2) Financing of the budget

— Article 269 establishes the principle of financing the budget from own resources and sets out the procedure for adopting decisions to implement it.

3) The stages in the budgetary procedure

— Article 272 describes in more detail the timetable and stages in the budgetary procedure, taking account of the powers conferred on each of the two arms of the budgetary authority (Council and Parliament) and on the Commission.

— Article 273 contains the provisions necessary to allow the Community's financial activities to continue if the budget is not adopted on schedule.

4) Execution and control of the budget

— Article 274 assigns to the Commission the essential powers and accountability for implementing the budget. It refers to the principle of sound financial management and cooperation between the Member States and the Commission on implementation of the budget.

— Article 275 lays down the procedures for the Commission to submit the accounts to the Council and to Parliament.

— Article 276 lays down the procedure for the discharge which Parliament gives to the Commission, acting on a recommendation by the Council, in respect of implementation of the budget.

— Article 278 sets out the conditions under which the Commission may transfer its assets between the currencies of the Member States.

5) Additional provisions

— Article 279 lays down the procedures for the Council to adopt supplementary rules for implementation of the Treaty in respect of financial matters: Financial Regulations, making available own resources and the responsibility of financial controllers, authorising officers and accounting officers.

— Finally, Article 280 defines the roles of the Commission and the Member States in combating fraud affecting the Community's financial interests. It lays down the procedure by which the Council adopts the measures needed in this area.

1.2. The Treaty on European Union (TEU)

1) Specific provisions under the second and third pillars

Articles 28 and 41 of the TEU contain provisions on financing operations under the common foreign and security policy and cooperation in the fields of justice and home affairs.

A distinction is made between the administrative expenditure arising from these operations and the operational expenditure. The administrative expenditure is automatically charged to the Community budget. As a rule, operational expenditure is also charged to the budget, unless the Council unanimously votes otherwise, in which case the operational expenditure will normally be financed by the Member States, scaled to gross national product, unless the Council again unanimously votes otherwise.

Article 28 rules out the possibility of charging to the Community budget expenditure under the common foreign and security policy relating to operations with military or defence implications. Such expenditure is therefore always financed by the Member States taking part in the operations.

The expenditure charged to the Community budget is covered by the budgetary procedure laid down in the EC Treaty. In particular, as this expenditure is non-compulsory, Parliament has the last say. This could lead to conflicts, as Parliament then has control over financing operations adopted and implemented by the Member States. For this reason, on 17 July 1997 Parliament, the Council and the Commission agreed to introduce a conciliation procedure between the two arms of the budgetary authority to deal with this type of expenditure and keep Parliament regularly up to date on the operations carried out and their financial implications. These provisions were incorporated into the Interinstitutional Agreements of 6 May 1999 and 17 May 2006.

2) Enhanced cooperation

The Amsterdam Treaty allows Member States which intend to establish enhanced cooperation between each other to make use of the institutions, procedures and mechanisms laid down by the EU and EC Treaties under certain conditions (see TEU, Article 44).

Article 44a of the TEU states that expenditure arising from implementation of enhanced cooperation, other than the administrative cost entailed for the institutions, is to be financed by the Member States taking part, unless the Council unanimously votes otherwise.

3) Non-participation by Member States in certain operations

Protocols annexed to the Treaties allow the United Kingdom, Ireland and Denmark not to take part in measures adopted pursuant to Title IV of the EC Treaty (on visas, asylum, immigration and other policies relating to free movement of persons). Denmark has also decided not to take part in operations under the common foreign and security policy with defence implications.

The abovementioned Member States therefore do not have to cover the financial consequences of these measures, except for the administrative costs arising for the institutions.

2. Secondary legislation

2.1. The decision on the own resources system and other instruments adopted in this field

1) The decision on the own resources system

In view of the specific way in which it is adopted, this decision is in fact equivalent to primary legislation.

The Member States have virtually absolute control over adoption of this decision, while Parliament is merely consulted. Not only must the Council act unanimously, thus giving each Member State a right of veto, but also the decision must be ratified by the national parliaments in the same way as the Treaties.

The first decision of this type was adopted in 1970. The most recent was taken by the Council on 7 June 2007 in the form of Decision 2007/436/EC, Euratom (¹).

2) Other instruments relating to implementation of the own resources system

This field is governed by four other instruments:

Council Regulation (EC, Euratom) No 1150/2000 of 22 May 2000 implementing the Council Decision on the system of the Communities' own resources (²). This regulation consolidates successive amendments to the previous Council Regulation (EEC, Euratom) No 1552/89 of 29 May 1989 (³);

Council Regulation (EEC, Euratom) No 1553/89 of 29 May 1989 on the definitive uniform arrangements for the collection of own resources accruing from value added tax (⁴);

Council Directive 89/130/EEC, Euratom of 13 February 1989 on the harmonisation of the compilation of gross national product at market prices (⁵); and

Council Regulation (EC, Euratom) No 1287/2003 of 15 July 2003 on the harmonisation of gross national income at market prices (GNI Regulation).

2.2. The Financial Regulation

In accordance with Article 279 of the EC Treaty, the Financial Regulation is adopted by the Council, acting unanimously after consulting Parliament and obtaining the opinion of the Court of Auditors.

The Financial Regulation was originally adopted on 21 December 1977 (⁶), but has been amended repeatedly since then. It mainly contains

---

(¹)   OJ L 163, 23.6.2007, p. 17.
(²)   OJ L 130, 31.5.2000, p. 1.
(³)   OJ L 155, 7.6.1989, p. 1.
(⁴)   OJ L 155, 7.6.1989, p. 9.
(⁵)   OJ L 49, 21.2.1989, p. 26.
(⁶)   OJ L 356, 31.12.1977, p. 1.

provisions applicable to the general budget: principles, establishment, structure, implementation and auditing of the accounts. The regulation deals exhaustively with implementation and control, as these aspects are not covered comprehensively in the Treaty.

In order to take account, in particular, of the requirements for legislative and administrative simplification and the tightening-up of management of Community finances, the Financial Regulation of 21 December 1977 was recast, in the interests of clarity, by Council Regulation (EC, Euratom) No 1605/2002 of 25 June 2002 [1].

It was recently amended by Council Regulation (EC, Euratom) No 1995/2006 of 13 December 2006 [2]. Its essential elements have been maintained and strengthened. Transparency, in particular, has been reinforced by laying down that information on all categories of recipients of all kinds of expenditure financed by the Community budget will be released, irrespective of the entity or authority involved in implementing the budget, thus including decentralised and joint management of the budget with non-EU countries and international organisations.

2.3. Regulation on budgetary discipline

The version adopted on 26 September 2000 [3] was recently repealed by Council Regulation (EC) No 1248/2007 of 22 October 2007 [4].

The first decision in this field was adopted in 1988 as part of the reform of the Community's finances [5].

The regulation dealt mainly with budgetary discipline in the agricultural sector.

It laid down the method for calculating the agricultural guideline which set an overall limit on the increase in total agricultural expenditure relating to the EAGGF Guarantee Section, the pre-accession agricultural instrument and the amounts shown in the financial framework for

---

[1] OJ L 248, 16.9.2002, p. 1.
[2] OJ L 390, 30.12.2006, p. 1.
[3] Regulation (EC) No 2040/2000 (OJ L 244, 29.9.2000, p. 27).
[4] OJ L 282, 26.10.2007, p. 3.
[5] See Chapter 3.

accession in respect of agriculture. But the ceilings set in the financial framework for 2007-13 in Annex I to the Interinstitutional Agreement of 17 May 2006 mean that there is now no need to maintain the agricultural guideline provided for therein.

The remaining provisions concerning budgetary discipline for agriculture in Regulation (EC) No 2040/2000 were superseded by Articles 18 to 20 of Council Regulation (EC) No 1290/2005 of 21 June 2005 on the financing of the common agricultural policy [1].

In order to ensure that the budget ceiling will not be exceeded, the new regulation lays down that the Commission will implement a monthly early-warning and monitoring system in respect of EAGF expenditure.

For that purpose, before the beginning of each financial year, the Commission will determine monthly expenditure profiles based, if necessary, on average monthly expenditure during the previous three years.

The Commission will present to the European Parliament and to the Council a monthly report examining the development of expenditure undertaken in relation to the profiles and containing an assessment of the foreseeable implementation for the current financial year.

2.4. The regulation setting up a guarantee fund for external actions

Borrowing and lending operations are conducted under non-budget financial instruments. However, the budget bears the risk of:

— the beneficiary defaulting under borrowing and lending operations for which the Commission plays the role of financial intermediary by contracting loans on the Community's behalf and onlending the proceeds in Member States or non-member countries;

— activation of the guarantee which the Community provides for loans granted by the European Investment Bank from its own resources to finance projects outside the Community.

---

[1]   OJ L 209, 11.8.2005, p. 1.

A guarantee fund was set up as part of the Delors II package to cover the risks involved in operations in countries outside the Community [1]. The volume of this fund, which is administered by the EIB, is now set at 9 % of the outstanding loans guaranteed. The fund is financed by transfers from the general budget (more precisely from the guarantee reserve) equivalent to 9 % of the new loans granted, by interest from investments and by amounts recovered from defaulting debtors. If the volume laid down is exceeded, the surplus is repaid to the budget. However, if the fund is unable to cover guarantees called in, the budget finances the additional amount necessary.

3. Rules adopted by agreement between the institutions

To prevent or overcome risks of conflict and gridlock in the budget procedures, the institutions concerned have often been prompted to conclude agreements on how to exercise the powers they are given by the Treaties. A number of agreements or joint declarations have thus been concluded since the mid-1970s [2]. They were incorporated, with certain updates or additions, into the Interinstitutional Agreement concluded in 1999, which in some ways constitutes a 'Charter' of agreements reached by the institutions on the budget.

The 1999 Interinstitutional Agreement was superseded by a new one signed on 17 May 2006 [3]. The purpose of the new Agreement, like the previous one, is to impose budgetary discipline, to improve the functioning of the annual budgetary procedure and cooperation between the institutions on budgetary matters and to ensure sound financial management. Budgetary discipline under this Agreement covers all expenditure. It is binding on all the institutions for as long as the Agreement is in force. These agreements have no legal basis in the Treaty. However, their legal significance may be considered far more than a simple political commitment.

---

[1] Council Regulation (EEC, Euratom) No 2728/94 (OJ L 293, 12.11.1994, p. 1), as last amended by Council Regulation (EC, Euratom) No 89/2007 of 30 January 2007 (OJ L 22, 31.1.2007, p. 1).

[2] See Chapters 2 and 4.

[3] OJ C139, 14.6.2006, p. 1.

They have been concluded by institutions which can enter into legal obligations under the powers conferred on them by the Treaties. In this respect, the agreements are perfectly consistent with the provisions of the Treaties.

— They contain rules which delineate the freedom of action of the institutions which have subscribed to them and therefore constitute specific commitments for them.

— They express the more general principle of true and honest cooperation provided for by the Treaty.

So far the Court of Justice has not ruled on the legal value of the Interinstitutional Agreements. It has, however, recognised the usefulness of this instrument and even that it is necessary in order to allow the institutions to carry out the tasks they have been given.

4. Developments concerning EU public finances in the institutional debate

The European Convention, which met between March 2002 and July 2003, drew up a Treaty establishing a Constitution for Europe which was intended to replace the existing treaties. Although this institutional debate did not focus specifically on budgetary matters, some of the changes envisaged could have a direct or indirect impact on the budgetary procedure or the budget itself.

The Constitutional Treaty [1] was subsequently submitted to an intergovernmental conference (IGC). It was adopted after some amendments in June 2004 and signed in October of the same year [2]. However, the failure of the referenda in France and the Netherlands effectively halted the ratification process and led the EU to a period of reflection on future institutional reforms.

---

[1] See Intergovernmental Conference document CIG 87/04
http://www.consilium.europa.eu/cms3_applications/Applications/igc/doc_register.asp?content=DOC&lang=FR&cmsid=754.
[2] See Intergovernmental Conference document CIG 87/2/04 REV2.

At its meeting on 21-22 June 2007, the European Council agreed to convene an IGC to prepare a Reform Treaty amending the existing treaties with a view to enhancing the efficiency and democratic legitimacy of the enlarged Union.

The draft Treaty amending the Treaty on European Union and the Treaty establishing the European Community (¹) was finally adopted at the inter-governmental conference of 18 October 2007 in Lisbon. The Lisbon Treaty was signed on 13 December 2007 in Lisbon.

Subject to ratification by the Member States (²), the Lisbon Treaty will introduce changes in the EU public finances architecture. The changes envisaged concern areas such as own resources procedures, the multi-annual financial framework and the annual budgetary procedure.

4.1. Own resources

The Lisbon Treaty reformulates the provisions concerning the system of own resources. Article 311 of the Treaty on the Functioning of the European Union (TFEU) (³) states that 'The Union shall provide itself with the means necessary to attain its objectives and carry through its policies'. The next paragraph provides the definition of 'the means' which is basically the current system of own resources of the European Union.

The Council, acting in accordance with a special legislative procedure and after consulting the European Parliament, may, unanimously, adopt a decision on the Community's own resources which, *inter alia,* may establish new categories of own resources or abolish existing ones.

As at present, any decision on the system of own resources will require approval by the Member States in accordance with their own constitutional requirements. Implementing measures in the form of regulations

---

(¹)   See Intergovernmental Conference document CIG 1/1/07 REV 1.

(²)   The Treaty of Lisbon is still in the process of being ratified by the Member States, in accordance with their respective constitutional requirements. As provided for in Article 6 thereof, the Treaty will enter into force on 1 January 2009, provided that all the instruments of ratification have been deposited, or, failing that, on the first day of the month following the deposit of the last instrument of ratification.

(³)   Ex Article 269 TEC – see Annex 1 for a comparative table of the provisions contained in the Treaty establishing the European Community and the Treaty on the functioning of the European Union (Lisbon Treaty).

will also be adopted following a special legislative procedure by the Council, acting after obtaining the consent of the European Parliament in so far as provided for in the own resources decision.

4.2. The multiannual financial framework (MAFF)

The multiannual financial framework, which until now was only included in the Interinstitutional Agreement and therefore – strictly speaking – was not legally binding, was incorporated into the Lisbon Treaty to enhance budgetary discipline and transparency (new Article 312 TFEU). The overall aim of the MAFF, covering at least five years and adopted in the form of a regulation, is to ensure that the European Union's expenditure develops in an orderly manner and within the limits of its own resources.

The Council, acting in accordance with a special legislative procedure and after obtaining the consent of the European Parliament, will adopt the MAFF regulation. Unanimity is required, although the European Council may, unanimously, adopt a decision authorising the Council to adopt the MAFF regulation by a qualified majority.

The financial framework must determine the annual ceilings on commitment appropriations by category of expenditure and the annual ceiling on payment appropriations. The categories of expenditure, limited in number, must correspond to the Union's major sectors of activity. In addition, the MAFF regulation will lay down any other provisions required for the annual budgetary procedure to run smoothly.

The provisions of the Lisbon Treaty underline the political responsibility of the budgetary authority and the Commission by stipulating that 'throughout the procedure leading to the adoption of the financial framework, the European Parliament, the Council and the Commission shall take any measure necessary to facilitate its adoption'.

4.3. The Union's annual budget

The Lisbon Treaty does not amend the provisions agreed upon in June 2004. As a rule, the new Treaty will simplify the budgetary procedure, on the one hand by removing the distinction between compulsory and non-compulsory expenditure and, on the other, by amending the budgetary procedure which becomes analogous to a co-decision procedure with one reading and conciliation.

The fundamental distinction between compulsory and non-compulsory expenditure will be abolished. The current distinction between these two types of expenditure results in a division of responsibility for the final adoption of any expenditure. The Council has the final word for compulsory expenditure which, *inter alia,* consists of common agricultural policy expenditure, contributions to international organisations or institutions, contributions provisioning the loan guarantee, expenditure resulting from international agreements, pensions and compensation. The European Parliament has the final decision on the rest of expenditure, which is non-compulsory.

Removal of this distinction should have a dual impact on the process of adoption of the annual budget. On the one hand, the responsibility of each arm of the budgetary authority will no longer be limited to its category of expenditure. Both arms of the budgetary authority will be fully and jointly accountable for the whole budget. On the other hand, the new provisions are likely to have an impact on the way the budget will be negotiated between the Council and the European Parliament.

The possibility for the Council or the European Parliament to reject the draft budget in the course of the procedure may increase the uncertainty of the outcome and open the risk of conflict between the two arms of the budgetary authority. On the other hand, the Commission may take all the necessary initiatives, e.g. it can call the Presidents of the European Parliament and the Council to meet for consultations and conciliation.

The Conciliation Committee can be convened to reach agreement on a joint text. Several scenarios are envisaged by the Lisbon Treaty in this respect, which may lead to two different results: either the budget is deemed to be adopted or a new draft budget has to be submitted by the Commission.

— If, within 21 days, the Conciliation Committee does not agree on a joint text, a new draft budget must be submitted by the Commission. Similarly, if the European Parliament and the Council both reject the joint text, or if one of these institutions rejects the joint text and the other fails to take a decision, a new draft budget must be submitted by the Commission. The same applies if the European Parliament rejects the joint text but the Council approves it.

— Any other outcome of the conciliation procedure leads to the budget being deemed to be adopted.

This new Treaty should result in balanced power-sharing between the Council and the European Parliament when it comes to adopting the annual budget. Moreover, the incorporation of the MAFF into the Lisbon Treaty and the removal of the distinction between non-compulsory and compulsory expenditure render the provisions concerning the maximum rate of increase obsolete.

4.4. Implementation of the budget and discharge

The Lisbon Treaty takes into account the obligations and resultant responsibilities of the Member States in respect of budget implementation and discharge. Regarding budget implementation, where the majority of budgetary appropriations are implemented under the shared management system, Article 317 TFEU (ex Article 274 TEC) stipulates that 'the Commission shall implement the budget in cooperation with the Member States'. The same article also provides that the appropriate regulations will lay down the control and audit obligations of the Member States in the implementation of the budget. Therefore the responsibility of the Member States emerging from close cooperation with the European Commission in implementation of the budget has been recognised.

Chapter 8

The financial autonomy of the European Union: the own resources system

The existence of own resources is one of the distinctive characteristics of the European Union and symbolises, in the budget sector, the originality of European integration: with the completion of the internal market, implementation of common policies and assertion of its separate identity in relations with non-member countries, the EU needs a means of finance of its own, independent of the Member States.

The EU's own resources may be defined in this connection as revenue allocated irrevocably to the Union to finance its budget and accruing to it automatically without the need for any subsequent decision by the national authorities.

The own resources system in its present form developed gradually[1]. Unlike the ECSC Treaty, the Treaties of Rome did not immediately set up a system of own resources for financing the Communities they were establishing: the two Communities (EEC and EAEC) were initially financed by contributions from the Member States. However, these Treaties did anticipate the creation at a later date of a system of own resources which would include, in particular, revenue from the Common Customs Tariff once it had been finally set up.

---

[1]   See Chapters 1 to 6.

This was the basis for the establishment of own resources, by the Decision of 21 April 1970, which progressively replaced national contributions. Subsequent own resources decisions have amended the system several times [1].

Until the own resources Decision of 7 June 2007, adopted in the wake of the financial framework for 2007-13 [2], takes effect, the system will be based on the Council Decision of 29 September 2000 and two implementing regulations (Council Regulation (EC, Euratom) No 1150/2000, as amended by Regulation (EC, Euratom) No 2028/2004, which lays down the provisions for implementing the decision, and Council Regulation (EEC, Euratom) No 1553/89 on the definitive uniform arrangements for the collection of own resources accruing from value added tax).

The main components of the current system are:

— traditional own resources, which result directly from the existence of a unified customs area and are not attributable to the Member States for legal – and practical – reasons; these resources are sugar levies and agricultural and customs duties. Member States retain 25 % of the amounts of traditional own resources collected as collection costs;

— VAT-based own resources, derived from application of a call rate to a VAT base determined uniformly for the Member States in accordance with EU rules;

— GNI-based own resources, resulting from application of a set call rate to total EU GNI, to match the total volume of resources to the total volume of expenditure;

— correction mechanisms, which grant particular Member States a reduction of their contribution to the EU budget [3].

Figure 8.1 shows the evolution of EU budget revenue by type of resource over the period 1997-2006.

---

[1]   Development of the own resources system is described in Chapter 12.
[2]   See Chapter 6.
[3]   These mechanisms are described in detail later in this chapter and also in Chapter 12.

FIGURE 8.1

EU budget revenue 1997-2006 (million EUR)

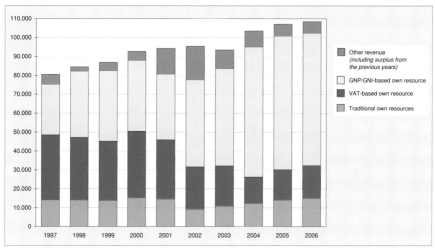

Figure 8.2 shows the split of own resources payments by Member States in 2006.

FIGURE 8.2

National contributions by Member State and traditional own resources collected on behalf of the EU (2006, million EUR)

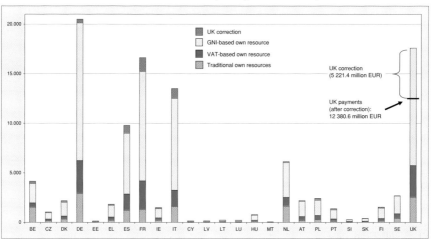

1. The essential characteristics of the present system of own resources

The system in place since 1988, when the GNI-based own resources were introduced, has three main objectives:

— financially, after the difficulties to secure a sufficient level of financing encountered several years in succession before 1988, it automatically ensures a level of resources in line with agreed expenditure;

— legally, it guarantees the specific nature of the EU's resources;

— economically, a number of provisions have been introduced to respect the principle, agreed at the 25 and 26 June 1984 Fontainebleau European Council, that 'any Member State sustaining a budgetary burden which is excessive in relation to its relative prosperity may benefit from a correction at the appropriate time' [1].

1.1 The financial dimension: a guaranteed level of resources for the European Union

The Community's financial difficulties in the early 1980s stemmed from the difficulty of meeting growing, inflexible expenditure requirements from the limited resources available (see Chapter 2). Until 1988, the amount of available own resources was not linked to expenditure requirements. This led to two diverging trends:

— limited availability of financing sources, due to a relative decrease in traditional own resources (on account of trade liberalisation) and the constraint imposed on the VAT-based resources by the ceiling;

— continually rising expenditure generated by the development of new policies and the reinforcement of existing ones.

The system put in place in 1988 introduced an overall own resources ceiling plus the GNP-based (later GNI-based) resources, which would func-

---

[1]   Bull. EC 6-1984, page 10.

tion as the residual resources, maintaining the necessary balance between revenue and expenditure.

1) The link between revenue and expenditure

The own resources decision sets an overall ceiling for own resources, expressed as a percentage of EU GNI (initially 1.27 % of ESA 79 GNP, recalculated as 1.24 % of ESA 95 GNI in 2001). This is an overall ceiling in that it applies to own resources taken as a whole, for all Member States. The maximum ceiling imposed on own resources remains applicable, unless the basic decision is amended, even if the financial framework is not renewed when it expires. This ensures the continuity of the financing system, whilst imposing a limit on any increase in expenditure.

The compatibility between the expenditure trend and the ceilings laid down for own resources is ensured by a number of provisions:

— under the provisions added to the Treaty of Rome by the Maastricht Treaty (Article 270), first the Commission must ensure that the proposals it presents or the implementing measures it adopts can be financed within the limit placed on the own resources;

— under Article 3(2) of the own resources decision, total appropriations for commitments entered in the budget may under no circumstances exceed a set percentage of EU GNI (initially 1.335 % of ESA 79 GNP, recalculated as 1.31 % of ESA 95 GNI in 2001);

— the ceilings on expenditure, in terms of appropriations for commitments in the financial framework, are established in such a way as to maintain orderly development in line with all the necessary appropriations for payments. The ensuing financial framework, which is set out in the Interinstitutional Agreement, 'is intended to ensure that, in the medium term, European Union expenditure, broken down by broad category, develops in an orderly manner and within the limits of own resources' (1).

---

(1)   See paragraph 10 of the Interinstitutional Agreement between the European Parliament, the Council and the Commission on budgetary discipline and sound financial management, OJ C 139, 14 June 2006, p. 1.

2) The GNI-based resources as a 'top-up'

In addition to the proceeds from traditional own resources and the VAT-based resources, which are determined by the rates applicable and the actual movement in the bases, expenditure is financed by revenue based on GNI. There is no particular limit on the rate of call for the GNI-based resources other than the own resources ceiling, which limits the total amount of all own resources to a maximum of 1.24 % of EU GNI.

These resources are therefore intended to balance the budget, which is why they are often referred to as 'additional resources' or 'residual resources' in budget documents.

1.2. The legal dimension: the specific nature of the resources

1) The legal basis: a definitive transfer of revenue by Member States under a specific procedure

Unlike the earlier system of financial contributions, the present system of own resources can be defined as a definitive transfer to the EU. Pursuant to Article 14 of the Financial Regulation([1]), final adoption of each year's budget imposes an obligation on each Member State to make over to the EU the payments due under this budget. The undertaking entered into by the Member States to supply the necessary resources explains the particularly cumbersome, formal procedure needed for adoption of basic decisions in this field, under Article 269 of the Treaty of Rome([2]).

2) The consequence: automatic payment

As the Community does not have its own tax authority, traditional own resources (customs duties, agricultural levies, sugar and isoglucose levies) are collected by the authorities of the Member States. In accordance with Article 2 of Regulation (EC, Euratom) No 1150/2000, these resources are established by the Member States as soon as the conditions provided for by the customs and sugar regulations for entry of the entitlement in the accounts and notification of the debtor have been met. The entitle-

---

([1])   Council Regulation (EC, Euratom) No 1995/2006 of 13 December 2006 amending Regulation (EC, Euratom) No 1605/2002 on the Financial Regulation applicable to the general budget of the European Communities (OJ L 390 of 30 December 2006).

([2])   See Chapter 6.

ments established are entered in the accounts and then credited to an own resources account opened in the name of the Commission with the Member State's Treasury or their appointed body.

On the other hand, since the VAT-based and GNP-based resources are not collected directly from taxpayers, they are made available on the first working day of each month at the rate of one-twelfth of the estimated amount appearing in the EU budget. This payment is guaranteed by Article 11 of Regulation (EC, Euratom) No 1150/2000, as amended by Regulation (EC, Euratom) No 2028/2004, which provides that interest payments will be imposed on any Member State which fails to credit the amounts on time.

The specific nature of the own resources, and consequently the EU's financial autonomy, are sometimes obscured by the fact that the own resources payments often appear in the national budgets and may therefore seem to be conditional on the vote of the national parliaments and to compete with national expenditure. This illusion has no foundation in law, whereby the transfer of resources is automatic.

1.3. The economic dimension: the search for more fairness

1) Partial and gradual replacement of the VAT-based own resources by GNP/GNI-based own resources

The VAT resources are structurally regressive, in that the proportion of consumption in GNI, and therefore in the VAT base, is often higher in the less prosperous Member States than in the richer States. Conversely, net exporting countries with high savings rates are favoured. Therefore, in an attempt to increase the fairness of Member States' gross contributions, the share of the VAT-based own resources in the financing of the budget has been progressively reduced. These resources have, to a large extent, been replaced by the GNP/GNI-based resources.

2) The issue of budgetary balances

The European Union is a community of solidarity, with parts of the EU budget serving a clear solidarity goal, while others fund measures to achieve specific objectives through EU agreed programmes. When considering each individual Member State, that gives rise to budgetary net balances (net benefits or net contributions) vis-à-vis the EU budget, although the policy benefits accrue to the Union as a whole. Budgetary net balances, measured by the difference between contributions to and receipts from the EU budget, obviously fail to account fully for the benefits resulting from EU membership and give a very limited view of them. The Commission has stressed this point on many occasions ([1]). Nevertheless, the size of some of these imbalances has been at the centre of political discussions.

Various measures have been introduced in the own resources system in attempts to redress the perceived excessive budgetary imbalances of certain Member States.

In 1984 the Fontainebleau European Council introduced a correction mechanism with regard to one Member State – the United Kingdom – whereby 66 % of the UK's net contribution is reimbursed. Although the correction was only for the UK, the Fontainebleau European Council acknowledged the general principle of entitlement to a correction, based on the size of the budgetary imbalance and the relative wealth of a Member State compared with the EU as a whole.

Other ad hoc measures were introduced over time, adding to the complexity of the system, in particular:

— limits on the financing of the UK correction: one third for Germany over 1985-2001 and three quarters for Germany, the Netherlands, Austria and Sweden since 2002;

— increase in the share retained as collection costs of traditional own resources from 10 % over 1970-2000 to 25 % since 2001, benefiting notably the Netherlands;

---

[1]   A full statement on this policy and its rationale was made in Chapter 2 of the 1998 Commission Report 'Financing of the European Union' (available on: http://ec.europa.eu/budget/documents/agenda_2000_reports_financing_en.htm) and in 'Budget Contributions, EU Expenditure, Budgetary Balances and Relative Prosperity of the Member States', a paper presented by President Santer to the EcoFin Council of 13 October 1997. The Presidency Conclusions of the Berlin European Council of 24 and 25 March 1999 endorsed this principle: '[...] it is recognised that the full benefits of Union membership cannot be measured solely in budgetary terms' (point 68).

— the own resources decision adopted on 7 June 2007 set a call rate of 0.3 % to be applied retroactively from 1 January 2007 when the decision entered into force. The same decision envisages, for the period 2007-13 only, a reduced call rate of 0.225 % for Austria, 0.15 % for Germany and 0.10 % for the Netherlands and Sweden;

— the new own resources decision provides for a gross reduction in the annual GNI contribution by the Netherlands and Sweden for the period 2007-13 only ([1]);

— downward adjustment of the UK correction, notably in relation to pre-accession expenditure and to expenditure in the Member States which joined the EU after 30 April 2004, so that the United Kingdom pays a fairer share of EU expenditure in the period of enlargement.

2. The existing situation and likely trends

2.1. Assessment criteria for the own resources system

The own resources system and individual own resources can be assessed against specific criteria. Many such criteria have been identified over time in European Commission or European Parliament documents and in academic research.

In its latest report on the operation of the own resources system ([2]), the Commission identified several assessment criteria, which it considers relevant to its analysis of the own resources system and any alternative to it:

— visibility and simplicity: the way in which the financing is achieved should be easy for the public to understand;

— financial autonomy: the financing of the EU budget should be secured and reliable;

([1])   See Article 2(5) of Council Decision 2007/436/EC, Euratom of 7 June 2007 on the system of the European Communities' own resources.

([2])   See 'Financing the European Union. Commission report on the operation of the own resources system', COM(2004) 505 final, Volume I, 14 July 2004.

— efficient allocation of economic resources: the financing should avoid distorting economic decisions unless this is deemed desirable, for instance due to the existence of external effects;

— sufficiency: the resources should meet the Union's financing needs and be able to match changes in these needs;

— administrative cost-effectiveness: the costs of levying and administering the resources should be low in relation to the income they generate;

— revenue stability: the resources should bring stable revenue to the budget;

— fairness in gross contributions: the budget burden should be distributed fairly between Member States.

It is virtually impossible for individual own resources or for a financing system considered as a whole, be it at local, national or EU level, to fully satisfy all possible assessment criteria. The choice of a specific financing system must therefore be based on a political judgment, taking into account the pros and cons of a variety of possible options.

2.2. A financing system which provides sufficient resources in a cost-effective way

According to the abovementioned Commission report, the current own resources system has performed well as regards the criteria of sufficiency and stability, but clearly failed to fulfil the visibility and simplicity criterion and has not contributed significantly to more efficient allocation of economic resources in the EU.

The own resources decision adopted on 7 June 2007 should make no significant difference to the functioning of the own resources system. In practice, adjustments are mainly made in favour of a limited group of net contributors to the budget, thereby further increasing the complexity and opacity of the financing system for the EU.

1) Sufficiency and stability

The problems encountered by the Community in the 1980s in bringing its revenue up to the level required to meet its increased expenditure have completely vanished thanks to the combined effect of two factors:

— introduction of the GNP-based (now GNI-based) resources as the balancing resource;

— the efforts made to contain expenditure during the 1990s and beyond. This has resulted, since 1996, in a positive and increasing margin between the own resources ceiling and the expenditure ceiling set in the financial framework and, even more so, between the own resources ceiling and the actual budget.

2) Cost-effectiveness

This is only called into question in the case of traditional resources. Collection of these resources is the responsibility of the Member States. It is complicated and entails a risk of fraud and irregularities[1]. By contrast, collection of the VAT-based resources, and especially the GNI-based resources, which together now make up over 80 % of total resources, costs very little. Taken as a whole, then, the present system is satisfactory from this point of view.

2.3. A system with room for improvement

In some respects, the present system has significant shortcomings.

1) Growing dependency on Member States' financial transfers

The Union's financial autonomy is a legal reality (see above), which is extremely important. However, the system puts too much emphasis on national contributions. Since own resources payments take the form of transfers from national budgets, they display many characteristics of 'contributions' from the Member States. The EU's growing dependence on these transfers creates a situation in which EU budget financing interferes with national budgetary policies and fuels demands from the Member

---

[1]   It should be noted, however, that, even if the yield from these duties did not accrue to the Communities, the Member States would still be required to apply the Customs Union legislation and would face the same problems.

States in terms of the benefits each country derives from the EU budget, even though this concept is difficult to define.

This lack of a direct link between EU budget financing and taxpayers has led to criticisms that budget decisions somehow lack legitimacy. Accountability of the budgetary authority would be enhanced by a financing system giving taxpayers/voters a clearer view of the cost of Europe.

2) Opacity and complexity

The financing system has grown increasingly complex over time, making it difficult even for the interested citizen to understand how it works. This complexity results in particular from the following features of the financing system.

— First, calculation of the VAT-based own resources is complex (the amounts collected depend on statistical calculations) and lacks transparency (de facto the capping transforms these VAT-based resources into GNI-based resources in all but name for many Member States)[1].

— Second, the various ad hoc corrections also tend to obscure the precise nature of the system and its effects.

— Third, the predominance of the GNI resources reveals the national origin of the resources but masks the categories of taxpayer concerned.

3) Absence of a link to EU policies

The financing system does not really support EU policies. Whereas the bulk of the own resources in the past were somehow related to EU policies (agricultural levies were related to the common agricultural policy, customs duties to the common customs area and common trade policy and the VAT-based resources to the process of VAT harmonisation), this is no longer the case. The GNI-based resources are linked to a measure of national income and the VAT-based resources are remotely linked to effective VAT in the Member States. As indicated below, alternative sources of financing have been suggested, which display a closer link to (and can support) EU policies.

---

[1]   See Chapter 12 for technical details.

2.4. Ways in which the system could develop

On the basis of these findings, there are two main possible approaches to reforming the EU financing system.

1) Developing a simple contribution-based system

The first approach would be to follow through to its conclusion the trend observed since 1988 with the introduction of the GNI resources and make them the main source for financing the European budget. This solution would have the advantage of financial efficiency and simplicity, particularly if correction mechanisms could be removed or phased out.

However, this evolution seems unlikely as, until today, the evolution of EU financing towards contributions has gone parallel with an ever increasing number of corrections and rebates. Moreover, it would accentuate the problems mentioned above (difficulty for taxpayers to identify how much they pay for Europe and no link between expenditure policies and financing of the budget).

2) Bringing the EU closer to its citizens

The second approach would be designed to bring the European Union closer to its citizens. In terms of the financing of EU activities, this step closer to the people could take two forms: on the one hand, increasing the European Parliament's responsibilities by extending its decision-making powers to the revenue side of the budget; on the other, restructuring revenue to increase the proportion of direct resources, with one or more taxes, parts of taxes or other resources (such as user fees) being clearly levied on taxpayers (or users) for the European Union.

Many different ideas have been put forward in the past as alternative means of providing funding for the EU budget, either to replace or to supplement existing resources, keeping in mind that Article 269 of the EC Treaty indicates that the EU budget is financed by own resources. These include, in particular, a modulated VAT; resources related to corporate income (EUCIT); energy or pollution charges, notably charges related to road transport and climate charges on aviation; revenue related to tradable permits; excise duties on tobacco and alcohol; transfer of seigniorage revenue; communication charges, including on telephony, e-mail or SMS; and resources related to personal income and financial transactions.

These options have been examined and assessed in detail in various studies[1]. These highlight the political nature of the debates on alternative sources of financing for the EU. For a number of options, technical preparations leading to introduction of the resources could be undertaken in a limited number of years[2]. This would, for instance, be the case for resources based on energy or VAT. Second, among the resources mentioned in past debates, the performance with regard to the assessment criteria would vary widely. For instance, some alternative resources would be highly visible to citizens, thereby contributing to the transparency of the system. Others would have a desired incentive effect on the behaviour of economic agents, thereby contributing directly to specific objectives for the EU.

In any event, every possible financing source for the EU envisaged in recent years has its pros and cons. They each perform well on some criteria and less well on others. The inability of specific options to meet certain criteria fully should not lead to the conclusion that they should all be dismissed, as has sometimes been argued in the past. On the contrary, the analyses of alternative financing systems highlight the fact that the choice made depends on a critical political decision on which criteria should be considered essential and which secondary, bearing in mind that a system based on a combination of resources of a differing nature may reasonably meet the main relevant criteria.

The choice between these two approaches still does not address the question of the individual Member States' net balances and how to correct them if necessary. This raises the problem of how much financial solidarity is desirable between Member States and in what areas, something which can only be tackled in a comprehensive manner if revenue and expenditure are considered together. This also raises questions about the possible interaction between the financing of the EU budget and the future development of solidarity (equalisation) mechanisms.

---

[1]   See, for instance, Cattoir, Ph. (2004), 'Tax-based EU own resources: an assessment', European Commission, Directorate-General for Taxation and Customs Union, *Taxation Papers*, Working Paper No 1/2004.

[2]   See 'Financing the European Union. Commission report on the operation of the own resources system', COM(2004) 505 final, Volume I, 14 July 2004.

Chapter 9

The framework
for Community expenditure

Since the 1988 reform, the budgetary procedure has been placed in a multiannual financial framework established at two levels.

The decision on own resources determines the nature of such resources and the method of calculating them, but also sets an overall annual ceiling on them. Since each year's budget has to be adopted and implemented in balance, disregarding miscellaneous revenue, the ceilings set in the decision on own resources determine the maximum amount of annual Community expenditure, in terms of appropriations for payments and commitments. They are both a limit, in economic terms, on the size of the Community budget and a guarantee that the Community will have a volume of financial resources at its disposal which will develop in line with economic activity in all the Member States.

Within the ceilings set in the decision on own resources, the financial framework determined by the Interinstitutional Agreement sets limits on the growth of expenditure by category for commitment appropriations and on total expenditure for payment appropriations.

The introduction of this financial framework has appreciably altered the parameters of the annual budgetary debate and has led to the development of multiannual financial programming instruments.

1. Ceilings on expenditure within the financial framework

1.1. Ceilings per heading

The financial framework breaks down commitment appropriations into broad categories (headings). There are also subheadings, which in fact possess the same characteristics as the headings themselves: each heading, or subheading, sets a maximum ceiling on expenditure. At the same time, it prevents appropriations or margins available under one heading/subheading from being used for expenditure under a different heading/subheading (ring-fencing). The present financial framework (2007-13) comprises six headings, two of which are subdivided into subheadings. A detailed description of these headings can be found in Chapter 13.

Heading 1 – Sustainable growth

This heading covers two separate subheadings:

— Subheading 1a – Competitiveness for growth and employment: Promoting competitiveness is a key strategic objective of the EU. It is reflected, in particular, in the renewed Lisbon strategy on growth and jobs, which provides a framework for an ambitious reform process in partnership with the Member States;

— Subheading 1b – Cohesion for growth and employment: The Union's cohesion policy aims at strengthening the economic and social cohesion of the enlarged Union in order to promote its harmonious, balanced and sustainable development. It is designed to reduce disparities between the levels of development of the various regions and Member States and the backwardness of the least favoured regions or islands, including rural areas.

Heading 2 – Preservation and management of natural resources

Funding is provided mainly to agriculture and rural development, and also to fisheries and to environment projects (Life+).

In order to clearly identify the ceiling for market-related expenditure and direct aid agreed by the European Council in Brussels in 2002, the Commission has proposed to introduce the corresponding sub-ceiling within heading 2. Like a subheading, the sub-ceiling sets the maximum level of expenditure for market-related expenditure and direct aid. However, unlike a subheading, the sub-ceiling leaves open the possibility of transferring part of the related appropriations to rural development (modulation) and, subject to the availability of unused margins and the authorisation of the budgetary authority, to other programmes/action under heading 2, without having to revise the financial framework.

Heading 3 – Citizenship, freedom, security and justice

This heading comprises two subheadings:

— Freedom, security and justice: funding within the current financial framework is mainly channelled via new framework funding programmes in the fields of solidarity in managing migration flows, security and safeguarding liberties, fundamental rights and justice;

— Citizenship: this covers action promoting active citizenship, health and consumer protection, programmes fostering European culture and diversity, including its cinematographic and audiovisual heritage, along with an instrument for major emergencies to increase the efficiency and effectiveness of civil protection and early-warning systems covering all types of hazards.

Heading 4 – The EU as a global player

This heading covers the financial instruments supporting the EU's external relations operations, e.g. the Instrument for Pre-Accession (IPA), the European Neighbourhood and Partnership Instrument (ENPI), the Development Cooperation Instrument (DCI), humanitarian aid, the Emergency Aid Reserve, etc. Expenditure in the field of the common foreign and security policy and loan guarantees for external action are also being funded under this heading.

Heading 5 – Administration

This heading sets the ceiling for administrative expenditure for all European institutions. It covers expenditure for active and retired staff, buildings, offices, equipment, furniture, European schools, missions or conference and meeting costs.

Heading 6 – Compensation

Compensation is paid to a new Member State as a temporary measure agreed in the Accession Treaty with the aim of improving its budgetary position vis-à-vis the EU budget in general.

Each heading must be sufficiently homogenous to allow the Community's political priorities to be identified and sufficiently wide to allow reallocation of expenditure between the various programmes under the same heading, as required. Each heading is complete in itself and covers a specific category of action. Consequently, as a budget item coming under one heading cannot be financed from another, revision may be necessary, even if raising the ceiling for one heading is offset by lowering the ceiling for another.

For each heading or subheading, the amount established, in terms of appropriations for commitments, sets an annual expenditure ceiling. The Interinstitutional Agreement provides that the institutions should ensure, as far as possible, that sufficient margins are left available beneath the ceilings for the various headings during the budgetary procedure and at the time of adoption of the budget, except for subheading 1B, for which the annual ceilings are expenditure targets which are to be entered in the budget each year.

1.2. Ceilings on total expenditure

An overall ceiling on appropriations for commitments is obtained by adding together the various ceilings for the individual headings.

An annual ceiling is established for appropriations for payments on the basis of a series of payment schedules established for the different categories of appropriations for commitments. This is an overall ceiling and is not broken down by heading.

Based on a forecast of the trend in Community GNI, it is possible to express the ceiling on appropriations for payments as a percentage of this estimated figure for GNI. In this way, it is possible to check that the estimates of Community expenditure are compatible with the own resources ceiling, which is also expressed as a percentage of GNI. This ceiling on own resources may not be exceeded. However, a 'margin for unforeseen expenditure' is inserted between the ceiling on own resources and the ceiling on appropriations for payments. This plays a twofold role:

— to allow revision of the financial framework should it be necessary to meet expenditure not originally foreseen; and

— to help to cushion the consequences of an unexpectedly low economic growth rate. In these circumstances, the volume of own resources actually available, with a ceiling set as a percentage of GNI, is smaller than envisaged at the outset, while the total ceiling for expenditure, which is set as an absolute amount, remains unchanged. The difference is taken from the margin for unforeseen expenditure.

In any event, the ceiling on own resources is an absolute limit. If the margin for unforeseen expenditure were completely used up, the budget adopted would still have to keep within that limit, which would mean that the total payment appropriations entered in the budget would be below the ceiling authorised in the financial framework. In such a situation, the budgetary authority would have to decide on the reductions needed in the ceilings set in the financial framework in order to comply with the own resources ceiling [1]. In the recent and current financial frameworks, however, the ceilings set for payment appropriations have been set well below the own resources ceiling. Such a situation therefore remains purely hypothetical.

2. Application of the multiannual financial framework

The terms for application of the multiannual financial framework are set out in the Interinstitutional Agreement (IIA) between the European Parliament, the Council and the Commission on budgetary discipline and sound financial management signed on 17 May 2006 [2], which, in particular, lays down the rules for the annual and other adjustments and for revision of the financial framework.

Other budgetary instruments enhancing flexibility and ensuring budgetary discipline have also been established or renewed by the IIA, namely

[1]   Point 15 of the Interinstitutional Agreement.
[2]   OJ C 139, 14.6.2006, p. 1.

the Emergency Aid Reserve, the European Union Solidarity Fund, the Flexibility Instrument and the European Globalisation Adjustment Fund. These instruments are mobilised only in case of need. In that case, the relevant commitment and payment appropriations can be entered in the budget over and above the ceilings set in the financial framework, within the limits set for each of those instruments.

2.1. Technical adjustments

Each year, the Commission makes a technical adjustment to the financial framework for the next year. This operation has a dual function:

— the financial framework is expressed at constant prices, so it has to be adjusted to take account of inflation each year in order to maintain the original purchasing power of the ceiling for each heading. Starting with the 2007-13 financial framework, this adjustment is based on a fixed deflator of 2 % a year, which means that the amounts in current prices are already set for the duration of the financial framework;

— the margin for unforeseen expenditure, expressed as a percentage of GNI, must be updated to take account of actual economic activity, on which the volume of own resources available depends. At this point it is possible to check the compatibility between total appropriations for payments and available own resources.

From the procedural point of view, this technical adjustment is made prior to the start of the budgetary procedure for year n+1 on the basis of the most recent economic data and forecasts available.

In order to set the annual budgetary procedure in a stable framework and to ensure budgetary discipline, no further adjustments are made for the year concerned.

A second (new) technical adjustment has been introduced in the IIA. If it is established in 2011 that a Member State's cumulated GNI for the years 2007-09 has diverged by more than +/- 5 % from the cumulated GNI estimated when drawing up the IIA, the Commission will adjust the amounts allocated from funds supporting cohesion to the Member State concerned for that period, within the limits set in the IIA (point 17).

2.2. Adjustments connected with implementation

When notifying the two arms of the budgetary authority of the technical adjustments to the financial framework, the Commission may also present proposals for adjusting the level of payment appropriations in the light of implementation of the programmes, to ensure an orderly progression in relation to commitment appropriations.

2.3. Adjustment of Structural Funds, Cohesion Fund, Rural Development and the European Fund for Fisheries

The IIA signed in May 2006 renewed the special measure introduced in the previous IIA in respect of structural measures at the start of the new programming period. In the event of a delay in adoption of these programmes, the budgetary authority undertakes to authorise before 1 May 2008, on a proposal from the Commission, the transfer to subsequent years of appropriations not used in 2007, in excess of the corresponding ceilings on expenditure (point 48 of the IIA).

2.4. Updating of forecasts for payment appropriations after 2013

The ceiling for appropriations for payments is established on the basis of payment schedules for the different categories of appropriations for commitments. Any incorrect estimate could cause an imbalance between the two corresponding ceilings. In particular, if commitments are not cleared as quickly as expected at the beginning of the period, payments may need to be stepped up later. In such cases steps must be taken to ensure sufficient means to meet the corresponding payments in the following years

The IIA sets 2010 as the year for updating the forecasts for payment appropriations after 2013. This update will take into account, inter alia, real implementation of budget appropriations for payments and commitments and the implementation forecasts.

2.5. Adjustments connected with excessive government deficit

If the Council has decided, in accordance with Article 104 of the Treaty establishing the European Community, that an excessive government deficit exists in a beneficiary Member State and has established that the

Member State has not taken effective action in response to a Council recommendation, it may decide to suspend some or all of the commitments from the Cohesion Fund to the Member State concerned with effect from 1 January of the year following the decision to suspend. In case of lifting such a suspension, the Council, acting on a proposal from the Commission, may decide on a transfer of suspended commitments to the following years. Suspended commitments from year n cannot be rebudgeted beyond year n+2.

2.6. Adjustment of the financial framework to cater for enlargement

If new Member States accede to the European Union during the period covered by the financial framework, the European Parliament and the Council, acting on a proposal from the Commission, will jointly adjust the financial framework to take account of the expenditure requirements resulting from the outcome of the accession negotiations.

2.7 Revision of the financial framework

In order to allow the Community to deal with unforeseen circumstances, the financial framework may be revised, provided the own resources ceiling is not exceeded (i.e. the revision must remain within the margin for unforeseen expenditure). The decision to proceed with such a revision is taken jointly by the two arms of the budgetary authority in accordance with the voting rules under Article 272(9) of the EC Treaty (i.e. with the Council acting by a qualified majority and the European Parliament by a majority of its members and three fifths of the votes cast), on a proposal from the Commission. However, if the revision equals an amount greater than 0.03 % of GNI, the Council's decision must be unanimous. Under the Interinstitutional Agreement, this procedure is subject to a series of conditions:

— as a general rule, the revision must be proposed and adopted before the start of the budgetary procedure for the year, or the first of the years, concerned;

— to ensure budgetary discipline, the institutions must, prior to any revision, examine the scope for reallocating appropriations either within the heading concerned or by offsetting appropriations between different headings of the financial framework;

— no revision affecting compulsory expenditure may lead to a reduction in the amount available for non-compulsory expenditure;

— finally, any revision must maintain an appropriate relationship between commitments and payments.

2.8. Emergency Aid Reserve

The purpose of the Emergency Aid Reserve is to provide a rapid response to specific aid requirements of non-member countries following events which could not be foreseen when the budget was established, first and foremost for humanitarian operations, but also for civil crisis management and protection where circumstances so require. The annual amount of the Reserve is set at EUR 221 million for the duration of the financial framework in constant prices. The Reserve is entered in the general budget as a provision. If some or all of the Reserve is to be mobilised, the corresponding commitment appropriations will be entered in the budget, if necessary over and above the ceilings laid down in the financial framework.

2.9. European Union Solidarity Fund

A special financial instrument was set up in November 2002 by means of a separate Interinstitutional Agreement(1) and renewed by point 26 of the current IIA to allow rapid financial assistance in the event of major disasters occurring on the territory of a Member State or of a candidate country. The annual amount to be budgeted to the Fund may not exceed EUR 1 billion each year in current prices. On 1 October each year, at least one-quarter of the annual amount should remain available in order to cover needs arising until the end of the year. The portion of the annual amount not entered in the budget may not be rolled over in the following years. If, on a proposal by the Commission based on the relevant legislative act, the two arms of the budgetary authority take a joint decision to deploy the Fund, the corresponding commitment appropriations are entered in the budget, if necessary over and above the ceilings laid down in the financial framework.

---

(1)   OJ C 283, 20.11.2002, p. 1.

2.10. Flexibility Instrument

This instrument, first introduced in the Interinstitutional Agreement of 6 May 1999 (¹), is intended to cover, for a given financial year, clearly identified expenditure which could not be financed within the limits of the ceilings available.

The Flexibility Instrument can be mobilised up to an annual ceiling of EUR 200 million in current prices. However, the portion of the amount which is not used in year n may be carried over up to year n+2.

The decision to deploy this instrument is taken jointly by the two arms of the budgetary authority in accordance with the voting rules under Article 272(9) of the EC Treaty, on a proposal from the Commission. The decision is taken, for a given year, during the corresponding budgetary procedure.

2.11. European Globalisation Adjustment Fund

The December 2005 European Council decided to establish a European Globalisation Adjustment Fund, which is intended to provide additional support for workers who suffer from the consequences of major structural changes in world trade patterns, to assist them with their reintegration into the labour market. The IIA (point 28) sets out the budgetary provisions required to deploy the Fund, which may not exceed a maximum annual amount of EUR 500 million in current prices. This amount can be drawn from any margin existing under the global expenditure ceiling of the previous year and/or from cancelled commitment appropriations from the previous two years, excluding those related to heading 1B of the financial framework ('Cohesion for growth and employment'). The appropriations will be entered in the general budget of the European Union as a provision through the normal budgetary procedure as soon as the Commission has identified the sufficient margins and/or cancelled commitments.

(¹)   OJ C 172, 18.6.1999, p. 1.

3. The implications of the financial framework

3.1. For the annual budget debate

1) Respect of the basic provisions of the Treaty

The multiannual financial framework currently in force does not call into question the basic provisions of the Treaty. The principle of annuality remains fully applicable. Budget appropriations are authorised and implemented on an annual basis. The ceilings set are annual limits on expenditure. Amounts not entered in the budget or not used for a particular year cannot be used in excess of the ceilings set for subsequent years.

The budgetary powers of the individual institutions are still those laid down in the Treaty. The object of the Interinstitutional Agreement is, by definition, to establish cooperation procedures or rules of conduct to help secure a consensus in order to forestall or resolve clashes. This means that the institutions agree to voluntary limitation of their powers in the areas concerned. However, if these procedures fail to produce agreement, or if the rules of conduct cannot be respected, each institution is free to use any room for manoeuvre available under the Treaty.

2) Impact on the budget debate

The financial framework has resulted in substantial changes in the budget debate. Establishing a multiannual financial framework implies holding regular detailed discussions on the broad lines of the Community's finances: the volume of the budget, the methods of financing and a shared political assessment of the priorities to be pursued.

Longer-term financial decisions are taken outside the annual budgetary procedure, in the form of a joint decision by the European Parliament and the Council. Community budget policy becomes more predictable, which leads to greater security for defining and implementing the various Community activities and allows Member States to manage their own national budget planning better in relation to the trends in Community expenditure.

This means that the annual discussion on the budget can focus more on the necessary political negotiations and on effective allocation of available resources between various Community operations, taking account of the results achieved in relation to the objectives pursued.

The existence, since 1988, of a financial framework and rules for management of this framework in the form of an Interinstitutional Agreement has greatly reduced the implications of some of the budgetary procedures provided for in Article 272 of the Treaty (¹).

The distinction between compulsory and non-compulsory expenditure, which is the basis for the division of responsibilities between the Council and the European Parliament, is becoming less significant.

— The financial framework encompasses both types of expenditure.

— The classification of expenditure between these two categories has largely been agreed between the two arms of the budgetary authority.

— The Interinstitutional Agreement in force contains a provision designed to prevent any increase in compulsory expenditure, as a result of revision of the financial framework, from 'crowding out' non-compulsory expenditure.

— The two arms of the budgetary authority have also agreed to accept, for each of the financial years covered by the financial framework, the maximum rates of increase for non-compulsory expenditure deriving from the budgets established within the expenditure ceilings set (point 13 of the Interinstitutional Agreement).

3.2. For budgetary management

The corollary of setting a ceiling on expenditure for the medium term endows the Community with resources ensuring compatibility at all times between current or new operations and the financial framework laid down.

(¹)   See Chapter 11.

1) The provisions

Article 270 of the EC Treaty provides that 'With a view to maintaining budgetary discipline, the Commission shall not make any proposal for a Community act, or alter its proposals, or adopt any implementing measure which is likely to have appreciable implications for the budget without providing the assurance that that proposal or that measure is capable of being financed within the limit of the Community's own resources ...'

Point 14 of the Interinstitutional Agreement also stipulates that 'No act adopted under the co-decision procedure by the European Parliament and the Council nor any act adopted by the Council which involves exceeding the appropriations available in the budget or the allocations available in the financial framework (...) may be implemented in financial terms until the budget has been amended and, if necessary, the financial framework has been appropriately revised in accordance with the relevant procedure for each of these cases'.

Point 13 of the Interinstitutional Agreement provides that 'for the purposes of sound financial management, the institutions will ensure as far as possible during the budgetary procedure (...) that sufficient margins are left available beneath the ceilings for the various headings'. This margin should allow supplementary appropriations to be entered as needed without having to revise the financial framework each time.

2) Financial planning of expenditure

The Commission must be in a position to know, at all times, the envisaged medium-term trend in expenditure regarding all Community operations, in order to be able to assess its compatibility with the financial framework laid down. To this end, rules were introduced on medium-term financial programming, starting in January 1991. More recently, point 46 of the IIA clearly defines how the financial programming is to be established by the Commission and transmitted to the budgetary authority.

Accordingly, the financial programming is to be established and transmitted twice a year and will contain, for all headings comprising operational expenditure:

— the latest known situation regarding expenditure programmes, either adopted or just proposed by the Commission and pending adoption, including their duration and reference amounts;

— multiannual estimates for all annual action (pilot projects, preparatory action, etc);

— the margins left under the different expenditure ceilings of the financial framework.

As the majority of the multiannual programmes under the current financial framework cover the period 2007-13, the financial programming tables are established for the same period, thus enabling both the Commission and the budgetary authority to assess the implications in the short and medium term of any decisions with financial consequences with regard to the expenditure ceilings. The financial programming provides guidance but does not pre-empt options to be taken in the course of the annual budget procedure.

In addition, the financial programming is the instrument for projecting and verifying compliance with the financial envelopes of multiannual programmes throughout the duration of the programmes.

Apart from testing the consistency between the envisaged trend in expenditure and the ceilings laid down, this instrument performs two other functions:

— it makes authorising departments take a more systematic approach to medium-term, objective-based management, based on cost-effectiveness and regular evaluation of programmes; and

— when the period covered by the financial framework comes to an end, the Commission is able to base its proposals for renewal of the framework on a reasoned, relatively detailed estimate of the requirements to be covered.

Part 3

ESTABLISHMENT OF THE GENERAL BUDGET

Chapter 10

The general principles governing the Community budget

1. The principle of unity of the Community budget

1.1. Definition of the principle of unity

The principle of unity of the Community budget stems from Article 268 of the EC Treaty, which lays down that:

'All items of revenue and expenditure of the Community ... shall be included in estimates to be drawn up for each financial year and shall be shown in the budget.'

All Community revenue and expenditure should therefore be incorporated in a single budget document. Article 4 of the Financial Regulation stipulates that 'the budget is the instrument which, for each financial year, forecasts and authorises all revenue and expenditure considered necessary for the European Community and the European Atomic Energy Community'.

The unity of the budget means that it is clear what expenditure and revenue are authorised: only the revenue and expenditure included in the budget are authorised.

1.2. Application of the principle of unity in the general budget

In practice, the principle of unity is not applied in full.

In the early years of the Communities[1], the autonomy of the Community institutions set up under the ECSC, and subsequently under the EEC and Euratom, meant that as many as five budgets could exist at any one time.

Since 1971, when the Treaty of Luxembourg of 22 April 1970 entered into force, the main financial activities of the Community institutions have been incorporated into a single document, the general budget of the European Communities, which now covers more than 95 % of authorised expenditure. Under Article 4 of the Financial Regulation, the revenue and expenditure of the Communities comprises:

— the revenue and expenditure of the European Community, including administrative expenditure occasioned for the institutions by the provisions of the Treaty on European Union relating to the common foreign and security policy and police and judicial cooperation in criminal matters, and the operational expenditure occasioned by implementation of those provisions where this is charged to the budget; and

— the revenue and expenditure of the European Atomic Energy Community.

In addition, the budget must record the guarantee for borrowing-and-lending operations entered into by the Communities[2] and payments to the Guarantee Fund for external actions.

1.3. Exceptions to the principle of unity

Financial activities not incorporated in the general budget currently include:

— borrowing-and-lending operations, although the general budget contains the guarantee for the Community's borrowing-and-lending operations[3];

---

[1]   See Chapter 1.
[2]   See Chapter 17.
[3]   See Chapter 17.

— the European Development Fund (¹);

— the financial activities of the European Investment Bank.

In addition, some of the Community's decentralised agencies operate independently on the basis of their own budgets. However, strictly speaking, these budgets are not exceptions to the principle of unity, as their revenue is drawn from a balancing subsidy entered in the general budget.

1.4. The special cases of the common foreign and security policy and police and judicial cooperation in criminal matters (²)

The common foreign and security policy (CFSP) and cooperation in the field of justice and home affairs constitute the second and third 'pillars', respectively, of the European Union, established by the Maastricht Treaty and amended by the Treaty of Amsterdam and by the Treaty of Nice, neither of which provided for full incorporation of these areas into the general budget.

In both cases, administrative expenditure is charged to the budget of the European Communities.

Article 28 of the Treaty on European Union provides for operating expenditure on the CFSP also to be charged to the budget, except for such expenditure arising from operations having military or defence implications and cases where the Council unanimously decides otherwise.

Expenditure which is not charged to the budget of the European Communities is charged to the Member States in accordance with the gross national product (GNP) scale, unless the Council unanimously decides otherwise. Some Member States (which have been given the right to opt out) are under no obligation to contribute to financing expenditure arising from operations with military or defence implications.

In the case of police and judicial cooperation in criminal matters, the Treaty of Amsterdam amended the provisions of the Maastricht Treaty, bringing cooperation on civil matters (such as immigration and asylum)

(¹)   See Chapter 18.
(²)   See Chapter 7.

under the first pillar. Activities in this area are therefore financed from the general budget. As regards police and judicial cooperation in criminal matters, Article 41 of the Treaty on European Union stipulates that operating expenditure is charged to the budget, except where the Council unanimously decides otherwise. In that case, the expenditure is charged to the Member States in accordance with the GNP scale, unless the Council unanimously decides otherwise.

For example, non-budget financing (i.e. financing divided between the Member States in accordance with the GNP scale) was used for the Europol agency, which organises police cooperation against organised crime, whereas the Schengen information system, which contains personal data collected during border checks, is financed by the general budget.

Whenever expenditure is charged to the general budget, the normal budgetary procedure applies.

2. The principle of accuracy of the Community budget

2.1. Definition of the principle of accuracy

The principle of accuracy basically means that the European Community will not spend more than is necessary. This principle is defined in different ways (in Article 5 of the Financial Regulation):

— 'no revenue shall be collected and no expenditure effected unless booked to a line in the budget;

— no expenditure may be committed or authorised in excess of the authorised appropriations;

— an appropriation may not be entered in the budget if it is not for an item of expenditure considered necessary'.

2.2. The specific case of interest generated by the funds which are the property of the Community

In line with this principle, interest yielded by the funds which are the property of the Communities will also be entered in the budget – as miscellaneous revenue (Article 5(4) of the Financial Regulation).

The issue of interest generated by Community funds is particularly acute in the case of pre-financing payments. Pre-financing is intended to provide the beneficiary with a float and may, depending on the rate of spending, generate interest.

If this pre-financing remains the property of the Communities, the principle is that any interest generated will be allocated to the programme or action concerned and deducted from the balance due to the beneficiary. In this case, the interest is neither recovered nor entered as miscellaneous revenue.

However, by way of exception, any interest will be recovered if the pre-financing payments exceed EUR 750 000 per agreement at the end of a financial year. In other cases, interest may nevertheless be recovered, taking account of the risks associated with the management environment and the nature of the action financed (Article 5a of the Financial Regulation and Article 4 of the Implementing Rules). Once recovered, the amounts corresponding to this interest are entered as miscellaneous revenue.

These rules do not apply in certain cases. Under Article 5a(2) of the Financial Regulation, interest is not due in cases of:

— pre-financing which does not represent a significant amount (currently set at EUR 50 000);

— pre-financing paid under a procurement contract;

— pre-financing paid to Member States;

— pre-financing paid under the pre-accession aid;

— advances paid to members of the institutions and to staff;

— pre-financing paid in the framework of joint management.

Finally, it is worth mentioning the specific situations for contributions considered earmarked revenue (listed in Article 18 of the Financial Regulation) and revenue received by way of fines, periodic penalty payments and other penalties and any accrued interest as long as the decisions imposing them may be annulled by the Court of Justice (Article 74 of the Financial Regulation). In these two cases, interest yielded by these funds is not entered as miscellaneous revenue.

3. The principle of universality of the Community budget

3.1. Definition of the principle of universality

The principle of universality is a corollary of the principle of unity. It does not stem directly from the Treaties, but from Article 17 of the Financial Regulation, which states that:

'Total revenue shall cover total payment appropriations ... All revenue and expenditure shall be entered in full [in the budget and in the accounts] without any adjustment against each other.'

In line with this principle, budget revenue may not be assigned to specific items of expenditure (non-assignment rule) and revenue and expenditure may not be set off against each other (gross budget rule). Consequently, revenue is pooled and used without distinction to finance all expenditure.

This principle supplements the unity principle by ensuring that budgetary authorisation for a given item of expenditure does not depend on the amount of a given item of revenue, which would restrict the scope of such authorisation and split the budget into watertight segments.

The non-assignment rule was enshrined in the Council Decision of 21 April 1970 creating own resources and was confirmed by subsequent decisions. In particular, Article 6 of the Council Decisions of 29 September 2000 and 7 June 2007 on the system of own resources states:

'The revenue ... shall be used without distinction to finance all expenditure entered in the ... budget ...'

3.2. Exceptions to the non-assignment rule

However, Article 18 of the Financial Regulation makes an exception to the non-assignment rule in the following cases:

— financial contributions from Member States to certain research programmes pursuant to the Council Regulation implementing the Decision on the system of the Communities' own resources; the reason for this is because not all Member States take part in the programmes concerned;

— financial contributions from Member States and other donor countries, including in both cases their public and parastatal agencies, or from international organisations to certain external aid projects or programmes financed by the Community and managed by the Commission on their behalf, pursuant to the relevant basic act;

— interest on deposits and the fines provided for in the Regulation on speeding up and clarifying the implementation of the excessive deficit procedure;

— revenue earmarked for a specific purpose, such as income from foundations, subsidies, gifts and bequests, including the earmarked revenue specific to each institution;

— contributions to Community activities from third countries or various bodies;

— revenue from third parties in respect of goods, services or work supplied at their request;

— proceeds from the sale of vehicles, equipment, installations, materials and scientific and technical apparatus which are being replaced or scrapped when the book value is fully depreciated;

— revenues arising from the repayment of amounts wrongly paid;

— proceeds from the supply of goods, services and works for other institutions or bodies, including refunds by other institutions or bodies of mission allowances paid on their behalf;

— insurance payments received;

— revenue from payments connected with lettings;

— revenue from the sale of publications and films, including those on an electronic medium.

Moreover, the basic act adopted by the legislative authority and laying down the basis for an EC programme may also assign the revenue for which it provides to specific items of expenditure (Article 18(2) of the Financial Regulation).

The abovementioned contributions to Community activities from non-member countries or various bodies include, for example, the contribution by the European Free Trade Association (EFTA) countries to financing certain Community policies, such as the research programmes in which they participate. Their participation began with the establishment of the European Economic Area in 1994.

Their contributions are calculated by applying a 'proportionality factor', based on the ratio between the GDP of the Member States of the Community and that of the EFTA member countries, and are allocated to the budget items concerned. These contributions and the expenditure they finance are not included in the budget and appear in it 'for information' only.

The same rule also applies to participation by the applicant countries in certain Community programmes as part of the pre-accession strategies. Their contributions are defined on a case-by-case basis in the association councils and allocated to the budget headings concerned.

3.3. Exceptions to the gross budget rule

Article 20 of the Financial Regulation makes the following exceptions to the gross budget rule:

— the following deductions may be made from payment requests, invoices or statements, which will then be passed for payment of the net amount: penalties imposed on parties to procurement contracts or beneficiaries of a grant; discounts, refunds and rebates on individual invoices and payment requests;

— moreover, the cost of products or services provided to the Communities incorporating taxes refunded by the Member States pursuant to the Protocol on the Privileges and Immunities of the European Communities or by third countries on the basis of the relevant agreements will be charged to the budget for the ex-tax amount;

— lastly, adjustments may be made in respect of exchange differences occurring in the implementation of the budget; the final balance will be included in the balance for the year.

All these exceptions are of a technical nature and are intended to simplify procedures.

3.4. The special case of agricultural co-responsibility levies (negative expenditure)

This negative expenditure was provided for in the sectoral agricultural regulations and divides up into different categories, such as amounts recovered in cases of fraud or irregularity.

In the recast Financial Regulation, 'negative expenditure' has been changed to assigned revenue to introduce greater transparency in the presentation of the budget and accounting, without detracting from the spending capacity in agriculture.

3.5. The special case of negative revenue

The budget may not contain negative revenue (Article 42 of the Financial Regulation). The own resources paid under the Council Decision on the system of the Communities' own resources must be net amounts and must be shown as such in the summary statement of revenue in the budget.

Nevertheless, Member States retain some amounts (10 % from 1971 to 2000 and 25 % since 2001) as collection costs for traditional own resources (i.e. sugar levies, customs duties and agricultural levies). From 1971 to 1987, these amounts were entered in the accounts as budgetary expenditure. From 1988 until 2002, the collection costs were entered as 'negative revenue' in the Community budget. From 2003 on, only the net amounts of the traditional own resources are indicated and the collection costs as such are no longer mentioned in the budget.

3.6. Impact of the exceptions to the gross budget rule on the multiannual expenditure framework

The abovementioned exceptions to the gross budget rule run counter to the constraints imposed by the multiannual financial framework, since they result in less expenditure being entered in the budget than would be the case if there were no offsetting of revenue and expenditure. The 2006 Interinstitutional Agreement (point 11) provides that the multiannual financial framework takes no account of budget items financed by earmarked revenue. If the offsetting of revenue and expenditure were abolished, this would therefore strengthen the constraints of the multiannual financial framework.

The multiannual financial framework itself adjusts revenue and expenditure against each other in the pensions field. A footnote to the table entitled 'Financial Framework 2007-13' in Annex I to the Interinstitutional Agreement states that 'the expenditure on pensions included under the ceiling for this heading is calculated net of the staff contributions to the relevant scheme, within the limit of EUR 500 million at 2004 prices for the period 2007-13'.

4. The principle of annuality of the Community budget

The principle of annuality requires budget operations to relate to a specific financial year. This makes it easier to monitor the activities of the Community executive.

It is defined by the EC Treaty from three angles:

— As regards estimates: 'All items of revenue and expenditure ... shall be included in estimates to be drawn up for each financial year' (first paragraph of Article 268 of the EC Treaty);

— As regards implementation: 'The expenditure shown in the budget shall be authorised for one financial year ...' (first paragraph of Article 271 of the EC Treaty and Article 6 of the Financial Regulation);

— As regards the financial year coinciding with the calendar year: 'The financial year shall run from 1 January to 31 December' (Article 272(1) of the EC Treaty and Article 6 of the Financial Regulation).

4.1. Annuality and differentiated appropriations

The Community budget, like any public authority budget, has to reconcile the principle of annuality with the need to engage in multiannual operations, which means that commitments have to be entered for a longer period than the financial year in which they are made.

1) Differentiated appropriations

The answer to this twin requirement is to enter differentiated appropriations, which consist of commitment appropriations and payment appropriations. This distinction goes back to Article 176(1) of the Euratom Treaty and is widely applied by Article 7 of the Financial Regulation.

(1)   Commitment appropriations cover the total cost of the legal commitments entered into, in principle, during the current financial year.

(2)   Payment appropriations cover payments made to honour the legal commitments entered into in the current financial year and/or earlier financial years.

In current budgetary practice, administrative expenditure (Article 179 of the Financial Regulation), most European Agricultural Guarantee Fund expenditure (Article 149 of the Financial Regulation) and loan guarantees, for example, are entered in the budget in the form of non-differentiated appropriations (the other categories of expenditure are made up of differentiated appropriations). The terms 'appropriations for commitments'/'appropriations for payments' are used when differentiated and non-differentiated commitment/payment appropriations are added together.

It must be stressed that the existence of differentiated appropriations does not constitute an exception to the principle of annuality. Commitment appropriations as such are authorised for one year under the annual budgetary procedure. It is simply the payments for the operations covered by these commitments which may extend over a number of financial years, the payment appropriations themselves being subject to budget authorisation each year. This dual annual authorisation of commitment and payment appropriations is a unique feature of the Community budget.

2) The gap between 'commitment appropriations' and 'payment appropriations' (concept of 'commitments outstanding')

The introduction of the concept of differentiated appropriations automatically opened up a 'gap' between commitments entered into and payments made: this gap is the result of the time lag between when the commitments are entered into and when the corresponding payments are made. The sum of appropriations committed but not yet paid is called 'commitments outstanding' (often referred to by the French acronym RAL). Outstanding commitments have grown steadily in recent decades as Community policies and the multiannual operations carried out to implement them have developed.

The phenomenon has been accentuated by the difficulties sometimes encountered in clearing commitments. Any delay in conclusion of contracts between the Community and the recipients of Community funding, as is often the case in the Community's external activities, or in implementation of such contracts or payment of the balance of Community funding (where it is contested, for example) has the effect of stretching the time lag between commitments and payments and, hence, increasing the amount of commitments outstanding. Outstanding commitments can therefore be said to include a normal component linked to the system of differentiated appropriations and an abnormal component linked to problems with implementing some multiannual activities.

The growth in outstanding commitments is worrying since it constitutes a growing liability for the Community budget and, hence, a medium-term constraint on the payment appropriations needed to honour this debt. The budgetary authority and the Commission, which is responsible for implementing the budget, are therefore gradually developing measures and tools to control this growth.

The Interinstitutional Agreement and the Council Decision on own resources (Decision 2000/597/EC, Euratom) require commitment appropriations entered in the budget to follow an orderly progression and a strict relationship to be maintained between commitment and payment appropriations so that they do not exceed a set percentage of the total GNP of the Member States.

Likewise, successive revisions of the Financial Regulation have laid down strict rules on deadlines for implementing multiannual projects.

— Article 77(3) of the Financial Regulation stipulates that the legal commitments entered into for multiannual measures must set a final date for implementation which must be specified to the recipient when the aid is granted.

— Similarly, as a rule, differentiated appropriations which have not been used by the end of the financial year are cancelled (Article 9 of the Financial Regulation).

— Lastly, to penalise inadequate monitoring of use of appropriations, Article 9 of the Financial Regulation introduces the idea of decommitment of appropriations not used by the end of the financial year for which they were entered.

4.2. Adjustments to the principle of annuality

The principle of annuality is generally respected. Pursuant to the Treaty, however, the Financial Regulation lays down a number of exceptions, or rather technical adjustments, to ensure more flexible budget management. The policy of tighter budgetary discipline and more transparent management of appropriations has, nonetheless, very much restricted application of these exceptions.

1) Carry-overs

Because of management constraints, use of appropriations cannot always be made to coincide with the calendar year. Article 271 of the EC Treaty therefore allows the pragmatic solution of authorising carry-overs, except, however, in the case of expenditure on staff or appropriations placed in reserve (see Article 9(6) of the Financial Regulation).

Article 9 of the Financial Regulation lays down the following rules:

— Automatic carry-overs:

- Non-differentiated appropriations corresponding to obligations duly contracted at the close of the financial year will be carried over automatically to the following financial year only.

— Non-automatic carry-overs:

- Commitment appropriations and non-differentiated appropriations not yet committed at the close of the financial year may be carried over in respect of amounts corresponding to commitment appropriations for which most of the preparatory stages of the commitment procedure have been completed by 31 December (these amounts may then be committed up to 31 March of the following year) or amounts which are necessary when the legislative authority has adopted a basic act in the final quarter of the financial year and the Commission has been unable to commit the appropriations provided for this purpose by 31 December.

- Payment appropriations may be carried over in respect of amounts needed to cover existing commitments or commitments linked to commitment appropriations carried over, when the appropriations provided for the relevant lines in the budget for the following financial year do not cover requirements. The institution concerned must first use the appropriations authorised for the current financial year and must not use the appropriations carried over until the former are exhausted (Article 9(3) of the Financial Regulation).

Requests for carry-overs of this type must be duly substantiated. The institution concerned must take the decision by 15 February of year n+1 at the latest (Article 9(1) of the Financial Regulation).

2) Additional periods

'Additional periods' means either an ad hoc extension of the financial year beyond the 12 months of the calendar year or an anticipation of the financial year.

At present, the general budget includes two types of additional period:

(1) entry in the accounts for the EAGF: because of the time needed at Community level to process the information supplied by the Member

States, entry of EAGF expenditure in the accounts may be extended by one month into year n+1 (Article 152 of the Financial Regulation);

(2) commitments of appropriations or payment in advance.

From 15 November each year, routine administrative expenditure and routine management expenditure for the EAGF may be committed in advance against the appropriations provided for the following financial year (Articles 178 and 150 of the Financial Regulation). Such commitments may not, however, exceed one-quarter (for administrative expenditure) and three quarters (for EAGF expenditure) of the appropriations decided by the budgetary authority on the corresponding budget line for the current financial year. For administrative expenditure, they may not apply to new expenditure of a kind not yet approved in principle in the last budget duly adopted, whereas for EAGF expenditure they may apply only to expenditure for which the principle is laid down in an existing basic act.

Expenditure which must be paid in advance pursuant to legal or contractual provisions, for example rents, may give rise to payments from 1 December onwards to be charged to the appropriations for the following financial year (Article 178 of the Financial Regulation).

3) Making appropriations available

Where amounts are decommitted as a result of total or partial non-implementation of the action for which they were earmarked, in any financial year after that in which the appropriations were entered in the budget, the appropriations concerned will be cancelled (Article 11 of the Financial Regulation).

However, two possible ways of making appropriations available are authorised by the Financial Regulation:

— Under Article 157 of the Financial Regulation and the specific regulation governing the Structural Funds, Cohesion Fund, European Fisheries Fund and European Agricultural Fund for Rural Development, the Commission will automatically decommit appropriations that have been committed. The decommitted appropriations may be made available again in the event of a manifest error attributable solely to the Commission. To this end, the Commission will examine decommitments made during the previous financial year and decide, by 15 February of the current year, on the basis of requirements, whether it is necessary to make the corresponding appropriations available again;

— The 2006 revision of the Financial Regulation introduced the new possibility of making funds available in the field of research and technological development (Article 160a):

'The commitment appropriations corresponding to the amount of the commitment decommitted as a result of total or partial non-implementation of the projects relating to research for which they were earmarked may, exceptionally and in duly substantiated cases, be made available again where it is essential to carry out the programme originally planned, unless the budget for the current financial year contains funds for this purpose ...

The Commission shall, at the beginning of each financial year, examine decommitments made during the previous financial year and assess, in the light of the requirements, the need for making the appropriations available again.

On the basis of this assessment, the Commission may submit appropriate proposals to the budgetary authority, by 15 February of each financial year, stating for each budget item the reasons for making these appropriations available again.

The budgetary authority shall decide on the Commission's proposals within six weeks. Where no decision is taken within this time limit, the proposals shall be deemed to be approved.

The amount of commitment appropriations to be made available again in year n shall in no case exceed 25 % of the total amount decommitted on the same budget line in year n-1. Commitment appropriations made available again shall not be carried over.

Legal commitments relating to the commitment appropriations which have been made available again shall be concluded by 31 December of year n. At the end of year n, the unused balance of the commitment appropriations made available again shall be definitively decommitted by the authorising officer responsible'.

4.3. Implications of annuality for revenue

The various decisions on own resources have established the principle that own resources are allocated to the Communities to finance their budget. Any surplus of revenue over total expenditure during a year is carried over to the following year.

Article 8(1) of the Financial Regulation also states that the revenue of a financial year is entered in the accounts for the financial year on the basis of the amounts collected during the financial year.

These provisions demonstrate the legislator's clear intention to apply the principle of annuality as strictly as possible to revenue. Budgetary implementation of the statement of revenue is therefore based on the principle of the 'cash budget': only the amounts collected between 1 January and 31 December are entered in the accounts.

As a result, the annual implementation of the budget will produce a balance at the end of the financial year consisting of the difference between the revenue actually collected and the payments actually made (see details given on the principle of budgetary equilibrium).

Article 8 of the Financial Regulation and Article 10(3) of Regulation 1150/2000 of 22 May 2000, as amended by Regulation 2028/2004 of 16 November 2004, provide for three cases where this strict annuality of revenue may be relaxed:

(1) Advance payments made in December of the preceding financial year in respect of traditional own resources for January are not entered in the accounts for that year in accordance with the usual 'cash budget' principle. Instead, they are entered for the year in which payment should normally have been made;

(2) The entries related to the EAGGF monetary reserve, to the reserve relating to loans and loan guarantees and to the reserve for emergency aid are also taken into account in the financial year to which they relate, irrespective of the date of payment;

(3) Lastly, any readjustments of the twelfths paid in respect of the VAT resources, of the correction granted to the United Kingdom for budgetary imbalances and of the GNP/GNI resources made in the course of the financial year, following adoption of a supplementary or amend-

ing budget affecting those resources, are also booked to the year to which they relate.

4.4. Annuality and medium-term financial framework

Since 1988, under the Interinstitutional Agreement renewed in 1993, 1999 and again in 2006, the budget of each financial year must be placed within the multiannual financial framework, a medium-term financial planning instrument. This mechanism cannot be considered to conflict with the principle of budget annuality.

(1) The multiannual financial framework sets expenditure ceilings for each year of the period covered, by heading for commitment appropriations and in the form of a total for payment appropriations. For structural measures, these amounts constitute the expenditure targets which the budgetary authority undertakes to enter in the budget each year. The amounts appearing in the multiannual financial framework do not therefore constitute expenditure authorisations, which are determined in the budget adopted annually.

(2) The annual ceilings apply to each financial year and may in no way be aggregated over the period. The calendar year, which is the same as the financial year, is therefore clearly the basic unit of time used for the multiannual financial framework.

5. The principle of equilibrium of the Community budget

The principle of equilibrium means that budget revenue must equal budget expenditure. This rule is enshrined in Article 268 of the EC Treaty. It was incorporated in the successive own resources decisions and in the Financial Regulation (Article 14). The Community, unlike its Member States, is not allowed to borrow to cover its expenditure.

5.1. Achievement of budgetary equilibrium

For technical reasons, it is inevitable that there will be differences between the forecasts made at the authorisation stage and the final outturn. A distinction should be drawn between:

— the authorisation stage: the equilibrium principle is strictly applied, both formally and mathematically, when the budget is established, i.e. at the estimates and authorisation stage. In the budget finally adopted, revenue and payment appropriations have to be in balance (Article 14 of the Financial Regulation);

— the implementation stage: the outturn, however, will inevitably diverge from the estimates on both the revenue and the expenditure sides. The revenue may in practice be either higher or lower than forecast. Since the appropriations authorised are absolute ceilings which, on no account, may be exceeded, actual expenditure will have to be below the estimates (or at best – which would be very rare – exactly the same as the estimates).

The revenue and expenditure account, which shows the end-of-year results, provides a comparison between estimates and outturn. The Communities must, nonetheless, do all they can to ensure that outturn also complies with the equilibrium principle. Corrections are therefore sometimes necessary during the year, involving either management measures or, if it is essential to alter the amounts authorised, adoption of a supplementary and/or amending budget.

5.2. Concept of budget balance

1) Definition of the balance

The balance for a given financial year consists of the difference between all the revenue collected in respect of that financial year and the amount of payments made against appropriations for that financial year, plus the amount of the appropriations for the same financial year carried over.

On the one side, the net amount of appropriations carried over from previous financial years which have been cancelled is added to this difference and, on the other, payments made in excess of non-differentiated appropriations carried over from the previous financial year as a result of variations in euro rates and the balance resulting from exchange gains and losses during the financial year are subtracted from it (Article 15 of Regulation (EC, Euratom) No 1150/2000, as amended by Regulation (EC, Euratom) No 2028/2004, implementing the decision on own resources).

2) Practical application

The balance from each financial year will be entered in the budget for the following financial year as revenue in the case of a surplus or as a payment appropriation in the case of a deficit (Article 15(1) of the Financial Regulation).

The estimates of such revenue or payment appropriations will be entered in the budget during the budgetary procedure and in a letter of amendment (Article 15(2) of the Financial Regulation).

Moreover, after presentation of the accounts for each financial year, any discrepancy with the estimates must be entered in the budget for the following financial year through an amending budget devoted solely to that discrepancy. In such a case, the preliminary draft amending budget must be submitted by the Commission within 15 days following the submission of the provisional accounts (Article 15(3) of the Financial Regulation).

Headings with token entries are accordingly included in the statement of revenue and in the statement of expenditure to accommodate the balance ('surplus available from the preceding financial year' or 'deficit carried over from previous year').

In practice, two situations are possible:

— Positive balance (surplus): this is the normal situation, where the revenue outturn (resources collected) covered all expenditure requirements on the basis of the rules applicable (in particular, coverage of carry-overs). In this case, the surplus is carried forward to the following year, where it is entered on the revenue side. The Financial Regulation provides for early entry in the budget for year n of the probable balance for year n-1, with the final adjustment being made after the closure of the accounts for year n-1 through a supplementary and/or amending budget;

— Negative balance (deficit): this is more of an exception (the last case was in 1986). However, the revenue outturn might prove to be less than the amount necessary to cover requirements determined in accordance with the rules applicable. When a deficit is recorded, a corresponding amount must be entered on the expenditure side of the following year's budget, by a procedure similar to that described in the event of a surplus.

5.3. Negative reserve

Under Article 44 of the Financial Regulation, the Commission section of the budget may include a 'negative reserve' limited to a maximum amount of EUR 200 million. A 'negative reserve' mechanism has helped, albeit indirectly, to keep the budget in balance, even though it really amounts to a failure to achieve such a balance. This mechanism consists of financing new expenditure by assuming that savings will be made somewhere in the budget during the financial year, without it being possible to identify which items will generate these savings when the budget is adopted. A negative amount is therefore included in the budget which must be covered during the year by transfers from headings which turn out to be in surplus.

The negative reserve first appeared in the 1986 budget as a way of securing agreement between the two arms of the budgetary authority on the rate of increase for non-compulsory expenditure. Appropriations not used (i.e. savings made) were transferred to this negative reserve. The concept of 'negative reserve' was formally enshrined for the first time in the revision of the Financial Regulation dated 24 June 1988, with the maximum amount limited to ECU 200 million.

6. The principle of specification of the Community budget

6.1. The principle of specification

The principle of specification of expenditure is enshrined in Article 271 of the EC Treaty. It means that each appropriation must have a given purpose and be assigned to a specific objective in order to prevent any confusion between appropriations, at both the authorisation and implementation stages, and thus to ensure that:

— the budget established is completely unambiguous; and

— it is executed in accordance with the wishes of the budgetary authority.

The principle of specification also applies to revenue and requires the various sources of revenue paid into the budget to be clearly identified.

Articles 40 and 41 of the Financial Regulation, which deal with the structure and presentation of the budget, describe very precisely how this principle is to be implemented. These articles were incorporated in 2002 to adapt the structure of the budget to the requirements stemming from the introduction of activity-based budgeting in the Commission.

6.2. Specification and structure of the budget

The principle of specification determines both the horizontal and the vertical structure of the budget.

1) The horizontal structure of the budget

The budget is divided into:

— a general statement of revenue;

— sections, subdivided into statements of revenue and of expenditure, for the European Parliament (Section I), the Council (Section II), the Commission (Section III), the Court of Justice (Section IV), the Court of Auditors (Section V), the Economic and Social Committee (Section VI), the Committee of the Regions (Section VII) and the European Ombudsman (Section VIII). The European Data Protection Supervisor, a new authority being created, should share the Ombudsman's section;

— in addition, Section III (Commission), which accounts for 95 % of expenditure, is organised under titles corresponding to the Commission's policy areas. Each title is, in turn, subdivided into chapters, of which the first includes all administrative appropriations for the policy area in question and the remainder correspond to the related activities. A general summary of administrative appropriations allocated to policy areas is also included. Finally, the budget includes a number of annexes with additional information on specific issues.

2) The vertical structure of the budget: the budget nomenclature

Depending on the type and purpose of the appropriations, each section is subdivided into titles, chapters, articles and items (third paragraph of Article 271 of the EC Treaty and Article 21 of the Financial Regulation).

Under Article 5 of the Financial Regulation 'no revenue shall be collected and no expenditure effected unless booked to a line in the budget'.

The article is therefore the slot to accommodate revenue and expenditure, while the real organisation by specific area, which the budgetary authority is responsible for determining, is at the level of chapters. As a rule, only the budgetary authority may make decisions on transfers between chapters.

The nomenclature is determined during the budgetary procedure. The broad outline is currently as follows:

(a) General statement of revenue

Title 1	Own resources
Title 3	Surpluses, balances and adjustments
Title 4	Revenue accruing from persons working with the institutions and other Community bodies
Title 5	Revenue accruing from the administrative operation of the institutions
Title 6	Contributions and refunds in connection with Community agreements and programmes
Title 7	Interest on late payments and fines
Title 8	Borrowing and lending operations
Title 9	Miscellaneous revenue

(b) Statements of revenue and expenditure for each section

On the revenue side, the nomenclature is identical to that of the general statement of revenue.

For the statement of each institution's administrative expenditure (in Sections I, II, IV, V, VI, VII and VIII), the nomenclature is as follows:

Title 1	Expenditure relating to persons working with the institution
Title 2	Buildings, equipment and miscellaneous operating expenditure
Title 3	Expenditure resulting from special functions carried out by the institution
Title 4	Interinstitutional cooperation, interinstitutional services and activities
Title 5	Data processing
Title 6	Staff and administrative expenditure of European Community delegations
Title 7	Decentralised expenditure on support staff and administration
Title 10	Other expenditure

However, the administrative expenditure of the Commission is found under the different titles of Section III, thereby providing a clear picture of the total expenditure on each of the Commission's policy areas. This administrative chapter follows a common structure across all policy areas:

Chapter NN 01

Article NN 01 01	Expenditure related to staff in active employment
Article NN 01 02	External staff and other management expenditure
Article NN 01 03	Expenditure related to equipment, furniture and services, and buildings of the Delegations of the Commission of the European Communities
Article NN 01 05	Expenditure related to staff in active employment for indirect research

Section III of the budget is therefore organised under titles corresponding to the Commission's policy areas. In the 2008 budget, the titles are as follows:

01 Economic and financial affairs
02 Enterprise
03 Competition
04 Employment and social affairs
05 Agriculture and rural development
06 Energy and transport
07 Environment
08 Research
09 Information society and media
10 Direct research
11 Fisheries and maritime affairs
12 Internal market
13 Regional policy
14 Taxation and customs union
15 Education and culture

16   Communication
17   Health and consumer protection
18   Area of freedom, security and justice
19   External relations
20   Trade
21   Development and relations with African, Caribbean and Pacific (ACP) States
22   Enlargement
23   Humanitarian aid
24   Fight against fraud
25   Commission's policy coordination and legal advice
26   Commission's administration
27   Budget
28   Audit
29   Statistics
30   Pensions
31   Language services
40   Reserves

3) Structure by article or item

The budget contains, for each individual item, article, chapter and title:

(1) the appropriations provided for the financial year in question (year n), in the form of commitment appropriations and payment appropriations for differentiated appropriations;

(2) the appropriations provided for the preceding financial year (year n-1);

(3) the actual expenditure in the last financial year for which the accounts have been closed (year n-2);

(4) appropriate remarks on each expenditure line. These remarks include the references of the basic legal instrument, if one exists, plus all necessary explanations concerning the nature and purpose of the appropriations.

In addition, the budget must include information on staff numbers and, in particular, the 'establishment plan' for each institution (Article 46 (1) of the Financial Regulation).

Lastly, in the absence of formal inclusion of borrowing-and-lending operations in the budget, these operations appear in the budget in the following form:

— in the general statement of revenue: the relevant budget headings carrying a token entry and accompanied by appropriate remarks;

— in the Commission section: the budget lines relating to the categories of operation and carrying a token entry, as long as no effective charge which has to be covered by specific resources has arisen, plus remarks giving references to the legal basis and indicating the volume and duration of the operations envisaged and the financial guarantee given by the Communities in respect of these operations;

— in a document annexed to the Commission section, as an indication: ongoing capital operations and debt management, plus the capital operations and debt management for the financial year in question.

6.3. Specification and entry of appropriations against headings

There are three types of entry against budget headings:

1) Headings with appropriations entered: this is the usual situation

2) Headings with a token entry (p.m.)

Token entries are used in the following three cases:

(1) where no legal basis exists at the time the budget is adopted and the measure envisaged cannot be undertaken without a legal basis [1];

(2) where it is difficult at the outset to cost new operations;

---

[1] See Chapter 10, Section 6.4 on legal bases.

(3) where the budgetary authority wishes to stop an operation temporarily.

In these three cases, appropriations may be entered in a specific 'reserves' title: Title 40.

Headings with a token entry may receive appropriations by transfer.

A token entry is therefore a sign that the budgetary authority accepts the principle of expenditure under the heading concerned, but that any expenditure is subject to certain conditions.

3) Headings with a dash

A dash is entered to indicate headings which are no longer operational, but for which the appropriations entered for year n-1 and the outturn for year n-2 still have to be shown for reasons of comparison and to satisfy the technical requirements of budgetary presentation.

Headings with a dash may not be given appropriations by means of transfers. A supplementary or amending budget must be adopted to allocate appropriations to these headings.

The dash therefore means that the budgetary authority no longer accepts the principle of expenditure under the heading, as it considers the operation to be finished.

6.4. Flexibility in application of the rule of specification: transfers of appropriations

Transfers of appropriations within the budget is the procedure used to correct the estimates made by the budgetary authority by moving appropriations from one heading to another (Article 274 of the EC Treaty).

Transfers therefore help to improve the prospects of budget implementation which comes in for particularly careful scrutiny on the part of the budgetary authority [1].

---

[1]   See Chapter 14.

The transfer mechanism is described in Articles 22 to 26 of the Financial Regulation and is sophisticated. In particular, these articles draw a distinction between transfers between titles, transfers between chapters and transfers between articles. They also differentiate between administrative and staff appropriations and operational appropriations, and between institutions covered by the budget.

1) Transfers between titles

(a) Operational expenditure of the Commission

Proposals are prepared by the Commission, then submitted to the budgetary authority, which takes a decision by the following procedure:

(1) non-compulsory expenditure: Parliament approves or rejects the transfer by an absolute majority after consulting the Council;

(2) compulsory expenditure: the Council approves or rejects the transfer by a qualified majority after consulting Parliament.

In both cases the Commission's proposals are deemed to be accepted if the budgetary authority has not taken a decision within six weeks.

Proposals for mixed transfers from compulsory expenditure to non-compulsory expenditure (or vice versa) are deemed to be approved unless:

(1) a veto is entered by one of the arms of the budgetary authority, in which case the proposal is rejected;

(2) Parliament or the Council reduces the amount, in which case the transfer is then deemed to be approved at the lowest amount.

The possibility of making such transfers between *non-differentiated and differentiated appropriations* is accepted in the Financial Regulation (Article 24).

(b) Expenditure on staff and administration of the Commission

For these transfers, different procedures may apply, given the impact of the transfers to be made. As is the case for operational expenditure, the Commission may propose transfers to the budgetary authority which then accepts or rejects the proposals, following the procedures described under point (a). There are nevertheless two specific procedures related to particular situations.

— The Commission makes the transfers itself after giving the budgetary authority three weeks' notice. This is the case for transfers from one title to another up to a maximum of 10 % of the appropriations for the year on the line from which the transfer is made, and up to a maximum of 30 % of the appropriations for the year on the line to which the transfer is made. However, this procedure does not apply if duly substantiated reasons are raised within the three-week period by either branch of the budgetary authority, in which case the budgetary authority takes a decision following the procedures described under point (a).

— The Commission makes transfers and informs the budgetary authority within two weeks after its decisions. This applies during the last two months of the financial year to expenditure on staff, external staff and other agents up to a total limit of 5 % of the appropriations for the financial year. This also applies to transfers of appropriations from the 'provisions' title, as soon as the basic act is adopted pursuant to the 'co-decision' procedure (laid down in Article 251 of the EC Treaty), in cases where no basic act existed for the action concerned when the budget was established.

(c) For institutions other than the Commission

The institution concerned may propose transfers within its own section to the budgetary authority, which then accepts or rejects the proposals, following the procedures described under point (a).

For transfers from one title to another up to a maximum of 10 % of the appropriations for the year on the line from which the transfer is made, the institution concerned makes the transfers itself after giving the budgetary authority three weeks' notice, except if duly substantiated reasons are raised within that three-week period by either branch of the budgetary authority, in which case the budgetary authority takes a decision following the procedures described under point (a).

2) Transfers between chapters

(a) For the Commission

As regards operational expenditure, proposals for transfers from one chapter to another are prepared by the Commission, then submitted to the budgetary authority, which takes a decision following the procedures described under point 1(a).

However, for transfers from one chapter to another within the same title up to a maximum of 10 % of the appropriations for the year on the line from which the transfer is made, the Commission makes the transfers itself after giving the budgetary authority three weeks' notice, except if duly substantiated reasons are raised within that three-week period by either branch of the budgetary authority, in which case the budgetary authority takes a decision following the procedures described under point 1(a).

(b) For other institutions

Without any limit, these institutions may, within their own sections of the budget, transfer appropriations from one chapter to another after giving the budgetary authority three weeks' notice, except if duly substantiated reasons are raised within that three-week period by either branch of the budgetary authority, in which case the budgetary authority takes a decision following the procedures described under point 1(a).

3) Transfers within chapters

(a) For the Commission

The Commission may transfer appropriations within articles and between articles within each chapter without any need to inform the budgetary authority and without any limit.

(b) For the other institutions

Without any limit, each institution may, within its own section of the budget, transfer appropriations from one article to another after giving the budgetary authority three weeks' notice, except if duly substantiated reasons are raised within that three-week period by either branch of the budgetary authority, in which case the budgetary authority takes a decision following the procedures described under point 1(a).

4) Specific rules for transfers of appropriations

(a) European Agricultural Guarantee Fund

The specific rules concern the time limits for submitting proposals to the budgetary authority or adopting decisions.

In cases where the Commission may transfer appropriations, it must take its decision by 31 January of the following financial year at the latest and inform the budgetary authority three weeks before making the transfers (Article 153(1) of the Financial Regulation).

Where the Commission is required to submit transfers to the budgetary authority, it must submit its proposals to the budgetary authority by 10 January of the following financial year at the latest. In this case, the budgetary authority takes a decision in accordance with the normal procedure, as described under point 1(a), but within a time limit of three weeks instead of six weeks (Article 153(2) of the Financial Regulation).

(b) Structural Funds, Cohesion Fund and European Fisheries Fund

With regard to the operational expenditure in these three fields, the Commission may make transfers from one title to another, provided the appropriations in question are for the same objective within the meaning of the Regulations governing these Funds or are technical assistance expenditure (Article 158 of the Financial Regulation).

These rules do not apply to the European Agricultural Fund for Rural Development.

(c) Research and technological development appropriations

With regard to operational expenditure for research and technological development appropriations, the Commission may make transfers from one title to another, provided the appropriations in question are used for the same purpose (Article 160 of the Financial Regulation).

(d) Reserve for emergency aid for third countries

Decisions on transfers to allow use of the reserve for emergency aid are taken by the budgetary authority on a proposal from the Commission. The procedure described under point 1(a) applies.

If the Commission proposal is not agreed to by both arms of the budgetary authority and they fail to reach a common position on use of this reserve, the European Parliament and the Council must refrain from acting on the Commission proposal for a transfer (Article 26(2) of the Financial Regulation).

(e) Humanitarian aid and crisis management

In duly substantiated exceptional cases of international humanitarian disasters and crises occurring after 15 December of the budgetary year, the Commission may transfer unused budgetary appropriations for the current budgetary year still available in the budget falling under heading 4 of the multiannual financial framework to the budget titles concerning the crisis management aid and humanitarian aid operations. The Commission must inform the two branches of the budgetary authority immediately after making such transfers (Article 26(3) of the Financial Regulation).

(f) Joint Research Centre

In this case, the Commission may, within the budget title relating to the policy area 'Direct action research', make transfers between chapters of up to 15 % of the appropriation on the line from which the transfer is made (Article 161(4) of the Financial Regulation).

(g) Offices

Specific rules also apply to European offices such as the Office for Official Publications (OPOCE). In such cases, the Director of each European office will take decisions on transfers within the statement of expenditure of the Office concerned. The Commission must inform the budgetary authority of such matters.

6.5. Reserves

The introduction of reserves in the budget can be considered an exception to the rule of specification from two points of view:

— in that the reserves set aside are not allocated to any precise purpose;

— in that the limit on authorised appropriations for a specific item of expenditure is weakened in this way.

Allowance is made in the Financial Regulation for three types of budget reserve:

(1) provisions (Article 43);

(2) a reserve for emergency aid for third countries (Article 45);

(3) a negative reserve (Article 44) ([1]).

The purpose of these reserves is to facilitate budget management. They make it possible, during the financial year, to endow a budget heading for operations for which full details had not been decided at the time the budget was adopted, or to increase authorised appropriations to meet unforeseen situations or to reduce them to make savings, depending on progress with implementation.

These reserves may be called upon only by means of a transfer procedure: the rule of specification is therefore restored in any case when the time comes to use them.

7. The principle of the unit of account of the Community budget

7.1. The principle of the unit of account

As in other international organisations, the question of which monetary unit to use arose for the Community budget.

([1])   For the definition of negative reserve, see Section 5 ('The principle of equilibrium').

The principle of adopting a unit of account distinct from the national currencies was established in the earliest days of the ECSC in Decision No 3/52 of 23 December 1952 and, in the case of the EEC and Euratom, by the Treaties themselves (Article 279 of the EC Treaty and Article 181 of the Euratom Treaty).

With the exceptions of 1958, 1959 and 1960, when preparations were being made for applying Article 279 of the EC Treaty and Article 181 of the Euratom Treaty and the EEC and Euratom budgets were drawn up in Belgian francs, the Community budget has always been expressed in units of account.

Finally, with economic and monetary union, the Community budget adopted the new single currency, the euro, as its unit of account on 1 January 1999, at the same time as the first Member States participating.

This principle is now enshrined in Article 16 of the Financial Regulation. Subject to two specific exceptions – in the case of imprest accounts or for the needs of administrative management of the Commission's External Service – the budget must be drawn up and implemented in euros and the accounts must be presented in euros.

7.2. From the dollar to the euro: successive units of account

1) 1951-58: the ECSC adopted the unit of account used by the European Payments Union, namely the US dollar.

2) 1958-60: The ECSC budget was expressed in a 'gold parity' unit of account which corresponded to a given weight of fine gold (0.88867088 grams) in accordance with the Bretton Woods Agreements.

3) 1961 onwards: Use of this 'gold parity' unit of account was extended to the EEC and Euratom. Following the crisis in the international monetary system in the early 1970s, all reference to gold was dropped, and so this unit of account was no longer of any use and the search started for a replacement.

4) 1977/78-80: A unit of account based on a 'basket' of different Community currencies was introduced; this was the European unit of account

(EUA) which, it was hoped, would be unaffected by external monetary fluctuations and therefore more stable.

5) 1981-98: The ecu was applied to the general budget; it was based on the same basket as the EUA but, unlike its predecessor, was subject to regular revision of the amounts.

6) 1999 onwards: The euro became the single currency of the new economic and monetary union and was applied to the EU's general budget.

7.3. Simplification brought about by use of the euro

The Community budget is now expressed in euros, which is a significant simplification. The euro is the only instrument used to express and settle the debts and claims of the Community, eliminating any exchange risks between the Community unit of account and national currencies, which still existed with the ecu. Exchange risks have been transferred from the EU to those Member States not participating in monetary union. Now the only exchange risks borne by the EU are in its relations with non-EU countries, where the corresponding debts or claims are expressed in a unit other than the euro.

The euro money market is the same as that of the participating Member States and is obviously much bigger than the ecu market, thus safeguarding its stability and the 'purchasing power' of the Community budget.

8. The principle of transparency and the Community budget

Articles 29 and 30 of the Financial Regulation enshrine the principle of transparency.

Under Article 29, the budget must be established and implemented and the accounts presented in compliance with the principle of transparency.

The budget, any amending budgets and the consolidated annual accounts must all be published in the Official Journal of the European Union.

Information on borrowing-and-lending operations contracted by the Communities for third parties must be given in an Annex to the budget and information on operations of the Guarantee Fund for external actions in the financial statement (Article 30(1) and (2) of the Financial Regulation).

The 2006 revision of the Financial Regulation added a new obligation relating to information on beneficiaries of funds from the EC budget. This obligation already existed for beneficiaries of funds managed by the institutions, either directly or indirectly (Articles 90 and 110 of the Financial Regulation). It has now been extended to all methods of managing the EC budget (Article 30(3) of the Financial Regulation).

9. The principle of sound financial management of the Community budget

The principle of sound financial management is based on Article 274 of the EC Treaty, which provides that 'the Commission shall implement the budget … on its own responsibility and within the limits of the appropriations, having regard to the principles of sound financial management'.

Article 27 of the Financial Regulation links this principle to the principles of economy, efficiency and effectiveness. The principle of economy requires that the resources used by the institution to engage in its activities be made available in due time, in appropriate quantity and quality and at the best price. The principle of efficiency is concerned with the best relationship between resources employed and results achieved. The principle of effectiveness is concerned with attaining the specific objectives set and achieving the intended results.

In practice, sound financial management is based on setting verifiable objectives which can be monitored by measurable indicators, in order to switch from means-based management to results-oriented management. Allocation of resources to activities (using activity-based budgeting or ABB) makes it possible to integrate the cost of the activities and their objectives.

Appropriate application of this principle requires that the planning, budgeting, management and reporting processes take place within a single common conceptual framework. Consequently, a common structure of activities and policy areas provides the framework for defining policy priorities, allocating and managing resources in line with those priorities and reporting the results achieved. In this context, activity-based budgeting is the budgetary component of a wider 'activity-based management' (ABM) approach. The main instruments of ABM are:

— the annual policy strategy (APS), the purpose of which is to set out the policy priorities and the overall resources required to meet them;

— the preliminary draft budget (PDB), which includes Activity Statements as the main instrument for justifying the appropriations proposed by the Commission in terms of objectives and indicators (see Chapter 11);

— the annual management plans (AMPs), which are prepared by all Commission departments and include specific objectives and performance indicators for all activities with the resources (financial and human), which are managed in line with predefined policy priorities; and

— the annual activity reports (AAR), with the declarations by Directors-General on the legality and regularity of operations and on achievement of the objectives.

10. Evaluation of Community action and sound financial management

The concept of evaluation is fully integrated throughout the programme cycle and is understood as a continuous process which must cover the entire duration of a measure: from the preparation stage in order to define the objectives and means, through allocation of resources in the budget to completion of the measure, when the results will be assessed and conclusions drawn on whether the measure should be renewed.

10.1. Legislative decisions

1) Ex ante *evaluation, an essential requirement for sound and efficient management of Community programmes*

Ex-ante evaluation is a process that supports preparation of proposals for new or renewed Community action. Its purpose is to gather information and carry out analyses which help to ensure the delivery of policy objectives, the cost-effectiveness of the instruments used and the possibility of reliable evaluation at a later stage.

An *ex ante* evaluation should be seen as an analytical process, which can stretch over a long period of time. Different steps can be followed separately. An *ex-ante* exercise is not necessarily a one-off project, which merely produces a report, but rather a process consisting of separate phases and different pieces of analysis.

Article 2 of the Financial Regulation of December 1977, as amended by Council Regulation (EC, Euratom, ECSC) No 2333/95 of September 1995, already stipulated that '… mobilisation of Community resources must be preceded by an evaluation to ensure that the resultant benefits are in proportion to the resources applied'.

This requirement was maintained in the Financial Regulation adopted in 2002 which states that *ex ante* and *ex post* evaluations 'shall be applied to all programmes and activities which entail significant spending and evaluation results disseminated to spending, legislative and budgetary authorities' (Article 27 of the Financial Regulation).

Ex ante evaluation must address:

— the need to be met in the short or long term;

— the added value of Community involvement;

— the objectives to be achieved;

— the policy options available, including the risks associated with them;

— the results and impact expected, in particular economic, social and environmental impact, and the indicators and evaluation arrangements needed to measure them;

— the most appropriate method of implementation for the preferred option(s);

— the internal coherence of the proposed programme or activity and its relations with other relevant instruments;

— the volume of appropriations, human resources and other administrative expenditure to be allocated with due regard for the cost-effectiveness principle;

— the lessons learned from similar experiences in the past.

In addition to this *ex ante* evaluation, each proposal for a programme or activities leading to budget expenditure must set out the monitoring, reporting and evaluation arrangements. These must take account of the responsibilities of each level of government that will be involved in implementing the proposed programme or activity. This will avoid any duplication of evaluations, in particular in case of shared management with Member States.

2) Legislative financial statement

At the Commission, proposals to be submitted to the legislative authority are assessed from both the financial and resources point of view by means of a financial statement, which is submitted to the budgetary authority with expenditure proposals. The same obligation is also imposed on Member States when they submit proposals in conformity with the relevant provisions of the EU Treaty and on any institution submitting an amendment to a proposal or initiative which may have appreciable implications for the budget, including changes in the number of posts (Article 28 of the Financial Regulation).

The financial statement is designed to provide information on both administrative and human resources and operational appropriations. A financial statement is referred to as 'budgetary' when it accompanies the preliminary draft budget and as 'legislative' when it accompanies legislative proposals with budgetary implications.

A legislative financial statement analyses the reasons for the appropriations requested in two different ways. Firstly, it demonstrates the need for the Community action envisaged by clarifying its general objective and value added. It also gives an overall description of the logic behind the proposal in order to give reasons for the particular action to be financed and demonstrate its cost-effectiveness in achieving the stated objectives. Secondly, the financial statement provides output and costing information by specifying the predicted nature and volume of output and establishing the unit cost. The purpose of this is to facilitate assessment of the proposed level of funding and of its impact on the expected results.

In addition to these explanations, the legislative financial statement will also provide information on the fraud prevention and protection measures in place or planned.

10.2. Budget decisions

In the Commission, the budgetary decision-making process starts with the annual policy strategy (APS) decision and ends with the preliminary draft budget (PDB). The role of evaluation is to support this process by providing fact-based evidence on the performance and progress of the Community programmes.

The findings of the individual evaluations provide relevant input for preparation of the annual policy strategy. In addition, the Commission decides annually on a limited number of strategic evaluations, designed specially to prepare its APS debate. These evaluations, which cut across a number of areas, are designed to supplement the results of the evaluations carried out by operational departments. They assess the impact of any policy that uses the resources of several departments.

10.3. Implementation of the budget

In order to provide relevant and timely information for subsequent decision-making, all programmes or activities, including pilot projects and preparatory action, mobilising resources exceeding EUR 5 million will be subject to an interim and/or *ex post* evaluation of the human and financial resources allocated and the results obtained (Article 27 of the Financial Regulation, as defined by the Implementing Rules).

In this context, mid-term and *ex post* evaluations need to be adapted both to decision-making needs and to the life-cycle and nature of each activity. However, as a general guideline, activities should be subject to an overall evaluation at least every six years. In the case of multiannual programmes or activities, at least one thorough evaluation during the life-cycle of the action is needed.

Mid-term evaluations carried out during implementation of a programme generally focus on the relevance of the objectives, the implementing arrangements and the initial results. Since new programmes are often prepared long before their predecessors are completed, mid-term evaluation is an important source of information for planning the next programme.

Ex post evaluation is typically carried out after the programme expires, focusing mainly on its impact and cost-effectiveness. Since it is not usually completed until after the following programme has started, its results can be used if any revisions or changes are made to the new programme during its life-cycle.

11. Internal control and sound financial management

The 2006 revision of the Financial Regulation added a new aspect to the principle of sound financial management.

Under Article 28a of the Financial Regulation, the budget must be implemented in compliance with effective and efficient internal control, which is defined as a process applicable at all levels of the management and designed to provide reasonable assurance of achieving the following objectives:

— effectiveness, efficiency and economy of operations;

— reliability of reporting;

— safeguarding of assets and information;

— prevention and detection of fraud and irregularities;

— adequate management of the risks related to the legality and regularity of the underlying transactions.

Chapter 11

The annual budgetary procedure

1. Preliminary remarks

1.1. The institutional and legal aspects of the budgetary procedure

The Treaty establishing the European Community (Article 272) defines the successive stages of the budgetary procedure. It establishes the powers of each of the two arms of the budgetary authority (European Parliament and Council) and the Commission in this procedure.

From a legal point of view, there are two key moments in the budgetary procedure: first, the adoption of the draft budget by the Council, which marks the formal opening of the procedure for the budgetary authority, and, second, the final adoption of the budget after Parliament's second reading, which closes the procedure.

Although the preliminary draft budget, produced by the Commission at the start of the budgetary procedure, does not have the legal status of a legislative proposal, it nonetheless reflects the Commission's power of initiative as regards the financial implications of Community policies.

1.2. The timetable for the budgetary procedure

Article 272 of the EC Treaty lays down a formal timetable for each stage of the procedure; this timetable is planned in such a way that the budget will normally be adopted by 1 January each year.

However, with the dual aim of ensuring that the draft budget can be examined properly and of making the best use of the time available to the budgetary authority, a degree of flexibility has since been built into the timetable; on the basis of a proposal made by the Commission on 19 March 1975, the budgetary authority agreed in 1976 to adjust the official timetable set by the Treaty.

The pragmatic timetable brings forward the official deadlines and provides for documents to be transmitted unofficially to each of the institutions concerned before the dates set in Article 272.

The letter of this article is still respected, but in practice the time given to the Council and Parliament during each stage of the budgetary procedure is appreciably longer.

This pragmatic timetable has been operating since the 1977 financial year.

1.3. The impact of the 1988 financial reform

The Interinstitutional Agreement (IIA) concluded in 1988 and renewed in 1993 brought about substantial changes to both the content and the implications of the budgetary procedure.

Apart from the fact that the annual debate on the budget must now be integrated into the financial framework defined([1]), new procedures for cooperation between the two arms of the budgetary authority have been introduced in the budgetary procedure to ensure greater consensus on its implementation.

Annex III to the 1999 Interinstitutional Agreement set out the arrangements for interinstitutional collaboration in the budgetary sector. These consist of four trialogue meetings and two conciliation meetings at the time of the two Council (Budgets) meetings which adopt the draft budget and subsequently give it a second reading. The trialogue meetings are attended by the Chairman of the European Parliament's Committee on Budgets, the President of the Council (Budgets) and the member of the Commission with responsibility for the budget. The conciliation meetings

---

([1])   See Part 2 'The characteristics of the present financial system'.

are attended by the members of the Council (Budgets) and a European Parliament delegation, with the Commission also taking part.

Annex II to the IIA of 17 May 2006 slightly adapted these provisions, making the trialogue prior to the first reading by the European Parliament optional and subject to need.

1.4. The impact of the Lisbon Treaty

The Lisbon Treaty includes changes to the annual budget timetable and procedure (see Section 4 of Chapter 7).

Under the new provisions, the draft budget will be prepared by the Commission and submitted to the Council. The current second reading procedure will be replaced by a conciliation procedure, similar to that used for legislative co-decision. The Council, followed by Parliament, will conduct a first reading, which will be followed by convening a conciliation committee. The budget will then be adopted on the basis of a joint text to be agreed by Parliament and the Council.

2. The stages in the budgetary procedure

2.1. Definition of the financial framework

1) Updating the financial framework ([1])

Under the Interinstitutional Agreement of 17 May 2006 (point 16), the Commission makes technical adjustments to the financial framework for the following year, in line with movements in GDP and prices. The results are communicated to the budgetary authority, usually towards the end of February. The technical adjustments are made on the basis of a fixed deflator of 2 % a year.

At the same time, the Commission submits its proposals to the budgetary authority for adjustment of the financial framework in the light of past implementation in accordance with point 18 of the Agreement. The

---

([1])   See Chapter 9.

budgetary authority must take decisions on these proposals before 1 May. In the absence of a decision, the existing financial framework, after technical adjustment, continues to apply.

The Interinstitutional Agreement (point 22) also provides that, as a rule, any proposal to revise the financial framework necessary to implement unforeseen measures must be presented and adopted before the start of the procedure for the year or the first of the years concerned. This provision is designed to ensure, as far as possible, that no procedure to revise the financial framework interferes with the annual budgetary procedure, with the risk of weakening the financial framework's function of setting a medium-term framework for spending.

2) Establishment of the maximum rate of increase for non-compulsory expenditure

In accordance with the EC Treaty (Article 272(9)), this rate is set by the Commission, after consulting the Economic Policy Committee, and communicated to the various institutions by 1 May. In practice, this also takes place towards the end of February.

The fourth and fifth subparagraphs of Article 272(9) of the EC Treaty allow the maximum rate of increase set by the Commission to be exceeded in two cases: (i) when the rate of increase for non-compulsory expenditure resulting from the draft budget established by the Council is over half the maximum rate, Parliament may further increase that expenditure up to a limit not exceeding half the maximum rate; (ii) when the Council, acting by a qualified majority, and the European Parliament, acting by a majority of its members and three-fifths of the votes cast, agree on a new rate.

2.2. Preparation of the preliminary draft budget by the Commission

1) The statements of estimates of the various institutions

As required by Article 272(2) of the EC Treaty, each institution draws up an estimate of its revenue and expenditure.

In practice, each institution has its own rules of procedure for examining and adopting its estimates; procedures are not, therefore, uniform. In the

Council, for instance, the estimates are adopted by a qualified majority, whereas a simple majority is sufficient in Parliament.

The Commission prepares its own statement of estimates and also receives those of the other institutions. In principle, the other institutions must send the Commission their statements of estimates before 1 July; in practice, however, under the pragmatic timetable, most institutions do this by 1 May.

The Commission consolidates all these estimates in a preliminary draft budget, which is the overall forecast of revenue and expenditure for the year ahead.

If it disagrees with any of the estimates submitted by the other institutions, it may attach a dissenting opinion and its own recommendations, in accordance with Article 272(2) of the Treaty.

However, this does not usually happen: the principle of institutional autonomy generally prevails. It would therefore be quite exceptional for the Commission to submit a duly substantiated dissenting opinion to the budgetary authority.

2) The internal Commission procedure for preparing the preliminary draft budget

The internal procedure for preparing the preliminary draft is organised by DG Budget, which gathers together the requests from the other directorates-general and departments, submits to the Commission problems which it was not possible to solve at a lower level and prepares the documents for compilation into the preliminary draft budget.

Stage 1: Annual policy strategy (APS)

The annual policy strategy is the Commission decision launching the yearly strategic planning and programming cycle. The objective is to set a limited number of policy priorities which will guide the work of the Commission throughout the year. Preparations begin in December of year 'n-2' with a policy debate by all the members of the Commission, of which the outcome is a limited number of policy priorities for the year in question. Commission departments then propose specific initiatives in relation to those priorities. The annual policy strategy decision, in February of year 'n-1', presents how the Commission proposes to act in relation to the priorities and what resources (human and financial) are necessary to ensure efficient delivery by policy area.

This decision guides the process for drawing up the preliminary draft budget and, at the same time, programming Commission activities for year n.

Stage 2: Submission of requests by Commission departments

In February, on the basis of the annual policy strategy decision, the Director-General for the Budget sends out a circular containing instructions for the spending departments and providing them with details of the overall economic and financial framework. This circular marks the start of the Commission's internal work on preparing the more detailed preliminary draft budget and specifies in particular:

— the information and documents to be presented for each activity or budget line to support the requests for appropriations. In this regard, it is important to underline the role of activity statements which, since the introduction of ABB, constitute the main supporting documents for the operational expenditure proposed by the Commission. Under Article 33(2)(d) of the Financial Regulation, the Commission must provide information on SMART [1] objectives measured by performance indicators to support the budget proposal. In addition, a cost-benefit approach should be applied to proposed changes in appropriations. Evaluation results should also underpin the Commission proposal. Activity statements are therefore at the very heart of ABM as they draw on all the instruments in the Commission's management cycle to demonstrate effective use of budgetary resources;

— the framework and parameters for drawing up the indicative financial programming for the medium term.

---

[1] Specific, measurable, achievable, relevant and timed.

By the end of February, the spending departments submit their quantified requests and all the information and grounds, in response to the budget circular.

Stage 3: Preparation of interdepartmental discussions

In March budget hearings are held between DG Budget and the spending departments. Given the constraints imposed by the financial framework and the annual policy strategy decision, the requests for appropriations are examined on the basis of the priority to be given to the various operations to be financed, the foreseeable trend in requirements (including payment appropriations and administrative resources) and the consistency, in terms of cost-effectiveness, between the resources considered necessary and the objectives pursued.

The medium-term indicative financial programmes also drawn up by departments allow the requests for appropriations to be put into perspective for the year in question and an assessment to be made of the compatibility of the envisaged trend in expenditure with the ceilings set by the financial framework.

Stage 4: Trialogue on the priorities for the budget

April: This stage was introduced by the Interinstitutional Agreement concluded in 1993 and renewed in 1999 and 2006. It is the first stage of the collaboration procedure set out in Annex II to the Agreement. This trialogue meeting between the representatives of Parliament, the Council and the Commission must take place after the technical adjustment of the financial framework and before the preliminary draft budget is established by the Commission, in order to discuss the possible priorities for the budget of the next financial year. It takes the form of an exchange of views on the main policies which may be adopted by each of the two arms of the budgetary authority at the next stage of the budgetary procedure, based on the economic and financial context already defined and the initial preparatory work started by the Commission departments.

Stage 5: Adoption and transmission of the preliminary draft budget

On the basis of the departmental hearings, DG Budget prepares a summary document and submits to the Commission its proposal for the preliminary draft budget (incorporating the other institutions' statements of estimates).

Early May: After making the technical adjustments to the financial framework (in February) and examining any decisions taken by the budgetary authority before 1 May concerning adjustment of the financial framework to reflect implementation, the Commission adopts the preliminary draft budget. Working versions of the documents adopted are then transmitted unofficially to the budgetary authority.

Mid-June: The preliminary draft budget is sent to the budgetary authority in all the Community languages.

Article 272(3) of the EC Treaty and Article 33(1) of the Financial Regulation provide that the Commission must send the preliminary draft budget to the Council by 1 September of year n-1; in practice (in the pragmatic timetable), the deadline is 15 June. The preliminary draft is also sent to Parliament for information.

In accordance with Article 33 of the Financial Regulation, the Commission prepares a general introduction to the preliminary draft budget, containing financial tables covering the entire budget, explanations and grounds for the requests for appropriations for the various policy areas and a detailed statement on borrowing and lending policy. It also produces various working documents: an analysis of financial management in the previous year and of commitments outstanding, an establishment plan of budgetary posts and staff, activity statements containing detailed information on the performance of the different activities, a summary of the schedule of payments due in future years, the statement of estimates of revenue and expenditure of subsidised agencies, etc. The revenue and expenditure account and financial balance sheet for the previous year are also available in early May.

Under the 2006 Interinstitutional Agreement, as regards compulsory expenditure, the Commission must identify in its preliminary draft budget:

— appropriations connected with new or planned legislation; and

— appropriations arising from the application of legislation existing when the previous budget was adopted.

All the documents making up the preliminary draft budget follow the approach of activity-based budgeting [1].

2.3. Adoption of the draft budget by the Council

1) Timetable

In practice, the procedure is conducted in accordance with the pragmatic timetable: after receiving the preliminary draft budget on 15 June, the Council adopts the draft by 31 July and sends it to Parliament in the first half of September (the official deadline set in Article 272(4) of the EC Treaty is 5 October).

2) Procedure

The Council decisions are prepared by the Budget Committee (made up of the financial attachés in the Permanent Representations), then by Coreper II (Permanent Representatives Committee – Deputy level).

Under Annex II to the 2006 Interinstitutional Agreement, the Council decision is preceded by ad hoc conciliation with Parliament. This conciliation forms the second stage of the institutional collaboration procedure introduced by the Agreement.

The conciliation is for compulsory expenditure, on the basis of the distinction made by the Commission in the preliminary draft budget, depending whether or not the appropriations are requested as a result of new or existing legislation. The 2006 IIA makes particular reference to this conciliation for expenditure relating to fisheries agreements (point 41) and financing of the common foreign and security policy (point 42). The purpose is to secure agreement on this subject between the two arms of the budgetary authority. The conciliation takes place in two stages.

Stage 1 consists of a trialogue meeting between the President of the Council (Budgets), the Chairman of Parliament's Committee on Budgets and the member of the Commission with responsibility for the budget.

---

[1]   See Chapter 11.

Formal conciliation between the Council and a Parliament delegation, with the Commission also taking part, takes place on the date set by the Council for establishing the draft budget. The institutions then ratify the results of the trialogue or take the opportunity to continue their efforts to reach agreement on the amount of compulsory expenditure. If no agreement is secured, the budgetary procedure continues, with each institution recovering its powers in full.

3) Voting rules

For adoption of the draft budget, a qualified majority (Article 205(2) of the EC Treaty) is required in the Council, 255 votes from a majority of the members, out of a total of 345 votes distributed in accordance with the weightings shown in Table 11.1.

TABLE 11.1

Qualified majority voting and country weights

Member State	Votes for each country	Total votes
DE, FR, IT, UK	29	116
ES, PL	27	54
RO	14	14
NL	13	13
BE, CZ, EL, HU, PT	12	60
BG, AT, SE	10	30
DK, IE, LT, SK, FI	7	35
EE, CY, LV, L, SL	4	20
MT	3	3
All Member States		345

These voting rules make it possible for 'blocking minorities' to be formed, when Member States with a combined total of 91 votes align.

If the Council fails to muster the majority necessary for adopting the draft budget by the official deadline of 5 October, Parliament and/or the

Commission may bring an action before the Court of Justice for failure to act (Article 232 of the EC Treaty).

Parliament made use of this possibility on 18 December 1987, followed five days later by the Commission, when the Council failed to adopt the draft 1988 budget on time; the Court ruled on 12 July 1988 that there was no need to give a judgment on the two actions, after the budget had been adopted on 18 May 1988.

2.4. Parliament's first reading of the budget (Article 272(4))

1) Timetable

The draft budget must be laid before Parliament not later than 5 October of the year preceding that in which it is to be implemented.

If Parliament gives its approval in the 45 days after the 5 October deadline (i.e. by 19 November), the budget stands as finally adopted.

If, within this time, Parliament has neither amended the draft budget nor proposed modifications to it, the budget is deemed to be finally adopted.

If Parliament adopts amendments or proposes modifications during these 45 days, the draft budget, together with the amendments or proposed modifications, is returned to the Council (Article 272(4)).

The EC Treaty thus sets a deadline of 19 November for sending the amendments and proposed modifications to the Council, but the unofficial time limit is around 25 October.

2) Procedure and voting rules

Parliament's internal procedure begins with its Secretary-General referring the draft budget to the Committee on Budgets.

The Committee on Budgets then consults the other parliamentary committees concerned and appoints two of its members as rapporteurs for the draft budget: one for the Commission section and one for the sections on the other institutions.

After studying all the material produced (opinions of the other committees and work of the rapporteurs), the Committee on Budgets proposes modifications of compulsory expenditure and amendments of non-compulsory expenditure. These are then laid before the plenary.

Parliament devotes a part-session at the end of October to this first reading and discusses the proposed modifications and amendments adopted by the Committee on Budgets. The draft amendments and proposed modifications rejected by the Committee on Budgets are put to a vote at the part-session only if another committee or at least 40 members so request.

The amendments to non-compulsory expenditure require an absolute majority of members (at least 393 votes in favour).

The proposed modifications to compulsory expenditure are approved by an absolute majority of votes cast.

One basic rule of this procedure should be noted: if, at any stage of the 'to-ing and fro-ing' between the Council and Parliament, the two arms of the budgetary authority reach agreement on the amounts (on the line and in reserve) and on the remarks on a budget line, no subsequent changes may be made (except by means of a letter of amendment). The matter is considered closed. In other words, if Parliament does not modify compulsory expenditure on its first reading, the Council cannot return to it on its second reading unless changes have been proposed in the ad hoc letter of amendment from the Commission. Similarly, if Parliament accepts an item of non-compulsory expenditure entered in the draft budget on its first reading, neither the Council nor Parliament may return to it on its second reading. Finally, if, on its second reading, the Council accepts an amendment which Parliament has made to non-compulsory expenditure on its first reading, Parliament cannot return to it on its second reading.

2.5. The Council's second reading of the budget (Article 272(5))

1) Procedure

The procedure for the Council's second reading is very similar to that for the first reading.

This second reading takes place at a Council meeting (Budgets) during the third week of November, after a conciliation meeting with a delegation from Parliament.

The draft budget is revised on the basis of the proposed modifications accepted by the Council.

If, within 15 days after the draft budget has been returned by Parliament, the Council has not changed any of the amendments to non-compulsory expenditure adopted by Parliament and if the proposed modifications to compulsory expenditure have been accepted, the budget is deemed to be finally adopted. The Council informs Parliament that it has not changed any of the amendments and that the proposed modifications have been accepted.

If, within the same 15-day time limit, the Council changes one or more of Parliament's amendments or if Parliament's proposed modifications are rejected or altered, the draft budget, as amended, is returned to Parliament. The Council informs Parliament of the results of its deliberations.

In principle, the Council unofficially informs Parliament of its decision around 22 November, even if it is not formally transmitted until 4 December.

2) Voting rules

The Council's decisions on second reading are taken as follows:

For amendments (non-compulsory expenditure), the Council may alter, by qualified majority, each of the amendments adopted by Parliament.

For proposed modifications (compulsory expenditure):

— if a modification proposed by Parliament does not have the effect of increasing the total amount of expenditure of an institution, notably where the increase in expenditure involved is expressly offset by one or more proposed modifications involving a corresponding reduction in expenditure, the Council may, acting by a qualified majority, reject the proposed modification. If no decision is taken to reject it, the proposed modification stands as accepted;

— if a modification proposed by Parliament has the effect of increasing the total amount of expenditure of an institution, the Council may, acting by a qualified majority, accept this proposed modification. If no decision is taken to accept it, the proposed modification stands as rejected;

— if, as provided for in the two preceding subparagraphs, the Council has rejected a proposed modification, it may, acting by a qualified majority, either retain the amount shown in the draft budget or set another amount.

These qualified majority voting rules have given rise to the appearance of 'overthrown majorities' or 'minorities for acceptance', when the Council considers proposals for modifications of compulsory expenditure (not involving an increase in the total amount of expenditure) and amendments to non-compulsory expenditure. In these cases 26 votes are sufficient (the other countries cannot then muster the number of votes required to reject the proposal).

The results of the Council's second reading on compulsory expenditure produce what are, as a rule, the final amounts, since the Council has the last say on this category of expenditure, unless Parliament subsequently rejects the entire draft budget.

2.6. Parliament's second reading and adoption of the budget

1) Procedure, timetable and voting rules (Article 272(6) of the EC Treaty)

The internal procedure is practically the same as for the first reading.

However, as the Council has already had the last say on compulsory expenditure on its second reading, Parliament is mainly concerned with non-compulsory expenditure, where it can either accept or refuse the Council's proposals.

Within 15 days after the draft budget has been placed before it, Parliament, acting by a majority of its members and three fifths of the votes cast, may therefore amend or reject the changes made by the Council to its amendments and adopt the budget accordingly.

If Parliament does not act within these 15 days, the budget is deemed to be finally adopted in the form of the draft produced by the Council on second reading.

The timetable is such that Parliament generally gives the budget its second reading in the second week of December.

2) Parliament's second reading of the budget and establishment of the rate of increase for non-compulsory expenditure (Article 272(9) of the EC Treaty)

Section 2.1, point 2 of this chapter ('Establishment of the maximum rate of increase for non-compulsory expenditure') sets out the conditions under which the Commission sets the maximum rate of increase and under which the budgetary authority may exceed this level.

Until 1987, Parliament's second reading of the budget produced serious clashes between the two arms of the budgetary authority on the rate of increase for non-compulsory expenditure [1]. Parliament's endeavours to extend its budgetary powers (and, thus, to promote or influence certain Community policies) were directed in particular at the possibility of raising the rate of increase above the statistical maximum rate referred to in Article 272(9) of the Treaty.

The new budgetary rationale stemming from the Interinstitutional Agreements of 1988, 1993, 1999 and 2006 has contributed to 'neutralising' the maximum rate of increase.

3) Final adoption of the budget

Article 272(7) provides that, when the budgetary procedure has been completed, the President of Parliament declares the budget finally adopted.

After the final adoption of the budget, each Member State is bound to pay over to the Commission the sums due so that it can implement the budget (Article 17 of the Financial Regulation). This allows commitment of the appropriations entered in the budget with effect from 1 January (Article 8).

---

[1] See Part 1 'The development of the Community's financial system'.

The declaration of final adoption confirms the status of the budget as authentic.

In this connection, the Court of Justice stated in its judgment of 3 July 1986 in Case 34/86 that the President of Parliament was not an independent budgetary authority but simply an organ of one of the two arms of the budgetary authority. In the event of disagreement between the Council and Parliament, the President of Parliament should therefore refrain from declaring the budget finally adopted.

In practice, if there is no adverse reaction from the Council or its representatives during the vote in plenary, Parliament's President notes the Council's tacit agreement to the rate of increase for non-compulsory expenditure resulting from Parliament's second reading and accordingly adopts the budget.

3. Amending budgets

3.1. Definition and procedure

'If there are unavoidable, exceptional or unforeseen circumstances, the Commission may present preliminary draft amending budgets' (Article 37(1) of the Financial Regulation).

The purpose of amending budgets is to provide a suitable means of adjusting budget forecasts to real requirements during the year.

There are also amending budgets relating solely to revenue, which adjust the forecasts made in the initial budget either upwards or downwards in line with the actual own resources collected during the year.

Amending budgets are subject to the same rules of procedure as the general budget. As regards the date for presentation, Article 37(2) of the Financial Regulation states: 'The Commission shall, save in exceptional circumstances, submit any preliminary draft amending budget to the Council by 1 September each year at the latest'.

3.2. 'Balance' amending budget

Closure of the previous year's accounts on 1 May each year allows calculation of the positive or negative balance resulting from the differences between the receipts forecast in the budget and those which actually materialise, and from underspending of the payment appropriations provided for in the budget.

Article 15 of the Financial Regulation states that 'the balance from each financial year shall be entered in the budget for the following financial year as revenue in the case of a surplus or as a payment appropriation in the case of a deficit'.

Entry of the balance for year n in the budget is proposed in a preliminary draft supplementary and/or amending budget presented in late April or early May of year n+1 once the final balance is known. Part of this balance may be entered in advance in year n by means of a letter of amendment.

4. Letters of amendment

4.1. Definition and procedure

The Commission may, on its own initiative or at the request of the other institutions with their own budget section, present a letter of amendment to the preliminary draft budget in the light of information which was not available when the preliminary draft was established. Irrespective of the stage reached in the procedure, the letter of amendment always relates to the preliminary draft budget and is incorporated into the current budgetary procedure after two readings in both Parliament and the Council.

The object of letters of amendment is to adjust forecasts to any significant changes occurring between establishment of the preliminary draft and Parliament's first reading.

However, save in very exceptional circumstances, the Commission must put any such letter of amendment to the Council at least 30 days before Parliament's first reading of the draft budget, and the Council must put the letter of amendment to Parliament at least 15 days before the first reading (Article 34 of the Financial Regulation).

4.2. Ad hoc letters of amendment

Annex II to the Interinstitutional Agreement states that 'if it considers it necessary, the Commission may present to the budgetary authority an ad hoc letter of amendment to update the figures underlying the estimate of agricultural expenditure in the preliminary draft budget and/or to correct, on the basis of the most recent information available concerning fisheries agreements in force on 1 January of the financial year concerned, the breakdown between the appropriations entered in the operational items for international fisheries agreements and those entered in reserve. That letter of amendment must be sent to the budgetary authority before the end of October'. Given the pressure of time, it must usually be adopted after one reading and, as compulsory expenditure, is incorporated in the draft budget during the Council's second reading in November.

In view of the volume of agricultural expenditure in the budget, the ad hoc letter of amendment often has a considerable impact on the increase in payment appropriations. For this reason, the Council insists that the Commission includes an estimate of the balance in this letter of amendment; any surplus reduces the total payment appropriations.

Each year there are usually between one and three letters of amendment during the budgetary procedure, including the ad hoc letter of amendment.

5. Rejection of the budget and the consequences

Parliament, as one arm of the budgetary authority, has the power to reject the budget: this is one of its most important prerogatives.

It made use of this power in December 1979 for the 1980 budget and in December 1984 for the 1985 budget[1].

5.1. Conditions required to reject the budget

Article 272(8) of the EC Treaty states that Parliament, acting by a majority of its members and two thirds of the votes cast, may, if there are

---

[1]   See Part 1 'The development of the Community's financial system'.

important reasons, reject the draft budget and ask for a new draft to be submitted to it.

The expression 'if there are important reasons' has no real legal significance; rejection of the budget is a political act.

5.2. The consequences of rejection

1) The 'third reading' of the budget

In order to maintain continuity in the public service, it is necessary to extend the procedure until the budget is finally adopted. To this end, Article 272(8) of the Treaty provides that Parliament, when rejecting the budget, will ask for a new draft to be submitted to it.

There then arises a problem of interpretation as regards the stage of the budgetary procedure at which the deliberations of the budgetary authority should resume: should the Commission produce a new preliminary draft or is it sufficient for the Council and Parliament to return to the stage reached in the budgetary procedure just before the budget was rejected?

As the objective is to complete the procedure as soon as possible, the first solution has never prevailed (except in the very special case of rejection of supplementary and amending budget No 1/1982, when the Commission restarted the procedure by presenting supplementary and amending budget No 1/1983).

Generally speaking, after a budget has been rejected, the Commission presents 'new budget proposals' to amend the draft budget produced by the Council on its second reading.

These new proposals are put to the Council and Parliament so that they can come to an agreement as soon as possible during a 'third reading' for which the Treaties make neither provision nor formal arrangements. In practice, a pragmatic approach is adopted, the two arms of the budgetary authority having eventually to come to an agreement so that the Community can have a budget.

2) The provisional-twelfths arrangements

(a) The provisions of the Treaty

To ensure continuity of the public service, Article 273 of the EC Treaty established the provisional-twelfths arrangement.

If, at the beginning of a financial year, the budget has not yet been voted, a sum equivalent to not more than one-twelfth of the budget appropriations for the preceding financial year may be spent each month in respect of any chapter or other subdivision of the budget; this arrangement must not, however, have the effect of placing at the disposal of the Commission appropriations in excess of one-twelfth of those provided for in the draft budget being prepared.

The Council may, acting by a qualified majority, authorise expenditure in excess of one-twelfth.

If the decision relates to non-compulsory expenditure, the Council transmits it immediately to Parliament; within 30 days Parliament, acting by a majority of its members and three fifths of the votes cast, may adopt a different decision on the expenditure in excess of the one-twelfth referred to above. This part of the Council's decision is then suspended until Parliament has taken its decision.

If, at the end of the 30 days, Parliament has not taken a decision which differs from the Council's decision, the latter is deemed to be finally adopted.

(b) Article 13 of the Financial Regulation

Article 13 of the Financial Regulation also states that commitments may be made per chapter, up to a maximum of one-quarter of the total allotted appropriations in the chapter in question of the previous financial year plus one-twelfth for each month which has elapsed.

Payments may be made monthly per chapter, up to a maximum of one-twelfth of the allotted appropriations in the chapter in question of the preceding financial year.

The limit of the appropriations provided for in the draft budget in preparation may not be exceeded.

At the request of the Commission, and without prejudice to the above rules, to satisfy management requirements the Council, acting by a qualified majority, may, after consulting Parliament, authorise the simultaneous expenditure of two or more provisional twelfths.

(c) Problems with operating the provisional-twelfths arrangements

The different cases of application: the provisional-twelfths arrangements apply not only in the extreme case of rejection of the budget but also when the Council fails to adopt a draft budget on time (as was the case for 1988) and when the President of Parliament has not declared the budget finally adopted (as was the case for 1987).

Utilisation of appropriations by chapter: Article 273 of the Treaty provides for appropriations to be used by chapter under the provisional-twelfths arrangements. However, the Financial Regulation provides that the Council may, exceptionally, authorise the total for a specific chapter to be exceeded, provided it is offset against another chapter. In practice, this provision is equivalent to a transfer mechanism under the provisional-twelfths arrangements.

The dual limit rule determines the amounts available under the twelfths arrangements for any given budget chapter. The amount available must always be the lowest possible; as a rule, a level of one-twelfth of the appropriations provided in the budget for the preceding year must never be exceeded. However, if the appropriations entered in the draft budget are lower, then under the dual limit rule only one-twelfth of this lower amount is available to the Commission.

The object of the dual limit rule is to ensure continuity in the European public service, but without making available to the Commission more appropriations than are planned for the budget being prepared, which, in principle, reflect the Community's actual needs.

This rule poses a problem of interpretation when a budget is rejected: the Commission argues that once the budgetary procedure has started, account must be taken of the stages reached up to the point of rejection of the budget and that the limit should therefore be the amount proposed in the draft budget rejected or in the draft at the last stage of examination. The Council and Parliament, on the other hand, maintain that the entire budgetary procedure must begin again from the start and that there is therefore no real dual limit until the Commission has presented new budget proposals.

Making revenue available: on the revenue side of the budget, when the provisional-twelfths arrangements are in operation, there is no problem with making available traditional own resources (which are collected on behalf of the Community and made available automatically).

As regards VAT and GNI-based own resources, the own resources decision states that if, at the beginning of the financial year, the budget has not been adopted, the existing VAT and GNI rates of call shall remain applicable until the new rates enter into force.

Moreover, the twelfth subparagraph of Article 10(3) of Regulation (EC, Euratom) No 1150/2000 of 22 May 2000 implementing the system of the Communities' own resources provides for calculation of twelfths on the basis of the amount entered in the last budget finally adopted. The adjustment must be made on the first due date following final adoption of the budget if it is adopted before the 16th of the month. Otherwise, the adjustment must be made on the second due date following final adoption of the budget.

This arrangement provides the Community with sufficient resources to meet its day-to-day requirements.

6. Provisions of the Interinstitutional Agreement on improvement of the budgetary procedure

The Interinstitutional Agreements of 1988, 1993, 1999 and 2006 considerably improved the course of the budgetary procedure by establishing a formal procedure for interinstitutional collaboration, which provides a framework for discussing and resolving disputes between the two arms of the budgetary authority (see point 1.3 of this chapter: 'The impact of the 1988 financial reform' and Section 2 'The stages in the budgetary procedure'), and by setting out specific provisions in certain areas of dispute, such as the classification of expenditure, the maximum rate of increase for non-compulsory expenditure in the absence of a financial framework, the entry of financial provisions in legislative instruments, legal bases, expenditure relating to fisheries agreements and the financing of the common foreign and security policy (CFSP).

One of the fields for which the 2006 Interinstitutional Agreement does not include specific provisions is the 'third pillar' of the Maastricht and Amsterdam Treaties relating to cooperation in the fields of justice and home affairs, for which the expenditure may or may not be incorporated in the general budget [1].

6.1. Classification of expenditure

Point 35 of the 2006 Interinstitutional Agreement (IIA) states that 'the preliminary draft budget is to contain a proposal for the classification of each new budget item and of each item with an amended legal base'.

If they do not accept the classification proposed by the Commission in the preliminary draft budget, Parliament and the Council will examine the classification of the budget item concerned on the basis of Annex III, which forms an integral part of the IIA, and agreement will be sought during the interinstitutional conciliation procedure provided for in Annex II.

Annex III to the IIA (see Annex) therefore becomes the reference for classification of budget items, avoiding some of the difficulties with interpreting the definition of compulsory expenditure in the Treaty.

6.2. Maximum rate of increase for non-compulsory expenditure in the absence of a financial framework

In the absence of a financial framework, the provisions in Article 272(9) of the EC Treaty on the maximum rate of increase apply. The IIA makes the following arrangements for applying these provisions.

— Parliament's margin for manoeuvre, set by these provisions at half the maximum rate, applies as from the draft budget established by the Council on first reading. The maximum rate of increase must be respected in the annual budget, including any amending budgets.

---

[1] See Chapter 10 on the principle of unity and Chapter 13, Section 3.

— If so required, agreement on a new rate, higher than the maximum rate of increase, for commitment and/or payment appropriations for non-compulsory expenditure can be secured by means of the conciliation procedure.

6.3. Incorporation of financial provisions in legislative acts

Legislative instruments concerning multiannual programmes adopted under the co-decision procedure contain a provision laying down the financial allocation for the programme for its entire duration. That amount will be the prime reference figure during the annual budgetary procedure. The budgetary authority undertakes not to depart from this amount except in duly justified circumstances.

On the other hand, legislative instruments concerning multiannual programmes not subject to the co-decision procedure do not have to contain an 'amount deemed necessary'. If a financial reference is nevertheless included by the Council, it must be made clear that it is illustrative, and the relevant provision of the Interinstitutional Agreement must be cited (point 38).

These provisions reaffirm the role of the financial statement provided for in the Financial Regulation.

It reflects, in financial terms, the objectives of the programme and includes a schedule covering its entire duration.

It will be revised, where necessary, and forwarded to the budgetary authority when the preliminary draft budget is presented and after the budget is adopted.

6.4. Legal bases

Implementation of appropriations entered in the budget requires prior adoption of a basic act (an act of secondary legislation which provides a legal basis for the Community action – whether a regulation, directive or decision).

However, the following may be implemented, within certain limits, without a basic act:

— appropriations for pilot schemes of an experimental nature designed to test the feasibility of an action and its usefulness. The relevant commitment appropriations may be entered in the budget for not more than two successive financial years and may not exceed EUR 40 million a year for all the pilot projects;

— appropriations for preparatory action in the field of application of the EC Treaty and the Euratom Treaty and of Title VI of the Treaty on European Union, designed to prepare proposals with a view to the adoption of future action (subject to a limit of three financial years and EUR 50 million per financial year for the total amount of the new budget lines concerned, and a further limit of EUR 100 million for the total amount of appropriations actually committed);

— appropriations for preparatory measures in the field of Title V of the Treaty on European Union (concerning common foreign and security policy – CFSP). These measures must be limited to a short period of time and designed to establish the conditions for European Union action in fulfilment of the objectives of the CFSP and for the adoption of the necessary legal instruments;

— appropriations for one-off actions, or even actions for an indefinite duration, carried out by the Commission by virtue of tasks resulting from its prerogatives at institutional level pursuant to the EC Treaty and the Euratom Treaty other than its right of legislative initiative and under specific powers directly conferred on it by those Treaties;

— appropriations for the operation of each institution under its administrative autonomy.

The first two exceptions listed above – pilot projects and preparatory action – introduce an element of flexibility at both institutional and legislative levels: Parliament often initiates these activities, although not exclusively, thus breaching the Commission's monopoly of initiative within the strict limits provided for in the Interinstitutional Agreement. It should also be noted that the budgetary decision relating to these activities precedes and gives rise to the legislative decision, reversing the usual order.

The pilot projects and preparatory action must not relate to activities which are already covered by legal bases in force as this would introduce some redundancy and impair the budgetary decisions relating to the legal bases concerned. It is also routine to allow a pilot project to become preparatory action when there are plans to draw up a legal base. Finally, preparatory action cannot be adopted for three consecutive years unless a legal base for it has already been proposed, in which case the preparatory action would maintain continuity pending introduction of the legal base.

6.5. Expenditure relating to fisheries agreements and the financing of the common foreign and security policy (CFSP)

Amounts relating to the fisheries agreements in force on 1 January of the year in question will be entered on the appropriate budget line.

Amounts relating to agreements which are to come into force after that date are entered in the reserve.

The budgetary authority reaches agreement on these amounts within the conciliation procedure. If the amounts prove insufficient, a preliminary consultation takes place, based on information and, possibly, proposals presented by the Commission on what measures should be taken.

There is still some uncertainty about the classification of the reserve for fisheries agreements: while fisheries agreements which have already been concluded are classified in the Interinstitutional Agreement as compulsory expenditure, the appropriations placed in reserve for agreements which have not yet been concluded are placed in a reserve chapter which is usually considered to fall under non-compulsory expenditure. The appropriations in the reserve for fisheries agreements are therefore considered as compulsory expenditure by the Council and as non-compulsory expenditure by Parliament.

For the financing of the CFSP, the institutions must come to an agreement in the interinstitutional conciliation procedure on the amount of operational expenditure to be entered in the budget. In the absence of an agreement, the amount contained in the previous budget or the amount proposed in the preliminary draft budget is entered, whichever is the lower. Based on foreseeable needs and allowing a reasonable safety margin, these appropriations are entered on the budget lines specifically provided for the purpose and may not be placed in reserve.

Should the allocations prove insufficient in the course of the financial year, the two arms of the budgetary authority must seek a solution as a matter of urgency, on a proposal from the Commission.

Part 4

STRUCTURE OF THE COMMUNITY BUDGET

Chapter 12

Revenue

1. General overview

The revenue of the general budget of the European Union can be divided into two main categories: own resources and other revenue. This is laid down in Article 269 of the Treaty establishing the European Union, which states that: 'Without prejudice to other revenue, the budget shall be financed wholly from own resources'.

The main bulk of budgetary expenditure is financed by the system of own resources, as introduced in 1970 by Council Decision 70/243/ECSC, EEC, Euratom of 21 April 1970 (ORD 1970). Other revenue represents only a very minor part of total financing [1].

There are now three main categories of own resources: traditional own resources, the VAT-based resource and the GNI-based resource. These are supplemented by various correction mechanisms.

Revenue from traditional own resources is not sufficient to cover EU budget expenditure. On average, the share of traditional own resources (net 75 %, i.e. after deduction of 25 % retained as collection costs) in total own resources reached around 15 % over 2000-06.

---

[1] On average, other revenue amounted to around 3 % of total revenue over 2000-06 (excluding the surpluses carried over from the previous year, which themselves are mainly a consequence of the difference between the outturn of own resources payments and of expenditure in the preceding year). For detailed historical data on revenue, see the annexes of the 'EU Budget Financial Report', as available on: http://ec.europa.eu/ budget/publications/fin_reports_en.htm.

This is why ORD 1970 established a second own resource, based on value added tax (VAT), to finance the Community budget. Revenue from this resource, which accrued as of 1979, gradually became the main source of financing, but turned out also to be insufficient to cover Community expenditure in the mid-1980s. Thus Council Decision 88/376/EEC, Euratom of 24 June 1988 (ORD 1989) introduced a new resource based on Member States' wealth (ESA 79 GNP, later replaced in 2002 by ESA 95 GNI).

The GNI-based resource (the 'residual' resource) is determined so that total revenue balances total expenditure. The GNI-based resource has gradually become the most important source of financing of the EU budget, representing on average 60 % of total own resources payments over 2000-06.

The different own resources are explained in more detail in Section 2 and other revenue in Section 3 of this chapter. Finally, the sequential use of the different sources of revenue to finance budgeted expenditure is explained in Section 4. Figures and tables presenting the system of own resources can be found on the European Commission Internet site([1]).

2. Own resources

2.1. Traditional own resources

Traditional own resources (comprising customs duties, agricultural duties, and sugar and isoglucose levies) were introduced in 1970 and are levied on economic operators and collected by Members States on behalf of the EU. Member States retain 25 % of the amounts collected, to cover collection costs.

Revenue deriving from traditional own resources are: 'levies, premiums, additional or compensatory amounts, additional amounts or factors, Common Customs Tariff duties and other duties established or to be established by the institutions of the Communities in respect of trade with non-member countries ... as well as contributions and other duties provided for within the framework of the common organisation of the markets in sugar' (Article 2(1)(a) of Council Decision 2007/436/EC, Euratom of 7 June 2007 (ORD 2007)). Following the implementation

---

([1])   http://ec.europa.eu/budget/documents/annual_budgets_reports_accounts_en.htm.

into EU law of the Uruguay round agreements on multilateral trade, there will no longer be any material difference between agricultural duties and customs duties. Therefore this distinction will be removed when the ORD 2007 enters into force.

Assigning customs duties to the financing of common expenditure is the logical consequence of the free movement of goods within the EU.

Since 2001 Member States have retained, as collection costs, 25 % of the established amounts of traditional own resources. Before 2001, 10 % was retained, but this percentage was increased to 25 % by Council Decision 2000/597/EC, Euratom of 29 September 2000 (ORD 2000).

2.2. The VAT-based own resource

1) Definition

VAT-based payments derive from the application of a call rate to Member States' VAT bases set according to harmonised rules (see below).

However, VAT bases are capped at 50 % of GNI. This percentage was initially 55 % from 1988 to 1994, but was then gradually reduced to 50 % of GNP as of 1999 under Council Decision 94/728/EC, Euratom of 31 October 1994 (ORD 1994).

The capping of the VAT base reflects the intention to remedy the regressive aspects of the VAT-based resource, which is seen as penalising the less wealthy Member States.

2) Calculation of the base

The harmonised VAT base is calculated by the relevant Member State using what is known as the 'revenue method'. It consists of dividing the total annual net VAT revenue collected by the Member State in question by the weighted average rate of VAT, i.e. an estimate of the average rate applicable to the various categories of taxable goods and services, to obtain the intermediate VAT base. The intermediate base is subsequently adjusted with negative or positive compensations in order to obtain a harmonised VAT base pursuant to the Sixth Council Directive 77/388/EEC of 17 May 1977 and subsequent amendments.

3) The call rate of the VAT-based resource

ORD 2007 fixed the VAT call rate at 0.3 % (with, over the period 2007-13 only, a reduced rate of 0.225 % for Austria, 0.15 % for Germany and 0.10 % for the Netherlands and Sweden).

However, under ORD 2000, the actual VAT call rate (the 'uniform' rate) corresponded to the difference between the 'maximum' call rate and what is known as the 'frozen' rate (conditional upon the size of the UK correction, see hereafter).

The 'maximum' call rate, initially set at 1 % over the period 1974-79, was later increased to 1.4 % by ORD 1985 and then gradually reduced by ORD 1994 (by 0.08 % per year to 1.32 % in 1995, 1.24 % in 1996, 1.16 % in 1997, 1.08 % in 1998 and 1.0 % in 1999 and onwards). ORD 2000 further reduced the 'maximum' call rate to 0.75 % in 2002 and 2003 and, from 2004 onwards, to 0.50 %.

The 'frozen' rate is a relic from the pre-1988 period, when it was needed to ensure that no Member State would contribute more than the maximum rate of call for the VAT-based resource, including its contribution to the financing of the UK correction (which was added to Member States' VAT-based payments). The 'frozen rate' corresponds to the ratio between the amount of the UK correction ([1]) and the sum of the capped VAT bases of all the Member States, taking into account the fact that the United Kingdom is excluded from the financing of its correction and that the share of Austria, Germany, the Netherlands and Sweden in the financing of the correction is reduced by three-quarters. The 'frozen rate' is deducted from the maximum rate of call. The result gives the actual rate of call Member States have to pay (the 'uniform' rate).

ORD 2007 provided for significant improvements in transparency and simplicity, as compared to the very complex 'frozen' rate system, by fixing the VAT call rate at 0.30 % (with, for the period 2007-13 only, a reduced call rate of 0.225 % for Austria, 0.15 % for Germany and 0.10 % for the Netherlands and Sweden).

([1])   The UK correction in question is the one for the preceding year; see hereafter.

2.3. The GNI-based resource

1) Definition

Since 1988, GNP/GNI-based payments also constitute own resources. These payments result from the application of a call rate – set so that total revenue balances total expenditure – to Member States' GNP/GNI bases.

Since 1988, this resource has been the cornerstone of the own resources system for financing the EU budget, notably for the following reasons:

— The GNI-based resource is a 'residual' resource, providing the revenue required to cover expenditure in excess of the amount yielded by traditional own resources and VAT-based payments in any particular year. By implication, the GNI-based resource ensures that the EU budget is always balanced *ex ante*.

— The GNI-based resource guarantees stability in budget revenues in the medium term, within the overall ceiling for the total amount of own resources that may be assigned to the EU budget (1.24 % of EU GNI). ORD 1988 initially created this ceiling, fixed it at 1.15 % of GNP in 1988 and raised it to 1.20 % in 1992, a level which was further raised by ORD 1994 from 1.21 % in 1995 to 1.27 % in 1999, later recalculated as 1.24 % of GNI in 2001 – see COM(2001) 801 final of 28 December 2001.

— The GNI-based resource contributes to improving the equity of gross contributions across the Member States by making contributions more proportional to each Member State's ability to pay. The Berlin European Council of 24 and 25 March 1999, and resulting ORD 2000, took a step further in this direction by establishing the GNI-based resource as the dominant resource, thus improving the fairness of the EU budget financing system.

2) The call rate of the GNI-based resource

The GNI call rate is determined by the additional revenue needed to finance the budgeted expenditure not covered by the other resources (VAT-based payments, traditional own resources and other revenue). As in the case of VAT, a call rate is applied to the GNI of each of the Member States.

In addition, over the period 2007-13 only, ORD 2007 introduced a reduction in annual GNI-based payments for the Netherlands and Sweden corresponding to 'lump sums' of respectively EUR 605 million and EUR 150 million (in constant 2004 prices). These 'lump sums' are financed by all Member States, including the Netherlands, Sweden and the United Kingdom, since these lump sums are granted after calculation of the UK correction and therefore have no impact on the calculation of the UK correction.

2.4 The UK correction

The budgetary imbalance correction mechanism in favour of the United Kingdom (UK correction) was introduced by the European Council in Fontainebleau in June 1984 and the resulting ORD 1985. The purpose of the mechanism was to reduce the UK budgetary imbalance through a reduction in its payments to the Community. The imbalance was initially calculated as the difference between the UK share in total EU (uncapped) VAT-bases and the UK share in total EU expenditure allocated to Member States, this difference being then multiplied by total EU expenditure allocated to Member States. The UK contribution was subsequently reduced by 66 % of the budgetary imbalance thus calculated.

The mechanism was subsequently modified by ORD 1988 to neutralise the introduction of the GNP/GNI-based resource and the capping of the VAT-based resource. The idea behind this so-called 'UK advantage' is to neutralise for the UK all changes to own resources decisions since 1985, resulting in a global UK contribution to the Community budget as if the financing system created by the Fontainebleau European Council were still in force. ORD 1994 essentially confirmed the previous arrangements. ORD 2000 established new rules for the UK correction financing (further reducing the contribution of Germany, from two-thirds as was the case from 1985 to 2001, to one-quarter as of 2002, and extending this later reduction to the Netherlands, Austria and Sweden) and provided that certain windfall gains, resulting from changes extraneous to the UK correction mechanism but potentially benefiting the United Kingdom, should be neutralised (notably windfall gains related to the increase, from 10 % to 25 % as of 2001, in the share of traditional own resources retained as collection costs and windfall gains related to pre-accession expenditure in countries which joined the EU after 30 April 2004). ORD 2007 suppresses these later windfall gains from 2014 onwards and progressively introduces a new enlargement-related deduction from 2009 onwards.

1) Calculation of the amount of the correction

The initial steps, pursuant to ORD 1985, consist of:

(i) calculating the difference, in the preceding financial year, between:

— the UK share of total EU (uncapped) VAT bases, and

— the UK share of total EU expenditure allocated to Member States;

(ii) multiplying the difference thus obtained by total EU expenditure allocated to Member States;

(iii) multiplying the result under (ii) by 0.66.

The result obtained under (iii) is called the 'original amount' of the UK correction.

Additional steps were later introduced, by subtracting the following elements:

(iv) since 1988, from the result under (iii): the effect of the introduction, under ORD 1988, of the capping on VAT bases and of the GNP/GNI-based resource, namely the difference between:

— what the UK payments would have been in the absence of the GNP/ GNI resource and of the capping of VAT bases, and

— and the actual UK GNP/GNI- and VAT-based payments.

The difference referred to in step (iv) is called the 'UK advantage', since it corresponds to the (usually positive) effect for the UK following the reforms introduced by ORD 1988. By deducting this difference from the original amount of the UK correction, this effect is neutralised. The resulting amount is called the 'core UK correction'.

(v) since 2001, from the result under (iii): the effect of the increase, from 10 to 25 %, in the share of traditional own resources (TOR) retained by Member States as collection costs. This effect, referred to as 'TOR windfall gains' is the result of the multiplication between:

— 20 % of TOR collected, the percentage of 20 % being the ratio of the additional share of TOR (15 %) retained as collections costs divided by net TOR collected (75 %), and

— the difference between the UK share in total TOR collected and the UK share in EU (uncapped) VAT bases.

Introduced under ORD 2000, the increase in the share of TOR retained by Member States as collection costs implies a shortfall in EU revenue that is made up through additional GNI-based payments. Since Member States' share of EU GNI is different from their share of traditional own resources, this affects the level of their overall contribution. According to a logic similar to that of the 'UK advantage', the effect on the overall UK contribution is being neutralised by deducting the above difference from the 'core UK correction'.

(vi) over the period 2004-13, from total allocated expenditure, see (i) and (ii) above: the amount of EU pre-accession expenditure to each country which joined the EU after 30 April 2004, in the last year before its accession. These amounts are carried forward to subsequent years and adjusted annually by applying the EU GDP deflator.

From 2014 onwards, ORD 2007 removes the above deduction (vi) introduced under ORD 2000 and introduces, from 2009 onwards, a new enlargement-related deduction, see (vii) below.

Total allocated expenditure used for the calculation of the UK correction excludes expenditure in non-member countries (notably pre-accession expenditure in applicant countries) but includes, upon enlargement, EU expenditure allocated to new Member States. Accession of a new Member State therefore decreases the UK share in total allocated expenditure and increases total allocated expenditure, both leading to an increase in the UK correction. The above deduction from total allocated expenditure ensures that expenditure which is unabated before enlargement remains unabated after enlargement.

(vii) since 2009, from total allocated expenditure, see (i) and (ii) above: EU expenditure allocated to each Member State which joined the EU after 30 April 2004 except for agricultural expenditure[1]. Only 20 % of this expenditure will be deducted in 2009, 70 % in 2010 and 100 % onwards.

---

[1] This includes the share of rural development expenditure (EADRF) deemed to originate from the EAGGF Guarantee Section. The part originating from the EAGGF Guidance Section is deducted from allocated expenditure.

The above deduction aims at full UK participation in the financing of the costs of enlargement (except for agricultural expenditure). However, the additional UK contribution resulting from the above deduction may not exceed a ceiling of EUR 10.5 billion, in 2004 prices, during the period 2007-13. In the event of further enlargement between 2008 and 2013, this ceiling will be adjusted accordingly.

The final amount of the UK correction is obtained by deducting from (iii) the elements (iv) and (v) and by deducting from total allocated expenditure, as used in steps (i) and (ii), the elements (vi) and (vii).

2) Financing the correction

The financing of the UK correction is distributed among Member States according to their shares in EU GNI. The United Kingdom is excluded from the financing of its own correction. From 1985, Germany's contribution to financing the UK correction was limited to two-thirds of its normal share. Since 2002, this has been limited to one-quarter and extended to the Netherlands, Austria and Sweden.

This extension was introduced primarily in response to arguments by Austria, Germany, the Netherlands and Sweden that their EU budgetary burden was excessive and that they deserved more favourable budgetary treatment. An inevitable result of this arrangement is that the burden of financing the UK correction has now shifted to the remaining Member States, a group that includes those benefiting from the Cohesion Fund.

3. Other revenue

Other revenue is covered by Titles 4 to 9 of the general statement of revenue of the EU budget (¹).

Title 4 covers revenue accruing from persons working with the institutions and other EU bodies (taxes on salaries and pensions, and staff contributions to the pension scheme).

(¹)   The surplus available from the preceding financial year is recorded in Title 3 (Article 300). However, this surplus is itself mainly a consequence of the difference between the outturn of own resources payments and expenditure in the previous year.

246 EUROPEAN UNION PUBLIC FINANCE

Title 5 covers revenue accruing from the administrative operation of the institutions, such as proceeds from the sale of property, from letting and hiring, from the supply of services and from bank interest.

Title 6 covers contributions and refunds in connection with EU agreements and programmes (repayment of miscellaneous expenditure, revenue from services rendered against payment, contributions under specific agreements, financial corrections, and revenue relating to the European Agricultural Guarantee Fund, the European Agricultural Fund for Rural Development, and temporary restructuring amounts in the EU sugar sector).

Title 7 covers interest on late payments and fines (e.g. interest on late payment of own resources by Member States or fines on companies for infringing EU competition rules).

Title 8 covers revenue from EU borrowing and lending operations.

Title 9 covers miscellaneous revenue.

Other revenue is the result of the EU's normal activities; this revenue bears witness to the EU's status as a legal entity and its power of independent action.

4. The budgetary logic of financing the European Union

4.1. Equilibrium *ex ante*

The EU budget is known as an expenditure budget, in that expenditure is estimated prior to the calculation of the revenue that will be needed to finance it. The budget is always in balance *ex ante*.

Recourse to the different sources of revenue is sequential, i.e. a series of successive balances is calculated.

First, the expected proceeds from other revenue and any estimated surpluses from the previous year are subtracted from the total forecast volume of expenditure. The remaining expenditure is financed by own resources.

Within the category of own resources, the estimated revenue from traditional own resources is deducted first. The next step is to calculate the amount of the VAT-based resource. The remaining amount of expenditure is financed by the GNI-based resource. The GNI-based resource is the 'residual' resource that provides the revenue required to cover expenditure in excess of the sum of all the other sources of revenue.

4.2. Balance for the year

The balance of the budgetary year is determined by the actual outturn of revenue and expenditure. A surplus is carried over to the following budgetary year, thus reducing the amount of own resources needed in that year by means of a lower call rate for the GNI resource. A deficit would be likewise carried over, increasing the rate of call of GNI needed to balance the budget *ex ante*. A deficit is, however, exceptional and has occurred only three times, in 1977, 1984 and 1986.

The precise rules for drawing up the balance of the financial year are laid down in Council Regulation (EC, Euratom) No 1150/2000 of 22 May 2000 (¹) and in Council Regulation (EC, Euratom) No 1605/2002 of 25 June 2002.

The balance of a given financial year is made up of the difference between:

(1) all the revenue collected in respect of that financial year, which means traditional own resources established and made available to the Commission, called and paid VAT-based and GNI-based resources, and proceeds from other revenue; and

(2) payments made against appropriations for that financial year increased by the amount of appropriations for the same financial year carried over to the following budgetary year.

To this difference is then added (or subtracted from it if the difference is negative) the net amount of appropriations carried over from the previous

---

(¹) Council Regulation (EC, Euratom) No 1150/2000 of 22 May 2000 implementing Decision 94/728/EC, Euratom on the system of the Communities' own resources (OJ L 130, 31.5.2000, p.1).

financial year that have been cancelled, together with some other items resulting from exchange rate variations.

The resulting surplus is usually included in an amending budget in the following year. The Commission may, however, anticipate a surplus by proposing a letter of amendment to the preliminary draft budget in order to enter part of the expected surplus in the following year's budget.

4.3. VAT and GNI balances

Member States' VAT- and GNI-based payments are calculated using the VAT and GNI bases for the year in question, as forecast at the time of drafting of the preliminary draft budget. This forecast is later revised once during the budgetary year in question and budgeted in an amending budget. Member States' payments are adjusted accordingly.

However, final data for the VAT and GNI bases are not available until the end of the year following the budgetary year in question. The difference between what Member States should have paid according to the final bases and what they actually paid on the basis of the (revised) budgetary forecast is consequently called in the year after the budgetary year to which they refer. These VAT and GNI balances are calculated by the Commission, and Member States have to make the balances available for the first working day of December. Corrections to the final VAT and GNI bases can also be made in subsequent years. The previously calculated balances will then be adjusted and the difference called together with the VAT and GNI balances for the previous year.

Chapter 13

Expenditure by heading

1. Introduction

1.1. Content of the multiannual financial framework

The multiannual financial framework (MAFF) 2007-13 was formally adopted on 17 May 2006 when the European Parliament, the Council and the Commission signed the Interinstitutional Agreement (IIA) on budgetary discipline and sound financial management[1]. Three main priorities have been identified for the 2007-13 MAFF:

— integrating the single market into the broader objective of sustainable growth, mobilising economic, social, and environmental policies to that end; the goals for this priority are competitiveness, cohesion and the preservation and management of natural resources;

— giving more substance to the concept of European citizenship by joining up the area of freedom, justice, and security with access to basic public goods and services;

— establishing a coherent role for Europe as a global player – inspired by its core values – in assuming its regional responsibilities, promoting sustainable development and contributing to civilian and strategic security.

---

[1]   http://eur-lex.europa.eu/LexUriServ/site/en/oj/2006/c_139/c_13920060614en00010017.pdf.

1.2. Structure and ceilings of the multiannual financial framework 2007-13

Whereas Agenda 2000 ([1]) contained eight headings (11 including sub-headings), the framework for 2007-13 has six headings (eight including subheadings or sub-ceilings) and is therefore simpler and less rigid. Having a smaller number of headings not only reflects the broad policy goals, but also creates vital breathing space to allow for developments that cannot always be precisely predicted 10 years in advance.

— Heading 1: Sustainable growth

This heading is divided into two separate, but interlinked components:

1a. Competitiveness for growth and employment, encompassing expenditure on research and innovation, education and training, trans-European networks, social policy, the internal market and accompanying policies;

1b. Cohesion for growth and employment, designed to enhance convergence of the least developed Member States and regions, to complement the EU strategy for sustainable development outside the less prosperous regions and to support inter-regional cooperation.

— Heading 2: Preservation and management of natural resources

This includes the common agricultural and fisheries policies, rural development, environmental measures, and veterinary and phytosanitary actions.

— Heading 3: Citizenship, freedom, security and justice

This heading reflects the growing importance attached to two fields where the Union has been assigned new tasks:

3a. Freedom, Security and Justice: justice and home affairs, border protection, immigration and asylum policy;

3b. Citizenship: public health and consumer protection, culture, youth, information and dialogue with citizens.

([1])   http://ec.europa.eu/budget/faq/faq_fin_persp_en.htm#faq11.

— Heading 4: The European Union as a global player

This covers external action, including pre-accession instruments. Whereas the Commission proposed to bring the European Development Fund (EDF) into the financial framework, the European Council and the European Parliament agreed to leave it out.

— Heading 5: Administration

This heading covers administrative expenditure for all institutions, pensions and the European Schools.

— Heading 6: Compensation

Heading 6 includes some temporary post-accession amounts related to the latest enlargement of the Union (compensation over 2007-13 for Bulgaria and Romania).

Tables 13.1A and 13.1B present the commitment appropriations for the financial framework 2007-13 (in constant and current prices). The tables also take into account the revision of the framework for the financing of the European Navigation Satellite System programme 'Galileo' and the European Institute of Technology (EIT) (see Chapter 6).

2. Headings

2.1. Heading 1A – Competitiveness for growth and employment

Promoting competitiveness is a key strategic objective of the EU, reflected in the renewed Lisbon strategy on growth and jobs, which provides a framework for an ambitious reform process in partnership with the Member States. The EU budget to promote competitiveness for growth and employment for 2007-13 comes to EUR 85.6 billion in current prices, about 8.8 % of the total EU budget. Close to 65 % of this money is being spent on research and development (R & D). The other main expenditure areas are transport and energy networks, lifelong learning (education and training) and the competitiveness and innovation programme (CIP). Action contributing to the goals of competitiveness, sustainable growth and employment is being taken in the following areas: internal market, statistics, the fight against fraud, and taxation and the customs union.

Table 13.1: Financial framework 2007-13 (revised)

(million EUR at constant 2004 prices)

Commitment appropriations	2007	2008	2009	2010	2011	2012	2013	Total 2007-13
1. Sustainable growth	50 865	53 262	54 071	54 860	55 400	56 866	58 256	383 580
1a Competitiveness for growth and employment	8 404	9 595	10 209	11 000	11 306	12 122	12 914	75 550
1b Cohesion for growth and employment	42 461	43 667	43 862	43 860	44 094	44 744	45 342	308 030
2. Preservation and management of natural resources	51 962	54 685	54 017	53 379	52 528	51 901	51 284	369 756
of which: market related expenditure and direct payments	43 120	42 697	42 279	41 864	41 453	41 047	40 645	293 105
3. Citizenship, freedom, security and justice	1 199	1 258	1 380	1 503	1 645	1 797	1 988	10 770
3a Freedom, security and justice	600	690	790	910	1 050	1 200	1 390	6 630
3b Citizenship	599	568	590	593	595	597	598	4 140
4. EU as a global player	6 199	6 469	6 739	7 009	7 339	7 679	8 029	49 463
5. Administration (¹)	6 633	6 818	6 973	7 111	7 255	7 400	7 610	49 800
6. Compensations	419	191	190					800
Total commitment appropriations	117 277	122 683	123 370	123 862	124 167	125 643	127 167	864 169
as % of GNI	1.08 %	1.09 %	1.07 %	1.05 %	1.03 %	1.02 %	1.01 %	1.048 %
Total payment appropriations	115 142	119 805	112 182	118 549	116 178	119 659	119 161	820 676
as % of GNI	1.06 %	1.06 %	0.97 %	1.00 %	0.97 %	0.97 %	0.95 %	1.00 %
Margin available	0.18 %	0.18 %	0.27 %	0.24 %	0.27 %	0.27 %	0.29 %	0.24 %
Own Resources Ceiling as % of GNI	1.24 %	1.24 %	1.24 %	1.24 %	1.24 %	1.24 %	1.24 %	1.24 %

(¹) The expenditure on pensions included under the ceiling for this heading is calculated net of the staff contributions to the relevant scheme, within the limit of EUR 500 million at 2004 prices for the period 2007-13.

Table 13.2: Financial framework 2007-13 (revised)

(million EUR at current prices)

Commitment appropriations	2007	2008	2009	2010	2011	2012	2013	Total 2007-13
1. Sustainable growth	53 979	57 653	59 700	61 782	63 638	66 628	69 621	433 001
1a Competitiveness for growth and employment	8 918	10 386	11 272	12 388	12 987	14 203	15 433	85 587
1b Cohesion for growth and employment	45 061	47 267	48 428	49 394	50 651	52 425	54 188	347 414
2. Preservation and management of natural resources	55 143	59 193	59 639	60 113	60 338	60 810	61 289	416 525
of which: market related expenditure and direct payments	45 759	46 217	46 679	47 146	47 617	48 093	48 574	330 085
3. Citizenship, freedom, security and justice	1 273	1 362	1 523	1 693	1 889	2 105	2 376	12 221
3a Freedom, security and justice	637	747	872	1 025	1 206	1 406	1 661	7 554
3b Citizenship	636	615	651	668	683	699	715	4 667
4. EU as a global player	6 578	7 002	7 440	7 893	8 430	8 997	9 595	55 935
5. Administration ([1])	7 039	7 380	7 699	8 008	8 334	8 670	9 095	56 225
6. Compensations	445	207	210					862
Total commitment appropriations	124 457	132 797	136 211	139 489	142 629	147 210	151 976	974 769
as % of GNI	1.04 %	1.06 %	1.04 %	1.02 %	1.00 %	0.99 %	0.98 %	1.02 %
Total payment appropriations	122 190	129 681	123 858	133 505	133 452	140 200	142 408	925 294
as % of GNI	1.02 %	1.03 %	0.94 %	0.97 %	0.93 %	0.94 %	0.91 %	0.96 %
Margin available	0.22 %	0.21 %	0.30 %	0.27 %	0.31 %	0.30 %	0.33 %	0.28 %
Own Resources Ceiling as % of GNI	1.24 %	1.24 %	1.24 %	1.24 %	1.24 %	1.24 %	1.24 %	1.24 %

([1]) The expenditure on pensions included under the ceiling for this heading is calculated net of the staff contributions to the relevant scheme, within the limit of EUR 500 million at 2004 prices for the period 2007-13.

GRAPH 13.1

The structure of expenditure 2007-13

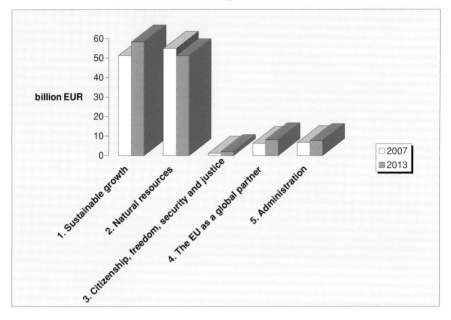

1) Key initiatives

— The seventh framework programmes (EC and Euratom) for research and technological development (FP7) set out all the activities of the Community in that area and in support of research and development activities in a broad range of scientific disciplines. The programmes are a crucial instrument in supporting the further development of a European Research Area (ERA). They play a leading role in supporting European research and stimulating cooperation across the Union. They finance collaborative research projects in areas such as health, nanotechnologies, energy, environment (including climate change) and transport, taking into account international science and technology cooperation policy. Another important objective of FP7 is to ensure optimal use and development of research infrastructure, supporting regional research-driven clusters and supporting research for the benefit of small and medium-sized enterprises (SMEs). Through their combined impact, these programmes will allow for the emergence and reinforcement of

European poles of excellence in various fields. FP7 also promote mobility among European researchers and fund individual projects of outstanding scientific excellence. Through a risk-sharing finance facility they allow a larger volume of European Investment Bank lending and guarantee operations, thus improving access to debt financing for private investment in research, technological development and demonstration. A central feature of FP7 is the European Research Council (ERC). It will be devoted to introducing a new dynamic in research, by putting a premium on excellence through competition and attracting outstanding scholars. Global amount set for research and technological development 2007-13: EUR 54.6 billion.

— With the Trans-European Networks (TEN) programme, the Union supports the linking of regions and national transport and energy networks through modern and efficient infrastructure. The main focus lies on interconnection and interoperability of national networks together with access to such networks. In the period 2007-13, TEN for transport will concentrate on 30 priority projects; special attention will be given to financing the cross-border sections and to projects aiming to eliminate bottlenecks. Total Community aid for TEN projects in the field of energy may not exceed 10 % of the total investment cost. For works in the field of transport, Community financial aid may not in general exceed 30 % for priority projects for cross-border sections or 20 % for other priority projects. In addition to the TEN budget line, trans-European networks are also supported through the Structural Funds, the Cohesion Fund and loans from the European Investment Bank. The Marco Polo II programme supports environmentally friendly forms of transport such as shipping, rail and inland waterways, especially over long distances, in urban areas and on congested corridors. Global amount set for TEN and Marco Polo 2007-13: EUR 8.6 billion.

— Galileo is a European flagship industrial project of strategic importance. It will consist of 30 satellites which will enable maximum coverage of the earth and generate a competitive advantage in measuring objects in time and space. Global amount 2007-13: EUR 3.4 billion, of which EUR 400 million is financed under FP7 (see Chapter 6).

— The Lifelong Learning Programme comprises four sectoral programmes on school education (Comenius), higher education (Erasmus), vocational training (Leonardo da Vinci) and adult education (Grundtvig). It contributes to the development of an advanced knowledge society within the Union, instrumental to sustainable economic growth, more and better jobs and greater social cohesion. In concrete terms, the programme offers opportunities for learners, teachers and trainers to study or teach in another Member State. Global amount 2007-13: EUR 7.0 billion.

— Erasmus Mundus and Erasmus Mundus II are cooperation and mobility programmes in the field of higher education, to enhance the quality of European higher education and to promote intercultural understanding through cooperation with non-Member States. They also contribute to increasing the attractiveness of European higher education worldwide. Global amount 2009-13 (Erasmus Mundus II): EUR 0.5 billion.

— The Competitiveness and Innovation Framework Programme (CIP) provides a coherent and integrated response to the objectives of the renewed Lisbon strategy for growth and jobs. The largest of its specific programmes, the Entrepreneurship and Innovation Programme (EIP), helps innovative enterprises by providing access to finance through the European Investment Fund. The EIP also gives SMEs easy access to the EU via the business support networks. The Information and Communication Technology (ICT) Policy Support Programme stimulates new markets for electronic networks, media content and digital technologies. The Intelligent Energy-Europe Programme supports actions to increase the uptake and demand for energy efficiency, to promote renewable energy sources, and to stimulate diversification of fuels and energy efficiency in transport. Global amount 2007-13: EUR 3.6 billion.

— The Community Programme for employment and social solidarity (PROGRESS) groups actions targeting anti-discrimination and diversity, gender equality, employment incentive measures, working conditions, social protection and the fight against social exclusion. It provides financial support for the Social Policy Agenda. Global amount 2007-13: EUR 0.7 billion.

— Nuclear Decommissioning. The programme aims at closing down old nuclear power plants and ensures adequate handling of contaminated elements and locations. Examples are V-1 Jaslovske Bohunice in Slovakia and Ignalia in Lithuania. Global amount 2007-13: EUR 1.3 billion.

— Fiscalis 2013 and Customs 2013. Customs will support the development of a pan-European electronic customs environment, contribute to the implementation of the modernised Customs Code, ensure the maintenance of the current operational trans-European IT systems, and support actions designed to increase cooperation between Member States' customs administrations. Fiscalis supports closer cooperation among tax authorities and better implementation of existing tax rules. It is also tackling tax fraud issues. Global amount 2007-13: EUR 0.5 billion.

2) New financial instruments

— The Interinstitutional Agreement between the European Parliament, the Council and the Commission on budgetary discipline and sound financial management introduced new co-financing mechanisms to reinforce the leverage effect of the EU budget by increasing the funding incentive. The three institutions agreed to encourage the development of appropriate multiannual financial instruments acting as catalysts for public and private investors with the European Investment Bank (EIB), the European Investment Fund and the European Bank for Reconstruction and Development to support investment in research and development, trans-European networks and small and medium-sized enterprises.

— The Risk-Sharing Finance Facility (RSFF) is an innovative debt-based EIB facility supported by the seventh Framework Programme to increase predominantly private investment in research, technological development and demonstration (RTD) and in innovation. The RSFF, which has been jointly developed by the European Commission and the EIB, will provide loans and guarantees for RTD and innovation projects (including support for research infrastructure) which would otherwise not receive sufficient finance because they are high-risk. The EC and the EIB, as risk-sharing partners, will make a contribution of up to EUR 1 billion each to the facility to cover the specific risks of financing RSFF projects. Based on this risk-sharing partnership, a total of up to EUR 10 billion could be provided to RTD and innovation projects under the RSFF. RSFF will increase the EIB's capacity to finance more R & D and innovation projects, and thus enable it to provide loans and guarantees with higher risk profiles than those readily financed on the European market. By reinforcing the EIB's financing capacity in the area of research and innovation, RSFF will facilitate and leverage the efforts of a large number of European financial institutions in RDI financing, thus increasing banking and capital markets financing in that sector. RSFF is demand driven. The EU and the EIB will be reimbursed for the risks taken. RSFF will benefit private and public organisations involved in research and innovation of any size and ownership, and in particular research-intensive mid-size companies, SMEs, and research infrastructure or other large research undertakings like Joint Technology Initiatives (JTIs). RSFF is open not only to legal entities involved in FP7 or EUREKA projects, but to all legal entities and projects carrying out RDI activities that contribute to FP7 objectives.

— As requested by the Council and the European Parliament, the EIB will make risk-sharing credit facilities available to its network of partner banks in all Member States and associated countries for smaller projects and promoters. Such facilities will increase the bank's lending capacity in support of eligible RDI projects. The Cooperation Agreement between the European Community (EC) and the European Investment Bank (EIB) on the Risk-Sharing Finance Facility (RSFF) was signed on 5 June 2007 by Commission member Janez Potočnik and EIB President Philippe Maystadt. At present, it covers the period 1 January 2007 to 31 December 2008; as from 2009 it will be amended annually taking into consideration the Decision on the seventh Framework Programme, the relevant decisions on the Specific Programmes 'Cooperation' and 'Capacities', and market demand.

— The Entrepreneurship and Innovation Programme, which is part of the Competitiveness and Innovation Framework Programme (CIP), promotes access to finance for SMEs with a view to encouraging early stage (seed and start-up) investment, expansion and business transfer. The Community's financial instruments for SMEs are notably the High Growth and Innovative SME Facility (GIF) and the SME Guarantee (SMEG) Facility; both are operated by the European Investment Fund (EIF) on behalf of the Commission.

— The GIF contributes to setting up and financing of SMEs and to reducing the equity and risk capital market gap which prevents SMEs from exploiting their growth potential; it also supports innovative SMEs with high growth potential, in particular those undertaking research, development and other innovation activities. The GIF invests in specialised venture capital funds which in turn provide capital to SMEs.

— The SMEG Facility provides support for guarantee schemes or direct guarantees to facilitate debt financing via loans or leasing, microcredit financing, guarantees for equity or quasi-equity investments in SMEs and securitisation of SME debt finance portfolios to mobilise additional debt financing for SMEs.

— A Loan Guarantee Instrument (LGTT) was created for TEN-T Projects. As stipulated in the Regulation laying down general rules for the granting of Community financial aid in the field of the trans-European transport and energy networks, the contribution from the general budget of the European Union to the LGTT may not exceed EUR 500 million for the period 2007-13. The EIB contributes an equal amount. The EIB is a risk-sharing partner and manages the Community contribution to the loan guarantee instrument on behalf of the Community. Community exposure to the loan guarantee instrument, including management fees and other eligible costs, is limited to the amount of the Community contribution to the loan guarantee instrument, with no further liability on the general budget of the European Union. The residual risk inherent in all operations is borne by the EIB.

— The overall goal of the LGTT is to leverage limited public resources and stimulate private capital investment in transport infrastructure projects of European significance whose financial viability is based, in whole or in part, on revenues, tolls or other income paid by or on behalf of the users or beneficiaries; the LGTT aims at countering the problem of the low private sector ability to assume initial traffic revenue risk. This objective is achieved by providing security for standby credit facilities aimed at covering post-construction risks during the early operational phase of the project.

2.2. Heading 1B – Cohesion for growth and employment

The EU's cohesion policy aims at strengthening the economic and social cohesion of the enlarged Union in order to promote balanced and sustainable development. It is designed to reduce disparities between the levels of development of the various regions and Member States and the backwardness of the least favoured regions or islands, including rural areas. Cohesion aid is implemented by the Commission and the Member States under shared management. The aid is intended to complement rather than replace structural expenditure by a Member State. Cohesion policy has undergone significant development over time. While the European Social Fund and the European Regional Development Fund were set up in 1958 and 1975 respectively, it was the Single European Act in 1986 that laid the basis for a genuine cohesion policy. One of the objectives of the policy was to counterbalance the effects of the completion of the internal market on less developed Member States. While the budget for cohesion amounted to about 17 % of the first financial framework, the EU cohesion budget for 2007-13 is EUR 347.4 billion (including EUR 0.8 billion for technical assistance), in current prices, about 36 % of the total EU budget.

1) Key initiatives

— Convergence is the main objective, representing just over 81 % of cohesion expenditure. It aims at stimulating the growth potential of the least developed Member States and regions, by improving the investment required to increase long-term competitiveness, job creation and sustainable development. Seventy-one per cent of convergence funding is allocated to regions whose gross domestic product (GDP) per capita is less than 75 % of the average GDP of the 25 Member States at the time of the adoption of the cohesion instruments (EU-25) and 24 % (Cohesion Fund) to Member States whose gross national income (GNI) per capita is less than 90 % of the average GNI of the EU-25. The remaining 5 % are allocated to transitional support to regions that lost eligibility due to the statistical effect of enlargement. Financial allocations for specific Member States are calculated on the basis of objective criteria such as the eligible population, regional prosperity, national prosperity, surface area and unemployment. Global amount 2007-13: EUR 282.9 billion.

— Regional competitiveness and employment capacity: 16 % of cohesion expenditure is dedicated to strengthening this area. It is invested in non-convergence regions through a menu of tools fostering innovation and the knowledge economy and reducing regional isolation from digital and transport networks. Seventy-nine per cent of these funds are distributed among Member States on the basis of eligible population, regional prosperity, employment and population density criteria, while the remaining 21 % are spent on transitional and specific support for regions whose GDP has risen above the 75 % average EU-25 threshold. Seventy-five per cent of regional competitiveness and employment expenditure on the EU-15 is earmarked for action directly contributing to the Lisbon strategy for growth and jobs. Global amount 2007-13: EUR 55.0 billion.

— Territorial cooperation: 3 % of cohesion expenditure goes on territorial cooperation at cross-border, trans-national and inter-regional levels. Together with the EU contribution to the International Fund for Ireland, the PEACE programme under the cross-border cooperation objective also promotes peace and reconciliation in Northern Ireland. Global amount 2007-13: EUR 8.7 billion.

2) Main financial instruments

Cohesion policy is implemented through three main financial instruments:

— The European Regional Development Fund operates in all Member States and co-finances infrastructure and productive investment together with other measures supporting regional and local development.

— The Cohesion Fund co-finances trans-European networks in the area of transport infrastructure and environment projects (including energy efficiency, renewable energy and sustainable transport modes) in Member States whose GDP per capita is less than 90 % of the average GNI of the EU-25.

— The European Social Fund supports measures to improve employment opportunities for workers to increase their mobility and to facilitate their adaptation to industrial change throughout the Union.

The Funds also provide technical assistance. This may be used to help regions and Member States prepare major funding projects (Jaspers), to leverage additional loan resources for public private partnerships in urban areas (Jessica) or to improve access to finance and risk capital for SMEs (Jeremie). These initiatives are implemented in close cooperation with the European Investment Bank Group, the European Bank for Reconstruction and Development and others.

2.3. Heading 2 – Preservation and management of natural resources

The EU has a strong mandate and policy responsibility in the fields of agriculture and rural development, fisheries, and the environment. The EU budget to preserve and manage natural resources for 2007-13 comes to EUR 416.5 billion, which is about 43 % of the total EU budget. Funding is provided mainly to agriculture, rural development, fisheries, environment projects and veterinary and phytosanitary actions with more than 79 % of the money going to agriculture.

In terms of funding mechanisms, 85 % of the budget for the common agricultural policy (CAP) will be channelled through direct payments to farmers subject to 'cross-compliance'. Most of the remaining funds will be used for interventions aimed at stabilising agricultural markets for various products.

Financing for rural development takes the form of co-financing. While overall priorities are agreed at EU level, there is plenty of scope for Member States and regions to design their programmes so they reflect an appropriate balance between the three principal objectives.

With regard to fisheries, the European Fisheries Fund (EFF) operations are mainly implemented by the Member States as a part of shared management.

1) Key initiatives

— The objectives of the CAP derive directly from the Treaty. The CAP should, in particular, ensure a fair standard of living in the farming community, stabilise markets and guarantee security of supplies. Over time, the CAP has undergone significant change, including substantial reforms and simplification efforts. The latest major reform took place in 2003 with an emphasis on:

- 'single farm payments' to farmers, irrespective of production;

- linking payment to environmental, food safety, animal and plant health, and animal welfare standards ('cross-compliance');

- a stronger rural development policy;

- a reduction in direct payments for bigger farms ('modulation');

- a ceiling on CAP expenditure until 2013;

- sectoral reforms.

The key aim of these reforms was to shift the slant of the farm economy towards the market in order to make the agricultural sector more competitive. Reflecting the multipurpose application of agricultural activity, the CAP must also be fully compatible with sustainable development, in particular by promoting environmentally friendly production methods and the effective use of resources. Over the last two decades the CAP's share of the EU budget has fallen from 70 % to less than 45 %. At the end of the 2007-13 period it should amount to 39 % of the EU budget. Global amount 2007-13: EUR 316.6 billion (after transfer to rural development).

— Rural development is considered to be a second pillar of the CAP. The rural development policy for 2007-13 will focus on three major themes:

• improving competitiveness for farming and forestry;

• enhancing the environment and the countryside through support for land management;

• improving the quality of life in rural areas while diversifying the rural economy.

Resources will be used to co-fund rural development, mainly through rural development programmes under the European Agricultural Fund for Rural Development (EAFRD). Part of these resources will co-fund the management of the Natura 2000 network, which is a European ecological network of sites set up to protect habitat types and plant and animal species of particular importance. Global amount 2007-13: EUR 92.0 billion.

— Of the budget for fishery and maritime affairs, 64 % will be invested in the EFF. The EFF contributes to the economic diversification of regions affected by a reduction in fishing activity, to the adjustment of fleet capacity and to fleet renewal that does not involve an increase in fishing. The remaining part of the budget will be used to fund fisheries and maritime affairs through other channels. Activities financed outside the EFF include expenditure arising from EC fisheries agreements with third countries, monitoring and controlling the Common Fisheries Policy (CFP), and support for the management of fishery resources through collection of basic data, studies and pilot projects. Global amount 2007-13: EUR 6.8 billion.

— The European environment programme LIFE+ promotes biodiversity, aims to develop environmental policy and governance, and will support information and communication activities. Forty per cent of the amount allocated to LIFE+ will fund projects promoting biodiversity, for example to conserve habitats or protect wild birds. Global amount 2007-13: EUR 2.1 billion.

2.4. Heading 3A – Freedom, Security and Justice

The protection of life, freedom and property of citizens is a core objective of the European Union. In a context of ever stronger security interdependence, responsibilities in that area include the management of the Union's external borders, the development of a common asylum area, cooperation between law enforcement agencies and judicial authorities to prevent and fight terrorism and crime, respect for fundamental rights and a global approach to drug issues.

Expenditure on freedom, security and justice will have increased in real terms by 163 % in 2013 compared with the last year of the previous financial framework. In the current financial framework, around 0.77 % of the EU's overall budget is being used for programmes in the fields of solidarity in managing migration flows, security and safeguarding liberties, and fundamental rights and justice. Global amount 2007-13: EUR 7.6 billion.

1) Key initiatives

Solidarity and management of migration flows

— The European External Borders Fund supports the implementation of the common integrated border management system and cooperation by consular services. Among the measures financed by that fund are the development and application of surveillance systems together with the setting up of strategic and operational coordination between authorities. Global amount 2007-13: EUR 1.82 billion.

— A European Refugee Fund aids Member States in receiving and bearing the consequences of receiving refugees and displaced persons, in accordance with their international protection obligations. It co-finances actions linked to reception conditions and asylum procedures, such as accommodation infrastructure, medical or legal assistance and integration measures. Global amount 2008-13: EUR 628 million.

— Support for integration and return policies is provided through the European Fund for the Integration of Third-country Nationals and the European Return Fund. The integration fund supports Member States in enabling third-country nationals to settle and actively take part in European societies. This includes measures conveying basic knowledge about the host society's language, institutions and fundamental values. The return fund assists Member States with improving the management of common return standards. Global amounts: EUR 825 million for the integration fund (2007-13), EUR 676 million for the return fund (2008-13).

— In addition, specific instruments allow for the development and operation of important large-scale IT systems, such as the second generation Schengen Information System, the Visa Information System or the EURODAC system for comparing the fingerprints of asylum seekers to determine the Member State responsible for an asylum application.

Security and safeguarding liberties

— A programme to help prevent, prepare for and manage the consequences of terrorism contributes to protecting citizens against acts that may threaten individual liberties, democratic society and the rule of law. Support measures include actions aiming at improved risk and threat assessment and enhanced cooperation between security services. Global amount 2007-13: EUR 139 million.

— A second security programme aims at promoting coordination, cooperation and best practice in the fields of law enforcement, crime prevention and criminology, together with witness and victim protection. Global amount 2007-13: EUR 606 million.

Fundamental rights and justice

— Actions combating violence, providing information on and preventing the use of drugs and actively promoting fundamental rights are financed under a framework programme on fundamental rights and justice. The same instrument also supports judicial cooperation in criminal and civil matters, aiming at promoting mutual recognition of judicial decisions, avoiding conflicts of jurisdiction, and promoting the rights of defendants. Global amounts 2007-13: EUR 117 million for actions combating violence, EUR 21 million for drugs prevention and information, EUR 97 million for fundamental rights and EUR 308 million for judicial cooperation.

— The EU budget also finances the Agency for Fundamental Rights in Vienna, the Agency for the Management of Operational Cooperation at the External Borders (Frontex) in Warsaw, the European Monitoring Centre for Drugs and Drug Addiction in Lisbon, the European Police College in Bramshill, the judicial cooperation network Eurojust in the Hague and, once it has been transformed into an EU body, the European Police Office Europol.

2.5. Heading 3B – Citizenship

The European Union currently invests around 0.5 % of its budget in actions promoting active citizenship, health and consumer protection, programmes fostering European culture and diversity and an instrument for major emergencies to increase the efficiency and effectiveness of civil protection. In the latter, the European Union carries out supporting, coordinating or complementary actions with the Member States – which retain primary responsibility. The most significant increase under the citizenship heading has been made for health and consumer policies (including the European Centre for Disease Prevention and Control in Stockholm and the European Food Safety Authority in Parma), the allocation of which will be 33 % higher (in 2004 prices) at the end of the current period than it was in 2006.

Financial assistance under the citizenship heading usually takes the form of grants, on the basis of calls for proposals, or public procurement contracts, depending on the specific needs. As a general rule, programmes are managed centrally by the Commission, but it may also delegate management to external bodies. Global amount 2007-13: EUR 4.7 billion.

1) Key initiatives (in current prices) for the period 2007-13

— Action in the field of public health is financed to promote healthier ways of living and generate and disseminate health knowledge. Concrete actions in this area include measures aiming to identify health threats posed by diseases or physical and chemical agents, the development of vaccination policies, EU surveillance of communicable diseases or the development of contingency or health emergency plans. Global amount 2008-13: EUR 322 million.

— Action in the field of consumer policy includes monitoring market developments, providing scientific advice and risk evaluation and promoting co-regulatory and self-regulatory initiatives. The EU budget also contributes to the functioning of European consumer organisations, the development of Community-wide standards for products and services and consumer education measures. Global amount 2007-13: EUR 157 million.

— The Youth in Action programme finances actions such as youth exchanges, measures to encourage active participation of young people in the democratic life of their community, expenses and subsistence costs for voluntary participation by young people in non-profit activities to the general benefit or support for youth bodies active Europe-wide. Global amount 2007-13: EUR 885 million.

— The Media 2007 programme contributes to the promotion of European cultural values and the creation of highly skilled jobs in the audiovisual sector. It aims at enhanced cultural and linguistic diversity, increased circulation of European audiovisual works and a more competitive audiovisual sector. Examples of co-financing are: training for audiovisual professionals, development of European projects, financing plans, dubbing and subtitling. Global amount 2007-13: EUR 755 million.

— The Culture 2007 programme promotes cultural exchange and cooperation, in particular the mobility of cultural players and transnational circulation of cultural and artistic products of European interest. It supports cultural bodies and cooperation projects in the form of festivals, master classes, international expositions, workshops, translations and conferences. Significant funding is also provided for the European Capitals of Culture to help implement activities stressing

European visibility and trans-European cultural cooperation. Global amount 2007-13: EUR 400 million.

— The Europe for Citizens programme promotes active European citizenship, giving citizens the opportunity to interact, developing a sense of European identity and enhancing tolerance and mutual understanding between Europeans. Examples are town-twinning activities, local trans-national citizens' projects and Europe-wide civil society organisations. Global amount 2007-13: EUR 215 million.

— The Union's civil protection financial instrument supports and complements the efforts of the Member States to protect people, the environment and property in the event of natural and man-made disasters and to facilitate cooperation in the field of civil protection. It finances studies, scenarios, exercises, staff exchanges and information provision, and also contributes to the development of detection and early warning systems. Global amount 2007-13: EUR 134 million.

— Further actions and initiatives include the EU visitors' programme, the European Year of Intercultural Dialogue in 2008 and pilot information networks.

2.6 Heading 4 – Europe as a global partner

The EU is founded on the values of liberty, democracy, respect for human rights and fundamental freedoms and the rule of law. The European Union has allocated around 5.8 % of the ceiling of the multiannual financial framework to the external projection of its policies, representing an overall amount of EUR 55.9 billion for the period 2007-13 (NB: all figures are in current prices at a standard deflator of 2 % per year). This money is being used, in particular:

— to support candidate countries and the western Balkans region on their path towards accession;

— to provide stability, security and prosperity in our neighbourhood;

— to support democracy and human rights across the globe;

— to provide economic and development assistance;

— to respond to 'global challenges' (the fight against HIV/AIDS or climate change);

— to respond to instability and crises;

— to provide humanitarian aid and macro financial assistance.

The European development aid policy is essentially channelled through the European Development Fund (see Chapter 18), which is an important part of external policy but is financed as a separate instrument and outside the general budget.

Further to enlargement, the EU has been entrusted with even greater responsibilities in the field of external actions. These responsibilities are channelled towards three main objectives: providing stability, security and prosperity in its neighbourhood ('The EU and its neighbourhood policy'); working actively to support sustainable development at international level ('The EU as a sustainable development partner'); and promoting global political governance and ensuring strategic and civilian security ('The EU as a global player'). In order to address these responsibilities, the Communication 'Building our Common Future – Policy Challenges and Budgetary Means of the Enlarged Union 2007-13' adopted on 10 February 2004 set an ambitious goal of a stronger voice for the Union, supported by more efficient tools. A further Communication on the Instruments for External Assistance under the future Financial Framework 2007-13, adopted on 29 September 2004, detailed the approach to be followed in order to achieve these political objectives and proposed the instruments to support them. In an effort to streamline the multitude of legal bases for external activities, a balance had to be struck between geographically focused and thematic instruments, and between policy-driven and crisis-reaction instruments.

1) Policy-driven instruments

The key action envisaged is the intensification, after the 2007 start-up of the new programmes, of assistance on the basis of the Instrument for Pre-accession (IPA), European Neighbourhood and Partnership Instrument (ENPI), Development Cooperation Instrument (DCI), Cooperation with Industrialised and High-income Countries (ICI) and the European Instrument for Democracy and Human Rights (EIDHR).

— The Pre-Accession Instrument. Recent progress and achievements on 'enlargement' notably include the accession of Bulgaria and Romania on 1 January 2007, which completed the fifth round of accession. The EU prepared the ground for future enlargement by opening accession negotiations with Croatia and Turkey, while the former Yugoslav Republic of Macedonia was granted candidate status. The key goals are to continue the accession negotiations with Croatia and Turkey, the preparation of the former Yugoslav Republic of Macedonia as a candidate country, and to strengthen the EU's relationship with the rest of the western Balkans through the Stabilisation and Association Process. A further and central important task will relate to the obligations that the EU is expected to take on as regards the implementation of the Kosovo status settlement. Since 1 January 2007, pre-accession assistance has been provided on basis of the new Instrument for Pre-accession (IPA), which replaced the range of former instruments (Phare, ISPA, Sapard, CARDS, and assistance to Turkey). Under IPA, pre-accession assistance is available to candidate countries and potential candidates. The instrument addresses the need for a flexible approach in order to accommodate new priorities quickly. It covers Institution Building, Regional and Cross-border Cooperation, Regional Development, Rural Development and Human Resources Development. The last three components are accessible only to recognised candidate countries as a preparation for the structural funds, the European Agricultural Guarantee Fund and the Rural Development Fund. They are budgeted under the respective policy areas: Enlargement, Regional Policy, Agriculture and Rural Development, and Employment and Social Affairs. Global amount 2007-13: EUR 11.5 billion.

— The European Neighbourhood and Partnership Instrument. The Commission will pursue its efforts to create an area of peace, stability and prosperity between the EU and its neighbours through the development of the partnerships in the framework of the European Neighbourhood Policy (ENP). The relationship between the EU and the Russian Federation is distinct from the ENP and is covered by a wide-ranging strategic partnership expressed through the Common Spaces[1]. Roadmaps for the achievement of the Common Spaces

---

[1]   There are four so-called 'common spaces' of cooperation between the EU and Russia: the common economic space, the common space of freedom, security and justice, the common space of cooperation in the field of external security, and the common space of research, education and culture.

have been agreed. Financial assistance is delivered through the new ENPI instrument, which covers the countries targeted by the European Neighbourhood Policy, i.e. the countries of the south and eastern Mediterranean, including Palestine, together with countries in Eastern Europe and the southern Caucasus. This instrument also supports the strategic partnership with Russia.

The ENPI has two main objectives, namely to:

— promote progressive economic integration and deeper political cooperation between the EU and partner countries;

— address the specific opportunities and challenges of the geographical proximity common to the EU and its neighbours.

The ENPI is a 'policy-driven' instrument which replaces MEDA, Tacis, and other, fragmented, former instruments. It supports the implementation of ENP Action Plans, in particular. A specific feature is the cross-border cooperation component, which will take the form of joint programmes bringing together regions of Member States and partner countries sharing a common border. The ENPI countries will benefit also from the thematic programmes covered by the Development Cooperation Instrument (DCI), for which part of their respective budgets is set aside, in particular as regards the migration and asylum programme. Global amount 2007-13: EUR 11.2 billion.

— The new Development Cooperation Instrument (DCI) was adopted on 18 December 2006 [1] with the overarching objective of supporting eligible developing countries, territories and regions in the eradication of poverty in the context of sustainable development, including pursuit of the Millennium Development Goals (MDGs), as well as the promotion of democracy, good governance and respect for human rights and for the rule of law. However, it does not include the 10th European Development Fund (EDF) covering the ACP countries, because the proposal for budgetisation of the EDF did not go through [2]. Nevertheless, the thematic programmes may include activities aimed at various

---

[1]   Regulation (EC) No 1905/2006 of the European Parliament and of the Council establishing a financing instrument for development cooperation (OJ L 378, 27.12.2006, p. 41).

[2]   See Chapter 18.

regions or groups of partner countries, or an international operation that is not geographically specific. Assistance will be given in line with the relevant strategy papers adopted and discussed with the Council under the comitology procedure and with the Parliament as part of the dialogue introduced under the democratic scrutiny mechanism. Reinforcing the political role of the EU in Asia will be one of the main priorities, in particular by reinforcing the partnerships with China and India, and concluding global agreements with key ASEAN countries. Cooperation with Latin America will continue under the strategic orientations set out in the December 2005 Communication([1]). Global amount 2007-13: EUR 16.9 billion.

— The European Instrument for Democracy and Human Rights (EIDHR). This instrument is designed to complement the various other tools of EU policy on democracy and human rights, which range from political dialogue and diplomatic demarches to various financial and technical cooperation instruments, including geographic and thematic programmes and the crisis-related Instrument for Stability. Interventions under the EIDHR have a specific complementary and additional role because it is global and does not require the consent of third country governments or other public authorities. This provides scope for cooperation with civil society and international interventions which are neither geographically linked nor crisis related, and which may require a transnational approach. It provides the necessary framework for operations such as support for independent EU Election Observation Missions, which contributes significantly and successfully to democratic processes in third countries. Global amount 2007-13: EUR 1.1 billion.

— The Instrument for Cooperation with Industrialised and Other High-Income Countries. Cooperation with these countries is an important factor in strengthening the European Union's role and place in the world, in consolidating multilateral institutions and in contributing to balanced development of the world economy. The overarching objectives are managing and developing the existing frameworks for bilateral relations with the EU's main industrialised partners and high-

---

([1]) Communication from the Commission to the Council and the European Parliament, 'A stronger partnership between the European Union and Latin America', COM(2005) 636 final.

income countries, enhancing the EU's economic interests through economic cooperation and business promotion activities, and facilitating people-to-people exchanges through educational, scientific and academic contacts. Global amount 2007-13: EUR 0.2 billion.

2) Specific crisis-response instruments

— The Instrument for Stability (IfS) is a new instrument designed to provide an adequate response both to instability and crises and to longer-term challenges with a stability or security aspect. It is complementary to the Pre-Accession, European Neighbourhood and Partnership and Development Cooperation instruments, and provides assistance designed to establish the necessary conditions for implementing policies supported by the IPA, ENPI and DCI. In particular, the Stability Instrument allows the Community to:

— deliver an effective, immediate and integrated response to situations of crisis and instability in third countries, within a single legal instrument, until normal cooperation under one of the general instruments for cooperation and assistance can resume; this will build on the added value already demonstrated by the Rapid Reaction Mechanism and on the emergency provisions already provided for in a number of existing external relations financial instruments;

— address global and regional trans-border challenges with a security or stability dimension arising in third countries, including issues such as nuclear safety and non-proliferation, the fight against trafficking, organised crime and terrorism, and unforeseen major threats to public health;

— deliver a timely response to any urgent policy challenges faced by the Union, by piloting measures unforeseen under the three policy-driven instruments, until such time as they can be adequately incorporated into the policy framework of those instruments.

The Stability Instrument operates purely under the first pillar. However, its design takes into account the need for effective operational coordination between Community actions and measures adopted under the Common Foreign and Security Policy. Global amount for the Stability Instrument 2007-13: EUR 2.1 billion.

— The new activity 'Crisis management and global threats to security' provides for funding to cover crisis-response and preparedness operations, action on non-proliferation of weapons of mass destruction, action on organised crime, trafficking, protection of critical infrastructure and threats to public health, and the fight against terrorism. Assistance in the nuclear sector, although governed by a distinct and specific regulation, is also budgeted under that activity, as are appropriations for civil protection intervention in third countries.

— The Humanitarian Aid Instrument. Humanitarian aid activities will continue to have the existing regulation on humanitarian aid as their sole legal basis. The Humanitarian Aid Instrument is regarded as being sufficiently clear in terms of objectives and as performing well in terms of delivery and efficiency. The year 2005 is remembered for the impact of two huge natural disasters – the tsunami in South-East Asia on 26 December 2004 and the earthquake in Pakistan in October 2005. However, the Commission also continues to fund assistance in forgotten and complex crisis situations; in 2006, the focus was mainly on Darfur, Sudan, and the Middle East, to assist the Lebanese population following the war and the Palestinian population, for whom additional resources needed to be mobilised. Since 2007, food aid activities and part of the aid to uprooted people which were funded under Development and External Relations have come under the Humanitarian Aid Instrument. Global amount 2007-13: EUR 5.6 billion.

3) Common foreign and security policy (CFSP)

Common foreign and security policy (CFSP) activities will continue with an increased budget, in line with the financial framework 2007-13. The bulk of the resources is likely to be used to finance the ESDP operation in Kosovo, where the EU is expected to play a central role in the implementation of the settlement. Increased involvement is also expected in Afghanistan, while the EU will still have to perform its international role in conflict resolution and stabilisation activities in the Middle East, Africa and other difficult regions of the globe. Since the CFSP is an 'intergovernmental' instrument not subject to first-pillar decision procedures, all CFSP expenditure has to be based on joint action under Title V of the EU Treaty. Global amount 2007-13: EUR 2.0 billion.

4) Macro-financial assistance and loan guarantee

Since its inception in 1990, Macro-Financial Assistance has proved to be an efficient instrument for economic stabilisation and a driver of structural reform in the beneficiary countries. Speeding up reform in neighbouring countries in line with the neighbourhood policy, and the adjustment and reform efforts of candidate and potential candidate countries during the pre-accession period, might increase external funding needs. The resources for provisioning the Guarantee Fund for External Actions are budgeted directly under Heading 4 in the regular annual budget procedure. Global amount 2007-13: EUR 0.8 billion.

5) Emergency aid reserve

The Emergency Aid Reserve is financed outside the budget (a more detailed explanation follows in part 3 of this chapter). For external action, the EU now has several new instruments at its disposal. They are designed to allow quick reaction and long-term investment in different political and geographical contexts, while maintaining the flexibility necessary in a dynamic global environment. These instruments will consequently see resources increase: by 2013, overall external relations expenditure under the financial framework will have increased by 29 % in real terms compared to 2006. The rate of increase for the common foreign and security policy over the same period is 245 %, for pre-accession assistance 52 %, for the neighbourhood policy and Russia 35 % and for development cooperation, economic cooperation and human rights policy 25 %. Nevertheless, the adequacy of the level of funding available for EU external relations in the light of its ambitious objectives remains a point of contention.

2.7. Heading 5 – Administration

Administrative expenditure for all institutions accounts for 5.8 % of the overall EU budget, covering expenditure on active and retired staff, buildings, offices, equipments, furniture, European schools, missions or conference and meeting costs. Of these appropriations 47 % are being spent on the Commission, 37 % on the other institutions and bodies (e.g. European Parliament, Council, etc) and the rest on Pensions and European Schools. The ceiling for administrative expenditure has been increased by 17 % in real terms between the last year of the previous financial framework (2006) and 2013.

Enlargement from 15 to 27 Member States, including the increase from 11 official languages in 2003 to 23 in 2007, the overall evolution of the Commission's responsibilities and the management of a larger spending volume over the period 2007-13 have been important factors influencing the workload and staffing requirements of the institutions.

The Commission has made considerable efforts in the follow-up to its 2000 proposals on administrative modernisation to focus on core activities and priorities and rationalise working methods. Since 2002, all needs with the exception of enlargement-related requirements have been covered by redeployments freed by efficiency gains. Between 2003 and 2007, excluding enlargement, the actual number of staff effectively declined. In its most recent report on planning and optimising Commission human resources to serve EU priorities([1]), the Commission committed itself to serving the priorities identified up to 2013 under constant human resources and to striving for a stronger concentration of resources on operational activities in priority policy areas.

In the annual budget, the Commission's administrative resources are largely included in the appropriations for each policy area. This provides a comprehensive view of the costs of the different EU policies and reflects the objective of matching resources to political priorities. Global amount 2007-13: EUR 56.2 billion.

2.8. Heading 6 – Compensation

Heading 6 (Compensation) is temporary and includes some compensation amounts related to the enlargement of the Union. Compensations, provided for in the accession treaties, ensure that new Member States retain a positive budgetary balance during the first three years of accession. For Bulgaria (resp. Romania), these compensations were fixed at EUR 130 million (resp. EUR 315 million) in 2007, EUR 64 million (resp. EUR 143 million) in 2008 and EUR 65 million (resp. EUR 145 million) in 2009, that is a total of EUR 862 million over 2007-09. Bulgaria and Romania will no longer receive compensations as of 2010. The 10 Member States that acceded in 2004, which received compensations over 2004-06, no longer receive compensations as of 2007.

---

[1]	See 'Planning and optimising Commission human resources to serve EU priorities', SEC(2007) 530 of 24.4.2007.

GRAPH 13.2

Long-term evolution of the financial framework (% of GNI and billion EUR)

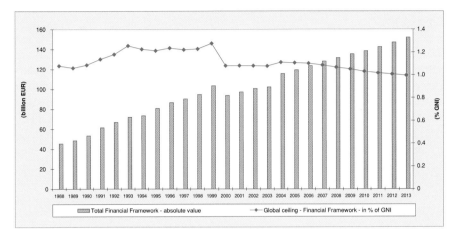

3. Other instruments outside the financial framework

Flexibility of the financial framework is enhanced by a number of instruments which are globally set outside the financial framework. The mechanisms concerned are the Emergency Aid Reserve, the EU Solidarity Fund, the Flexibility Instrument and the European Globalisation Adjustment Fund. However, the IIA lays down their management rules and mobilisation procedure.

The Emergency Aid Reserve is intended to allow a rapid response to the specific aid requirements of third countries following events which could not be foreseen when the budget was drawn up, first and foremost for humanitarian operations, but also for civil crisis management and protection where circumstances so require. The annual reserve is set at EUR 221 million.

The EU Solidarity Fund provides rapid financial assistance in the event of major disasters occurring on the territory of a Member State or of a candidate country. Payments made by this fund are implemented under the responsibility of the beneficiary state to restore basic infrastructures, pay for emergency services, provisional housing and clean-up operations, or to protect the population against imminent health threats. The amount available annually for extraordinary regional disasters is 7.5 % of the EUSF's annual budget (or EUR 75 million). Global amount 2007-13: EUR 7 billion.

The Flexibility Instrument: the resources available for external action have in the past often proved insufficient to adequately react to the rapidly changing and volatile policy environment. This situation has repeatedly led to the mobilisation of the flexibility instrument. This instrument is intended to allow the financing, for a given financial year and up to the amount of EUR 200 million, of clearly identified expenditure which could not be financed within the ceilings available for one or more headings.

The European Globalisation Adjustment Fund: the funding provided under this title is intended to provide additional support for workers who suffer from the consequences of major structural changes in world trade patterns, to assist them with their reintegration into the labour market. The maximum annual amount available under this fund is EUR 500 million.

4. Bodies with legal personality set up by the Commission

The 'bodies' set up by the Communities are also called 'decentralised bodies', 'traditional agencies' or 'regulatory agencies'.

They are independent bodies, with their own legal personality and their own legal base – so all have been set up on the basis of a Commission proposal, adopted by the Council or by Council and Parliament. Their legal basis defines their mandate and structure, and the Commission's role in their work – but always with the agency working at arm's length from the Commission.

They include different types of bodies: they were created to meet specific needs on a case-by-case basis over a period spanning more than 30 years of EC/EU history (the eldest were created in 1975, the youngest in 2007; most of them started up in two waves following the Brussels Councils of October 1993 and October 2003).

The first regulatory agencies, Cedefop (Vocational training) and Eurofound (Improvement of living and working conditions), were created in 1975. During the 1990s, the deepening of the internal market led to a series of new agencies with roles more focused on tasks of a technical and/or scientific nature, such as authorisation of plant varieties and medicines. Extra tasks – and perhaps also the wish to see agencies spread around the EU – led to further waves of agencies.

Decentralised bodies exert a wide range of functions: undertaking strategic or applied studies, monitoring developments, networking and pooling good practice, self-regulation and co-regulation, policy and regulatory recommendations, and referral to scientific authority. Frequently they represent a pooling at EU level – with a view to achieving greater effectiveness – of competences formerly exercised by Member States' departments in areas of shared competence, rather than performing tasks previously carried out by Commission departments. Grants to decentralised agencies are financed from appropriations in the relevant expenditure headings under the relevant Policy Area(s).

The EU budget contributes to the funding of the decentralised agencies by granting a subsidy to their individual budgets. The extent to which their budgets depend on the EU subsidy varies considerably: two are financially independent from EU grants, while others rely totally on them.

The 2007 budget provided for 25 regulatory agencies [1]. Two of these are 'third pillar' agencies dealing with issues under freedom, security and justice.

According to the establishment plans these regulatory agencies employ some 3 495 staff, with an annual budget of around EUR 852.7 million, of which Community contributions amount to EUR 441.8 million [2].

---

[1] There exists another group of agencies not financed under the EU budget, which fall under the second (foreign and security policy) and third (police and judicial cooperation in criminal matters) pillars of the Treaty on the European Union. The second-pillar agencies are the European Institute for Security Studies, located in Paris (France), European Union Satellite Centre, located in Torrejón de Ardoz (Spain), and European Defence Agency, located in Brussels (Belgium). The third-pillar agency not entered in or financed by the Community budget is the European Police Office (Europol), located in The Hague (the Netherlands).

[2] Figures for first and second-pillar agencies only.

The agencies vary widely in size, from 20 people in the case of the Gender Institute to over 647 in the case of OHIM (Community trademarks). Most of the agencies are financed entirely from the EU budget but four are mainly or entirely self-financed (¹).

Heading 1A covers 12 agencies with total revenues estimated at EUR 575.0 million, of which Community contributions amount to EUR 217.8 million. Heading 2 covers three agencies with total revenues estimated at EUR 51.9 million, of which Community contributions amount to EUR 34.0 million. Heading 3A covers five agencies with total revenues estimated at EUR 87.8 million, of which Community contributions amount to EUR 86.8 million. Heading 3B covers two agencies with total revenues estimated at EUR 83.5 million; this amount is equal to Community contributions. Heading 4 covers two agencies with total revenues estimated at EUR 19.7 million; this amount is equal to Community contributions (²). Heading 5 covers one agency with revenues estimated at EUR 34.7 million and no contribution from the EU budget.

As decentralised bodies, the agencies publish their budgets separately in the EU Official Journal under their own responsibility. However, the EU budget also includes extensive information on their budget parameters: the authorised EU subsidy to their respective budgets, an estimate of each body's own budget and their authorised establishment plans.

(¹)   EMEA, OHIM, CVPO, all of which are able to charge fees, and the Translation Centre for the Bodies of the European Union, which receives financial contributions from its clients (the other agencies in particular).

(²)   The Heading 4 amount does not include the budget for the European Agency for Reconstruction. In 2007 this agency was already being phased out and no contribution was provided for in the EU budget.

Part 5

IMPLEMENTATION AND EXTERNAL CONTROL

Chapter 14

Implementation of the budget

1. Assignment of implementing powers

1.1. The role of the Commission

1) Principle: Commission responsibility

Under Article 274 of the EC Treaty:

'The Commission shall implement the budget, in accordance with the provisions of the regulations made pursuant to Article 279, on its own responsibility and within the limits of the appropriations, having regard to the principles of sound financial management. Member States shall cooperate with the Commission to ensure that the appropriations are used in accordance with the principles of sound financial management.'

2) Application of the principle

The way in which this principle is applied is determined by the provisions laid down in Articles 48 to 52, 56, 57 and 59 of the 2003 Financial Regulation (¹), which are more detailed and explicit than in the previous 1977 Financial Regulation.

(¹)   Council Regulation (EC, Euratom) No 1605/2002 of 25 June 2002 (OJ L 248, 16.9.2002,
        p. 1) on the Financial Regulation applicable to the general budget of the European Com-
        munities entered into force on 1 January 2003. It was last amended by Council Regula-
        tion (EC, Euratom) No 1995/2006 of 13 December 2006 (OJ L 390, 30.12.2006, p. 1),
        which entered into force for the majority of its provisions on 1 May 2007.

(a) Prior adoption of a basic act

The Financial Regulation requires a legal basis separate from the budget for the implementation of appropriations for any action, with the exception of certain cases defined in the Financial Regulation (pilot schemes, preparatory actions, etc). The notion of 'basic act' is defined in Article 49 of the Financial Regulation.

(b) Delegation of implementing powers

The Financial Regulation provides for delegation of the budgetary implementation powers of the institutions in accordance with the conditions they lay down in their internal rules and within the limits of the act of delegation.

The Financial Regulation clarifies the conditions under which the Commission may delegate powers [1]: the Commission may not delegate to third parties the implementing powers it enjoys under the Treaties where they involve a large measure of discretion implying political choices. Within these limits, the Commission may delegate tasks of public authority, and in particular budget implementation tasks, to certain entities (see point 2.1 below); in any case, the implementing tasks delegated must be clearly defined and fully supervised as to the use made of them.

As a general rule, the Commission may not entrust measures for the implementation of funds deriving from the budget, including payment and recovery, to external private-sector entities unless they have a public service mission. Only technical expertise tasks and administrative, preparatory or ancillary tasks involving neither the exercise of public authority nor the use of discretionary powers of judgment can be entrusted, by contract, to external private-sector entities.

1.2. Limits to the Commission's implementing powers

1) Principle of institutional autonomy

Under Article 50 of the Financial Regulation, the Commission's implementing powers do not extend to the sections of the budget relating to the other institutions, given the principle of institutional autonomy on budgetary

---

[1]   See Section 2.

matters: each institution exercises the requisite powers for the implementation of these sections, in accordance with the Financial Regulation.

2) Committee procedures

The existence of management committees set up by various regulations represents a further, more political restriction.

(a) The first management committees

These committees, consisting of national experts appointed by the Member States, are intended to help the Commission with its implementation tasks; in practice, they often reduce the Commission's implementing powers.

Such committees were set up in the earliest days of the Community. For instance, Article 124 of the Treaty of Rome stipulates that 'the (European Social) Fund shall be administered by the Commission', but that 'the Commission shall be assisted in this task by a committee'. This committee has a purely advisory role and if the Commission does not wish to follow its opinions, it has only to inform it of this within six weeks.

In the case of the committees associated with the common agricultural policy, the Commission must, if it wishes to go against a committee's opinion, first inform the Council, which has one month in which to take a decision.

On the other hand, the European Development Fund (EDF) Committee, set up for the implementation of the revised Cotonou Agreement, is more restrictive of the Commission's powers: the Commission must ask the EDF Committee's opinion for the adoption of programming and implementation decisions regarding national, regional or intra-ACP strategies, as well as for their modification where this involves more than 20 % of the initial amount or more than EUR 10 million. If the Committee's opinion differs from the Commission proposal, the matter is then brought to the Council, which can adopt a different decision.

(b) The Council's desire for control

The EC Treaty provides that:

— 'the Council shall confer on the Commission in the acts which the Council adopts, powers for the implementation of the rules which the

Council lays down. The Council may impose certain requirements in respect of the exercise of these powers. The Council may also reserve the right, in specific cases, to exercise directly implementing powers itself. The procedures referred to above must be consonant with the principles and rules to be laid down in advance by the Council, acting unanimously on a proposal from the Commission and after obtaining the opinion of the European Parliament.' (Article 202)

— 'the Commission shall ... exercise the powers conferred on it by the Council for the implementation of the rules laid down by the latter.' (Article 211)

On the strength of these provisions, the Council has sought to control the manner in which the Commission implements the budget, by setting up management committees to take part in the implementation procedure. The existence and operation of these committees have been the source of many conflicts between the Council, on the one hand, and the Parliament and Commission, on the other, which would prefer to confine the committees to an advisory role.

After the Single Act had strengthened the Commission's implementing powers, Council Decision 87/373/EEC of 13 July 1987 (the original Comitology Decision) laid down the main types of committee. This decision was replaced by Decision 1999/468/EC of 28 June 1999 [1]. The implementation of this decision is still a regular source of contention, in particular on the part of the European Parliament, which sees the existence of any committees other than advisory ones as an obstacle to the sound management of the Community budget. This Decision was amended by Decision 2006/512/EC of 17 July 2006 [2] in order to create a new procedure, the regulatory procedure with scrutiny, and in order to ensure that the European Parliament receives better information on the work of the committees.

(c) The committees provided for in the Comitology Decision

This decision provides for the following four procedures.

— *The advisory procedure*, at the end of which the Commission must take the utmost account of the opinion delivered by the committee (but is not bound by it), and informs the committee of the manner in which the opinion has been taken into account.

---

[1]   OJ L 269, 29.10.1999, p. 45.
[2]   OJ L 200, 22.07.2006, p. 11.

— *The management procedure*, at the end of which the Commission adopts measures that apply immediately. However, if these measures are not in accordance with the opinion of the committee, they are communicated to the Council, which may take a different decision within a period laid down in the basic instrument, but which may not exceed three months. The Commission may defer application of the measures decided.

— *The regulatory procedure*, at the end of which the Commission adopts the measures envisaged if they are in accordance with the opinion of the committee, or, if the measures are not in accordance with the opinion of the committee or if no opinion is delivered, submits a proposal to the Council on the measures to be taken. The Council acts by a qualified majority on this proposal within a period laid down in the basic instrument, but which may not exceed three months. Where the basic instrument has been adopted by the co-decision procedure, the European Parliament may inform the Council of its position if it feels that the measures proposed exceed the Commission's implementing powers as provided for in the basic instrument. The Council may, but need not, take account of Parliament's position. If the Council opposes the Commission's proposal, the Commission may present an amended proposal, resubmit its proposal or present a legislative proposal based on the Treaty. If the Council has not taken a position upon expiry of the period allowed, the Commission takes the implementing measures.

— *The regulatory procedure with scrutiny*, at the end of which the Commission adopts the measures proposed only if they are in accordance with the opinion of the committee, and if the legislative authority does not oppose them. Whatever the position of the committee regarding the measures proposed by the Commission, the legislative authority is fully involved, and required to react.

The 1999 Decision also provides that the choice of procedure in the basic instrument is guided by the following criteria.

— *The management procedure* applies in respect of the common agricultural and common fisheries policies and for the implementation of programmes with substantial budgetary implications.

— *The regulatory procedure* applies in respect of the essential provisions of basic instruments (including measures concerning the protection of the health or safety of humans, animals and plants) and for the adaptation or updating of non-essential provisions of the basic instrument, where that instrument provides for such adaptation or updating.

— *The advisory procedure* applies 'in any case in which it is considered to be the most appropriate'.

— *The regulatory procedure with scrutiny* applies for measures of general scope designed to amend non-essential elements of a basic instrument adopted in accordance with the procedure referred to in Article 251 of the Treaty, including by deleting some of those elements or by supplementing the instrument by the addition of new non-essential elements.

Since 1999, the basic instruments providing for the establishment of a committee have been renewed, and now comply with these criteria. It is worth noting that a given committee may apply more than one of the procedures provided for in the Decision, depending on the type of measures presented by the Commission.

It should also be noted that Parliament was given some say in the operation of these committees for the first time in 1999, at least for committees applying the regulatory procedure and where the basic instrument was adopted by the co-decision procedure (in which Parliament carries the same weight as the Council). However, Parliament's involvement concerns compliance with this basic instrument, not the substance of the measures proposed. The 2006 Decision has reinforced the powers of the legislative authority, especially the Parliament.

3) Non-centralised implementation of the budget

The extent of the Commission's powers in the field of budget implementation is also limited by the fact that the Commission manages only a very small part of the budget directly. The 2003 Financial Regulation takes full account of this fact in defining the different methods for the management of the Community budget, spelling out their characteristics and establishing the criteria and conditions under which they are to be used.

(a) Expenditure

The bulk of budget funds are spent either by virtue of powers delegated or assigned to Member States, through economic organisations, agencies or national authorities (common agricultural policy, Structural Funds), or in conjunction with third countries (external action). However, some budget implementing tasks are directly delegated to national or international entities, under different modes of management.

(b) Revenue

Responsibility for the collection of own resources, which make up the bulk of revenue, is delegated to the national authorities. The rules are laid down in the own resources decision and the implementing regulation (see Section 3 of this chapter).

Under Article 256 of the EC Treaty, Council or Commission decisions which impose a pecuniary obligation on persons other than States are enforceable.

Enforcement is governed by the rules of civil procedure in force in the State in whose territory it is carried out. The enforcement order is attached to the decision, without any formality other than verification of the authenticity of the decision by the national authority designated by the government of each Member State for this purpose and notified to the Commission and the Court of Justice.

When these formalities have been completed upon application by the party concerned, that party may proceed to enforcement in accordance with the national law by bringing the matter directly before the competent authority.

Enforcement may be suspended only by a decision of the Court of Justice. However, the courts of the country concerned have jurisdiction over complaints that enforcement is being carried out in an irregular manner.

2. Implementation of expenditure

2.1. The principles governing the various management methods

These principles were reviewed in the financial reform undertaken by the Commission in 2000. A particular aim was to provide a clearer definition of the various methods of management involving partners outside the Commission.

1) Three different types of management

Enlargement of the European Union, the growing volume of amounts to administer and, in particular, the gradual extension of the Commission's tasks as Community policies have developed have prompted the Commission to adopt a variety of management methods. The Financial Regulation provides for three types of management:

— shared or decentralised;

— joint;

— centralised.

(a) Shared and decentralised management

Shared management receives only partial recognition in the Treaty, which provides that 'the Commission shall implement the budget ... on its own responsibility', although it adds that 'Member States shall cooperate with the Commission to ensure that the appropriations are used in accordance with the principles of sound financial management' (Article 274 EC). Discharge is granted to the Commission alone (Article 276 EC).

Although shared management has been a long-established practice, it was governed for a long time only by rules laid down in secondary legislation which stipulate, for each sector, the respective roles of the Commission and the national authorities[1]. The same applied to management decentralised to non-member countries[2], where the respective roles of the Commission and the beneficiary countries and the various types of

---

[1] The obligation on Member States to supply the Commission with information, the Commission's powers of control and the clearance of accounts procedure in the common agricultural policy are laid down in Council Regulation (EC) No 1290/2005 of 21 June 2005 on the financing of the common agricultural policy (OJ L 209, 11.8.2005, p. 1). For the Structural Funds the relevant provisions are those in Council Regulation (EC) No 1083/2006 of 11 July 2006 laying down general provisions on the European Regional Development Fund, the European Social Fund and the Cohesion Fund (OJ L 210, 31.7.2006, p. 25).

[2] See in particular the provisions of Council Regulation (EC) No 1085/2006 of 17 July 2006 establishing an Instrument for Pre-Accession Assistance (IPA) (OJ L 210, 31.7.2006, p. 82) and those of Commission Regulation (EC) No 718/2007 of 12 June 2007 implementing Council Regulation (EC) No 1085/2006 establishing an Instrument for Pre-Accession Assistance (OJ L 170, 29.6.2007, p. 1).

control applicable depend on the agreements signed by the Commission and these countries.

Management shared with Member States now applies to the bulk of the budget: the EAGGF Guarantee Section and the Structural Funds. It is understood to refer to 'the management of those Community programmes where the Commission and the Member States have distinct administrative tasks which are interdependent and set down in legislation and where both the Commission and the national administrations need to discharge their respective tasks for the Community policy to be implemented successfully' (¹). This expenditure, which is financed in full or in part by the EU budget, is handled by the Member States in accordance with the Community rules via national structures. A check is conducted to establish the eligibility of such expenditure. It is also audited by the Court of Auditors. Some expenditure is also managed in a similar way, in particular under pre-accession programmes, by non-member countries. This is known as decentralised management.

The relevant provisions of the Financial Regulation (Articles 53b and 53c) determine, without prejudice to complementary provisions in relevant sector-specific regulations, the main principles applicable to shared and decentralised management:

— the responsibilities of the Member States and third countries, which are required to take all the legislative, regulatory and administrative or other measures necessary for protecting the Communities' financial interests;

— the setting up by the Member States and third countries of an effective and efficient internal control system, and presentation by the Member States of an annual summary of the available audits and declarations;

— the clearance of accounts and financial corrections, for the Member States and third countries.

These provisions are in line with the EC Treaty, which, since the Treaty of Amsterdam, imposes obligations on Member States for the implemen-

---

(¹)   The definition given by the Committee of Independent Experts in its second report.

tation of the budget: cooperation with the Commission to ensure sound financial management (Article 274) and combating fraud (Article 280).

(b) Joint management

Joint management is the implementation of the budget by an international organisation in the following cases:

— wherever the Commission and the international organisation are bound by a long-term framework agreement laying down the administrative and financial arrangements for their cooperation;

— wherever the Commission and the international organisation elaborate a joint project or programme;

— where the funds of several donors are pooled and are not earmarked for specific items or categories of expenditure, that is to say, in the case of multi-donor actions.

(c) Centralised management

Finally, the Commission may implement the budget on a centralised basis, which means that implementation is handled:

— directly by its departments (implementation tasks performed by the financial actors as explained in point 2.2 below); in this case the Commission and its departments perform the operations required to carry out the measures concerned without any involvement of the Member States or non-member countries where the recipients of the expenditure reside; this method of management concerns the administrative appropriations and some operational appropriations (mainly for the internal policies under heading 3 of the multiannual financial framework 2007-13 and some external actions);

— or indirectly, by various entities to which such tasks have been entrusted.

This last form, further developed and refined as part of the reform of the Commission, needs further detailed explanation.

2) Indirect centralised management and externalisation

(a) Concept of externalisation

The multiplication and diversification of the management tasks of the Commission, along with the impossibility to expand indefinitely the number of officials, has justified the recourse to an externalisation policy.

Up to the end of the 1990s, externalisation also took the form of technical assistance offices (TAOs), i.e. private-law bodies entrusted with technical tasks or the management of large numbers of minor operations, including payments to recipients. This form of externalisation was criticised on two grounds: because tasks involving public service missions were performed by private bodies, including tasks involving budget implementation, and also because the Commission's control mechanisms were inadequate.

The reform of the Commission offered an opportunity to develop and refine this concept of externalisation, understood as the delegation of tasks, in whole or in part, to entities outside the Commission.

First, the 2003 Financial Regulation provides for strict limits on externalisation by subcontracting, specifying that the implementation of funds deriving from the budget, including payment and recovery, may not be entrusted to external private-sector entities or bodies.

Secondly, the Financial Regulation defines the different categories of entities to which the implementation of tasks, especially budgetary tasks, may be delegated.

The first criterion to be met is that the delegation of budget implementation tasks must comply with the principle of sound financial management. This obligation requires effective and efficient internal control and compliance with the principles of non-discrimination and the transparency of Community action. No implementing tasks delegated in this way may give rise to conflicts of interests.

Externalised management today applies, in a variety of forms, to a large number of programmes.

(b) Entities to which the implementation of the budget may be externalised

— First of all, a new category of entities acting on behalf of the Commission has been created: the executive agencies, intended to replace the TAOs. Executive agencies are legal persons under Community law, created by Commission Decision, to which powers may be delegated to implement all or part of a Community programme or project on behalf of the Commission and under its responsibility in accordance with a statute adopted by the Council (¹) (²). The originality of the executive agency concept lies in the combination of the autonomy of the agency (with a legal personality), which allows more flexible management, and supervision by the Commission (of the Steering Committee and the performance of the tasks), which guarantees the protection of Community interests.

The specific feature of these executive agencies is that they are considered to be authorising officers for the Community budget: the director of each agency implements directly the operational appropriations in the Community budget for the programmes or projects the management of which has been entrusted to the agency, in accordance with the rules of the Financial Regulation.

— Secondly, existing bodies already set up by the Communities (³), and other specialised Community bodies such as the European Investment Bank or the European Investment Fund, may be entrusted with the management of Community funds, provided that this is compatible with the tasks of each body as defined in the basic act in question. Unlike with the executive agencies, funds are transferred globally to these bodies for the implementation of their tasks.

— Thirdly, 'national agencies', i.e. national public-sector bodies or bodies governed by private law with a public-service mission which pro-

---

(¹)   Regulation (EC) No 58/2003 of 19 December 2002.

(²)   OJ L 11, 16.1.2003, p. 1.

(³)   Almost 30 Community agencies managing a wide range of activities are potentially concerned. These agencies are engaged in a Community activity on behalf of the European Union, but under specific arrangements adapted to the features of this activity: they have legal personality and their own budget, separate from the general budget of the Communities, even though in many cases all or part of the revenue comes from a subsidy paid from the general budget.

vide adequate financial guarantees and comply with the conditions provided for in the implementing rules, may be designated:

— by the Member State or the country concerned in accordance with the provisions of the relevant basic act in the case of management by a network, requiring the designation of at least one body or entity by the Member State or country concerned;

— by the Commission in all other cases, in agreement with the Member States or countries concerned.

This management method had already been used in certain sectors (education and culture), and has now been extended since its inclusion in the Financial Regulation.

— Fourthly, a new possibility of delegation was added in the triennial revision of the Financial Regulation in December 2006, to allow the delegation of tasks to persons entrusted with the implementation of specific actions pursuant to Title V of the Treaty on European Union, and identified in the relevant basic act within the meaning of Article 49 of the Regulation. These persons are designated by the Council.

2.2. Roles of the various actors

Expenditure operations are governed by a set of technical rules for using appropriations which are contained in the Financial Regulation and its Implementing Rules([1]). The management reform put in place since 2003 has been designed to enhance the responsibility of authorising officers, under the supervision of the internal audit service, and to do away with centralised *ex ante* controls.

([1])   Commission Regulation (EC, Euratom) No 2342/2002 of 23 December 2002 (OJ L 357, 31.12.2002, p. 1) laying down detailed rules for the implementation of Council Regulation (EC, Euratom) No 1605/2002 on the Financial Regulation applicable to the general budget of the European Communities, as last amended by Commission Regulation (EC, Euratom) No 478/2007 of 23 April 2007 (OJ L 111, 28.4.2007, p. 13).

1) Separation of duties

The budget is implemented by the two actors referred to in Article 279 of the Treaty: the authorising officer and the accounting officer. Their tasks and responsibilities are set out in the Financial Regulation.

The financial controller referred to in Article 279 of the Treaty no longer exists and has been replaced by the internal auditor. The internal auditor is not an actor involved in financial operations and does not exercise control over these operations, which are under the full responsibility of the authorising officers, who now assume complete responsibility for such decisions. The internal auditor performs his or her duties in accordance with international audit standards. His/her role is to verify the proper functioning of the management and control systems put in place by the authorising officers.

The principle of the segregation of duties is clearly stated in Article 58 of the Financial Regulation, as the basic rule for the implementation of the budget.

(a) Role of the authorising officer

The institution performs the duties of authorising officer, but may delegate these duties to staff. The scope of the powers delegated and the possibility for persons to whom these powers are delegated to subdelegate them are laid down in the internal administrative rules of the institution.

The authorising officers are now responsible for the entire management process, from determining the measures deemed necessary to meet the targets set by the institution to the production of results and the evaluation of these results.

To this end, authorising officers should themselves, more so and more effectively than before, perform a whole series of control functions within their departments. They must therefore put in place the appropriate organisational structures (internal management and control systems) and equip their departments with practical instruments and tools satisfying minimum standards in terms of rules and effectiveness, control lists, etc. Authorising officers should also be able to benefit at all times from advice given by horizontal departments. For this reason, a central financial service has been set up within Budget DG.

The tasks of authorising officers by delegation are to implement revenue and expenditure in accordance with the principles of sound financial management and to ensure that the requirements of legality and regularity are complied with. To do so, they:

— make budgetary commitments and legal commitments that bind the institution to third parties;

— validate expenditure and authorise payments;

— undertake the preliminaries for the implementation of appropriations;

— establish entitlements to be recovered and issue recovery orders.

Authorising officers by delegation report to their institution on the performance of their duties in the form of an annual activity report together with financial and management information, confirming that the information contained in the report presents a true and fair view except as otherwise specified in any reservations regarding certain areas of revenue and expenditure. The report sets out the results of the operations performed with reference to the objectives set, the risks associated with these operations, the use made of the resources provided, and the efficiency and effectiveness of the internal control system. The internal auditor takes note of the annual report and any other items of information supplied. No later than 15 June of every year, the Commission sends to the budgetary authority a summary of the annual reports for the previous year.

In the performance of their duties, authorising officers have to apply the principles of legality, regularity and sound financial management, and to set up and maintain local management systems to ensure compliance with these principles and the quality of the financial information relating to these operations.

In compliance with the minimum standards adopted by each institution and having due regard to the risks associated with the management environment and the nature of the actions financed, they must put in place the organisational structure and the internal management and control procedures suited to the performance of their duties, including where appropriate *ex post* verifications. Before an operation is authorised, the operational and financial aspects have to be verified by members of staff other than the person who initiated the operation. The initiation and the *ex ante* and *ex post* verification of an operation must be separate functions. These responsibilities have been reinforced since the financial controller no longer exists following the 2003 Financial Regulation.

(b) Role of the accounting officer

In each institution, the accounting officer is responsible for:

— proper implementation of payments, collection of revenue and recovery of amounts established as being receivable;

— keeping the accounts; preparing and presenting the accounts;

— laying down the accounting rules and methods and the chart of accounts;

— laying down and validating the accounting systems and, where appropriate, validating systems put in place by the authorising officer to supply or justify accounting information, whereby the accounting officer is empowered to verify compliance with validation criteria;

— treasury management.

The 2003 Financial Regulation has enhanced the powers of the accounting officer in relation to the authorising officer at the level of accounting rules and the supply of accounting information. Authorising officers will, for example, be formally required to supply whatever information the accounting officer requests in specific cases.

To ensure harmonisation, the Commission accounting officer has to lay down accounting standards (accounting and consolidation methods) to apply to the accounts of all the institutions. It is also the duty of the Commission accounting officer, in the presentation of the accounts process, to consolidate the financial statements prepared by each institution.

Finally, following the triennial revision of the Financial Regulation, the role of the accounting officer has been further extended: before the adoption of the accounts by the institution, the accounting officer has to sign them off, thereby certifying that (s)he has a reasonable assurance that the accounts present a true and fair view of the financial situation of the institution.

For that purpose, the accounting officer must satisfy him/herself that the accounts have been prepared in accordance with the accounting rules, methods and accounting systems established under his/her responsibility as laid down in the Financial Regulation for the accounts of his or her institution, and that all revenue and expenditure is entered in the accounts. For that purpose, the accounting officer is empowered to check the information received as well as to carry out any further checks (s)he deems necessary in order to sign off the accounts.

(c) Role of the internal auditor

At central level, an internal auditor is required to supply the institution, in accordance with international standards, with an assurance concerning the sound operation of budget implementation systems and procedures. This auditor is responsible for evaluating the effectiveness and efficiency of internal control and management systems put in place by authorising officers. In order to be able to work effectively, the internal auditor must have a strong and independent position within the institution, in accordance with the principle of the separation of duties. His or her independence is guaranteed by the Financial Regulation.

Unlike the financial controller, the internal auditor is not involved in the implementation of the budget and is not therefore a financial actor.

An audit progress committee has the task of ensuring that Commission departments take appropriate action to improve internal control systems in response to the Internal Audit Service's recommendations. This committee is chaired by the commissioner with responsibility for the budget, with the head of the Internal Audit Service as vice-chair. The committee has three other members: two commissioners designated by the institution and an outside person with the necessary experience and qualifications in internal audit and business management.

2) Liability

(a) General principles

The responsibilities of authorising officers or the accounting officer may be withdrawn at any time temporarily or definitively by the authority that appointed them.

Following the reform, there are no longer any special rules of liability in financial matters. The staff regulations, themselves to be revised, will apply, with the general rule that officials are liable to disciplinary action for any negligence on their part and may be required to pay compensation in cases of serious misconduct.

For the first time, the 2003 Financial Regulation prohibits any conflict of interests and defines the concept, which applies not only to the financial actors but to every person involved in budget implementation.

Finally, the Financial Regulation provides for cases where financial actors carry liability.

(b) Authorising officers

The obligation to pay compensation applies in particular:

— if the authorising officer determines entitlements to be recovered or issues recovery orders, commits expenditure or signs a payment order without complying with the Financial Regulation and its Implementing Rules;

— if the authorising officer omits to draw up a document establishing an amount receivable, neglects to issue a recovery order or is late in issuing it, or is late in issuing a payment order, thereby rendering the institution liable to civil action by third parties.

Each institution is to set up a specialised financial irregularities panel or participate in a joint panel established by several institutions, the role of which should be to determine whether a financial irregularity has occurred and what the consequences, if any, should be. On the basis of the opinion of this panel, the institution decides whether to initiate proceedings leading to disciplinary action or to payment of compensation. In addition, if the panel detects systemic problems, it is to send a report with recommendations.

(c) Accounting officer

For the accounting officer, any of the following forms of misconduct may render him or her liable to disciplinary action and payment of compensation:

— (s)he loses or damages monies, assets and documents in his/her keeping;

— (s)he wrongly alters bank accounts or postal giro accounts;

— (s)he recovers or pays amounts that are not in conformity with the corresponding recovery or payment orders;

— (s)he fails to collect revenue due.

3) OLAF

(a) The role of OLAF

In order to step up the fight against fraud, the Commission replaced the Task Force for the Coordination of the Fight against Fraud (UCLAF) in the Secretariat-General, which was set up in 1988, by a new department, OLAF (French acronym for the European Anti-Fraud Office)[1]. OLAF began operating on 1 June 1999, and the institutions have granted it independence in its investigation function[2]. OLAF continues to be a Commission department under the authority of the Commissioner with responsibility for the budget. Given its special independence in its investigation function, however, it is subject to scrutiny by a supervisory committee made up of five independent persons from outside the Community institutions, qualified in the fight against fraud.

In order to coordinate Member States' action in combating fraud against the Communities' interests, OLAF organises close and regular cooperation between the relevant national authorities.

Outside the Community institutions, OLAF exercises the investigation powers conferred by the Regulation on checks and inspections in Member States for the protection of the Communities' financial interests against

---

[1]   1999/352/EC, ECSC, Euratom: Commission decision of 28 April 1999 establishing the European Anti-Fraud Office (OLAF) (OJ L 136, 31.5.1999, p. 20).

[2]   Regulation (EC) No 1073/1999 of the European Parliament and of the Council of 25 May 1999 and Council Regulation (Euratom) No 1074/1999 of 25 May 1999 concerning investigations conducted by OLAF.

fraud and other irregularities(¹) and performs the checks and inspections provided for by the Regulation on the protection of the European Communities' financial interests(²). Where cooperation agreements exist, OLAF may also carry out such checks and inspections in non-member countries and on the premises of business operators(³).

Within the institutions, OLAF may conduct administrative investigations into any activities of departments of Community institutions and bodies which could be detrimental to the Communities' financial interests(⁴).

(b) New developments

The Commission reform puts the accent on preventing fraud as far upstream as possible.

The action proposed in the Reform White Paper concerning 'Fraud-proofing of legislation and contract management' requires Commission departments, before proposing new legislation with a potential impact on the Community budget, to submit proposals to OLAF for a risk assessment. Similarly, OLAF must advise all the institution's departments on fraud prevention aspects throughout the legislative process and must also advise Budget DG on setting up its central database on contracts and contractors.

(¹) Council Regulation (Euratom, EC) No 2185/96 of 11 November 1996 concerning on-the-spot checks and inspections carried out by the Commission in order to protect the European Communities' financial interests against fraud and other irregularities (OJ L 292, 15.11.1996, p. 2).

(²) Council Regulation (EC, Euratom) No 2988/95 of 18 December 1995 on the protection of the European Communities' financial interests (OJ L 312, 23.12.1995, p. 1).

(³) Council Regulation (Euratom, EC) No 2185/96 of 11 November 1996 concerning on-the-spot checks and inspections carried out by the Commission in order to protect the European Communities' financial interests against fraud and other irregularities (OJ L 292, 15.11.1996, p. 2).

(⁴) 1999/394/EC, Euratom: Council Decision of 25 May 1999 concerning the terms and conditions for internal investigations in relation to the prevention of fraud, corruption and any illegal activity detrimental to the Communities' interests (OJ L 149, 16.6.1999, p. 36); 1999/396/EC, ECSC, Euratom: Commission Decision of 2 June 1999 concerning the terms and conditions for internal investigations in relation to the prevention of fraud, corruption and any illegal activity detrimental to the Community's interests (OJ L 149, 16.6.1999, p. 57).

Any department launching a legislative proposal is thus required to submit drafts of instruments to OLAF if they concern sectors identified as being at risk on the basis of criteria laid down by OLAF and the reports of the Court of Auditors. OLAF is also to be involved in the work of Budget DG in drafting a set of harmonised standard contracts. It will also feed into the central contract and contractors database whatever information comes to its notice.

Various other actions in the White Paper are designed to improve coordination between OLAF and other departments.

2.3. Stages in the expenditure procedure

1) The stages in the expenditure procedure

An expenditure operation is divided into four parts: every item of expenditure has to be committed, validated, authorised and paid.

— *Commitment of expenditure by the authorising officer*: the budgetary commitment is the operation reserving the appropriation necessary to cover subsequent payments to honour a legal commitment[1]. The commitment may be individual (when the beneficiary and the amount are known in advance), global (if one of these elements is still not known), or provisional (for administrative and agriculture expenditure). The definition of the various forms of commitments marks a clear improvement compared with the previous Financial Regulation.

— *Validation of expenditure*: the act whereby the authorising officer verifies the existence of the creditor's entitlement, and determines or verifies the reality and the amount of the sum due and the conditions under which payment is due. Validation is based on supporting documents within the meaning of Article 104 of the Implementing rules of the Financial Regulation attesting the creditor's entitlement, and is confirmed by the signing of a 'passed for payment' voucher by the authorising officer.

---

[1] Confusion has to be avoided with the concept of legal commitment, which is the act whereby the authorising officer enters into or establishes an obligation that results in a charge.

— *Authorisation:* the act whereby the authorising officer, by issuing a payment order after having verified that the appropriations are available, instructs the accounting officer to pay an item of expenditure that he or she has validated.

— *Payment:* the final action whereby the institution is discharged of its obligations towards its creditors; payment is made by the accounting officer within the limits of the funds available. For payment of certain categories of expenditure, imprest accounts may be set up. Payments are divided into four types: payment of the entire amount due; payment of part of the amount due in any of the following ways: pre-financing, which may be divided into a number of payments, one or more interim payments, and payment of the balance of the amount due.

2) Conditions under which expenditure is made

The completion of these different stages is subject to compliance with certain conditions. The main conditions are the following:

— the budget commitment must come before the legal commitment. However, in order to bring the Financial Regulation into line with sectoral provisions authorising the use of annual instalments, the Financial Regulation provides explicitly for the possibility of splitting budget commitments where they relate to operations that will extend over more than one financial year, provided this is allowed by the relevant basic act;

— every payment has to be justified by supporting documents;

— the stages in the expenditure procedure must be completed within certain time limits, whereby creditors paid late are entitled to receive default interest charged to the Community budget.

3. The own resources collection system

Under Article 8 of the Decision on the own resources system, Member States collect own resources in accordance with their national provisions, which must be adapted to Community requirements.

The various categories of own resources (traditional own resources, the resource accruing from VAT and the GNI-based own resource) are assigned to the Communities in order to finance the budget of the European Union.

Member States can be required to make good any shortfall in traditional own resources resulting from deficiencies in the way they manage the collection system.

The detailed rules for making available own resources are spelt out in Regulation (EC, Euratom) No 1150/2000 (¹) implementing the basic own resources decision.

3.1. The procedure for making available own resources

1) Collection

Own resources are collected by the Member States' administrative authorities, acting on behalf of the Community, which does not have its own customs and tax authorities to carry out these tasks.

2) Establishment and entry in the accounts

(a) Establishment of own resources by the Member States

— *Traditional own resources:* In accordance with Article 2 of Regulation (EEC, Euratom) No 1150/2000, these resources are established as soon as the conditions provided for in the customs regulations have been met for the entry of the entitlement in the accounts and the notification of the debtor (for sugar levies, the relevant date is that of the notification provided for in the Community regulations governing the sugar sector).

— *VAT own resources:* Member States inform the Commission of the calculations made under Regulation (EEC, Euratom) No 1553/89 of 29 May 1989 (²).

(¹)   Council Regulation (EC, Euratom) No 1150/2000 of 22 May 2000 implementing Decision 2000/597/EC, Euratom on the system of the Communities' own resources (OJ L 130, 31.5.2000, p. 1), as amended by Regulation (EC, Euratom) No 2028/2004 (OJ L 352, 27.11.2004, p. 1).

(²)   Council Regulation (EEC, Euratom) No 1553/89 of 29 May 1989 on the definitive uniform arrangements for the collection of own resources accruing from value added tax (OJ L 155, 7.6.1989, p. 9).

— *GNI-based own resource:* Member States inform the Commission of the calculations made under Council Directive 89/130/EEC of 13 February 1989 (¹) and Council Regulation (EC, Euratom) No 1287/2003 of 15 July 2003 (²).

(b) Entry of own resources in the accounts

— *Traditional own resources:* All established amounts of traditional own resources must be entered in one or other of the accounts kept by the competent authorities.

— In the ordinary account provided for in Article 6(3)(a) of Regulation (EC, Euratom) No 1150/2000: all amounts recovered or secured and not challenged.

— In the separate account provided for in Article 6(3)(b) of Regulation (EC, Euratom) No 1150/2000: all amounts that have not yet been recovered and for which no security has been provided; amounts for which security has been provided and that have been challenged and might, upon settlement of the disputes, be subject to change may also be entered in this account.

Traditional own resources must be entered in the accounts no later than the first working day after the 19th of the second month following the month in which the entitlements were established.

— VAT resource and GNI-based resource: one-twelfth of the total amount of such resources appearing in the Community budget must be entered in the accounts on the first working day of each month. The balances of VAT and GNI resources are adjusted each year on the first working day of December.

(c) Making resources available to the Commission

Member States make available own resources to the Commission by crediting the amounts of traditional own resources and VAT and GNI-based own resources to an account opened in the name of the Commission with

---

(¹)   Council Directive 89/130/EEC, Euratom of 13 February 1989 on the harmonisation of the compilation of gross national product at market prices (OJ L 49, 21.2.1989, p. 26).

(²)   Council Regulation (EC, Euratom) No 1287/2003 of 15 July 2003 on the harmonisation of gross national income at market prices (OJ L 181, 19.7.2003, p. 1).

their treasury or other appointed body. For traditional own resources payments, however, Member States deduct 25 % in order to cover the collection costs borne by them.

Member States belonging to the Economic and Monetary Union make their own resources payments in euros and other Member States in their national currency. Any delay in making own resources available gives rise to the payment of interest by the Member State concerned.

3.2. System of scrutiny

As resources are collected at national level, it is firstly for the Member States' authorities to put in place an appropriate (internal) control infrastructure. As the Commission is the authorising body for revenue and therefore accountable to the budgetary authority, it must, of course, obtain assurances that the Member States collect own resources in accordance with the Community rules. It may therefore ask to be associated with national inspections and also ask Member States to conduct additional inspections. For traditional own resources, the Commission may, itself and on its own initiative, carry out on-the-spot inspections. For VAT own resources the Commission checks that the national authorities have correctly performed the calculations for determining the amounts.

These controls and inspections are carried out on behalf of the Community by agents authorised by the Commission under Regulation (EC, Euratom) No 1026/1999 of 10 May 1999 [1].

Inspection findings are set out in a report sent to the Member State concerned. This report, together with the Member State's comments, is then considered by the Advisory Committee on Own Resources (ACOR), made up of representatives of the Member States and the Commission (which chairs the meetings and provides secretariat services). This ensures openness, as each Member State is aware of the findings of controls carried out in the other Member States. After discussion in ACOR, the Commission finalises its position and follows up the observations made until the matter is settled.

---

[1]   Council Regulation (EC, Euratom) No 1026/1999 of 10 May 1999 determining the powers and obligations of agents authorised by the Commission to carry out controls and inspections of the Communities' own resources (OJ L 116, 20.5.1999, p. 1).

ACOR can also examine any matters relating to the collection of own resources.

For the control of VAT resources, the Commission draws up a report every three years on the procedures applied in the Member States and on any improvements envisaged. A similar report on the system for collecting traditional own resources is also produced every three years and sent to the budgetary authority.

4. Management of cash resources

The Commission has different types of accounts where its funds are kept and from which its treasury transactions are executed.

4.1. Accounts with Member State treasuries or with national central banks (pursuant to Article 9 of Council Regulation (EC, Euratom) No 1150/2000 on own resources) (¹)

Article 9 of Council Regulation (EC, Euratom) No 1150/2000 requires each Member State to credit own resources to an account opened in the name of the Commission with its treasury or the body it has appointed.

A number of Member States have opened these accounts with their national treasuries while in other cases they have been opened at national central banks.

The national treasuries do not usually operate as banks. Consequently, where 'Article 9' accounts are opened with them, most of the Commission's transfers of funds from these accounts are routed through the national central banks, where the Commission also has accounts.

The 'Article 9' accounts are kept in euros for Member States whose currency is the euro and in national currencies in the other Member States. These accounts serve for collecting own resources and, in several cases,

---

(¹)   Council Regulation (EC, Euratom) No 1150/2000 of 22 May 2000 implementing Decision 94/728/EC, Euratom on the system of the Communities' own resources, as amended by Council Regulation (EC, Euratom) No 2028/2004 of 16 November 2004.

for payments to Member State governments (in particular for the EAGGF and the Structural Funds).

'Article 9' accounts are not interest-bearing but are free of charge (Article 9(1) of Council Regulation (EC, Euratom) No 1150/2000). Article 12(1) of this Regulation requires that the Commission funds be kept on these accounts and be drawn on only to meet budgetary needs.

This means that only funds actually needed for immediate payments are placed on commercial bank accounts (see below). The remainder is kept on the accounts opened with the Member State treasuries and/or national central banks.

Under Article 12(4) of Regulation (EC, Euratom) No 1150/2000, the funds are divided among accounts held in the different Member States in proportion to the estimated budget revenue from each of them.

While the main own resources, i.e. those based on VAT and GNI, are generally credited to the Commission's account in equal monthly instalments, the Commission's payments are not spread evenly over the year. At present, around half of EAGGF payments are made in January and February. As a consequence, additional amounts may have to be called in from the Member States during the first months of each year. This is authorised by Article 10(3) of Regulation (EC, Euratom) No 1150/2000. Depending on the Commission's cash position, Member States may be invited to bring forward by one or two months in the first quarter of a budget year the entry in the Commission account of the VAT resource and/or the GNI-based resource. After the first quarter the monthly entry may not exceed one-twelfth of the VAT and GNI-based resources. These advance payments are calculated each month on the basis of actual cash flow and credited at the same time as the current VAT and GNI resources. An aboveaverage proportion of non-EAGGF payments are usually made in the month of December.

4.2. Accounts with commercial banks

At present there is at least one such account, chosen by open tender, in each Member State, with few exceptions.

These accounts are used for payments to beneficiaries with accounts in the Member State concerned.

They are held in euros and, where still necessary, in national currency and are interest-bearing.

Even with the introduction of the euro, the Commission has, up to now, kept its accounts in each Member State. The main reason for this is that cross-border payments normally attract higher charges than domestic payments. The cash needs of commercial bank accounts are covered by funds transferred from the 'Article 9' accounts in the Member States concerned.

The adoption of SEPA (Single Euro Payments Area) is expected to result, in the course of the next couple of years, in a reduction in the number of accounts held by the Commission with commercial banks for the execution of its payments within the EU.

The Commission's accounts must not go into debit.

Since most Commission payments (with very few exceptions) are made in euros, the majority of currency exchange operations concern the conversion into euros of own resources paid in national currency by the Member States not belonging to the euro zone. All such currency conversions are currently performed, on the instruction of the Commission, by national central banks.

All payments ordered by the Commission's treasury are sent to banks electronically.

The Commission is a member of SWIFT (Society of Worldwide Interbank Financial Telecommunication), has its own SWIFT code, and uses the SWIFT network to communicate with banks.

For transactions with national treasuries, which are not connected to SWIFT, messages in SWIFT format are generated and sent via secured email.

The number of payments executed by the Commission in 2006 was approximately 1.5 million.

Chapter 15

Consolidated annual accounts of the European Union

The annual accounts of the European Communities are drawn up in accordance with Articles 121 to 129 of Council Regulation (EC, Euratom) No 1605/2002 of 25 June 2002. The annual accounts of the European Communities are set out in two volumes:

Volume I   Consolidated financial statements and consolidated reports on implementation of the budget

Volume II   Commission: financial statements and reports on implementation of the budget

Each volume of the annual accounts has two distinct parts: the financial statements (based on accrual accounting rules) and the reports on budget implementation (prepared on a modified cash basis). Volume I represents the consolidated annual accounts of the European Communities including explanatory notes, while Volume II is the same but for the Commission alone, while also providing more details on the implementation of the budget.

A dual accounting system is thus in place in the European Communities so as to produce these two sets of accounts – there is both a general accounting system (based on accrual accounting rules) and a budgetary accounting system (based on cash accounting principles).

The general accounting system and rules framework as well as the financial statements were modernised in 2005 as part of a move to full accrual-based accounting financial statements – more details are given below. No changes were made to the budgetary accounting system, which continues to follow a (modified) cash basis of accounting.

1. Content of the financial statements

The financial statements of the European Communities comprise the following elements:

1.1. Balance sheet

The balance sheet shows the financial position of the European Communities at the end of each year, differentiated between assets and liabilities. Both the assets and liabilities are further differentiated between current and non-current amounts. The difference between total assets and total liabilities is referred to as the 'net assets' of the European Communities.

1.2. Economic Outturn Account

The economic outturn account presents the income and expenditure of the European Communities, on an accrual basis, for a given year. Both income and expenditure are recorded when the income is earned and the expenditure is incurred, rather than simply when the cash is received or paid out.

Income is split on the face of the economic outturn account between own resource and contribution revenue (such as VAT and other Member State contributions) and operating revenue. Operating revenues include such amounts as fines issued, agricultural levies and the recovery of amounts previously paid out.

Expenditure is shown on the face of the economic outturn account under the headings 'Administrative expenses' (such as staff and building costs) and the more significant 'Operating expenses'. Information is given on the split of operating expenses between the different types of management.

Finally, information is also presented in a 'segment' report, which provides a breakdown of operating revenues and expenses by policy area.

1.3. Cashflow table

The cashflow table provides an overview of the cash movements during the year. Cashflow information is used to assess the ability of the Communities to generate cash and cash equivalents, and its need to utilise such cash flows.

1.4. Statement of changes in net assets

The statement of changes in net assets shows the movements in reserves and net assets during the year.

1.5. Notes to the financial statements

The notes to the financial statements provide further details and explanations of the items mentioned above, including accounting policies and other disclosures. The notes also include the off-balance sheet, which provides details of the contingent assets and liabilities of the European Communities.

2. Accounting principles

The objective of financial statements is to provide information about the financial position, performance and cashflows of an entity in a form useful to a wide range of users. For a public sector entity such as the European Communities, the objectives are more specifically to provide information useful for decision-making, and to demonstrate the accountability of the entity for the resources entrusted to it.

If they are to present a true and fair view, financial statements must not only supply relevant information to describe the nature and range of an entity's activities, explain how it is financed and supply definitive information on its operations, but also do so in a clear and comprehensible manner allowing comparisons between financial years. It is with these goals in mind that the European Communities' financial statements are drawn up.

The general accounting system allows for the preparation of the financial statements as it contains all charges and income recorded for the financial year (shown in the economic outturn account) and all assets and liabilities recorded (used to establish the financial position in the form of a balance sheet as at 31 December). It also provides the necessary accounting information for the preparation of the cashflow table and the statement of changes in net assets.

Article 124 of the Financial Regulation sets out the accounting principles to be applied in drawing up the financial statements:

— Going-concern basis;

— prudence;

— consistent accounting methods;

— comparability of information;

— materiality;

— no netting;

— reality over appearance;

— accrual-based accounting.

3. The Financial Regulation and accounting rules

3.1. The Financial Regulation

The accounts are kept in accordance with Council Regulation (EC, Euratom) No 1605/2002 of 25 June 2002 (OJ L 248 of 16 September 2002, p. 1, last amended by Council Regulation (EC, Euratom) No 1995/2006 of 13 December 2006, OJ L390 of 30 December 2006) on the Financial Regulation applicable to the general budget of the European Communities and Commission Regulation (EC, Euratom) No 2342/2002 of 23 December 2002 laying down detailed rules for the implementation of this Financial Regulation, last modified on 28 March 2007.

3.2. The European Communities' accounting rules

In accordance with Article 133 of the Financial Regulation, all bodies that are included in the European Communities consolidated annual accounts apply the European Communities accounting rules, as adopted by the Accounting Officer of the Commission. These rules are based on the International Public Sector Accounting Standards (IPSAS) and, for accounting transactions not yet covered by IPSAS, on the relevant International Accounting Standards (IAS)/International Financial Reporting Standards (IFRS). These accrual-based rules were adopted following the opinion of an Advisory Expert Group for Accounting Standards, which provided independent professional guidance on this matter.

4. Accounting policies

A summary of the most important accounting policies applied in the European Communities is provided below.

4.1. Consolidation

The scope of consolidation for the European Communities comprises controlled entities, associates and joint ventures. The complete list of consolidated entities can be found in the financial statements. Controlled entities are all entities over which the European Communities have the power to govern their financial and operating policies so as to be able to benefit from their activities. This power must be currently exercisable. In practise this means the institutions, bodies and executive agencies of the European Communities. These entities are consolidated using the full consolidation method.

4.2. Currency and basis for conversion

The consolidated financial statements are presented in euros, the euro being the European Communities' functional and reporting currency. Foreign currency transactions are converted into euros using the exchange rates prevailing at the dates of the transactions. Year-end balances of monetary assets and liabilities denominated in foreign currencies are converted into euros on the basis of the exchange rates applying on 31 December of that year.

4.3. Balance sheet

1) Tangible and intangible fixed assets

Fixed assets are stated at historical cost less depreciation (excluding land) and impairment. Leases of tangible assets, where the European Communities have substantially all the risks and rewards of ownership, are classified as financial leases.

2) Investments and loans

Investments in associates (for example the European Investment Fund) and joint ventures are accounted for using the equity method. Other investments such as financial assets held at fair value and available-for-sale assets are carried at fair value. Loans and receivables and held-to-maturity investments are carried at amortised cost.

3) Stocks

Stocks are stated at the lower of cost and net realisable value, cost being determined using the first-in, first-out (FIFO) method. Net realisable value is the estimated selling price in the ordinary course of business, less the costs of completion and selling expenses.

4) Pre-financing amounts

Pre-financing is a payment intended to provide the beneficiary with a cash advance, i.e. a float. At year-end, outstanding pre-financing amounts are valued at the original amount(s) paid, less amounts returned, eligible amounts cleared, estimated eligible amounts not yet cleared at year-end, and value reductions.

5) Receivables

Receivables are carried at original amount less write-down for impairment. A write-down for impairment of receivables is established when there is objective evidence that the European Communities may not be able to collect all amounts due under the original terms of receivables. This does not mean that the European Communities will not continue its efforts to recover these amounts.

6) Cash and cash equivalents

Cash and cash equivalents are defined as short-term assets. They are valued at their face value converted into euros at the rate applying at the end of the year.

7) Employee benefit obligations

The European Communities include a liability on its balance sheet to cover its employee benefit obligations, primarily pensions. The liability is valued at each year-end using actuarial techniques, in accordance with international accounting rules.

8) Provisions for risks and charges

Provisions for risks and charges are recognised when the European Communities have a present legal or constructive obligation as a result of past events, it is more likely than not that an outflow of resources will be required to settle the obligation, and the amount can be reliably estimated.

9) Financial liabilities

Financial liabilities include borrowings and 'held for trading' liabilities. Borrowings are recognised initially at fair value, i.e. their issue proceeds (fair value of consideration received) net of transaction costs incurred, then subsequently carried at amortised cost using the effective interest method. 'Held for trading' liabilities include derivatives that do not qualify for hedge accounting when their fair value is negative.

10) Payables

A significant amount of the payables of the Communities are not related to the purchase of goods or services – instead they are unpaid cost claims from beneficiaries of grants or other Community funding. They are valued at the accepted and eligible amount.

11) Accrued and deferred income and charges

In applying accrual accounting, it is necessary to ensure that income and expenditure are included in the correct accounting periods, regardless of when the cash is received or paid out. Therefore a significant effort is needed at each year-end to identify such amounts. In particular, an assessment has to be made of eligible expenses incurred by beneficiaries of Community funds but not yet reported to the Communities (accrued charges). Different methods are used depending on the type of activities and the information available so as to arrive at a best estimate of these amounts. Conversely, some expenses are recorded in the current year although they relate to subsequent periods (deferred charges), so they have to be identified and included in the relevant future period.

Revenue should also be accounted for in the period to which it relates. At year-end, when a service has been rendered or supplies have been delivered or a contractual agreement exists (i.e. by reference to a contract) even though the invoice has not been sent, the amount should be assessed and recorded in the financial statements as accrued revenue. Conversely, when an invoice has been sent but does not relate to the reporting period, the amount should be deferred to a future period.

4.4. Revenue

Exchange revenue: revenue from the sale of goods is recognised when the significant risks and rewards of ownership of the goods are transferred to the purchaser. Revenue from a transaction involving the provision of services is recognised by reference to the stage of completion of the transaction at the reporting date.

Non-exchange revenue makes up the vast majority of the Communities' revenue and includes mainly direct and indirect taxes and own resource amounts. In addition to taxes, the European Communities may also receive payments from other parties, such as duties, fines and donations.

4.5. Expenditure

Exchange expenses arising from the purchase of goods are recognised when the supplies are delivered and accepted by the European Communities and are valued at original invoice cost.

Non-exchange expenses account for the majority of the expenditure of the European Communities. They relate to transfers to beneficiaries and can be of three types: entitlements, transfers under agreement, and discretionary grants, contributions and donations.

Transfers are recognised as expenses in the period during which the events giving rise to the transfer occurred, on condition that: the nature of the transfer is allowed by regulation (Financial Regulation, Staff Regulations, or other regulation) or a contract has been signed authorising the transfer; any eligibility criteria have been met by the beneficiary; and a reasonable estimate of the amount can be made.

When a request for payment or cost claim is received and meets the recognition criteria, it is recognised as an expense for the eligible amount. At year-end, incurred eligible expenses already due to the beneficiaries but not yet reported are estimated and recorded as accrued expenses.

4.6. Off-balance sheet

1) Contingent assets

A contingent asset is a possible asset that arises from past events and whose existence will be confirmed only by the occurrence or non-occurrence of one or more uncertain future events not wholly within the control of the European Communities. A contingent asset is disclosed when an inflow of economic benefits or service potential is probable.

2) Contingent liabilities

A contingent liability is a possible obligation that arises from past events and whose existence will be confirmed only by the occurrence or non-occurrence of one or more uncertain future events not wholly within the control of the European Communities. In addition, a contingent liability may be a present obligation that arises from past events but is not recognised, either because an outflow of resources embodying economic benefits or service potential is unlikely to be required to settle the obligation or, very rarely, because the amount of the obligation cannot be measured with sufficient reliability. A contingent liability is disclosed unless the possibility of an outflow of resources embodying economic benefits or service potential is remote.

3) Commitments for future funding

A commitment for future funding represents a legal or constructive commitment, usually contractual, that the European Communities have entered into and which may require a future outflow of resources.

4) Guarantees

Guarantees are possible assets or obligations that arise from past events and whose existence will be confirmed by the occurrence or non-occurrence of the object of the guarantee. Guarantees thus qualify as contingent assets or liabilities.

4.7. Use of estimates

In accordance with generally accepted accounting principles, the European Communities' financial statements necessarily include amounts based on estimates and assumptions by management based on the most reliable information available. Significant estimates include, but are not limited to, amounts for pensions, provision for future charges, valuation of publication stocks, financial risk on inventories and accounts receivable, accrued income and charges, contingent assets and liabilities, and degree of impairment of fixed assets. The methodology applied must be consistent. Actual results could differ from those estimates. Changes in estimates are reflected in the period in which they become known.

5. Budgetary accounts

The budgetary accounts give a detailed picture of the implementation of the budget. They are designed to establish the consolidated reports on the implementation of the budget, as referred to in Article 121 of the Financial Regulation. The budgetary accounts are based on the modified cash accounting principle (¹). The budget implementation reports comprise the budgetary outturn account and annexes (which provide more detail and comment on the information presented).

(¹)   This differs from pure cash-based implementation because of elements such as carry-overs.

5.1. Budgetary principles

The budgetary principles are explained in Chapter 10, but in summary they are: unity and budget accuracy; annuality; equilibrium; unit of account; universality; specification; sound financial management; and transparency.

5.2. The budgetary outturn account

Under Article 127 of the Financial Regulation, the budgetary outturn account sets out all budgetary operations for a year in terms of revenue and expenditure. Its structure is the same as that of the budget itself.

The budget outturn comprises the result of the European Union and the result of the participation of the EFTA countries. It represents the difference between total revenue received for that year and total payments made against that year's appropriations plus the total amount of that year's appropriations carried over to the following year.

The following are added to or subtracted from the resulting figure:

— the net balance of cancellations of payment appropriations carried over from previous years and any payments which, because of fluctuations in the euro rate, exceed non-differentiated appropriations carried over from the previous year,

— the balance of exchange-rate gains and losses recorded during the year.

A budget outturn surplus is paid back to the Member States the following year by deduction of their contributions for that year.

5.3. Revenue

The amounts of own resources entered in the accounts are those credited in the course of the year to the accounts opened in the Commission's name by the national treasuries and other bodies appointed by the Member States. The difference between the amount of VAT own resources and GNI-based resources entered in the budget and the amount actually due is calculated by the Commission and the resulting amount has to be settled by 1 December of the following year. This amount can be entered in the budget of that year via an amending budget. Other revenue entered in the accounts is the amount actually received in the course of the year.

5.4. Expenditure

For calculating the budget outturn for the year, expenditure comprises payments made against the year's appropriations for payments plus any of these appropriations that are carried over. Payments made against the year's appropriations for payments are payments validated by the authorising officer by 31 December. The payments taken into account for the European Agricultural Guarantee Fund and the European Agricultural Fund for Rural Development are those made by the Member States between 16 October year n and 15 October year n+1.

6. Modernisation of the European Communities' accounting system

6.1. Why change?

As an information system, public-sector accounting has substantially broadened its objectives from a mere record of budget execution to a more dynamic and complete management tool, setting out the economic, financial and asset/liability implications that arise. The European Communities therefore decided to fall into line with the approach adopted by many states, and supported by international bodies such as the International Federation of Accounts (IFAC) and the OECD, by modernising their accounts. This entailed a change from a system of accounts focusing on a cash-based description of budget expenditure and revenue operations, to an accrual accounting system.

The objective was to provide better information to management for their decision-making and to improve the transparency and quality of the accounting information presented annually. A new system was envisaged so as to ensure that both the internal users of the system and the external readers of the accounts have more reliable and relevant information.

6.2. The work done

Work began in earnest in 2003 with the commencement of the 'modernisation of the accounting system' project, which aimed to place the European Communities at the forefront of the international movement towards the modernisation of public sector accounting. As planned, the new accounting system came into use in January 2005, together with a new set of accounting rules and a new chart of accounts. Since 2005, therefore, the financial statements of the European Communities have been prepared under full accrual accounting rules as explained in point 3.2 above. It should be noted that the budget accounts are still based on movements of cash, so a dual system is in operation to allow all reporting requirements to be met.

The IT architecture was also updated to ensure that each accounting event, and not just cash movement, would be fully registered when it occurs. Improvements continue to be made to the IT systems to further the integration of systems, to improve the quality of accounting data and to provide better management reporting.

All services made an inventory of their assets and liabilities as at 31 December 2004. The end result of this was the complete restatement of the European Communities' balance sheet as at 31 December 2004 based on accrual accounting rules.

6.3. Main impact on the financial statements

The application of accrual accounting principles essentially means that income and expenditure are recorded in the accounts when earned/incurred and not just if cash is received/paid. This change in accounting rules has had five major impacts on the financial statements:

1) Pre-financing amounts shown as an asset on the balance sheet

An asset called 'pre-financing' is recognised on the Communities' balance sheet representing advances paid to beneficiaries with the intention to provide them with a float. The amount on the balance sheet represents money that beneficiaries have not yet used or for which they have not yet submitted reports or claims detailing how the money was spent. These amounts are quite significant as they concern the core of the Communities' activities.

2) Current payables

Under accrual accounting rules, amounts are recognised in the accounting system as costs and payables as soon as they are deemed incurred and eligible by the authorising services. Therefore the amount of payables on the Communities' balance sheet is considerably higher than before full accrual methods were used.

3) Year-end cut-off exercise

A key element of accrual accounting is ensuring that income and expenses are recorded in the accounting period to which they relate. Therefore, a significant exercise has to be performed by the European Communities at each year-end to estimate the accounting entries that need to be made to assign income and expenses to the correct accounting periods. The result of this exercise is a very significant amount of accrued expenses appearing on the Communities' balance sheet.

4) Amounts to be called in from Member States

Based on its accounting rules, the Communities must evaluate and recognise in its financial statements the expenditure to be financed by the general budget but which has not yet been declared by year-end. Consequently, many expenses are recognised under accrual accounting rules in the year n although they may be actually paid in year n+1 using the budget of year n+1. Nevertheless, the Communities can only call in resources from the Member States when they need money to pay an amount due. This inclusion of the Communities' liabilities in the accounts, coupled with the fact that the corresponding amounts needed to fund these are only recognised in future years, results in liabilities greatly exceeding assets at year-end (i.e. negative net assets).

To present this situation in the most comprehensible way, a vertical balance sheet showing the Communities' assets first, then its liabilities, was adopted. The difference represents principally the amounts to be called in from Member States. The existence of negative net assets simply reflects the difference between cash-based accounting and accrual accounting for an entity financed according to its cash-flow needs by the general budget. The budget does not take into account the obligation of Member States to provide the necessary resources in the future to pay for the expenditure incurred when it falls due. It should be remembered that the Communities cannot make a payment unless it is provided for in the budget, and all budgeted expenditure is covered by budgeted revenue from the Member States.

5) Disclosures and explanations

The financial statements of the European Communities now provide more complete and clear explanations and notes that should allow for a better understanding of the financial position and results of the Communities for a given year.

Chapter 16

Internal control and external scrutiny of the budget

1. Principles

1.1. Internal control

Article 274 of the EC Treaty (¹) states:

'The Commission shall implement the budget:

— in accordance with the provisions of the regulations made pursuant to Article 279;

— on its own responsibility; and

— within the limits of the appropriations, having regard to the principles of sound financial management.

Member States shall cooperate with the Commission to ensure that the appropriations are used in accordance with the principles of sound financial management.'

(¹)   See European Union – Consolidated versions of the Treaty on European Union and of the Treaty establishing the European Community (2002) (OJ 2002/C325/01, 24.12.2002).

The principle of sound financial management is spelled out in the Financial Regulation (¹), which requires that appropriations are used in accordance with the principles of economy, efficiency, and effectiveness.

The Commission has a wide range of financial and managerial tasks. In line with existing financial rules, the internal arrangements set up by the Commission constitute a structure of robust controls and management tools that enable the Commission to assume its political responsibilities for management by its Directors-General and heads of service. The overall responsibility for the implementation of the budget lies with the European Commission.

While parts of the operational budget are implemented directly by the Commission services (centralised direct management), a high proportion of the budget is managed in association with the Member States, notably for the structural funds and agriculture (shared management) (²). Some tasks are also delegated to agencies (centralised indirect management), implemented through the Commission delegations in third countries (decentralised management), or carried out jointly with international organisations (joint management). In all these cases, the control mechanisms to ensure the legality and regularity of the underlying transactions and the reliability of the accounts have to be defined.

In order to ensure that the funds are used in accordance with the applicable rules, the Commission applies clearance-of-accounts procedures or financial correction mechanisms that enable it to assume final responsibility for the implementation of the budget. These procedures, like the control procedures for programmes and actions, are multiannual in nature.

(¹) Council Regulation (EC, Euratom) No 1605/2002 of June 2002 on the Financial Regulation applicable to the general budget of the European Communities (OJ L 248, 16.9.2002, p. 1), as last amended by Council Regulation (EC, Euratom) No 1995/2006 of 13 December 2006 (OJ L 390, 30.12.2006), Articles 27-28a, 'principle of sound financial management'.

(²) Council Regulation (EC, Euratom) No 1605/2002 of June 2002 on the Financial Regulation applicable to the general budget of the European Communities (OJ L 248, 16.9.2002, p. 1), as last amended by Council Regulation (EC, Euratom) No 1995/2006 of 13 December 2006 (OJ L 390, 30.12.2006), Articles 53-57, 'methods of implementation'.

1.2. External scrutiny and accountability

Democratic control of the executive means, among other things, that the executive has to account in public to the parliament for its use of the public funds voted by parliament for its activities. This is the crucial moment for the executive. Does the democratically elected body consider that the executive has correctly used the funds voted by it for the policy purposes it agreed? The parliament needs an independent examiner or auditor to scrutinise what the executive has done and verify whether it has done what it was instructed to do and to report to parliament. If the executive is judged not to have acted as instructed, the parliament can, in the extreme case, sack the executive.

These principles are also reflected in the Treaties. Article 274 of the EC Treaty requires the Commission to implement the annual budget voted by Parliament and Council in accordance with Article 272 of the EC Treaty. Article 275 requires the Commission to submit the annual accounts and a financial statement of assets and liabilities to the Council and the European Parliament. Articles 246, 247 and 248 establish an independent Court of Auditors that carries out the annual audit and reports to Parliament each year. Article 276 gives the European Parliament the power to discharge the budget implemented by the Commission each year, upon a recommendation from the Council and taking into account the work of the Court of Auditors. Finally, Article 201 gives the European Parliament the power to censure the Commission, and if the motion of censure is passed then the Commission must resign as a body.

However, the reality is not as simple as that described. The Council is also part of the budgetary authority that votes the budget for the following year. Though the Commission has the final responsibility for implementing the budget, about 80 % of the budget – agriculture and structural actions – is in fact managed by the Member States themselves. So the Council also represents the implementers. Furthermore, it makes recommendations on how the budget has to be implemented in the discharge procedure. Parliament and Council agree the laws governing the Union's activities, though the Council has the final say on the financial rules (see Chapter 11), at least until the new treaty is adopted.[19]

Parliament is helped in the discharge procedure by the European Court of Auditors, which 'shall carry out the audit' (Article 246 of the EC Treaty). The Court is an independent institution of the Union (Article 247) and assists the European Parliament and the Council in exercising their powers of control over the implementation of the budget (Article 248).

2. Internal control in the Commission

The European Commission's governance structure is defined by the treaties. It has evolved to match the Commission's changing role and to reflect advances in European governance. In the reform launched in the year 2000, the Commission established a new governance framework, fully empowering authorising officers by delegation and specifying the control and accountability structures to be put in place to facilitate sound management. Over the years, this framework has been adapted in the light of experience.

2.1. Decentralised accountability arrangements

The EC Treaty (Articles 211-219) sets out in detail what is required of Commissioners – as a college and as individuals – under law. The College of Commissioners represents the apex of this architecture, defining policy and taking decisions: it carries political responsibility for the actions of the Commission.

The operational implementation of the budget is formally delegated to the various Directors-General or heads of service. The Financial Regulation constitutes the legal basis for such decentralised financial and accountability arrangements and defines the responsibilities of each financial actor. This delegation is decided annually via the Commission's internal rules, based on the approved budget structure for the year. Delegated Authorising Officers are responsible for the sound and efficient management of their resources and for setting up adequate and efficient control systems to ensure the legality and regularity of expenditure in their departments. Delegated Authorising Officers may formally sub-delegate responsibility to appropriate staff to authorise expenditure and revenue on their behalf.

In executing the budget, Delegated Authorising Officers must respect the provisions of the Financial Regulation and its Implementing Rules and should establish appropriate internal control systems in line with the Commission's Internal Control Standards for Effective Management. These Standards constitute the basic internal control principles and practices to be applied across the whole Commission. The standards specify the requirements, actions and expectations necessary to build an effective internal control system.

The control system is intended to provide reasonable assurance that operational activities are effective and efficient, that transactions are legal and regular, that financial and management reporting is reliable, that fraud and irregularities are prevented or detected, and, finally, that assets and information are safeguarded.

Internal control systems are reviewed regularly to ensure effective control at a reasonable cost. Each Delegated Authorising Officer is supported by a Resource Director and/or an Internal Control Coordinator to oversee and monitor the implementation of internal control systems within the Commission department in question. The competent Commissioner supervises the implementation of the budget by the Director-General or head of service.

At the end of each year, the Directors-General and heads of service must give an account to the Commission in an Annual Activity Report of the achievement of key policy objectives and provide a management report and a declaration of assurance on the exercise of their responsibility as Delegated Authorising Officers. The Director-General defines the necessary control mechanisms and includes in the Annual Activity Reports a description of the control environment and of the different tasks and responsibilities of all actors involved. The Director-General also declares that the information contained in the report gives a true and fair view and confirms that resources were used as intended and in accordance with sound financial management and that the internal control procedures in place give reasonable assurance as to the legality and regularity of the underlying transactions. The declaration may contain reservations regarding the assurance provided where there are particular issues affecting internal control. In all cases, action plans must be established to address any weaknesses identified.

Subsequently, the Commission adopts every year a 'synthesis of management achievements', through which it assumes its political responsibility under Article 274 of the EC Treaty for management by its Directors-General and heads of service, on the basis of their Annual Activity Reports. In cases where the Directors-General or heads of service have made reservations regarding their declaration of assurance, the annual synthesis presents a first analysis of how these shortcomings will be addressed.

It also examines important cross-cutting issues raised by other bodies, including the Internal Auditor, the European Court of Auditors, the European Parliament and the Council of Ministers.

The synthesis is transmitted to the Discharge Authority and to the European Court of Auditors at the latest by 15 June following each budget year.

The Commission's Accounting Officer executes payment and recovery orders approved by authorising officers and is responsible for managing the treasury, laying down accounting rules and methods, validating accounting systems, keeping the accounts and drawing up the institution's financial statements, as well as for consolidating these accounts with those of the other institutions. The Accounting Officer also signs off the accounts, certifying that (s)he has made the checks that (s)he considers necessary and is satisfied that they have been prepared in accordance with the accounting rules, methods and accounting systems established under his/her responsibility, that (s)he has made any adjustments necessary for a true and fair presentation of the accounts in accordance with the financial rules, and that they are therefore reliable.

The Central Financial Service of the Commission is the lead service as regards the Financial Regulation and the internal control framework. It also provides support and advice to other services on matters relating to financial management, including interpretation of legislation and internal control and risk management. The Service develops standards and guidelines, and facilitates the exchange of good practices in the field to help authorising officers to assume their financial management responsibilities.

2.2. Internal audit architecture

Following the administrative reform in 2000 the internal audit architecture was restructured to include a centralised internal audit function (Internal Audit service), a decentralised audit function within the services (Internal Audit Capabilities) and an Audit Progress Committee.

The Internal Audit Service (IAS) is a service of the Commission headed by the Internal Auditor of the Commission, whose mission is to issue independent audit opinions on the quality of management and internal control systems and to present recommendations aimed at ensuring the efficient and effective achievement of the Commission's objectives.

Internal Audit Capabilities (IAC) exist for all Commission departments. Their role is to assist Director-Generals and management within the Directorates-General in controlling risks and monitoring compliance with internal control standards. They provide an independent and objective opinion on the quality of management and internal control systems and make recommendations in order to improve the efficiency of operations and to ensure economic use of the Directorate-Generals' resources.

The Audit Progress Committee (APC) is composed of a number of Commissioners, some of whom are responsible for the management of large parts of the EU budget, together with external experts in audit matters. Under its Charter, the Audit Progress Committee reports annually to the College of the Commission on the quality of internal audit work and on the follow-up given by Commission departments to recommendations from a variety of sources: the Internal Auditor, the Internal Audit Capabilities, the European Court of Auditors [1], and audit-related matters in the resolutions adopted by the Discharge Authority [2]. Beyond these formal reporting obligations, the APC's role is preventive, drawing attention to situations which, if left unattended by the Commission departments, could seriously affect the reputation of the Commission. Accordingly, the Committee strives to increase the effectiveness of follow-up given by Commission departments to relevant audit recommendations, whatever their source.

2.3. Actions to improve the internal control framework

The Commission adopted an Action Plan towards an Integrated Internal Control Framework [3] in January 2006 to strengthen its internal control architecture. Drawing on recommendations by the European Court of

---

[1]   The European Court of Auditors provides, amongst others, the European Parliament and the Council with a statement of assurance as to the reliability of the accounts and the legality and regularity of the underlying transactions.

[2]   The Discharge Authority is made up of the European Council and the European Parliament. The European Parliament adopts a yearly discharge resolution, upon recommendation by the Council. The Commission follows up the recommendations contained in the discharge resolution.

[3]   Communication from the Commission to the Council, the European Parliament and the European Court of Auditors: Commission Action Plan towards an Integrated Internal Control Framework [COM(2006) 9 of 17.1.2006].

Auditors[1] and on work with experts from Member States, this Plan underlined the Commission's determination to further improve financial management and to ensure an effective and efficient control framework. The Action Plan addresses identified gaps with regard to simplifying legal and control frameworks, obtaining improved assurance from all actors in the management chain, sharing audit results and addressing specific issues that lead to a negative statement of assurance from the European Court of Auditors. The different actions are programmed to be completed by the end of 2007 and their results are then expected to become progressively visible and demonstrable in terms of increased assurance. This should lead to a reduction in the error rate through improved prevention, detection and correction.

3. External scrutiny by the European Court of Auditors

3.1. Historical background and Treaty mandate

The Court of Auditors was set up by the 1975 Brussels Treaty and was installed on 1 July 1977, meeting for the first time on 18 October 1977.

The Maastricht Treaty promoted the Court of Auditors in 1993 to the rank of a European Community institution (Article 7 of the EC Treaty) and introduced the requirement for the Court to publish an annual statement of assurance (known as DAS, from the French *declaration d'assurance*) on the reliability of the Communities' accounts and on the legality and regularity of the transactions underlying these accounts.

The Amsterdam Treaty gave the Court the status of a European Union institution, thus enlarging the Court's audit scope to include the second and third pillars of the Union (foreign and security policy, and justice and home affairs).

The Nice Treaty provided that the statement of assurance 'may be supplemented by specific assessments for each major area of Community activity'.

---

[1] Opinion No 2/2004 on the 'single audit' model (and a proposal for a Community Internal Control Framework) OJ C 107, 30.4.2004.

Unlike certain national supreme audit courts, the Court has no judicial powers. Nor does it have any power to take decisions, impose penalties or give orders. Article 248 of the EC Treaty requires the European Court of Auditors to examine the accounts and audit the revenue and expenditure of the European Union. The Court aims to contribute to improving the financial management of European Union funds, so as to ensure maximum value for money for all citizens of the Union. All bodies set up by the Community are included where the relevant constituent instrument does not preclude such examination.

The Treaty provisions appear to give greater emphasis in the Court's scrutiny work to compliance audits – whether the Commission has followed the rules – rather than to performance audits – whether the funding has achieved the aims for which it was intended.

Since the Maastricht Treaty, the Court has had to provide the European Parliament and the Council with public statements of assurance as to the reliability of the accounts and to the legality and regularity of the underlying transactions. This statement is published as part of the annual report. The Amsterdam Treaty extended the Court's mandate, asking it to assess the assurance by major sector of the budget. The statement of assurance (DAS) constitutes a genuine certification of the accounts, a task very different in nature from the traditional tasks of the Court, which were preparing and publishing observations or drawing up opinions on legislative and other proposals with important financial consequences. The Court also provides a separate statement of assurance relating to the accounts of the European Development Fund (EDF) and the underlying transactions.

The Court can also prepare special reports and may give an opinion on draft legislation; it is required to do so particularly on matters with financial and control provisions.

3.2. The Court's mission

The European Court of Auditors audits independently the collection and spending of European Union funds and, through this, assesses the way that the European institutions discharge these functions. It examines whether financial operations have been properly recorded, legally and regularly executed, and managed so as to ensure economy, efficiency and effectiveness. It makes the results of its work known through the publication of relevant, objective and timely reports. In its work, the Court aims to contribute to improving the financial management of European Union funds at all levels, so as to ensure maximum value for money for the citizens of the Union.

1) Coverage of the annual audit

The accounts of the European Community to be scrutinised comprise the financial statements and reports on the implementation of the budget of the institutions as set out in Article 126 of the Financial Regulation, those of the bodies set up by the Community (¹), where the relevant constituent instrument does not preclude such scrutiny (Article 248(1) EC) (²), and those of other bodies whose accounts must be consolidated in accordance with Article 121 of the Financial Regulation and Community accounting rules, together with the consolidated financial statements and consolidated reports on the implementation of the budget. A description of the content of these annual accounts is to be found in Chapter 15.

The annual audit covers these accounts relating to the general budget and the accounts of the EDF (Statement No 1 attached to the Brussels Treaty of 22 July 1975), which is not included in the budget.

The Commission also has to present a report on financial and budgetary management for the financial year in question with the provisional accounts, which are sent to the Court by 31 March of the following year.

The audit also encompasses borrowing and lending operations carried out outside the general budget.

(¹) Article 185 of the Financial Regulation.
(²) For example, the statute of the European Investment Bank (EIB) precludes scrutiny by the Court of Auditors of accounts and commitments from the EIB's own resources (the Court's audit powers cover only Community funds for which management has been delegated to the EIB; pursuant to Article 248(3) third subparagraph, EC, the detailed rules governing such audits are laid down in a tripartite agreement between the Court of Auditors, the EIB and the Commission). Another example is the Statute of the European Central Bank, which places strict limits on the prerogatives of the Court of Auditors.

Its coverage of the 'second and third pillars' (common foreign and security policy, cooperation in the field of justice and home affairs) is confined to operations financed from the general budget.

It covers revenue and expenditure operations that have already been carried out. On the revenue side, the yardsticks used are established entitlements and payments to the Community, while for expenditure, commitments and payments are taken into account. The audit is therefore an *ex post* exercise, although it may be carried out before the closure of accounts for the budgetary year in question.

2) Documentation and information required

The Court's investigative powers are very extensive [1]. It may, among other things, request the institutions, the Member States, Community bodies, beneficiaries, and the national audit bodies to provide any document or information it considers necessary to carry out the tasks entrusted to it by the Treaties.

The audit is based on records and, if necessary, performed on the spot in the Community institutions and in the Member States, at the premises of any body that manages revenue and expenditure on behalf of the Community or any natural or legal person in receipt of payments from the Community budget.

The Court receives regular information about the implementation of the budget throughout the year. Once a month within 10 working days following the end of each month, the Commission's accounting officer sends to the European Parliament and to the Council, as well as to the Court, in electronic form, figures, aggregated at chapter level at least, on the implementation of the budget, both for revenue and for expenditure against all appropriations.

Three times a year, within the 30 working days following 31 May, 31 August and 31 December, the Commission's accounting officer sends to the European Parliament and to the Council, as well as to the Court, a report on the implementation of the budget, covering both revenue and

---

[1]   Set out in Article 248(3) of the EC Treaty and detailed in Articles 139 to 144 of the Financial Regulation.

expenditure broken down by chapter, article and item (Article 131 of the Financial Regulation).

The Commission also sends to the European Parliament and to the Council, as well as to the Court, information twice a year on budgetary guarantees and the corresponding risks (Article 130 of the Financial Regulation).

The Commission also provides to the Court the annual activity reports of the Directors-General and heads of service, the 'Synthesis' report and the Commission's annual summary of the audits undertaken by the Internal Audit Service, which keeps the Court fully informed of the work it undertakes.

3) The Court's reports

The findings of the Court's audit are set out in an annual report (¹), the draft of which is sent to the institutions not later than 30 June of the year following the closure of the year under audit.

They are based on statements of preliminary findings (SPFs) or 'sector letters' to Commissioners, Commission Directorates-General or national government departments, via their supreme audit institutions, in which it sets down its observations arising from findings made during audits. The statements are sent to the auditees to obtain their replies, and can form part of the content of a special report or part of the annual report. The Court requests confirmation of the accuracy of its findings, proof where the findings are contested, the provision of further details or even that particular action be taken.

The annual report is published in the *Official Journal of the European Communities*, together with the replies of the institutions, by 15 November of the same year (²) (31 October for the report on the activities funded by the EDF).

In addition to this annual report, the Court may at any time submit observations on specific questions – for example in the form of special reports –

(¹)   Article 248(3) EC Treaty.
(²)   First subparagraph of Article 248(4) of the EC Treaty and Article 143(5) of the Financial Regulation.

and deliver opinions at the request of a Community institution ([1]). These too are published as a rule.

The Court adopts its reports and opinions by a majority of its 27 members ([2]).

4) The work of the Court of Auditors has three facets

These clearly reflect the two complementary approaches that generally underpin the external scrutiny of public finances:

a) Audits of the annual accounts – the more traditional approach – are common to all external audit bodies. This involves examining the accounts and supporting documents to assess whether the annual accounts provide a true and fair view of the Community's financial activities during the year and the Community's financial position at year-end.

b) Audit of the underlying transactions to ensure that the accounting and financial operations have been conducted in a proper manner and in accordance with the relevant legal rules (treaties, secondary legislation, agreements, contracts, etc). This is the 'financial audit' in the strict sense of the term. This leads to statements of compliance.

c) The audit of sound financial management represents a higher level of scrutiny that is essentially qualitative: the object is to ensure that the internal control systems and decisions and the decisions actually taken by the Community executive allow an optimum balance to be achieved between attaining a given objective and the means used, in terms of economy, efficiency and effectiveness:

— the check on economy consists of verifying that the resources used are acquired at the most appropriate time and at the lowest cost;

— the check on efficiency seeks to determine the degree to which the objectives assigned to the body under audit have been attained;

— the measurement of effectiveness consists of comparing the results obtained with the means used, i.e. ensuring that the resources were used in optimum fashion.

---

[1]   Second subparagraph of Article 248(4) of the EC Treaty.
[2]   Third subparagraph of Article 248(4) of the EC Treaty.

d) The statement of assurance as to the reliability of the accounts and the legality and regularity of the underlying transactions, which encompasses two conceptually independent tasks.

The Court's own DAS audit manual([1]) describes the method as follows.

An audit of the accounts

The opinion on the reliability of the accounts states whether the final consolidated accounts of the European Communities for a given year completely and accurately report the cash flows and financial results for that particular year and whether assets and liabilities at year-end are properly registered so as to reflect faithfully the financial position.

Here, the Court sets out to establish whether the European Commission has ensured the effective application of the relevant accounting rules and whether the consolidated final accounts give a true and fair view of the EU finances within the framework of the generally accepted accounting principles and methods.

The approach followed by the Court in auditing the accounts of the European Communities follows standard financial audit methodology, i.e. comprises the following basic elements:

a) evaluating the central accounting system;

b) checking the functioning of the key accounting procedures;

c) analytical checks (consistency and reasonableness) on the main accounting data;

d) analyses and reconciliations of accounts and/or balances;

e) substantive tests of commitments, payments and certain balance sheet items.

([1])   http://eca.europa.eu/portal/pls/portal/docs/1/348495.PDF.

Audit of the legality and regularity of the underlying transactions (¹)

The second task concerns the legality and regularity of the underlying transactions. The audit examines whether EU funds have been received and spent in conformity with contractual and legislative conditions and have been correctly and accurately calculated. Payments are audited down to the level of the final beneficiaries, given that a high percentage of Community expenditure payments are made on the basis of claims submitted by the final beneficiaries themselves.

The resulting audit opinion, presented in the form of an overall conclusion covering all revenue and expenditure transactions, is derived from audits of the major areas of EU revenue and expenditure (called specific assessments).

The task presents significant challenges, for example:

— about 80 % of the budget is implemented under shared management between the Commission and the Member States;

— much of the expenditure concerns claims made by many diverse final beneficiaries in the Member States and some even in third countries;

— the complexity of the rules applied in the implementation of so many different expenditure programmes in the 27 Member States.

The Court's DAS methodology has evolved since the DAS was first submitted on 15 November 1995, relating to the implementation of the 1994 budget. It was accompanied by a special report published at the same time as its annual report.

The statements of assurance for the general budget provided by the Court in more recent years can be summarised as follows. The Court has declared, albeit with certain reservations or observations attached, that the Communities' accounts accurately reflected their revenue and expenditure and financial position and that the transactions underlying the revenue and commitment of expenditure operations were in order and

---

(¹)   This text is drawn from the European Court of Auditors DAS Methodology manual (April 2007 © European Court of Auditors).

in accordance with the law. This was also the case with the new accrual accounting system in its first years in 2005 and 2006.

However, the Court felt unable to issue a positive statement of assurance for payment operations. Since the Amsterdam Treaty its statement has become more nuanced, since it has been able to give positive statements for own resources, commitments, administrative expenditure and, in more recent years, part of the payments (agricultural expenditure covered by the integrated administration and control system, where properly applied, external actions at the level of Commission delegations, and pre-accession aid, except recently Sapard).

5) Legality

While it assesses the legality and regularity of underlying transactions, the European Court of Auditors nevertheless cannot make any pronouncements on the legality or otherwise of acts by the institutions. Only the Court of Justice, the Court of First Instance and the Civil Service Tribunal have jurisdiction in this field.

In preparing its reports, the Court of Auditors often makes critical assessments of the legislative provisions with financial implications adopted by the Council. Also, since the entry into force of the Amsterdam Treaty, it must report on any cases of irregularity it uncovers in the course of its audits (first subparagraph of Article 248(2) of the EC Treaty). In recent DAS audits, of the 800 samples taken only four appeared to be irregularities to be reported to the European Anti-Fraud Office and only two were taken up for investigation by that body.

6) Cooperation with national supreme audit courts

The European Court of Auditors, as the EU's external audit institution, seeks good contacts and working relations with similar organisations all over the world. Particular attention is given to the Supreme Audit Institutions (SAIs) in Europe, where cooperation with the SAIs of EU Member States (required under Article 248(3) of the EC Treaty [1]) and EU candidate

---

[1] Since the Amsterdam Treaty, EC Treaty Article 248(3) calls on the Court and national audit institutions to 'cooperate in a spirit of trust while maintaining their independence'.

and potential candidate countries is amply justified by the fact that the Member States collect and pay out the lion's share of Community revenue and expenditure and that accession states also have control responsibilities over pre-accession funding.

The objective of this cooperation is closely linked to the Court's responsibility for the audit of EU funds. As these funds generally pass through the national administrations of the countries concerned and the respective SAIs audit those administrations, close cooperation between the Court and national SAIs is essential for effective and efficient implementation of the Court's tasks.

The Court applies generally accepted international public sector auditing standards, and international cooperation provides valuable opportunities to exchange views and experiences on their use.

4. Political control exercised by the European Parliament

Although budgetary powers are shared between the Council and the European Parliament, the latter assumes the essential responsibility for political control over the implementation of the budget under Article 276 of the EC Treaty and Article 180b of the Euratom Treaty, and under Articles 145 to 147 of the Financial Regulation.

4.1. Constant monitoring of budget implementation during the financial year

1) Development of the procedure

Historically, Parliament as an institution was first given responsibility for *ex post* control through preparation of the decision giving discharge. Parliament set up a specialised committee, the Committee on Budgetary Control (which began life as a mere subcommittee of the Committee on Budgets), which gradually imposed a system whereby budget implementation is monitored constantly.

The Maastricht Treaty enshrined this in law through changes to Article 276(2) of the EC Treaty, which introduced a system for hearing evidence from the Commission on the implementation of expenditure or the operation of financial control systems, as part of the preparation of the discharge. This Article also provides that the Parliament can ask for documents concerning 'any other purpose in connection with the exercise of [the Commission's] powers over the implementation of the budget'.

In practice, in agreement with the Commission, the Committee on Budgetary Control acquired the right to obtain relevant documents or information from the Commission departments in the field of budgetary control, subject to specific request and confidential handling in a secure archive upon agreement between the Parliament or its relevant body and the Commission. The Commission also accepted that Community officials could be called on by the committee to give evidence.

Since 1 January 2001, the Framework Agreement of 5 July 2000 on relations between the European Parliament and the Commission formalised the arrangements for transmitting information to Parliament, particularly as regards the annual discharge procedure (see Article 17 and Annex III). These provisions have been taken over in the new Framework Agreement of 26 May 2005 and its Annex I.

The Committee of Budgetary Control has also been refining its competences and responsibilities in successive revisions of Parliament's internal rules of procedure (see Annex VI for a full list). These permit scrutiny on many different fronts, although the discharge procedure forms the main component. The Committee on Budgetary Control examines the accounts, financial statements and analyses mentioned above and submits its conclusions to the full House, which adopts the decision giving discharge (see Section 4.2. below).

2) Powers of inquiry

Since the entry into force of the Treaty on European Union, Parliament also has extensive powers of investigation under Article 193 of the EC Treaty, which reads as follows:

'In the course of its duties, the European Parliament may, at the request of a quarter of its Members, set up a temporary committee of inquiry to investigate, without prejudice to the powers conferred by this Treaty on other institutions or bodies, alleged contraventions or maladministration in the implementation of Community law, except where the alleged facts are being examined before a court and while the case is still subject to legal proceedings.

The temporary committee of inquiry shall cease to exist on the submission of its report.

The detailed provisions governing the exercise of the right of inquiry shall be determined by common accord of the European Parliament, the Council and the Commission.'

Although this article is not designed exclusively to cover financial matters, it may enable Parliament, in appropriate cases, to examine the substance of allegations of infringements or maladministration relating to budget implementation.

3) The traditional 'Notenboom procedure' and the global transfer

The examination of the Commission's regular implementation reports and a motion for a resolution prepared by the Committee on Budgetary Control used to give rise, each year, to a major debate in the House on the implementation of the budget for the current year in September or early October.

The 'global transfer' has now become the responsibility of the Parliament's Committee on Budgets, and has assumed importance in the annual budget procedure. The procedure generally concludes with a series of transfers of appropriations being voted with a view to adjusting budget appropriations in line with the rate of implementation in the final months of the year.

4) Budget implementation and control following reforms since 1988

The 1988 Interinstitutional Agreement, including the 1988-92 financial framework, aimed to improve budgetary discipline and sound financial management. Provisions in successive agreements concluded between Parliament, the Council and the Commission have tightened control of budget implementation:

— The financial framework now places ceilings on commitment appropriations for particular policies or major categories of expenditure;

— More systematic spending forecasts are made in agriculture (the early warning system);

— Tighter control is exercised over implementation during the year; and

— A strict check is made of the existence of a proper legal basis for expenditure.

Under paragraphs 10, 28 and 29 of the Interinstitutional Agreement (IIA) of 6 May 1999 on budgetary discipline and improvement of the budgetary procedure, which entered into force on 1 January 2000, the Commission was obliged to ensure that preliminary draft budgets were consistent with the Community's actual financing requirements. To do so, it had to take account of the following considerations (strictly observing the 2000-06 financial framework while allowing for some flexibility):

— the capacity for using appropriations, maintaining a strict relationship between appropriations for commitments and appropriations for payments;

— the possibilities for launching new policies or new preparatory operations or continuing multiannual operations that were coming to an end;

— the need to ensure that any change in expenditure in relation to the previous year was in accordance with the constraints of budgetary discipline;

— the need to avoid entering items in the budget carrying insignificant amounts of expenditure on operations.

Under the terms of Annex III to the IIA of 6 May 1999, as regards compulsory expenditure, the Commission had to assess and, where necessary, adapt proposals for appropriations in line with the financial implications of existing legislation or legislation about to be adopted. Under paragraph 29 of the IIA, the Council and Parliament had to bear in mind the assessment of the scope for implementing the budget made by the Commission in its preliminary draft.

These provisions focused on improved forecasting, rapid feedback on problems of implementation identified during the process of establishing the budget, more rigorous financial programming, and a closer tie-up between the financial and budgetary processes and the legislative process. They have been considerably extended under parts II and III and Annex II of the new Interinstitutional Agreement (IIA) of May 2006 (¹). Articles 33, 44 and 46 are perhaps the most noteworthy. Though Parliament's Committee on Budgets is mainly involved in these matters, the Committee on Budgetary Control may also pursue such matters particularly in the discharge procedure.

In particular, the three institutions agreed to incorporate aspects of the developing integrated internal control framework within the IIA, for the first time in soft law measures (point 44):

'The institutions agree on the importance of strengthening internal control without adding to the administrative burden for which the simplification of the underlying legislation is a prerequisite. In this context, priority will be given to sound financial management aiming at a positive Statement of Assurance, for funds under shared management. Provisions to this end could be laid down, as appropriate, in the basic legislative acts concerned. As part of their enhanced responsibilities for structural funds and in accordance with national constitutional requirements, the relevant audit authorities in Member States will produce an assessment concerning the compliance of management and control systems with the regulations of the Community. Member States therefore undertake to produce an annual summary at the appropriate national level of the available audits and declarations.'

These soft law provisions have now been included in the Financial Regulation, with the unanimous approval of the Member States, and in the implementing rules.

Under Article 53a(3) of the Financial Regulation that came into force in May 2007, Member States are required, in cases of shared management, to produce an annual summary at the appropriate national level of the available audits and declarations.

(¹) Interinstitutional Agreement between the European Parliament, the Council and the Commission on budgetary discipline and sound financial management (OJ C 139, 14.6.2006).

Article 42a of the implementing rules specify that the summary is to be provided by the appropriate authority or body designated by the Member State for the area of expenditure concerned in accordance with the sector-specific rules. It further states that:

'2. The part related to audits shall:

— include, as concerns agriculture, the certificates established by the certification bodies, and, as concerns structural and other similar measures, the audit opinions provided by the audit authorities;

— be provided by 15 February of the year following the year of the audit activity for agricultural expenditure and for structural and other similar measures.

3. The part related to declarations shall:

— include, as concerns agriculture, the statements of assurance provided by the paying agencies, and, as concerns structural and other similar measures, certifications by the certifying authorities;

— be provided by 15 February of the following financial year for agricultural expenditure and for structural and other similar measures.'

These innovations are likely to have effects on the controls exercised by Member States in these areas and on the assurance given by the Member States to the Commission for the latter's reporting to the discharge authority.

4.2. Budget discharge

1) Definition and significance

The discharge is the decision taken by the authority empowered to do so (Parliament), after having received a recommendation from the Council, releasing the executive (Commission) from any further liability in respect of its management of the budget, thus marking final closure of the budget. It is a decisive moment. At worst, it can lead to a vote of no confidence in the Commission or similar actions.

The discharge procedure is provided for in Article 276 EC and set out in detail in Articles 145 to 147 of the Financial Regulation and in Annex V of Parliament's rules of procedure, to which Rule 93 of these rules refers.

The discharge decision is the culmination of a procedure that starts in year n+1 (n being the year in which the budget concerned is implemented) and is normally completed by 30 April of year n+2.

After the Council has drawn up a recommendation, Parliament examines the accounts and the balance sheet referred to in Article 275 EC, the annual report and any relevant special reports by the Court of Auditors, together with the replies of the audited institutions to the observations of the Court of Auditors, and the statement of assurance referred to in Article 248 EC. For this purpose, the Court of Auditors examines whether revenue and expenditure have been properly and lawfully received and incurred, checks that financial management has been sound and, in particular, points out any irregularities. The statement of assurance deals specifically with the reliability of the accounts and the legality and regularity of the underlying transactions.

By 30 April of year n+2 Parliament gives a discharge by voting on the draft decision and resolution drawn up by its Committee on Budgetary Control. In accordance with Article 198 EC, Parliament takes the decision by an absolute majority of the votes cast.

The Commission must take all appropriate steps to act on the observations in the decision giving discharge and on the comments accompanying the Council's discharge recommendations. If so requested by the European Parliament or the Council, the Commission must report on the measures taken in the light of these observations and in particular on the instructions given to the departments responsible for the implementation of the budget. These reports are also sent to the Court of Auditors.

In preparation for the discharge debate, Parliament (or the Council in the course of drawing up its recommendations) may request further information. In this event, it postpones the discharge decision and notifies the Commission of the reasons, so that it can take as quickly as possible whatever steps may be necessary to overcome the obstacles preventing Parliament from taking action.

The discharge decision has a double significance. First, it is the budgetary authority's political verdict on the manner in which the Commission exercises its responsibility for implementing the budget. Secondly, in a purely technical, accounting sense, it paves the way for the final closure of the accounts.

As a rule, discharge is based on the examination of:

— the accounts, the balance sheet and the analysis of financial management transmitted by the Commission;

— the annual report and relevant special reports by the Court of Auditors;

— the statement of assurance as to the reliability of the accounts and the legality and regularity of the underlying transactions, as provided for in Article 248(1) of the EC Treaty;

— the Council's recommendation prior to discharge;

— the reports and information provided by the Commission on the implementation of the budget.

2) Annual discharge procedure

In accordance with Article 276 of the EC Treaty, the Financial Regulation (various articles from 128 to 147) lays down the following stages and timetable.

— The accounting officers of the other institutions and bodies send to the Commission's accounting officer and to the Court of Auditors by 1 March of the following year at the latest their provisional accounts together with the report on budgetary and financial management during the year.

— The Commission's accounting officer consolidates these provisional accounts with the Commission's provisional accounts and sends to the Court of Auditors, by 31 March of the following year at the latest, the Commission's provisional accounts accompanied by its report on budgetary and financial management during the year together with the provisional consolidated accounts.

— The accounting officer of each institution and body also sends a report on budgetary and financial management to the European Parliament and the Council by 31 March of the following year.

— By 15 June at the latest, the Court of Auditors makes its observations on the provisional accounts of each institution and each body.

— The institutions other than the Commission and each of the Community bodies draw up their final accounts in accordance with Article 61 of the Financial Regulation and send them to the Commission's accounting officer and the Court of Auditors by 1 July of the following year at the latest for the final consolidated accounts to be drawn up.

— The Commission's accounting officer prepares the final consolidated accounts on the basis of this information presented by the other institutions. The final consolidated accounts are accompanied by a note drawn up by the Commission's accounting officer in which he/she declares that they were prepared in accordance with Title VII and with the accounting principles, rules and methods set out in annex to the financial statements.

— After approving the final consolidated accounts and its own final accounts, the Commission sends them both to the European Parliament, the Council and the Court of Auditors before 31 July of the following financial year.

— The final consolidated accounts are published in the Official Journal of the European Communities together with the statement of assurance given by the Court of Auditors in accordance with Article 248 of the EC Treaty and Article 160c of the Euratom Treaty by 15 November of the following financial year.

— The Court of Auditors transmits to the Commission and the institutions concerned, by 30 June at the latest, any observations that are in its opinion such that they should appear in the annual report. These observations must remain confidential. Each institution sends its reply to the Court of Auditors by 15 October at the latest. The replies of institutions other than the Commission are sent to the Commission at the same time.

— The Court of Auditors transmits to the authorities responsible for giving discharge and to the other institutions, by 15 November at the latest, its annual report accompanied by the replies of the institutions and ensures their publication in the *Official Journal of the European Union*.

— As soon as the Court of Auditors has transmitted the annual report, the Commission informs the Member States concerned immediately of the details in the report which relate to the management of the funds for which they are responsible under the applicable rules. Following receipt of this information, the Member States must reply to the Commission within 60 days. The latter transmits a summary to the Court of Auditors, the Council and the European Parliament before 28 February.

— The European Parliament may ask to hear the Commission give evidence on the execution of expenditure or the operation of financial control systems. After having heard the Commission and assessing the information provided, and upon a recommendation from the Council acting by a qualified majority, the Parliament gives discharge to the Commission, by 15 May of year n+2, for the implementation of the budget for year n.

— If this date cannot be met, the European Parliament or the Council informs the Commission of the reasons for postponement (Article 145 of the Financial Regulation). If the European Parliament postpones the decision giving discharge, the Commission has to make every effort to take measures, as soon as possible, to remove or facilitate removal of the obstacles to that decision.

— Parliament decides on the discharge by voting on the draft decisions and motions for a resolution prepared by its Committee on Budgetary Control by a majority of votes cast (in accordance with the general rules in Article 198 of the EC Treaty). Parliament gives discharge not only in respect of the implementation of the general budget, by the Commission and by each of the other institutions and consultative bodies, but also for the budgets of the agencies or satellite bodies and for operations under the various European Development Funds (internal financing agreements annexed to the Lomé Conventions).

3) The role of the Council

The Council's scope for intervention as the other arm of the budgetary authority is, formally speaking, limited to the drafting of the recommendation addressed to Parliament at the outset of the discharge procedure. Although not legally binding, this recommendation is significant. In practical terms, the Council's Budgets Committee analyses the annual report of the Court of Auditors and questions the Commission and the Court before submitting a draft recommendation to the ECOFIN Council. The Council President presents the recommendation to the Parliament's Budgetary Control Committee before that committee votes its discharge report.

Parliament pays close attention to the technical analysis underpinning the recommendation, and the Commission is required to follow up the recommendation.

4) The role of the Member States

Since the Member States are entrusted with the management of a large portion of Community funds, it is reasonable that they should be involved, albeit modestly, in the process leading up to discharge.

The Commission therefore sends them a questionnaire to obtain their opinions on the observations of the Court of Auditors that directly concern them. In their replies, the Member States must give the Commission all the information it needs to make a sound assessment of the reasons for the shortcomings identified by the Court.

5) Postponement and refusal of discharge

Parliament has gradually and substantially expanded the political dimension of discharge by using it as a lever to obtain much more influence over the way in which the Commission exercises its prerogatives and manages the business entrusted to it. As a result, events that can prevent the adoption of the discharge decision by the prescribed deadlines are now more than just textbook cases.

(a) Postponement of discharge

When preparing the discharge debate, Parliament (possibly assisted by the Council's work in drafting its recommendation) may find that certain points relating to implementation have not been made sufficiently clear. In this case, the discharge decision is postponed and the Commission is informed of the reasons for this postponement (Article 145 of the Financial Regulation).

Thus, Parliament may postpone the discharge decision:

— in order to impose on the Commission certain conditions which must be fulfilled beforehand (1996 discharge) (¹);

— in order to have more time to examine all the documents (as was the case, on the eve of the June 1979 elections, with the discharge for 1977);

— when the Commission has been asked to amend some of the documents on which the discharge is to be based (as was the case for the 1980 and 1985 discharges) or to provide further information (1990 discharge). The procedure for dialogue between the Commission and Parliament laid down in Article 276 of the EC Treaty, introduced by the Maastricht Treaty, is designed to avoid recourse to refusal of discharge where Parliament's reluctance to vote the discharge may be overcome by obtaining supplementary information.

Should it be decided to postpone the discharge, Article 145 of the Financial Regulation calls for the rapid removal of the obstacles.

(b) Refusal of discharge

Neither Article 276 of the EC Treaty nor the Financial Regulation makes any provision for the principle of refusing discharge, let alone the procedure for doing so. These points are covered by Articles 3 and 5 of Annex V to Parliament's rules of procedure.

A decision by Parliament to refuse the Commission a discharge because of serious objections must be considered exceptional. Discharge has in fact only been refused twice – in 1984 in respect of the 1982 financial year and more recently in 1998 in respect of the 1996 financial year.

(¹)   Resolution of 31 March 1998 (OJ C 138, 4.5.1998, p. 29).

When Article 276 of the EC Treaty entered into force in 1977, it was argued that such a refusal amounted to the expression of a vote of no confidence in the Commission and, like a censure motion, would therefore mean that the Commission had to resign.

Experience has shown that this political reasoning has no legal relevance. First, after the discharge for 1982 was refused in November 1984, the Commission (presided over by Gaston Thorn and only a few weeks from the end of its term) did not resign. Acknowledging that the closure of the budgetary cycle was unavoidable, Parliament eventually gave the discharge for 1982 on 15 March 1985.

Second, when the discharge for 1996 was refused in 1998, the Commission, under Jacques Santer, did not resign until March 1999 following a report by a 'Committee of Independent Experts', the content of which suggested that Parliament might adopt a censure motion.

A special procedure governs the adoption of a censure motion, which requires a majority of Parliament's members and two thirds of the votes cast.

6) Follow-up

Article 276 of the EC Treaty requires that:

'The Commission shall take all appropriate steps to act on the observations in the decisions giving discharge and on other observations by the European Parliament relating to the execution of expenditure, as well as on comments accompanying the recommendations on discharge adopted by the Council.'

Article 147 of the Financial Regulation provides that the institutions must take all appropriate steps to act on the observations on the implementation of expenditure appearing in the decisions giving discharge and the comments accompanying the recommendations for discharge adopted by the Council. At the request of Parliament or the Council, they must report on measures taken in the light of these comments and, in particular, on the instructions given to their departments. These reports are also sent to the Court of Auditors.

Part 6

OPERATIONS OUTSIDE THE GENERAL BUDGET

Chapter 17

Community borrowing and lending operations

1. General presentation and development of lending operations

Under the principle of budgetary equilibrium, the Community may not finance its activities by borrowing. A budget deficit cannot therefore be financed through recourse to borrowing. However, a certain number of express provisions of the Treaties establishing the Communities, together with the need to achieve the Treaty objectives, have led to the gradual creation of various instruments authorising the Commission, on behalf of the Community, to borrow on the financial markets to make loans in order to enable their final recipients to benefit from the advantageous conditions which the Community can secure with its very high credit rating.

The Community has developed several instruments enabling it to obtain access to the capital markets to finance various categories of loan.

Several periods can be identified in the development of the Community's financial instruments supported by the general budget.

— The first period is characterised by the total absence of activities of this type under the EEC Treaty, since they were only carried out by the ECSC, Euratom and the EIB.

— Towards the end of the 1960s, the need for Community solidarity within the Customs Union that had been created led to the emergence of operations to support Member States facing balance-of-payments problems. Euratom operations were also integrated into the general budget. The economic crisis that arose in 1973 after the first oil price shock gave rise to an even greater need to strengthen solidarity within the Community.

— In the 1970s, two instruments emerged. First, there was the New Community Instrument (NCI) to support investment by small and medium-sized firms. The second instrument was the blanket guarantee given from the general budget to EIB loans for microeconomic purposes in Mediterranean countries.

— The events that started in eastern Europe in 1989 led to an extension of the guarantee given to the EIB, enabling it to grant loans in central and eastern Europe (Poland and Hungary, to start with, then Czechoslovakia, Bulgaria and Romania) and to start the first borrowing and lending operation for a third country, Hungary, at the start of 1990.

— The European Parliament, the Council and the Commission agreed under point 49 of the new Interinstitutional Agreement of 17 May 2007 on budgetary discipline and sound financial management to encourage the development of new financial instruments to act as catalysts for public and private investors. Three new instruments were created under three Community programmes (Research, Competitiveness and Innovation, and Trans-European Networks – Transport). These instruments and their objectives are described in Chapter 13.2.

In addition, other borrowing and lending operations for macroeconomic purposes have been launched, not only for the countries of central and eastern Europe but also for Mediterranean countries such as Israel and Algeria.

2. Characteristics of borrowing and lending instruments

2.1. Sectoral instruments

1) ECSC

Article 49 of the ECSC Treaty empowered the High Authority to borrow funds, provided they were used solely to grant loans.

Loans were granted for three main purposes:

— To finance investment in the coal and steel sector;

— To finance conversion programmes for restructuring the coal and steel industry;

— To finance the construction of subsidised housing for workers in the coal and steel industries (second paragraph of Article 54).

In 1990 and 1991, the scope for loans was extended to certain eastern European countries, principally to finance projects promoting the sale of Community steel and industrial products which could be implemented within joint ventures.

Under the second paragraph of Article 54, the ECSC financed major infrastructure projects of Community interest between 1990 and 1994.

In 1994, the ECSC decided to review its borrowing and lending policy in preparation for the expiry of the Treaty (23 July 2002). On the basis of this decision, the last loans were made in 1997, except for loans for subsidised housing, which ended in 1998 with the 12th programme.

Over the course of its existence, the ECSC disbursed loans amounting to EUR 24.7 billion, of which EUR 24.08 billion came from borrowed funds and EUR 644 million from own funds (special reserve and former pension fund). On 31 December 2006, loans from borrowed funds worth EUR 281.8 million and loans from own funds worth EUR 55.5 million were still outstanding.

2) Euratom

Borrowing and lending operations are authorised under Article 172 of the Euratom Treaty of 25 March 1957.

Council Decision 77/270/Euratom of 29 March 1977 empowers the Commission to issue Euratom loans to finance investment projects in the Member States relating to industrial nuclear fuel cycle installations (mainly for the production of electricity).

Council Decision 94/179/Euratom of 21 March 1994 introduced a similar possibility for certain non-EU countries, for projects to increase the safety and efficiency of installations that are in service or under construction and for the dismantling of installations that cannot be preserved for technical or economical reasons.

The non-EU countries eligible for such loans were Armenia, Bulgaria, the Czech Republic, Hungary, Lithuania, Romania, Slovenia, Slovakia, the Russian Federation and Ukraine, some of which later became Member States.

Council Decision 77/271/Euratom of 29 March 1977, last amended in 1990, set a ceiling on the borrowing operations required for the funding of Euratom loans. The overall ceiling is EUR 4 000 million. Loans approved since 1977 total EUR 3 414 million.

2.2. Macroeconomic instruments

1) Borrowing and lending for balance-of-payments support

After the first oil shock, a Community borrowing facility was devised to help Member States whose balance of payments had been upset as a result of the rise in oil prices. The first loans were granted in 1976. The Council increased the volume of Community borrowings authorised under this facility to EUR 8 billion in 1984 and to EUR 16 billion in 1988. By 31 December 2000, all borrowings had been repaid. Under Regulation (EC) No 332/2002, the European Union may grant loans to Member States that are experiencing, or are seriously threatened with, difficulties in their balance of current payments or capital movements. Only Member States that have not adopted the euro may benefit from this Community facility. The outstanding amount of loans is limited to EUR 12 billion in principal. As of 31 December 2006, the outstanding amount under this instrument was zero.

2) Borrowing and lending in connection with cooperation with non-member countries

The Community grants financial assistance in the form of medium-term loans to a number of non-EU countries experiencing serious but generally short-term balance-of-payments or budget difficulties. This assistance is designed to support the implementation of strong adjustment and structural reform measures to remedy these difficulties, but is to be discontinued as soon as the country's external financial situation has been brought back onto a sustainable path. The loans are financed from the Community borrowing operations. They are in some cases complemented or combined with a grant component.

This form of cooperation started in the early 1990s to help the countries of central and eastern Europe to implement economic reforms (Hungary, Czechoslovakia, the Baltic states, Bulgaria, and Romania) and was subsequently extended to some Mediterranean countries (Israel, Algeria). In the second half of the 1990s, it was mainly the New Independent States which benefited from such assistance (Ukraine, Moldova, Belarus, Georgia, Armenia, and Tajikistan). In the years 2000-06, the main recipients of macro-financial assistance were the Balkan countries for the reconstruction and stabilisation of the region.

For the central and eastern European recipients, which have since become Member States, the total volume of loans disbursed amounted to EUR 2 780 million, which have been almost fully repaid. At the end of 31 December 2006, the outstanding loans for these countries totalled EUR 365 million.

For the New Independent States, the total volume of loans disbursed amounted to EUR 631 million, which have been almost fully repaid. At the end of 31 December 2006, the outstanding loans for these countries totalled EUR 185 million.

For the Balkan countries, the total volume of loans disbursed amounted to EUR 419 million. At the end of 31 December 2006, the outstanding loans for these countries totalled EUR 419 million.

2.3. European Investment Bank (EIB) loans outside the Community

These loans from EIB own resources are covered by a Community guarantee underwritten by the general budget against possible default by beneficiary countries. A guarantee agreement signed between the Community and the European Investment Bank specifies the conditions of the Community guarantee. The use of such guaranteed loans dates from the 1990s under various mandates to support the Community's external policies. A more structured Community guarantee was established for the period 2000-07 by Council Decision 2000/24/EC of 22 December 1999 for EIB loans outside the Community. The total ceilings for each area under this general mandate, after modifications to take into account the enlargement of the EU and the European Neighbourhood Policy, amounted to EUR 19 460 million, broken down between the 'South-Eastern Neighbours' and Turkey (EUR 9 635 million), Mediterranean countries (EUR 6 520 million), Latin America and Asia (EUR 2 480 million), and the Republic of South Africa (EUR 825 million). This general mandate was supplemented by Council Decision 2001/777/EC on the Baltic Sea basin of Russia under the Northern Dimension (EUR 100 million) and Council Decision 2005/48/EC for specific lending actions in Russia, Ukraine, Moldova and Belarus (EUR 500 million).

At the end of 2006, the EIB had signed loan agreements for a total amount corresponding to 96 % of the ceilings under the second general mandate.

The third general mandate to cover the period 2007-13 was adopted under Council Decision 2006/1016/EC of 19 December 2006. The maximum ceiling for EIB financing operations carried out under this mandate is EUR 27 800 million, consisting of a basic ceiling of EUR 25 800 million and an optional mandate of EUR 2 000 million, the activation of which will be decided by the Council based on the outcome of the midterm review in 2010.

The different regional ceilings (with indicative sub-ceilings) are as follows (in EUR million):

— Pre-Accession countries: EUR 8 700 million;

— Neighbourhood and Partnership countries: EUR 12 400 million (of which Mediterranean countries EUR 8 700 million and Eastern Europe, Southern Caucasus and Russia EUR 3 700 million);

— Asia and Latin America: EUR 3 800 million (of which Latin America EUR 2 800 million and Asia EUR 1 000 million);

— Republic of South Africa: EUR 900 million,

— Optional mandate: EUR 2 000 million.

The Council Decision calls for strengthening of the consistency of the EIB outside lending mandate with the external policy objectives of the EU in order to maximise synergies between EIB financing and the budgetary resources of the EU available under the various instruments (IPA, ENPI, Instrument for Stability, DCI for South Africa). This objective is to be reached through regular dialogues and consultations on strategic programming between the Bank and the Commission. The EIB loans are intended to support investment in sectors such as the environment, transport, telecommunications and energy infrastructure, depending on the specific characteristics and priorities of each region.

For pre-accession countries, the objective is to help facilitate their integration within the EU and prepare them for accession, in particular by financing investment to integrate their infrastructure with that of the EU, and by assisting SMEs.

In the Mediterranean region, the EIB is to continue and consolidate its focus on support for the private sector and on creating an investment-friendly environment, mainly by financing infrastructure that will enable economic development.

In Eastern Europe, the Southern Caucasus and Russia, the EIB is to finance projects of significant interest to the European Union in transport, energy, telecommunications and environmental infrastructure with priority for the major Trans-European network (TEN) axes. In Central Asia, the focus is on major energy supply and energy transport projects with cross-border implications.

In Asia and Latin America, the Bank is to finance projects that are of interest to both the Community and the countries concerned – cofinancing with EU promoters, transfer of technology and know-how, and cooperation in the fields of energy and environmental protection.

In the Republic of South Africa, the Bank is to focus on infrastructure projects of public interest and private sector support, including SMEs. The Bank's operations also have to complement Community assistance policies, programmes and instruments in South Africa, the overriding objective of which is the reduction of poverty and inequality.

3. The guarantee provided by the Community's general budget for borrowing operations

3.1. Borrowing and lending operations

This involves borrowings contracted by the Commission on behalf of the Community, which are then on-lent to third parties on the same conditions regarding the amount, term, rate and dates of payment of interest. The risk for the budget therefore derives from the need to ensure reimbursement of the sum borrowed by the Community in the event of default by the beneficiary of the loan on the due date of payment.

This type of guarantee to lenders concerns the macroeconomic-type 'balance-of-payments' and 'medium-term financial assistance' loans and the microeconomic loans (Euratom).

3.2. Loan guarantees

In the other cases, the Community provides a guarantee for loans granted by the European Investment Bank to finance projects outside the Community. The guarantee covers all or part of the amount of the loans granted. Depending on the protocol concerned, the guarantee covers between 100 % and 65 % of the amount. Most current outstanding loans are guaranteed at a rate of 65 %.

In these cases, the Community's undertaking is in the form of the signing of a contract of guarantee between the Community and the institution thus secured.

4. The relationship between the general budget and borrowing and lending operations and loan guarantees

4.1. The budget and lending operations

1) The non-inclusion of borrowing and lending operations in the budget

Unlike the first Euratom borrowings, current borrowing and lending operations do not appear in the budget as revenue and expenditure. In

1978, at the instigation of the European Parliament, the Commission proposed that these operations be shown in full in the budget, assimilating borrowing to revenue and loans to expenditure, in a 'part II' of the general budget. The Council's rejection of this proposal was one of the 'important reasons' which led Parliament to reject the draft budget for 1979. The Council's stance derived from the wish to maintain exclusive control over decisions concerning borrowing and lending.

2) Limited consequences for the budget

Under its structure resulting from the Financial Regulation as last amended on 13 December 2006 (Council Regulation (EC, Euratom) No 1995/2006), the budget does, however, contain a document showing all borrowing and lending operations, which is annexed to the Commission section. This document serves solely for guidance.

Furthermore, while the basic decision authorising an operation is adopted by the Council, after Parliament has given its opinion, it is the budgetary authority which authorises the granting of the guarantee. This 'performance guarantee' is granted by including a budget heading carrying a token entry in the 'expenditure' side of the Budget. When the guarantee is activated, appropriations are allocated to these headings by transfer or by means of a supplementary and amending budget.

4.2. The search for greater transparency in the treatment of these operations in the budget and providing against the risk of default

A statement annexed to the Financial Regulation resulting from the 1990 revision specifies that: 'The Commission undertakes to study the possibility of improving the treatment of borrowing/lending operations in Community budget documents. It will submit the conclusions of its study before the end of 1991'. Although the outcome of this exercise was then incorporated in the procedure for establishing the budget, the principles of transparency and sound financial management were introduced in the Financial Regulation of 2002, setting out clear requirements in this respect. Moreover, the development of the Community's external action and the growing use of the budget guarantee instrument made it necessary to apply the rules of budgetary discipline to these operations as well: the economic, social and political instability of certain countries benefiting from the Community guarantee for their loans increases the probability that the guarantee will in fact be activated. For example, the Community has had to pay the EIB substantial amounts under this guarantee following the defaults of Lebanon, Syria and the Republics of the former Yugoslavia between 1988 and 1993, and in relation to loans granted to the Federal Republic of Yugoslavia and to Bosnia and Herzegovina between 1992 and 2000. The latter eventually paid the amounts due. In 2003 and 2004, the guarantee was called upon to cover EIB loans to Argentina.

1) A new structure for budget documents

Articles 30 and 46 of the Financial Regulation ensure greater transparency in the presentation of budget documents by providing that information on borrowing and lending operations contracted by the Communities for third parties is to appear in an Annex to the budget. In addition to the information in this annex, the Financial Regulation requires the budget to show:

— In the general statement of revenue, the budget lines that correspond to the relevant operations and are intended to record any reimbursements received from beneficiaries who have initially defaulted, leading to activation of the performance guarantee. These lines carry a token entry (p.m.) and are accompanied by appropriate remarks;

— In the Commission section, the budget lines containing the Communities' performance guarantees in respect of the operations in question. These lines carry a token entry (p.m.), so long as no effective charge to be covered by actual resources has arisen, and are accompanied by remarks indicating the basic act and the volume of the operations envisaged, the duration, and the financial guarantee given by the Communities in respect of these operations.

2) Better cover of potential risks related to loan guarantees for non-member countries

(a) Guarantee Fund for external actions

The Guarantee Fund, introduced by Council Regulation (EC, Euratom) No 2728/94 of 31 October 1994, is intended to cover the activation of general budget guarantees for non-member countries in order to avoid possible disruptions to the implementation of the budget in the event of defaults. Its function is to provide a cushion for external shocks that would otherwise affect the budget directly. It intervenes in cases of default and activation of the Community guarantee for the following three types of loans guaranteed by the budget (as described in the above sections):

— Euratom loans to certain non-EU countries, for projects to increase the safety and efficiency of installations that are in service or under construction or for the dismantling of installations that cannot be preserved for technical or economical reasons;

— Macro-financial assistance loans to non-EU countries to tackle short-term balance-of-payments or budget difficulties;

— EIB loans to non-EU countries covered by a Community guarantee.

EIB loans represent the bulk of the loans with around 90 % of the outstanding volume.

(b) The budget provisioning of the Guarantee Fund

The Regulation was amended by Council Regulation (EC, Euratom) No 89/2007 of 30 January 2007 to adjust the provisioning rules of the Guarantee Fund to the suppression of the reserve for loan guarantees to non-member countries. Under the new financial framework 2007-13, it was decided that the financial resources necessary to provision the Guarantee Fund would be budgeted directly under the heading for external actions 'The EU as a global player', since such expenditure directly supports the Community's external policies. The basic principle of the Guarantee Fund is not affected by the new provisioning mechanism. The relationship between the amount of outstanding loans and the Guarantee Fund at the target level of 9 % is maintained. It reflects the best assessment of the risk profile of the Guarantee Fund. Under the new provisioning rules, the amount necessary to keep the Fund at its target level is now budgeted directly on the basis of the amount in the Fund and the amount of outstanding loans as at 31 December of the year n-1. This budgetary treatment is fully transparent, following the normal budgetary procedure as for any other expenditure, replacing the provisioning of the Fund on an ongoing basis throughout the year. There is to be a mid-term review of the functioning of the new provisioning mechanism and the target level. The indicative financial envelope under the heading 'EU as a global player' over the period 2007-13 amounts to EUR 200 million per year.

TABLE 16.1

Total annual risk borne by the budget in million EUR due under all loans disbursed as at 31.12.2006

Total annual risk borne by the budget in million EUR based on the amounts (capital and interest) due under all operations (MFA, Euratom and EIB) disbursed at 31.12.2006

Ranking	Country	2007	2008	2009	2010	2011	2012	2013	2014 until 2035	Total outstanding
1	Romania*	263.4	252.0	238.7	228.9	239.7	185.6	185.4	1,191.5	2,785.2
2	Turkey	151.0	189.0	195.0	217.7	221.2	213.2	196.5	1,070.8	2,454.6
3	Egypt	152.9	183.8	184.2	164.0	144.7	136.7	121.7	743.9	1,831.8
4	Morocco	117.4	120.7	121.9	121.9	124.3	121.6	118.9	833.9	1,680.6
5	Tunisia	112.2	115.6	117.2	121.4	116.2	114.0	110.2	604.3	1,411.0
6	Serbia and Montenegro	43.5	50.3	53.7	55.4	61.9	99.4	96.3	587.4	1,047.9
7	Bulgaria*	155.7	149.5	85.2	75.2	58.8	71.4	56.9	319.5	972.1
8	Czech Republic	102.2	97.8	151.5	90.8	81.6	79.7	74.5	232.1	910.3
9	Poland	98.4	89.0	81.8	77.9	75.4	73.0	67.3	237.7	800.5
10	South Africa	93.6	74.2	122.2	76.9	58.2	70.5	41.2	250.0	786.9
11	Slovakia	72.8	73.2	67.9	66.8	66.3	51.4	37.7	115.1	551.1
12	Croatia	33.3	35.2	27.8	27.8	36.2	37.9	37.2	314.9	550.5
13	Brazil	130.3	105.2	77.8	61.6	45.5	39.3	29.3	51.5	540.5
14	Lebanon	56.4	56.7	62.2	51.5	50.0	38.4	33.6	52.2	401.0
15	Jordan	44.8	44.2	45.2	41.0	39.3	36.0	29.4	78.8	358.8
16	Syria	16.1	19.5	20.2	23.6	23.6	23.6	21.6	167.0	315.2
17	Bosnia and Herzegovina	23.3	23.7	23.5	25.2	24.6	23.6	20.6	119.4	283.9
18	former Yugoslav Republic of Macedonia	17.1	23.1	24.5	23.2	22.0	23.7	20.4	106.6	260.6
19	Hungary	35.6	31.0	29.0	26.2	25.3	22.8	13.9	24.2	208.0
20	Slovenia	39.2	38.2	25.9	20.8	14.3	11.4	9.4	13.9	173.2
21	Indonesia	12.7	12.3	16.1	19.9	12.3	9.6	9.6	43.0	135.4
22	Lithuania	14.8	14.3	13.5	12.4	11.9	11.4	10.9	39.9	129.0
23	Albania	8.1	8.8	9.8	10.0	10.0	9.8	7.3	59.0	122.8
24	Argentina	19.5	21.0	18.1	11.5	11.3	10.9	11.1	7.7	111.0
25	Mexico	4.2	24.5	24.5	24.9	3.5	3.5	3.5	21.0	109.6
26	China	10.0	9.6	9.7	9.9	8.6	7.4	7.5	38.7	101.3
27	Pakistan	3.7	8.8	10.7	12.6	12.6	12.6	9.6	27.1	97.9
28	Cyprus	15.7	15.7	15.8	15.9	15.5	9.0	5.0	3.4	96.0
29	Georgia	30.5	2.3	24.3	23.4	14.0	0.0	0.0	0.0	94.6
30	Peru	8.4	7.4	7.2	10.3	10.1	9.9	9.7	21.6	84.5
31	Vietnam	6.9	6.6	9.6	10.1	10.0	9.9	9.8	16.0	79.0
32	Philippines	10.8	10.8	10.8	10.9	10.9	11.0	3.3	4.3	72.9
33	Latvia	8.5	8.1	7.3	7.1	6.9	5.3	5.2	24.4	72.8
34	Ukraine	36.8	15.7	15.1	0.0	0.0	0.0	0.0	0.0	67.5
35	Russia	2.7	2.0	4.4	4.4	4.4	5.9	5.9	34.8	64.6
36	Sri Lanka	1.4	1.3	2.8	3.4	5.0	6.6	6.6	37.4	64.6
37	Algeria	8.0	7.8	7.5	7.3	7.1	6.3	5.6	2.4	51.9
38	Gaza-Westbank	3.6	3.6	4.4	4.4	4.4	4.4	4.4	19.6	48.8
39	Thailand	6.0	5.7	6.3	5.3	4.9	6.6	9.1	2.2	46.1
40	Tajikistan	9.2	1.1	1.1	1.1	1.1	12.9	12.4	4.1	43.1
41	Panama	0.5	0.0	1.7	2.6	2.6	2.6	2.6	25.9	38.5
42	Laos	0.0	0.0	0.0	0.0	0.2	0.4	0.4	34.1	35.1
43	Bangladesh	4.4	4.4	4.4	4.4	4.4	4.4	4.4	0.0	31.1
44	Costa Rica	3.9	3.9	3.9	3.9	3.9	3.9	3.9	0.0	27.1
45	Israel	4.2	3.0	3.0	3.0	3.0	3.0	3.0	4.5	26.8
46	Regional -Central America	6.6	5.1	3.3	2.6	2.6	1.4	1.4	2.7	25.7
47	India	3.2	3.2	3.2	3.2	3.2	3.2	3.2	0.0	22.5
48	Estonia	4.7	4.2	3.4	2.5	2.4	1.9	1.3	0.6	21.1
49	Regional -Andean Pact	3.4	3.2	3.2	3.2	1.9	1.9	1.0	0.0	17.9
50	Maldives	0.4	1.1	1.8	1.8	1.8	1.8	1.8	5.3	15.6
51	Malta	1.0	0.8	0.7	0.7	0.7	0.7	0.3	0.0	4.7
52	Uruguay	1.7	0.0	0.0	0.0	0.0	0.0	0.0	0.0	1.7
	Total Outstanding	2 015.2	1 988.4	2 003.4	1 830.5	1 720.2	1 651.3	1 481.6	7 594.5	20 285.1
	Sub-total for Member States	812.1	773.8	720.7	625.1	598.7	523.5	467.8	2 202.3	6 724.1

*　Member State
*　Member State as of 01.01.2007.

Chapter 18

The European Development Fund

1. The European Development Fund (EDF) and agreements with the ACP (African, Caribbean and Pacific) countries

Since 1958, the European Development Fund has been the main geographic instrument for financial and technical cooperation between the European Community and developing countries and territories which, for historic reasons, maintained special links with certain Member States. Unlike other external policy actions (see Chapter 13), the EDF is not financed from the general budget of the European Community.

The EDF comes within the broader context of comprehensive cooperation agreements signed between the Community and the group of African, Caribbean and Pacific States (ACP), the Member States being signatories to these Conventions independently of the Community. Seventy-eight ACP countries are now parties to the ACP-EC Partnership Agreement (¹) and 21 overseas countries and territories (OCTs) come under the Council Decision on the association of overseas countries and territories.

Apart from the EDF, the ACP Partnership Agreement covers the following:

(¹)   Geographic cooperation with South Africa, although signatory to the Agreement, is funded from the Community budget and not from the European Development Fund.

— at financial level: loans from the own resources of the European Investment Bank to finance national and regional development programmes;

— at trade level: a trade regime based on duty-free entry, without quotas, to the EC market for almost all ACP exports and specific protocols for sugar, beef, veal and bananas, which expires on 31 December 2007 and will be replaced by WTO-compatible Economic Partnership Agreements or the Generalised System of Preferences as from 1 January 2008 onwards.

First EDF:	1959-64	Convention on overseas countries and territories annexed to the Treaty
Second EDF:	1964-70	First Yaoundé Convention
Third EDF:	1970-75	Second Yaoundé Convention
Fourth EDF:	1975-80	First Lomé Convention
Fifth EDF:	1980-85	Second Lomé Convention
Sixth EDF:	1985-90	Third Lomé Convention
Seventh EDF:	1990-95	Fourth Lomé Convention
Eighth EDF:	1995-2000	Fourth (revised) Lomé Convention
Ninth EDF:	2000-07	Cotonou Agreement
Tenth EDF:	2008-13	Revised Cotonou Agreement

The Partnership Agreement, known as the 'Cotonou Agreement', signed on 23 June 2000 and revised on 25 June 2005, replaces all previous conventions and is notable for the long period it covers (20 years). It contains all the principles, objectives and rules governing cooperation between the EC and ACP states. Its financial aspects are specified in a financial protocol annexed to the Partnership Agreement (ninth EDF) and in a multiannual financial framework for the period 2008 to 2013 determined by a separate decision of the ACP-EC Council of Ministers, funded from the tenth EDF. Such a protocol or financial framework determines the contribution key and volume of resources that Member States commit to make available to the EDF and the EIB.

2. The resources of the EDF

The Member States provide resources amounting to nearly EUR 22 billion (excluding support expenditure) to the ACP countries under the tenth EDF, of which EUR 1.5 billion are contributions to risk capital, (concessional) loans and quasi-capital managed by the EIB through the Investment Facility. The ninth EDF, which entered into force on 1 April 2003, had an initial allocation of EUR 13.5 billion, plus EUR 4.0 billion uncommitted or decommitted funds from previous EDFs. In addition, EUR 286 million are available to the overseas countries and territories under the tenth EDF, as against EUR 175 million under the ninth EDF, increasing to EUR 325 million after taking into account the transfers from previous EDFs.

3. The financial regime of the EDF

3.1. Non-inclusion in the budget

Like the rest of Community expenditure, the resources of the EDF originally came from financial contributions by the Member States, but the cost-sharing formula or contribution keys were different from those used to determine the expenditure of the general budget. This EDF formula took into account the special relations between certain Member States and the ACP countries.

With the introduction of the own resources system, designed to replace the Member States' contributions, the Commission proposed on 12 June 1973 that the financing of the EDF by contributions be replaced by own resources as well, so that the EDF could be integrated into the Community's general budget. The Council rejected this idea.

The Commission likewise proposed the incorporation of the fifth EDF in the budget. The Council did not concur and maintained the contribution scheme based on a political scale through another internal agreement signed on 20 November 1979. This refusal to incorporate the EDF in the budget was one of the 'important reasons' put forward by Parliament when rejecting the budget for 1980 on 13 December 1979. In seeking an agreement on the 1980 budget, the Commission annexed to its new budget proposal of 29 February 1980 a document providing annual estimates for the EDF together with other budget information and ever since has provided the two arms of the budgetary authority with a document entitled 'Financial information' on the EDF together with its preliminary draft budget. Furthermore, Parliament, using its power to create new budget headings for non-compulsory expenditure, has since the 1977 budget added two headings with token entries that could be used to accommodate the EDF if it were incorporated in the budget.

The non-inclusion of the EDF in the budget has since been confirmed on several occasions: on 11-13 February 1988 in Brussels, the European Council affirmed that the EDF would continue to be financed outside the budget. Furthermore, the Final Act of the Intergovernmental Conference leading to the Maastricht Treaty (7 February 1992) 'agrees that the European Development Fund will continue to be financed by national contributions in accordance with the current provisions'.

Following the 2003 Commission communication assessing the advantages and disadvantages of incorporating the EDF in the budget, the Commission proposed the incorporation of the EDF into the general budget together with its proposals for the new financial framework 2007-13. The European Council of December 2005 confirmed its position on financing the EDF separately from the budget. However, it adopted contribution keys closer to those used for the budget, which might facilitate future integration of the EDF within the budget.

The headings concerning the EDF nevertheless remain in the budget documents (some years with a token entry, others with a dash), together with comments providing precise information on the financial activities organised under the Fund.

3.2. The cost-sharing formula for national contributions of Member States to the financing of the tenth EDF

The scale applicable to the tenth EDF following the latest enlargement of the EU:

Code	Country	%
BE	Belgium	3.53
BG	Bulgaria	0.14
CZ	Czech Republic	0.51
DK	Denmark	2.00
DE	Germany	20.50
EE	Estonia	0.05
IE	Ireland	0.91
EL	Greece	1.47
ES	Spain	7.85
FR	France	19.55
IT	Italy	12.86
CY	Cyprus	0.09
LV	Latvia	0.07
LT	Lithuania	0.12
LU	Luxembourg	0.27
HU	Hungary	0.55
MT	Malta	0.03
NL	Netherlands	4.85
AT	Austria	2.41
PL	Poland	1.30
PT	Portugal	1.15
RO	Romania	0.37
SI	Slovenia	0.18
SK	Slovakia	0.21
FI	Finland	1.47
SE	Sweden	2.74
UK	United Kingdom	14.82

3.3. A distinctive financial regime

1) Control by the Member States

Through the Council of Ministers and Committee of Ambassadors, set up by the Cotonou Agreement itself, and the EDF Committee, which issues an opinion prior to any Commission decision on country or regional strategy papers and on annual action programmes prepared jointly with the ACP partners, the Member States retain a direct influence on these financial measures.

2) Financial execution

Although the European Development Fund, unlike the other European funds (EAGGF, ESF, ERDF, Cohesion Fund, etc), is a true financial instrument separate from the general budget, it has neither legal personality nor real autonomy of management since its administrators are Commission departments: the Directorate-General for Development, which is responsible for programming, and the EuropeAid Cooperation Office, which is responsible for implementation.

Given the specificities of the EDF rules, the EDF accounts are not consolidated with those of the general budget. However, financial statements comply with accrual accounting principles, i.e. conform to accounting rules and methods drawn up for the EDF on the basis of International Accounting Standards (IPSAS/IAS) and Generally Accepted Accounting Principles (GAAPs). The rules of valuation and the accounting methods adopted by the Accounting Officer of the European Development Fund were validated by the Accounting Standards Committee in July 2006.

The EDF also has an accounting officer, in accordance with the principle that authorising officers and accounting officers should not be one and the same person, responsible for collecting revenue and disbursing expenditure. To make this principle of separate roles more consistent, the EDF accounting officer's department has been made part of DG Budget and the Commission's accounting officer has taken on the role of EDF accounting officer.

However, a large proportion of expenditure is implemented at local level through the decentralised management method, by a national authorising officer designated by each ACP country and under the supervision of a Commission delegation.

The implementing rules for expenditure and revenue under each EDF are the subject of a specific Financial Regulation, as far as possible aligned with the Community Financial Regulation.

The EDF's revenue and expenditure, like operations under the general budget, are subject to internal financial control and to the external control of the Court of Auditors, the latter regularly devoting a special chapter of its annual report to the management of the EDF.

3.4. Multiannual management

Unlike the management of the general budget, the principle of annuality is not applicable to the implementation of the EDF. After commitment, expenditure may be executed over several calendar years. This is the reason for the distinction between 'global commitments' (which consist in setting aside overall allocations for projects and programmes on the basis of a financing agreement) and 'specific commitments' (which are the actual actions giving rise to expenditure).

The European Development Fund is thus an important part of the EU's spending, even though it remains outside the general budget. Political pressure from the European Parliament for the inclusion of the EDF is high, but the different priorities of Member States make such a decision difficult. The simultaneous execution of several EDFs also introduces confusion and leads to criticism. However, the EDF also has a distinctive financial regime and has proven its usefulness. Reforming it would therefore be a very sensitive issue.

ANNEXES

Comparison of existing budgetary Treaty provisions with the provisions of the Treaty on the Functioning of the European Union (Lisbon Treaty)

Note to the reader: this annex contains abstracts of the consolidated version of the Treaty on the Functioning of the European Union as it will result from the amendments introduced by the Treaty of Lisbon, signed on 13 December 2007 in Lisbon. The Treaty of Lisbon is still in the process of being ratified by the Member States, in accordance with their respective constitutional requirements. As provided for in Article 6 thereof, the Treaty will enter into force on 1 January 2009, provided that all the instruments of ratification have been deposited, or, failing that, on the first day of the month following the deposit of the last instrument of ratification. This publication is provisional in nature. Until the entry into force of the Treaty of Lisbon, a number of rectifications may be made to one or other language version of the text, in order to correct possible errors which may come to light in the Treaty of Lisbon or in the prior treaties. This text has been produced for documentary purposes and does not involve the responsibility of the institutions of the European Union.

Consolidated version of the Treaty establishing the European Community	Treaty on the Functioning of the European Union
Article 268	*Article 310* (ex Article 268 TEC)
All items of revenue and expenditure of the Community, including those relating to the European Social Fund, shall be included in estimates to be drawn up for each financial year and shall be shown in the budget.	1. All items of revenue and expenditure of the Union shall be included in estimates to be drawn up for each financial year and shall be shown in the budget.
Administrative expenditure occasioned for the institutions by the provisions of the Treaty on European Union relating to common foreign and security policy and to cooperation in the fields of justice and home affairs shall be charged to the budget. The operational expenditure occasioned by the implementation of the said provisions may, under the conditions referred to therein, be charged to the budget.	The Union's annual budget shall be established by the European Parliament and the Council in accordance with Article 314.

The revenue and expenditure shown in the budget shall be in balance.

2. The expenditure shown in the budget shall be authorised for the annual budgetary period in accordance with the regulation referred to in Article 322. |

The revenue and expenditure shown in the budget shall be in balance.	3. The implementation of expenditure shown in the budget shall require the prior adoption of a legally binding Union act providing a legal basis for its action and for the implementation of the corresponding expenditure in accordance with the regulation referred to in Article 322, except in cases for which that law provides. 4. With a view to maintaining budgetary discipline, the Union shall not adopt any act which is likely to have appreciable implications for the budget without providing an assurance that the expenditure arising from such an act is capable of being financed within the limit of the Union's own resources and in compliance with the multiannual financial framework referred to in Article 312. 5. The budget shall be implemented in accordance with the principle of sound financial management. Member States shall cooperate with the Union to ensure that the appropriations entered in the budget are used in accordance with this principle. 6. The Union and the Member States, in accordance with Article 325, shall counter fraud and any other illegal activities affecting the financial interests of the Union.
	CHAPTER 1 THE UNION'S OWN RESOURCES
Article 269	*Article 311* (ex Article 269 TEC)
Without prejudice to other revenue, the budget shall be financed wholly from own resources.	The Union shall provide itself with the means necessary to attain its objectives and carry through its policies.

The Council, acting unanimously on a proposal from the Commission and after consulting the European Parliament, shall lay down provisions relating to the system of own resources of the Community, which it shall recommend to the Member States for adoption in accordance with their respective constitutional requirements.	Without prejudice to other revenue, the budget shall be financed wholly from own resources. The Council, acting in accordance with a special legislative procedure, shall unanimously and after consulting the European Parliament adopt a decision laying down the provisions relating to the system of own resources of the Union. In this context it may establish new categories of own resources or abolish an existing category. That decision shall not enter into force until it is approved by the Member States in accordance with their respective constitutional requirements. The Council, acting by means of regulations in accordance with a special legislative procedure, shall lay down implementing measures for the Union's own resources system in so far as this is provided for in the decision adopted on the basis of the third paragraph. The Council shall act after obtaining the consent of the European Parliament.
<div align="center">Article 270</div> With a view to maintaining budgetary discipline, the Commission shall not make any proposal for a Community act, or alter its proposals, or adopt any implementing measure which is likely to have appreciable implications for the budget without providing the assurance that that proposal or that measure is capable of being financed within the limit of the Community's own resources arising under provisions laid down by the Council pursuant to Article 269.	<div align="center">Repealed *Content included in Article 310(4)*</div>

CHAPTER 2

THE MULTIANNUAL FINANCIAL FRAMEWORK

Article 312

1. The multiannual financial framework shall ensure that Union expenditure develops in an orderly manner and within the limits of its own resources.

It shall be established for a period of at least five years.

The annual budget of the Union shall comply with the multiannual financial framework.

2. The Council, acting in accordance with a special legislative procedure, shall adopt a regulation laying down the multiannual financial framework. The Council shall act unanimously after obtaining the consent of the European Parliament, which shall be given by a majority of its component members.

The European Council may, unanimously, adopt a decision authorising the Council to act by a qualified majority when adopting the regulation referred to in the first subparagraph(*).

3. The financial framework shall determine the amounts of the annual ceilings on commitment appropriations by category of expenditure and of the annual ceiling on payment appropriations. The categories of expenditure, limited in number, shall correspond to the Union's major sectors of activity.

(*) Subject to a Procès-Verbal of Rectification under examination at the time of editing this book.

	The financial framework shall lay down any other provisions required for the annual budgetary procedure to run smoothly. 4. Where no Council regulation determining a new financial framework has been adopted by the end of the previous financial framework, the ceilings and other provisions corresponding to the last year of that framework shall be extended until such time as that act is adopted. 5. Throughout the procedure leading to the adoption of the financial framework, the European Parliament, the Council and the Commission shall take any measure necessary to facilitate its adoption.
Article 271	Becomes Article 316
The expenditure shown in the budget shall be authorised for one financial year, unless the regulations made pursuant to Article 279 provide otherwise. In accordance with conditions to be laid down pursuant to Article 279, any appropriations, other than those relating to staff expenditure, that are unexpended at the end of the financial year may be carried forward to the next financial year only. Appropriations shall be classified under different chapters grouping items of expenditure according to their nature or purpose and subdivided, as far as may be necessary, in accordance with the regulations made pursuant to Article 279.	

The expenditure of the European Parliament, the Council, the Commission and the Court of Justice shall be set out in separate parts of the budget, without prejudice to special arrangements for certain common items of expenditure.	
	CHAPTER 3 **THE UNION'S ANNUAL BUDGET**
Article 272	*Article 313* (ex Article 272(1), TEC)
1. The financial year shall run from 1 January to 31 December.	The financial year shall run from 1 January to 31 December.
	Article 314 (ex Article 272(2) to (10), TEC) The European Parliament and the Council, acting in accordance with a special legislative procedure, shall establish the Union's annual budget in accordance with the following provisions.
2. Each institution of the Community shall, before 1 July, draw up estimates of its expenditure. The Commission shall consolidate these estimates in a preliminary draft budget. It shall attach thereto an opinion which may contain different estimates. The preliminary draft budget shall contain an estimate of revenue and an estimate of expenditure.	1. With the exception of the European Central Bank, each institution shall, before 1 July, draw up estimates of its expenditure for the following financial year. The Commission shall consolidate these estimates in a draft budget. which may contain different estimates. The draft budget shall contain an estimate of revenue and an estimate of expenditure.
3. The Commission shall place the preliminary draft budget before the Council not later than 1 September of the year preceding that in which the budget is to be implemented.	

The Council shall consult the Commission and, where appropriate, the other institutions concerned whenever it intends to depart from the preliminary draft budget.

The Council, acting by a qualified majority, shall establish the draft budget and forward it to the European Parliament.

4. The draft budget shall be placed before the European Parliament not later than 5 October of the year preceding that in which the budget is to be implemented.

The European Parliament shall have the right to amend the draft budget, acting by a majority of its Members, and to propose to the Council, acting by an absolute majority of the votes cast, modifications to the draft budget relating to expenditure necessarily resulting from this Treaty or from acts adopted in accordance therewith.

If, within 45 days of the draft budget being placed before it, the European Parliament has given its approval, the budget shall stand as finally adopted. If within this period the European Parliament has not amended the draft budget nor proposed any modifications thereto, the budget shall be deemed to be finally adopted.

If within this period the European Parliament has adopted amendments or proposed modifications, the draft budget together with the amendments or proposed modifications shall be forwarded to the Council.

5. After discussing the draft budget with the Commission and, where appropriate, with the other institutions concerned, the Council shall act under the following conditions:

2. The Commission shall submit a proposal containing the draft budget to the European Parliament and to the Council not later than 1 September of the year preceding that in which the budget is to be implemented.

The Commission may amend the draft budget during the procedure until such time as the Conciliation Committee, referred to in paragraph 5, is convened.

3. The Council shall adopt its position on the draft budget and forward it to the European Parliament not later than 1 October of the year preceding that in which the budget is to be implemented. The Council shall inform the European Parliament in full of the reasons which led it to adopt its position.

4. If, within 42 days of such communication, the European Parliament:

(a) approves the position of the Council, the budget shall be adopted;

(b) has not taken a decision, the budget shall be deemed to have been adopted;

(c) adopts amendments by a majority of its component members, the amended draft shall be forwarded to the Council and to the Commission. The President of the European Parliament, in agreement with the President of the Council, shall immediately convene a meeting of the Conciliation Committee. However, if within 10 days of the draft being forwarded the Council informs the European Parliament that it has approved all its amendments, the Conciliation Committee shall not meet.

(a) the Council may, acting by a qualified majority, modify any of the amendments adopted by the European Parliament;

(b) with regard to the proposed modifications:

– where a modification proposed by the European Parliament does not have the effect of increasing the total amount of the expenditure of an institution, owing in particular to the fact that the increase in expenditure which it would involve would be expressly compensated by one or more proposed modifications correspondingly reducing expenditure, the Council may, acting by a qualified majority, reject the proposed modification. In the absence of a decision to reject it, the proposed modification shall stand as accepted;

– where a modification proposed by the European Parliament has the effect of increasing the total amount of the expenditure of an institution, the Council may, acting by a qualified majority, accept this proposed modification. In the absence of a decision to accept it, the proposed modification shall stand as rejected;

– where, in pursuance of one of the two preceding subparagraphs, the Council has rejected a proposed modification, it may, acting by a qualified majority, either retain the amount shown in the draft budget or fix another amount.

The draft budget shall be modified on the basis of the proposed modifications accepted by the Council.

5. The Conciliation Committee, which shall be composed of the members of the Council or their representatives and an equal number of members representing the European Parliament, shall have the task of reaching agreement on a joint text, by a qualified majority of the members of the Council or their representatives and by a majority of the representatives of the European Parliament within 21 days of its being convened, on the basis of the positions of the European Parliament and the Council.

The Commission shall take part in the Conciliation Committee's proceedings and shall take all the necessary initiatives with a view to reconciling the positions of the European Parliament and the Council.

6. If, within the 21 days referred to in paragraph 5, the Conciliation Committee agrees on a joint text, the European Parliament and the Council shall each have a period of 14 days from the date of that agreement in which to approve the joint text.

7. If, within the period of 14 days referred to in paragraph 6:

(a) the European Parliament and the Council both approve the joint text or fail to take a decision, or if one of these institutions approves the joint text while the other one fails to take a decision, the budget shall be deemed to be definitively adopted in accordance with the joint text; or

If, within 15 days of the draft being placed before it, the Council has not modified any of the amendments adopted by the European Parliament and if the modifications proposed by the latter have been accepted, the budget shall be deemed to be finally adopted. The Council shall inform the European Parliament that it has not modified any of the amendments and that the proposed modifications have been accepted.

If within this period the Council has modified one or more of the amendments adopted by the European Parliament or if the modifications proposed by the latter have been rejected or modified, the modified draft budget shall again be forwarded to the European Parliament. The Council shall inform the European Parliament of the results of its deliberations.

6. Within 15 days of the draft budget being placed before it, the European Parliament, which shall have been notified of the action taken on its proposed modifications, may, acting by a majority of its Members and three fifths of the votes cast, amend or reject the modifications to its amendments made by the Council and shall adopt the budget accordingly. If within this period the European Parliament has not acted, the budget shall be deemed to be finally adopted.

7. When the procedure provided for in this Article has been completed, the President of the European Parliament shall declare that the budget has been finally adopted.

(b) the European Parliament, acting by a majority of its component members, and the Council both reject the joint text, or if one of these institutions rejects the joint text while the other one fails to take a decision, a new draft budget shall be submitted by the Commission; or

(c) the European Parliament, acting by a majority of its component members, rejects the joint text while the Council approves it, a new draft budget shall be submitted by the Commission; or

(d) the European Parliament approves the joint text whilst the Council rejects it, the European Parliament may, within 14 days from the date of the rejection by the Council and acting by a majority of its component members and three-fifths of the votes cast, decide to confirm all or some of the amendments referred to in paragraph 4(c). Where a European Parliament amendment is not confirmed, the position agreed in the Conciliation Committee on the budget heading which is the subject of the amendment shall be retained. The budget shall be deemed to be definitively adopted on this basis.

8. If, within the 21 days referred to in paragraph 5, the Conciliation Committee does not agree on a joint text, a new draft budget shall be submitted by the Commission.

9. When the procedure provided for in this Article has been completed, the President of the European Parliament shall declare that the budget has been definitively adopted.

8. However, the European Parliament, acting by a majority of its Members and two thirds of the votes cast, may, if there are important reasons, reject the draft budget and ask for a new draft to be submitted to it.

9. A maximum rate of increase in relation to the expenditure of the same type to be incurred during the current year shall be fixed annually for the total expenditure other than that necessarily resulting from this Treaty or from acts adopted in accordance therewith.

The Commission shall, after consulting the Economic Policy Committee, declare what this maximum rate is as it results from:

- the trend, in terms of volume, of the gross national product within the Community;

- the average variation in the budgets of the Member States; and the trend of the cost of living during the preceding financial year.

The maximum rate shall be communicated, before 1 May, to all the institutions of the Community. The latter shall be required to conform to this during the budgetary procedure, subject to the provisions of the fourth and fifth subparagraphs of this paragraph.

If, in respect of expenditure other than that necessarily resulting from this Treaty or from acts adopted in accordance therewith, the actual rate of increase in the draft budget established by the Council is over half the maximum rate, the European Parliament may, exercising its right of amendment, further increase the total amount of that expenditure to a limit not exceeding half the maximum rate.

10. Each institution shall exercise the powers conferred upon it under this Article in compliance with the treaties and the acts adopted thereunder, with particular regard to the Union's own resources and the balance between revenue and expenditure.

Where the European Parliament, the Council or the Commission consider that the activities of the Communities require that the rate determined according to the procedure laid down in this paragraph should be exceeded, another rate may be fixed by agreement between the Council, acting by a qualified majority, and the European Parliament, acting by a majority of its Members and three fifths of the votes cast. 10. Each institution shall exercise the powers conferred upon it by this Article, with due regard for the provisions of the Treaty and for acts adopted in accordance therewith, in particular those relating to the Communities' own resources and to the balance between revenue and expenditure.	
<div align="center">Article 273</div>	<div align="center">*Article 315* (ex Article 273 TEC)</div>
If, at the beginning of a financial year, the budget has not yet been voted, a sum equivalent to not more than one twelfth of the budget appropriations for the preceding financial year may be spent each month in respect of any chapter or other subdivision of the budget in accordance with the provisions of the Regulations made pursuant to Article 279; this arrangement shall not, however, have the effect of placing at the disposal of the Commission appropriations in excess of one twelfth of those provided for in the draft budget in course of preparation. The Council may, acting by a qualified majority, provided that the other conditions laid down in the first subparagraph are observed, authorise expenditure in excess of one twelfth.	If, at the beginning of a financial year, the budget has not yet been definitively adopted, a sum equivalent to not more than one twelfth of the budget appropriations for the preceding financial year may be spent each month in respect of any chapter of the budget in accordance with the provisions of the regulations made pursuant to Article 322; that sum shall not, however, exceed one twelfth of the appropriations provided for in the same chapter of the draft budget. The Council on a proposal by the Commission, may, provided that the other conditions laid down in the first paragraph are observed, authorise expenditure in excess of one twelfth in accordance with the regulations made pursuant to Article 322. The Council shall forward the decision immediately to the European Parliament.

If the decision relates to expenditure which does not necessarily result from this Treaty or from acts adopted in accordance therewith, the Council shall forward it immediately to the European Parliament; within 30 days the European Parliament, acting by a majority of its Members and three fifths of the votes cast, may adopt a different decision on the expenditure in excess of the one twelfth referred to in the first subparagraph. This part of the decision of the Council shall be suspended until the European Parliament has taken its decision. If within the said period the European Parliament has not taken a decision which differs from the decision of the Council, the latter shall be deemed to be finally adopted.

The decisions referred to in the second and third subparagraphs shall lay down the necessary measures relating to resources to ensure application of this Article.

The decision referred to in the second paragraph shall lay down the necessary measures relating to resources to ensure application of this Article, in accordance with the acts referred to in Article 311.

It shall enter into force 30 days following its adoption if the European Parliament, acting by a majority of its component Members, has not decided to reduce this expenditure within that time-limit.

Article 316
(ex Article 271 TEC)

In accordance with conditions to be laid down pursuant to Article 322, any appropriations, other than those relating to staff expenditure, that are unexpended at the end of the financial year may be carried forward to the next financial year only.

Appropriations shall be classified under different chapters grouping items of expenditure according to their nature or purpose and subdivided in accordance with the regulations made pursuant to Article 322.

	The expenditure of the European Parliament, the European Council and the Council, the Commission and the Court of Justice of the European Union shall be set out in separate parts of the budget, without prejudice to special arrangements for certain common items of expenditure.
	CHAPTER 4 IMPLEMENTATION OF THE BUDGET AND DISCHARGE *Article 317*
Article 274	(ex Article 274 TEC)
The Commission shall implement the budget, in accordance with the provisions of the regulations made pursuant to Article 279, on its own responsibility and within the limits of the appropriations, having regard to the principles of sound financial management. Member States shall cooperate with the Commission to ensure that the appropriations are used in accordance with the principles of sound financial management. The regulations shall lay down detailed rules for each institution concerning its part in effecting its own expenditure. Within the budget, the Commission may, subject to the limits and conditions laid down in the regulations made pursuant to Article 279, transfer appropriations from one chapter to another or from one subdivision to another.	The Commission shall implement the budget in cooperation with the Member States, in accordance with the provisions of the regulations made pursuant to Article 322, on its own responsibility and within the limits of the appropriations, having regard to the principles of sound financial management. Member States shall cooperate with the Commission to ensure that the appropriations are used in accordance with the principles of sound financial management. The regulations shall lay down the control and audit obligations of the Member States in the implementation of the budget and the resulting responsibilities. They shall also lay down the responsibilities and detailed rules for each institution concerning its part in effecting its own expenditure. Within the budget, the Commission may, subject to the limits and conditions laid down in the regulations made pursuant to Article 322, transfer appropriations from one chapter to another or from one subdivision to another.

Article 275	Article 318 (ex Article 275 TEC)
The Commission shall submit annually to the Council and to the European Parliament the accounts of the preceding financial year relating to the implementation of the budget. The Commission shall also forward to them a financial statement of the assets and liabilities of the Community.	The Commission shall submit annually to the European Parliament and to the Council the accounts of the preceding financial year relating to the implementation of the budget. The Commission shall also forward to them a financial statement of the assets and liabilities of the Union. The Commission shall also submit to the European Parliament and to the Council an evaluation report on the Union's finances based on the results achieved, in particular in relation to the indications given by the European Parliament and the Council pursuant to Article 319.
Article 276	Article 319 (ex Article 276 TEC)
1. The European Parliament, acting on a recommendation from the Council which shall act by a qualified majority, shall give a discharge to the Commission in respect of the implementation of the budget. To this end, the Council and the European Parliament in turn shall examine the accounts and the financial statement referred to in Article 275, the annual report by the Court of Auditors together with the replies of the institutions under audit to the observations of the Court of Auditors, the statement of assurance referred to in Article 248(1), second subparagraph and any relevant special reports by the Court of Auditors.	1. The European Parliament, acting on a recommendation from the Council, shall give a discharge to the Commission in respect of the implementation of the budget. To this end, the Council and the European Parliament in turn shall examine the accounts, the financial statement and the evaluation report referred to in Article 318, the annual report by the Court of Auditors together with the replies of the institutions under audit to the observations of the Court of Auditors, the statement of assurance referred to in Article 287(1), second subparagraph, and any relevant special reports by the Court of Auditors.

2. Before giving a discharge to the Commission, or for any other purpose in connection with the exercise of its powers over the implementation of the budget, the European Parliament may ask to hear the Commission give evidence with regard to the execution of expenditure or the operation of financial control systems. The Commission shall submit any necessary information to the European Parliament at the latter's request.	2. Before giving a discharge to the Commission, or for any other purpose in connection with the exercise of its powers over the implementation of the budget, the European Parliament may ask to hear the Commission give evidence with regard to the execution of expenditure or the operation of financial control systems. The Commission shall submit any necessary information to the European Parliament at the latter's request.
3. The Commission shall take all appropriate steps to act on the observations in the decisions giving discharge and on other observations by the European Parliament relating to the execution of expenditure, as well as on comments accompanying the recommendations on discharge adopted by the Council.	3. The Commission shall take all appropriate steps to act on the observations in the decisions giving discharge and on other observations by the European Parliament relating to the execution of expenditure, as well as on comments accompanying the recommendations on discharge adopted by the Council.
At the request of the European Parliament or the Council, the Commission shall report on the measures taken in the light of these observations and comments and in particular on the instructions given to the departments which are responsible for the implementation of the budget. These reports shall also be forwarded to the Court of Auditors.	At the request of the European Parliament or the Council, the Commission shall report on the measures taken in the light of these observations and comments and in particular on the instructions given to the departments which are responsible for the implementation of the budget. These reports shall also be forwarded to the Court of Auditors.
	CHAPTER 5 COMMON PROVISIONS
Article 277	*Article 320* (ex Article 277 TEC)
The budget shall be drawn up in the unit of account determined in accordance with the provisions of the regulations made pursuant to Article 279.	The multiannual financial framework and the annual budget shall be drawn up in euro.

Article 278	Article 321 (ex Article 278 TEC)
The Commission may, provided it notifies the competent authorities of the Member States concerned, transfer into the currency of one of the Member States its holdings in the currency of another Member State, to the extent necessary to enable them to be used for purposes which come within the scope of this Treaty. The Commission shall as far as possible avoid making such transfers if it possesses cash or liquid assets in the currencies which it needs.	The Commission may, provided it notifies the competent authorities of the Member States concerned, transfer into the currency of one of the Member States its holdings in the currency of another Member State, to the extent necessary to enable them to be used for purposes which come within the scope of the Treaties. The Commission shall as far as possible avoid making such transfers if it possesses cash or liquid assets in the currencies which it needs.
The Commission shall deal with each Member State through the authority designated by the State concerned. In carrying out financial operations the Commission shall employ the services of the bank of issue of the Member State concerned or of any other financial institution approved by that State.	The Commission shall deal with each Member State through the authority designated by the State concerned. In carrying out financial operations the Commission shall employ the services of the bank of issue of the Member State concerned or of any other financial institution approved by that State.
Article 279	Article 322 (ex Article 279 TEC)
The Council, acting unanimously on a proposal from the Commission and after consulting the European Parliament and obtaining the opinion of the Court of Auditors, shall:	1. The European Parliament and the Council, acting in accordance with the ordinary legislative procedure, and after consulting the Court of Auditors, shall adopt by means of regulations:
(a) make Financial Regulations specifying in particular the procedure to be adopted for establishing and implementing the budget and for presenting and auditing accounts;	(a) the financial rules which determine in particular the procedure to be adopted for establishing and implementing the budget and for presenting and auditing accounts;
(b) lay down rules concerning the responsibility of financial controllers, authorising officers and accounting officers, and concerning appropriate arrangements for inspection.	(b) rules providing for checks on the responsibility of financial actors, in particular authorising officers and accounting officers.

From 1 January 2007, the Council shall act by a qualified majority on a proposal from the Commission and after consulting the European Parliament and obtaining the opinion of the Court of Auditors.	
2. The Council, acting unanimously on a proposal from the Commission and after consulting the European Parliament and obtaining the opinion of the Court of Auditors, shall determine the methods and procedure whereby the budget revenue provided under the arrangements relating to the Community's own resources shall be made available to the Commission, and determine the measures to be applied if need be, to meet cash requirements.	2. The Council, acting on a proposal from the Commission and after consulting the European Parliament and the Court of Auditors, shall determine the methods and procedure whereby the budget revenue provided under the arrangements relating to the Union's own resources shall be made available to the Commission, and determine the measures to be applied, if need be, to meet cash requirements.
	Article 323 The European Parliament, the Council and the Commission shall ensure that the financial means are made available to allow the Union to fulfil its legal obligations in respect of third parties.
	Article 324 Regular meetings between the Presidents of the European Parliament, the Council and the Commission shall be convened, on the initiative of the Commission, under the budgetary procedures referred to in this Title (*). The Presidents shall take all the necessary steps to promote consultation and the reconciliation of the positions of the institutions over which they preside in order to facilitate the implementation of this Title.

(*) Subject to a Procès-Verbal of Rectification under examination.

CHAPTER 6

COMBATTING FRAUD

Article 280	Article 325 (ex Article 280 TEC)
1. The Community and the Member States shall counter fraud and any other illegal activities affecting the financial interests of the Community through measures to be taken in accordance with this Article, which shall act as a deterrent and be such as to afford effective protection in the Member States.	1. The Union and the Member States shall counter fraud and any other illegal activities affecting the financial interests of the Union through measures to be taken in accordance with this Article, which shall act as a deterrent and be such as to afford effective protection in the Member States, and in all the Union's institutions, bodies, offices and agencies.
2. Member States shall take the same measures to counter fraud affecting the financial interests of the Community as they take to counter fraud affecting their own financial interests.	2. Member States shall take the same measures to counter fraud affecting the financial interests of the Union as they take to counter fraud affecting their own financial interests.
3. Without prejudice to other provisions of this Treaty, the Member States shall coordinate their action aimed at protecting the financial interests of the Community against fraud. To this end they shall organise, together with the Commission, close and regular cooperation between the competent authorities.	3. Without prejudice to other provisions of the Treaties, the Member States shall coordinate their action aimed at protecting the financial interests of the Union against fraud. To this end they shall organise, together with the Commission, close and regular cooperation between the competent authorities.
4. The Council, acting in accordance with the procedure referred to in Article 251, after consulting the Court of Auditors, shall adopt the necessary measures in the fields of the prevention of and fight against fraud affecting the financial interests of the Community with a view to affording effective and equivalent protection in the Member States. These measures shall not concern the application of national criminal law or the national administration of justice.	4. The European Parliament and the Council, acting in accordance with the ordinary legislative procedure, after consulting the Court of Auditors, shall adopt the necessary measures in the fields of the prevention of and fight against fraud affecting the financial interests of the Union with a view to affording effective and equivalent protection in the Member States and in all the Union's institutions, bodies, offices and agencies.
5. The Commission, in cooperation with Member States, shall each year submit to the European Parliament and to the Council a report on the measures taken for the implementation of this Article.	5. The Commission, in cooperation with Member States, shall each year submit to the European Parliament and to the Council a report on the measures taken for the implementation of this Article.

L 253/42   [EN]   Official Journal of the European Communities   7.10.2000

II

(Acts whose publication is not obligatory)

COUNCIL

COUNCIL DECISION

of 29 September 2000

on the system of the European Communities' own resources

(2000/597/EC, Euratom)

THE COUNCIL OF THE EUROPEAN UNION,

Having regard to the Treaty establishing the European Community, and in particular Article 269 thereof,

Having regard to the Treaty establishing the European Atomic Energy Community, and in particular Article 173 thereof,

Having regard to the proposal from the Commission (¹),

Having regard to the opinion of the European Parliament (²),

Having regard to the opinion of the Court of Auditors (³),

Having regard to the opinion of the Economic and Social Committee (⁴),

Whereas:

(1) The European Council meeting in Berlin on 24 and 25 March 1999 concluded, *inter alia*, that the system of the Communities' own resources should be equitable, transparent, cost-effective, simple and based on criteria which best express each Member State's ability to contribute.

(2) The Communities' own resources system must ensure adequate resources for the orderly development of the Communities' policies, subject to the need for strict budgetary discipline.

(3) It is appropriate that the best quality data be used for the purposes of the budget of the European Union and the Communities' own resources. The application of the European system of integrated economic accounts (hereinafter referred to as the 'ESA 95') in accordance with

Council Regulation (EC) No 2223/96 (⁵) will improve the quality of measurement of national accounts data.

(4) It is appropriate to use the most recent statistical concepts for the purposes of own resources and accordingly to define gross national product (GNP) as being equal for these purposes to gross national income (GNI) as provided by the Commission in application of the ESA 95 in accordance with Regulation (EC) No 2223/96.

(5) It is, moreover, appropriate, should modifications to the ESA 95 result in significant changes in GNI as provided by the Commission in accordance with Regulation (EC) No 2223/96, that the Council decide whether these modifications apply for the purposes of own resources.

(6) According to Council Decision 94/728/EC, Euratom of 31 October 1994 on the system of the European Communities' own resources (⁶), the maximum ceiling of own resources for 1999 was set equal to 1,27 % of the Communities' GNP at market prices and an overall ceiling of 1,335 % of the Communities' GNP was set for appropriations for commitments.

(7) It is appropriate to adapt these ceilings expressed as a percent of GNP in order to maintain unchanged the amount of financial resources put at the disposal of the Communities by establishing a formula for the determination of the new ceilings, in relation to GNP as defined for the present purposes, to be applied after the entry into force of this Decision.

(¹) OJ C 274 E, 28.9.1999, p. 39.
(²) Opinion delivered on 17 November 1999 (OJ C 189, 7.7.2000, p. 79).
(³) OJ C 310, 28.10.1999, p. 1.
(⁴) OJ C 368, 20.12.1999, p. 16.

(⁵) OJ L 310, 30.11.1996, p. 1. Regulation as amended by Regulation (EC) No 448/98 (OJ L 58, 27.2.1998, p. 1).
(⁶) OJ L 293, 12.11.1994, p. 9.

7.10.2000 | EN | Official Journal of the European Communities   L 253/43

(8) It is appropriate that the same method be used in the future on the occasion of changes in the ESA 95 which may have effects on the level of GNP.

(9) In order further to continue the process of making allowance for each Member State's ability to contribute to the system of own resources and of correcting the regressive aspects of the current system for the least prosperous Member States, the European Council meeting in Berlin of 24 and 25 March 1999 concluded that the Union's financing rules would be amended as follows:

— the maximum rate of call of the VAT resource would be reduced from 1 % to 0,75 % in 2002 and 2003 and to 0,50 % from 2004 onwards,

— the value added tax base of the Member States would continue to be restricted to 50 % of their GNP.

(10) The European Council of 24 and 25 March 1999 concluded that it is appropriate to adapt the amount retained by Member States to cover the costs related to collection in connection with the so-called traditional own resources paid to the budget of the European Union.

(11) Budgetary imbalances should be corrected in such a way as not to affect the own resources available for the Communities' policies and be resolved, to the extent possible, by means of expenditure policy.

(12) The European Council of 24 and 25 March 1999 concluded that the manner for calculating the correction of budgetary imbalances in favour of the United Kingdom as defined in Decision 88/376/EEC, Euratom (¹) and confirmed by Decision 94/728/EC, Euratom, should not include the windfall gains resulting from changes in the financing systems and from future enlargement. Accordingly, at the time of enlargement, an adjustment will reduce 'total Allocated Expenditure' by an amount equivalent to the annual pre-accession expenditure in the acceding countries, thereby ensuring that expenditure which is unabated remains so.

(13) For reasons of clarity, the description of the calculation of the correction in respect of budgetary imbalances granted to the United Kingdom has been simplified. This simplification has no impact on the determination of the amount of this correction granted to the United Kingdom.

(14) The European Council of 24 and 25 March 1999 concluded that the financing of the correction of budgetary imbalances in favour of the United Kingdom should be modified to allow Austria, Germany, the Netherlands and Sweden to see a reduction in their financing share to 25 % of the normal share.

(15) The monetary reserve, hereinafter referred to as 'the EAGGF monetary reserve', the reserve for the financing of the Loan Guarantee Fund and the reserve for emer-

(¹) OJ L 185, 15.7.1988, p. 24.

gency aid in non-member countries are covered by specific provisions.

(16) The Commission should undertake, before 1 January 2006, a general review of the operation of the own resources system, accompanied, if necessary, by appropriate proposals, in the light of all relevant factors including the effects of enlargement on the financing of the budget of the European Union, the possibility of modifying the own resources structure by creating new autonomous own resources and the correction of budgetary imbalances granted to the United Kingdom as well as the granting to Austria, Germany, the Netherlands and Sweden of the reduction in the financing of the budgetary imbalances in favour of the United Kingdom.

(17) Provisions must be laid down to cover the changeover from the system introduced by Decision 94/728/EC, Euratom to that arising from this Decision.

(18) The European Council of 24 and 25 March 1999 concluded that this Decision should take effect on 1 January 2002,

HAS LAID DOWN THESE PROVISIONS, WHICH IT RECOMMENDS TO THE MEMBER STATES FOR ADOPTION:

Article 1

The Communities shall be allocated own resources in accordance with the rules laid down in the following Articles in order to ensure, in accordance with Article 269 of the Treaty establishing the European Community (hereinafter referred to as the 'EC Treaty') and Article 173 of the Treaty establishing the European Atomic Energy Community (hereinafter referred to as the 'Euratom Treaty'), the financing of the budget of the European Union.

The budget of the European Union shall, without prejudice to other revenue, be financed wholly from the Communities' own resources.

Article 2

1. Revenue from the following shall constitute own resources entered in the budget of the European Union:

(a) levies, premiums, additional or compensatory amounts, additional amounts or factors and other duties established or to be established by the institutions of the Communities in respect of trade with non-member countries within the framework of the common agricultural policy, and also contributions and other duties provided for within the framework of the common organisation of the markets in sugar;

(b) Common Customs Tariff duties and other duties established or to be established by the institutions of the Communities in respect of trade with non-member countries and customs duties on products coming under the Treaty establishing the European Coal and Steel Community;

(c) the application of a uniform rate valid for all Member States to the harmonised VAT assessment bases determined according to Community rules. The assessment base to be taken into account for this purpose shall not exceed 50 % of GNP for each Member State, as defined in paragraph 7;

(d) the application of a rate — to be determined pursuant to the budgetary procedure in the light of the total of all other revenue — to the sum of all the Member States' GNPs.

2. Revenue deriving from any new charges introduced within the framework of a common policy, in accordance with the EC Treaty or the Euratom Treaty, provided that the procedure laid down in Article 269 of the EC Treaty or in Article 173 of the Euratom Treaty has been followed, shall also constitute own resources entered in the budget of the European Union.

3. Member States shall retain, by way of collection costs, 25 % of the amounts referred to in paragraph 1(a) and (b), which shall be established after 31 December 2000.

4. The uniform rate referred to in paragraph 1(c) shall correspond to the rate resulting from the difference between:

(a) the maximum rate of call of the VAT resource, which is fixed at:

0,75 % in 2002 and 2003,

0,50 % from 2004 onwards,

and

(b) a rate ('frozen rate') equivalent to the ratio between the amount of the compensation referred to in Article 4 and the sum of the VAT assessment bases (established in accordance with paragraph (1)(c)) of all Member States, taking into account the fact that the United Kingdom is excluded from the financing of its correction and that the share of Austria, Germany, the Netherlands and Sweden in the financing of the United Kingdom correction is reduced to one fourth of its normal value.

5. The rate fixed under paragraph 1(d) shall apply to the GNP of each Member State.

6. If, at the beginning of the financial year, the budget has not been adopted, the previous uniform VAT rate and rate applicable to Member States' GNPs, without prejudice to the provisions adopted in accordance with Article 8(2) as regards the EAGGF monetary reserve, the reserve for financing the Loan Guarantee Fund and the reserve for emergency aid in third countries, shall remain applicable until the entry into force of the new rates.

7. For the purposes of applying this Decision, GNP shall mean GNI for the year at market prices as provided by the Commission in application of the ESA 95 in accordance with Regulation (EC) No 2223/96.

Should modifications to the ESA 95 result in significant changes in the GNI as provided by the Commission, the Council, acting unanimously on a proposal of the Commission

and after consulting the European Parliament, shall decide whether these modifications shall apply for the purposes of this Decision.

Article 3

1. The total amount of own resources assigned to the Communities to cover appropriations for payments may not exceed a certain percentage of the total GNPs of the Member States. This percentage, expressed in two decimal places, will be calculated by the Commission in December 2001 on the basis of the following formula:

Maximum own resources =

$$1,27 \% \times \frac{1998 + 1999 + 2000 \text{ GNP ESA second edition}}{1998 + 1999 + 2000 \text{ GNP ESA 95}}$$

2. Appropriations for commitments entered in the general budget of the European Union must follow an orderly progression resulting in a total amount, which does not exceed a certain percentage of the total GNPs of the Member States. This percentage, expressed in two decimal places, shall be calculated by the Commission in December 2001 on the basis of the following formula:

Maximum appropriations for commitments =

$$1,335 \% \times \frac{1998 + 1999 + 2000 \text{ GNP ESA second edition}}{1998 + 1999 + 2000 \text{ GNP ESA 95}}$$

An orderly ratio between appropriations for commitments and appropriations for payments shall be maintained to guarantee their compatibility and to enable the ceilings pursuant to paragraph 1 to be respected in subsequent years.

3. The Commission shall communicate to the budgetary authority the new ceilings for own resources before 31 December 2001.

4. The method described in paragraphs 1 and 2 will be followed in the case of modifications to the ESA 95 which result in changes in the level of GNP.

Article 4

The United Kingdom shall be granted a correction in respect of budgetary imbalances.

This correction shall be established by:

(a) calculating the difference, in the preceding financial year, between:

— the percentage share of the United Kingdom in the sum of uncapped VAT assessment bases, and

— the percentage share of the United Kingdom in total allocated expenditure;

7.10.2000   [EN]   Official Journal of the European Communities   L 253/45

(b) multiplying the difference thus obtained by total allocated expenditure;

(c) multiplying the result under (b) by 0,66;

(d) subtracting from the result under (c) the effects arising for the United Kingdom from the changeover to capped VAT and the payments referred to in Article 2(1)(d), namely the difference between:

— what the United Kingdom would have had to pay for the amounts financed by the resources referred to in Article 2(1)(c) and (d), if the uniform rate had been applied to non-capped VAT bases, and

— the payments of the United Kingdom pursuant to Article 2(1)(c) and (d);

(e) from the year 2001 onwards, subtracting from the result under (d) the net gains of the United Kingdom resulting from the increase in the percentage of resources referred to in Article 2(1)(a) and (b) retained by Member States to cover collection and related costs;

(f) calculating, at the time of each enlargement of the European Union, an adjustment to the result under (e) so as to reduce the compensation, thereby ensuring that expenditure which is unabated before enlargement remains so after enlargement. This adjustment shall be made by reducing total allocated expenditure by an amount equivalent to the annual pre-accession expenditure in the acceding countries. All amounts so calculated shall be carried forward to subsequent years and shall be adjusted annually by applying the euro GNP deflator used for the adaptation of the Financial Perspective.

Article 5

1. The cost of the correction shall be borne by the other Member States in accordance with the following arrangements:

The distribution of the cost shall first be calculated by reference to each Member State's share of the payments referred to in Article 2(1)(d), the United Kingdom being excluded; it shall then be adjusted in such a way as to restrict the financing share of Austria, Germany, the Netherlands and Sweden to one fourth of their normal share resulting from this calculation.

2. The correction shall be granted to the United Kingdom by a reduction in its payments resulting from the application of Article 2(1)(c) and (d). The costs borne by the other Member States shall be added to their payments resulting from the application for each Member State of Article 2(1)(c) and (d).

3. The Commission shall perform the calculations required for the application of Article 4 and this Article.

4. If, at the beginning of the financial year, the budget has not been adopted, the correction granted to the United Kingdom and the costs borne by the other Member States as

entered in the last budget finally adopted shall remain applicable.

Article 6

The revenue referred to in Article 2 shall be used without distinction to finance all expenditure entered in the budget. The revenue needed to cover in full or in part the EAGGF monetary reserve, the reserve for the financing of the Loan Guarantee Fund and the reserve for emergency aid in third countries, entered in the budget shall not be called up from the Member States until the reserves are implemented. Provisions for the operation of those reserves shall be adopted as necessary in accordance with Article 8(2).

Article 7

Any surplus of the Communities' revenue over total actual expenditure during a financial year shall be carried over to the following financial year.

Any surpluses generated by a transfer from EAGGF Guarantee Section chapters, or surplus from the Guarantee Fund arising from external measures, transferred to the revenue account in the budget, shall be regarded as constituting own resources.

Article 8

1. The Communities' own resources referred to in Article 2(1)(a) and (b) shall be collected by the Member States in accordance with the national provisions imposed by law, regulation or administrative action, which shall, where appropriate, be adapted to meet the requirements of Community rules.

The Commission shall examine at regular intervals the national provisions communicated to it by the Member States, transmit to the Member States the adjustments it deems necessary in order to ensure that they comply with Community rules and report to the budget authority.

Member States shall make the resources provided for in Article 2(1)(a) to (d) available to the Commission.

2. Without prejudice to the auditing of the accounts and to checks that they are lawful and regular as laid down in Article 248 of the EC Treaty and Article 160C of the Euratom Treaty, such auditing and checks being mainly concerned with the reliability and effectiveness of national systems and procedures for determining the base for own resources accruing from VAT and GNP and without prejudice to the inspection arrangements made pursuant to Article 279(c) of the EC Treaty and Article 183 point (c) of the Euratom Treaty, the Council shall, acting unanimously on a proposal from the Commission and after consulting the European Parliament, adopt the provisions necessary to apply this Decision and to make possible the inspection of the collection, the making available to the Commission and payment of the revenue referred to in Articles 2 and 5.

Article 9

The Commission shall undertake, before 1 January 2006, a general review of the own resources system, accompanied, if necessary, by appropriate proposals, in the light of all relevant factors, including the effects of enlargement on the financing of the budget, the possibility of modifying the structure of the own resources by creating new autonomous own resources and the correction of budgetary imbalances granted to the United Kingdom as well as the granting to Austria, Germany, the Netherlands and Sweden of the reduction pursuant to Article 5(1).

Article 10

1.   Member States shall be notified of this Decision by the Secretary-General of the Council and the Decision shall be published in the *Official Journal of the European Communities*.

Member States shall notify the Secretary-General of the Council without delay of the completion of the procedures for the adoption of this Decision in accordance with their respective constitutional requirements.

This Decision shall enter into force on the first day of the month following receipt of the last of the notifications referred to in the second subparagraph. It shall take effect on 1 January 2002 except for Article 2(3) and Article 4, which shall take effect on 1 January 2001.

2.   (a)   Subject to (b), Decision 94/728/EC, Euratom shall be repealed as of 1 January 2002. Any references to the Council Decision of 21 April 1970 on the replacement of financial contributions from Member States by the Communities' own resources (¹), to Council Decision 85/257/EEC, Euratom of 7 May 1985 on the Communities' system of own resources (²), to Decision 88/376/EEC, Euratom, or to Decision 94/728/EC, Euratom shall be construed as references to this Decision.

(b)   Articles 2, 4 and 5 of Decisions 88/376/EEC, Euratom and 94/728/EC, Euratom shall continue to apply to the calculation and adjustment of revenue accruing from the application of a uniform rate valid for all Member States to the VAT base determined in a uniform manner and limited between 50 % to 55 % of the GNP of each Member State, depending on the relevant year, and to the calculation of the correction of budgetary imbalances granted to the United Kingdom for the years 1988 to 2000.

(c)   For amounts referred to in Article 2(1)(a) and (b) which should have been made available by the Member States before 28 February 2001 in accordance with the applicable Community rules, Member States shall continue to retain 10 % of these amounts by way of collection costs.

Done at Brussels, 29 September 2000.

For the Council

The President

L. FABIUS

(¹) OJ L 94, 28.4.1970, p. 19.
(²) OJ L 128, 14.5.1985, p. 15. Decision repealed by Decision 88/376/EEC, Euratom.

23.6.2007   [EN]   Official Journal of the European Union   L 163/17

II

(Acts adopted under the EC Treaty/Euratom Treaty whose publication is not obligatory)

DECISIONS

COUNCIL

COUNCIL DECISION

of 7 June 2007

on the system of the European Communities' own resources

(2007/436/EC, Euratom)

THE COUNCIL OF THE EUROPEAN UNION,

Having regard to the Treaty establishing the European Community, and in particular Article 269 thereof,

Having regard to the Treaty establishing the European Atomic Energy Community, and in particular Article 173 thereof,

Having regard to the proposal from the Commission,

Having regard to the opinion of the European Parliament (¹),

Having regard to the opinion of the Court of Auditors (²),

Having regard to the opinion of the European Economic and Social Committee (³),

Whereas:

(1) The European Council meeting in Brussels on 15 and 16 December 2005 concluded, *inter alia*, that the own resources arrangements should be guided by the overall objective of equity. Those arrangements should therefore ensure, in line with the relevant conclusions of the 1984 Fontainebleau European Council, that no Member State sustains a budgetary burden which is excessive in relation to its relative prosperity. It is therefore appropriate to introduce provisions covering specific Member States.

(2) The Communities' own resources system must ensure adequate resources for the orderly development of the Communities' policies, subject to the need for strict budgetary discipline.

(3) For the purposes of this Decision, gross national income (GNI) should be defined as annual GNI at market prices as provided by the Commission in application of the European system of national and regional accounts in the Community (hereinafter referred to as the ESA 95) in accordance with Council Regulation (EC) No 2223/96 (⁴).

(4) In view of the changeover from ESA 79 to ESA 95 for budgetary and own resources purposes, and in order to maintain unchanged the amount of financial resources put at the disposal of the Communities the Commission recalculated, in accordance with Article 3(1) and 3(2) of Council Decision 2000/597/EC, Euratom of 29 September 2000 on the system of the European Communities' own resources (⁵), the ceiling of own resources and the ceiling for appropriations for commitments, expressed to two decimal places, on the basis of the formula in that Article. The Commission communicated the new ceilings to the Council and the European Parliament on 28 December 2001. The ceiling of own resources was set at 1,24 % of the total GNIs of the Member States at market prices and a ceiling of 1,31 % of the total GNIs of the Member States was set for appropriations for commitments. The European Council of 15 and 16 December 2005 concluded that these ceilings should be maintained at their current levels.

(¹) Opinion delivered on 4 July 2006 (not yet published in the Official Journal).
(²) OJ C 203, 25.8.2006, p. 50.
(³) OJ C 309, 16.12.2006, p. 103.

(⁴) OJ L 310, 30.11.1996, p. 1. Regulation as last amended by Regulation (EC) No 1267/2003 of the European Parliament and of the Council (OJ L 180, 18.7.2003, p. 1).
(⁵) OJ L 253, 7.10.2000, p. 42.

L 163/18   EN   Official Journal of the European Union   23.6.2007

(5)   In order to maintain unchanged the amount of financial resources put at the disposal of the Communities, it is appropriate to adapt those ceilings expressed in per cent of GNI in case of modifications to the ESA 95 which entail a significant change in the level of GNI.

(6)   Following the implementation in European Union law of the agreements concluded during the Uruguay round of multilateral trade negotiations there is no longer any material difference between agricultural duties and customs duties. It is therefore appropriate to remove this distinction from the field of the general budget of the European Union.

(7)   In the interests of transparency and simplicity, the European Council of 15 and 16 December 2005 concluded that the uniform rate of call of the Value Added Tax (VAT) resource shall be fixed at 0,30 %.

(8)   The European Council of 15 and 16 December 2005 concluded that Austria, Germany, the Netherlands and Sweden shall benefit from reduced VAT rates of call during the period 2007-2013 and that the Netherlands and Sweden shall benefit from gross reductions in their annual GNI-based contributions during the same period.

(9)   The European Council of 15 and 16 December 2005 concluded that the correction mechanism in favour of the United Kingdom shall remain, along with the reduced financing of the correction benefiting Germany, Austria, Sweden and the Netherlands. However, after a phasing-in period between 2009 and 2011, the United Kingdom shall participate fully in the financing of the costs of enlargement, except for agricultural direct payments and market-related expenditure, and that part of rural development expenditure originating from the European Agricultural Guidance and Guarantee Fund (EAGGF), Guarantee Section. The calculation of the correction in favour of the United Kingdom shall therefore be adjusted by progressively excluding expenditure allocated to Member States which have acceded to the EU after 30 April 2004, except for the agricultural and rural development expenditure mentioned above. The additional contribution of the United Kingdom resulting from the reduction in allocated expenditure shall not exceed EU-10,5 billion in 2004 prices during the period 2007-2013. In the event of further enlargement before 2013, except for the accession of Bulgaria and Romania, the amount will be adjusted accordingly.

(10)   The European Council of 15 and 16 December 2005 concluded that point (f) of the second paragraph of Article 4 of Decision 2000/597/EC, Euratom regarding the exclusion of the annual pre-accession expenditure in acceding countries from the calculation of the correction in favour of the United Kingdom shall cease to apply at the end of 2013.

(11)   The European Council of 15 and 16 December 2005 invited the Commission to undertake a full, wide-ranging review covering all aspects of EU spending, including the Common Agricultural Policy (CAP), and of resources, including the United Kingdom rebate, and to report in 2008/2009.

(12)   Provisions should be laid down to cover the changeover from the system laid down by Decision 2000/597/EC, Euratom to that introduced by this Decision.

(13)   The European Council of 15 and 16 December 2005 concluded that this Decision shall take effect on 1 January 2007,

HAS LAID DOWN THESE PROVISIONS, WHICH IT RECOMMENDS TO THE MEMBER STATES FOR ADOPTION:

Article 1

The Communities shall be allocated own resources in accordance with the rules laid down in the following Articles in order to ensure, in accordance with Article 269 of the Treaty establishing the European Community (hereinafter referred to as the EC Treaty) and Article 173 of the Treaty establishing the European Atomic Energy Community (hereinafter referred to as the Euratom Treaty), the financing of the general budget of the European Union.

The general budget of the European Union shall, without prejudice to other revenue, be financed wholly from the Communities' own resources.

Article 2

1.   Revenue from the following shall constitute own resources entered in the general budget of the European Union:

(a)   levies, premiums, additional or compensatory amounts, additional amounts or factors, Common Customs Tariff duties and other duties established or to be established by the institutions of the Communities in respect of trade with non-member countries, customs duties on products under the expired Treaty establishing the European Coal and Steel Community as well as contributions and other duties provided for within the framework of the common organisation of the markets in sugar;

23.6.2007   EN   Official Journal of the European Union   L 163/19

(b) without prejudice to the second subparagraph of paragraph 4, the application of a uniform rate valid for all Member States to the harmonised VAT assessment bases determined according to Community rules. The assessment base to be taken into account for this purpose shall not exceed 50 % of GNI for each Member State, as defined in paragraph 7;

(c) without prejudice to the second subparagraph of paragraph 5, the application of a uniform rate — to be determined pursuant to the budgetary procedure in the light of the total of all other revenue — to the sum of all the Member States' GNIs.

2. Revenue deriving from any new charges introduced within the framework of a common policy, in accordance with the EC Treaty or the Euratom Treaty, provided that the procedure laid down in Article 269 of the EC Treaty or in Article 173 of the Euratom Treaty has been followed, shall also constitute own resources entered in the general budget of the European Union.

3. Member States shall retain, by way of collection costs, 25 % of the amounts referred to in paragraph 1(a).

4. The uniform rate referred to in paragraph 1(b) shall be fixed at 0,30 %.

For the period 2007-2013 only, the rate of call of the VAT resource for Austria shall be fixed at 0,225 %, for Germany at 0,15 % and for the Netherlands and Sweden at 0,10 %.

5. The uniform rate referred to in paragraph 1(c) shall apply to the GNI of each Member State.

For the period 2007-2013 only, the Netherlands shall benefit from a gross reduction in its annual GNI contribution of EUR 605 million and Sweden from a gross reduction in its annual GNI contribution of EUR 150 million, measured in 2004 prices. These amounts shall be adjusted to current prices by applying the most recent GDP deflator for the EU expressed in euro, as provided by the Commission, which is available when the preliminary draft budget is drawn up. These gross reductions shall be granted after the calculation of the correction in favour of the United Kingdom and its financing referred to in Articles 4 and 5 of this Decision and shall have no impact thereupon.

6. If, at the beginning of the financial year, the budget has not been adopted, the existing VAT and GNI rates of call shall remain applicable until the entry into force of the new rates.

7. For the purposes of this Decision, GNI shall mean GNI for the year at market prices as provided by the Commission in application of the ESA 95 in accordance with Regulation (EC) No 2223/96.

Should modifications to the ESA 95 result in significant changes in the GNI as provided by the Commission, the Council, acting unanimously on a proposal of the Commission and after consulting the European Parliament, shall decide whether these modifications shall apply for the purposes of this Decision.

Article 3

1. The total amount of own resources allocated to the Communities to cover annual appropriations for payments shall not exceed 1,24 % of the sum of all the Member States' GNIs.

2. The total annual amount of appropriations for commitments entered in the general budget of the European Union shall not exceed 1,31 % of the sum of all the Member States' GNIs.

An orderly ratio between appropriations for commitments and appropriations for payments shall be maintained to guarantee their compatibility and to enable the ceiling pursuant to paragraph 1 to be respected in subsequent years.

3. Should modifications to the ESA 95 result in significant changes in the GNI that apply for the purposes of this Decision, the ceilings for payments and commitments as determined in paragraphs 1 and 2 shall be recalculated by the Commission on the basis of the following formula:

$$1,24\ \%\ (1,31\ \%) \times \frac{GNI_{t-2} + GNI_{t-1} + GNI_t\ ESA\ current}{GNI_{t-2} + GNI_{t-1} + GNI_t\ ESA\ modified}$$

where t is the latest full year for which data according to Council Regulation (EC, Euratom) No 1287/2003 of 15 July 2003 on the harmonisation of gross national income at market prices (GNI Regulation) ([1]) is available.

Article 4

1. The United Kingdom shall be granted a correction in respect of budgetary imbalances.

This correction shall be established by:

(a) calculating the difference, in the preceding financial year, between:

— the percentage share of the United Kingdom in the sum of uncapped VAT assessment bases, and

_____
([1]) OJ L 181, 19.7.2003, p. 1.

— the percentage share of the United Kingdom in total allocated expenditure;

(b) multiplying the difference thus obtained by total allocated expenditure;

(c) multiplying the result under (b) by 0,66;

(d) subtracting from the result under (c) the effects arising for the United Kingdom from the changeover to capped VAT and the payments referred to in Article 2(1)(c), namely the difference between:

— what the United Kingdom would have had to pay for the amounts financed by the resources referred to in Article 2(1)(b) and (c), if the uniform rate had been applied to non-capped VAT bases, and

— the payments of the United Kingdom pursuant to Article 2(1)(b) and (c);

(e) subtracting from the result under (d) the net gains of the United Kingdom resulting from the increase in the percentage of resources referred to in Article 2(1)(a) retained by Member States to cover collection and related costs;

(f) calculating, at the time of each enlargement of the EU, an adjustment to the result under (e) so as to reduce the compensation, thereby ensuring that expenditure which is unabated before enlargement remains so after enlargement. This adjustment shall be made by reducing total allocated expenditure by an amount equivalent to the annual pre-accession expenditure in the acceding countries. All amounts so calculated shall be carried forward to subsequent years and shall be adjusted annually by applying the latest available GDP deflator for the EU expressed in euro, as provided by the Commission. This point shall cease to apply as from the correction to be budgeted for the first time in 2014;

(g) adjusting the calculation, by reducing total allocated expenditure by total allocated expenditure in Member States that have acceded to the EU after 30 April 2004, except for agricultural direct payments and market-related expenditure as well as that part of rural development expenditure originating from the EAGGF, Guarantee Section.

This reduction shall be phased in progressively according to the schedule below:

United Kingdom correction to be budgeted for the first time in the year	Percentage of enlargement-related expenditure (as defined above) to be excluded from the calculation of the correction in favour of the United Kingdom
2009	20
2010	70
2011	100

2. During the period 2007-2013 the additional contribution of the United Kingdom resulting from the reduction of allocated expenditure referred to in paragraph (1)(g) shall not exceed EU-10,5 billion, measured in 2004 prices. Each year, the Commission services shall verify whether the cumulated adjustment of the correction exceeds this amount. For the purpose of this calculation, amounts in current prices shall be converted into 2004 prices by applying the latest available GDP deflator for the EU expressed in euro, as provided by the Commission. If the ceiling of EU-10,5 billion is exceeded, the United Kingdom's contribution shall be reduced accordingly.

In the event of further enlargement before 2013, the ceiling of EU-10,5 billion shall be adjusted upwards accordingly.

Article 5

1. The cost of the correction shall be borne by the other Member States in accordance with the following arrangements:

(a) the distribution of the cost shall first be calculated by reference to each Member State's share of the payments referred to in Article 2(1)(c), the United Kingdom being excluded and without taking account of the gross reductions in the GNI-based contributions of the Netherlands and Sweden referred to in Article 2(5);

(b) it shall then be adjusted in such a way as to restrict the financing share of Austria, Germany, the Netherlands and Sweden to one fourth of their normal share resulting from this calculation.

2. The correction shall be granted to the United Kingdom by a reduction in its payments resulting from the application of Article 2(1)(c). The costs borne by the other Member States shall be added to their payments resulting from the application for each Member State of Article 2(1)(c).

3. The Commission shall perform the calculations required for the application of Article 2(5), Article 4 and this Article.

4. If, at the beginning of the financial year, the budget has not been adopted, the correction granted to the United Kingdom and the costs borne by the other Member States as entered in the last budget finally adopted shall remain applicable.

Article 6

The revenue referred to in Article 2 shall be used without distinction to finance all expenditure entered in the general budget of the European Union.

Article 7

Any surplus of the Communities' revenue over total actual expenditure during a financial year shall be carried over to the following financial year.

Article 8

1. The Communities' own resources referred to in Article 2(1)(a) shall be collected by the Member States in accordance with the national provisions imposed by law, regulation or administrative action, which shall, where appropriate, be adapted to meet the requirements of Community rules.

The Commission shall examine at regular intervals the national provisions communicated to it by the Member States, transmit to the Member States the adjustments it deems necessary in order to ensure that they comply with Community rules and report to the budgetary authority.

Member States shall make the resources provided for in Article 2(1)(a), (b) and (c) available to the Commission.

2. The Council shall, in accordance with the procedures laid down in Article 279(2) of the EC Treaty and Article 183 of the Euratom Treaty, adopt the provisions necessary to apply this Decision and to make possible the inspection of the collection, the making available to the Commission and payment of the revenue referred to in Articles 2 and 5.

Article 9

In the framework of the full, wide-ranging review covering all aspects of EU spending, including the CAP, and of resources, including the United Kingdom rebate, on which it shall report in 2008/2009, the Commission shall undertake a general review of the own resources system.

Article 10

1. Subject to paragraph 2, Decision 2000/597/EC, Euratom shall be repealed as of 1 January 2007. Any references to the Council Decision of 21 April 1970 on the replacement of financial contributions from Member States by the Communities' own resources [(¹)], to Council Decision 85/257/EEC, Euratom of 7 May 1985 on the Communities' system of own resources [(²)], to Council Decision 88/376/EEC, Euratom of 24 June 1988 on the system of the Communities' own resources [(³)], to Council Decision 94/728/EC, Euratom of 31

October 1994 on the system of the European Communities' own resources [(⁴)] or to Decision 2000/597/EC, Euratom shall be construed as references to this Decision.

2. Articles 2, 4 and 5 of Decisions 88/376/EEC, Euratom, 94/728/EC, Euratom and 2000/597/EC, Euratom shall continue to apply to the calculation and adjustment of revenue accruing from the application of a uniform rate valid for all Member States to the VAT base determined in a uniform manner and limited between 50 % and 55 % of the GNP or GNI of each Member State, depending on the relevant year, and to the calculation of the correction of budgetary imbalances granted to the United Kingdom for the years 1988 to 2006.

3. Member States shall continue to retain, by way of collection costs, 10 % of the amounts referred to in Article 2(1)(a) which should have been made available by the Member States before 28 February 2001 in accordance with the applicable Community rules.

Article 11

Member States shall be notified of this Decision by the Secretary-General of the Council.

Member States shall notify the Secretary-General of the Council without delay of the completion of the procedures for the adoption of this Decision in accordance with their respective constitutional requirements.

This Decision shall enter into force on the first day of the month following receipt of the last of the notifications referred to in the second subparagraph.

It shall take effect on 1 January 2007.

Article 12

This Decision shall be published in the *Official Journal of the European Union*.

Done at Luxembourg, 7 June 2007.

For the Council
The President
M. GLOS

(¹) OJ L 94, 28.4.1970, p. 19.
(²) OJ L 128, 14.5.1985, p. 15.
(³) OJ L 185, 15.7.1988, p. 24.

(⁴) OJ L 293, 12.11.1994, p. 9.

14.6.2006 | EN | Official Journal of the European Union | C 139/1

I

(Information)

EUROPEAN PARLIAMENT

COUNCIL

COMMISSION

INTERINSTITUTIONAL AGREEMENT

between the European Parliament, the Council and the Commission on budgetary discipline and sound financial management

(2006/C 139/01)

THE EUROPEAN PARLIAMENT, THE COUNCIL OF THE EUROPEAN UNION AND THE COMMISSION OF THE EUROPEAN COMMUNITIES,

hereinafter referred to as the 'institutions',

HAVE AGREED AS FOLLOWS:

1. The purpose of this Agreement is to implement budgetary discipline and to improve the functioning of the annual budgetary procedure and cooperation between the institutions on budgetary matters as well as to ensure sound financial management.

2. Budgetary discipline under this Agreement covers all expenditure. It is binding on all the institutions for as long as this Agreement is in force.

3. This Agreement does not alter the respective budgetary powers of the institutions, as laid down in the Treaties. Where reference is made to this Point, the Council will act by a qualified majority and the European Parliament by a majority of its members and three fifths of the votes cast, in compliance with the voting rules laid down in the fifth subparagraph of Article 272(9) of the Treaty establishing the European Community (hereinafter referred to as the 'EC Treaty').

4. Should a Treaty revision with budgetary implications occur during the multiannual financial framework 2007 to 2013 (hereinafter referred to as 'the financial framework'), the necessary adjustments will be made accordingly.

5. Any amendment of this Agreement requires the consent of all the institutions. Changes to the financial framework must be made in accordance with the procedures laid down for that purpose in this Agreement.

6. This Agreement is in three parts:

 — Part I contains a definition and implementing provisions for the financial framework and applies for the duration of that financial framework.

 — Part II relates to improvement of interinstitutional collaboration during the budgetary procedure.

 — Part III contains provisions related to sound financial management of EU funds.

7. The Commission will, whenever it considers it necessary and in any event at the same time as it presents a proposal for a new financial framework pursuant to Point 30, submit a report on the application of this Agreement, accompanied where necessary by a proposal for amendments.

8. This Agreement enters into force on 1 January 2007 and replaces:

 — the Interinstitutional Agreement of 6 May 1999 between the European Parliament, the Council and the Commission on budgetary discipline and improvement of the budgetary procedure [1],

---

[1] OJ C 172, 18.6.1999, p. 1.

C 139/2 | EN | Official Journal of the European Union | 14.6.2006

— the Interinstitutional Agreement of 7 November 2002 between the European Parliament, the Council and the Commission on the financing of the European Union Solidarity Fund supplementing the Interinstitutional Agreement of 6 May 1999 on budgetary discipline and improvement of the budgetary procedure (¹).

PART I — FINANCIAL FRAMEWORK

DEFINITION AND IMPLEMENTING PROVISIONS

A. Contents and scope of the financial framework

9. The financial framework is set out in Annex I. It constitutes the reference framework for interinstitutional budgetary discipline.

10. The financial framework is intended to ensure that, in the medium term, European Union expenditure, broken down by broad category, develops in an orderly manner and within the limits of own resources.

11. The financial framework establishes, for each of the years 2007 to 2013 and for each heading or subheading, amounts of expenditure in terms of appropriations for commitments. Overall annual totals of expenditure are also shown in terms of both appropriations for commitments and appropriations for payments.

All those amounts are expressed in 2004 prices.

The financial framework does not take account of budget items financed by revenue earmarked within the meaning of Article 18 of the Financial Regulation of 25 June 2002 applicable to the general budget of the European Communities (²), hereinafter referred to as the 'Financial Regulation'

Information relating to operations not included in the general budget of the European Union and the foreseeable development of the various categories of Community own resources is set out, by way of indication, in separate tables. This information will be updated annually when the technical adjustment is made to the financial framework.

12. The institutions acknowledge that each of the absolute amounts shown in the financial framework represents an annual ceiling on expenditure under the general budget of the European Union. Without prejudice to any changes in those ceilings in accordance with the provisions of this Agreement, the institutions undertake to use their respective powers in such a way as to comply with the various annual expenditure ceilings during each budgetary procedure and when implementing the budget for the year concerned.

13. By concluding this Agreement, the two arms of the budgetary authority agree to accept the rates of increase

for non-compulsory expenditure deriving from the budgets established within the ceilings set by the financial framework for its entire duration.

Except in sub-heading 1B 'Cohesion for growth and employment' of the financial framework, for the purposes of sound financial management, the institutions will ensure as far as possible during the budgetary procedure and at the time of the budget's adoption that sufficient margins are left available beneath the ceilings for the various headings.

14. No act adopted under the codecision procedure by the European Parliament and the Council nor any act adopted by the Council which involves exceeding the appropriations available in the budget or the allocations available in the financial framework in accordance with Point 12 may be implemented in financial terms until the budget has been amended and, if necessary, the financial framework has been appropriately revised in accordance with the relevant procedure for each of these cases.

15. For each of the years covered by the financial framework, the total appropriations for payments required, after annual adjustment and taking account of any other adjustments or revisions, must not be such as to produce a call-in rate for own resources that exceeds the own resources ceiling.

If need be, the two arms of the budgetary authority will decide, in accordance with Point 3, to lower the ceilings set in the financial framework in order to ensure compliance with the own resources ceiling.

B. Annual adjustments of the financial framework

Technical adjustments

16. Each year the Commission, acting ahead of the budgetary procedure for year n+1, will make the following technical adjustments to the financial framework:

    (a) revaluation, at year n+1 prices, of the ceilings and of the overall figures for appropriations for commitments and appropriations for payments;

    (b) calculation of the margin available under the own resources ceiling.

The Commission will make those technical adjustments on the basis of a fixed deflator of 2 % a year.

The results of those technical adjustments and the underlying economic forecasts will be communicated to the two arms of the budgetary authority.

No further technical adjustments will be made in respect of the year concerned, either during the year or as ex-post corrections during subsequent years.

(¹) OJ C 283, 20.11.2002, p. 1.
(²) OJ L 248, 16.9.2002, p. 1.

14.6.2006   EN   Official Journal of the European Union   C 139/3

17. In its technical adjustment for the year 2011, if it is established that any Member State's cumulated GDP for the years 2007-2009 has diverged by more than +/- 5 % from the cumulated GDP estimated when drawing up this Agreement, the Commission will adjust the amounts allocated from funds supporting cohesion to the Member State concerned for that period. The total net effect, whether positive or negative, of those adjustments may not exceed EUR 3 billion. If the net effect is positive, total additional resources shall be limited to the level of underspending against the ceilings for sub-heading 1B for the years 2007-2010. The required adjustments will be spread in equal proportions over the years 2011-2013 and the corresponding ceilings will be modified accordingly.

Adjustments connected with implementation

18. When notifying the two arms of the budgetary authority of the technical adjustments to the financial framework, the Commission will present any proposals for adjustments to the total appropriations for payments which it considers necessary, in the light of implementation, to ensure an orderly progression in relation to the appropriations for commitments. The European Parliament and the Council will take decisions on those proposals before 1 May of year n, in accordance with Point 3.

Updating of forecasts for payment appropriations after 2013

19. In 2010, the Commission will update the forecasts for payment appropriations after 2013. That update will take into account the real implementation of budget appropriations for commitments and budget appropriations for payments, as well as the implementation forecasts. It will also consider the rules defined to ensure that payment appropriations develop in an orderly manner compared to commitment appropriations and the growth forecasts of the European Union Gross National Income (GNI).

Adjustments connected with excessive government deficit

20. In the case of the lifting of a suspension of budgetary commitments concerning the Cohesion Fund in the context of an excessive government deficit procedure, the Council, on a proposal from the Commission and in compliance with the relevant basic act, will decide on a transfer of suspended commitments to the following years. Suspended commitments of year n cannot be re-budgeted beyond year n+2.

C. Revision of the financial framework

21. In addition to the regular technical adjustments and adjustments in line with the conditions of implementation, in the event of unforeseen circumstances the financial framework may, on a proposal from the Commission, be revised in compliance with the own resources ceiling.

22. As a general rule, any proposal for revision under Point 21 must be presented and adopted before the start of the budgetary procedure for the year or the first of the years concerned.

Any decision to revise the financial framework by up to 0,03 % of the European Union GNI within the margin for unforeseen expenditure will be taken jointly by the two arms of the budgetary authority acting in accordance with Point 3.

Any revision of the financial framework above 0,03 % of the European Union GNI within the margin for unforeseen expenditure will be taken jointly by the two arms of the budgetary authority, with the Council acting unanimously.

23. Without prejudice to Point 40, the institutions will examine the scope for reallocating expenditure between the programmes covered by the heading concerned by the revision, with particular reference to any expected underutilisation of appropriations. The objective should be that a significant amount, in absolute terms and as a percentage of the new expenditure planned, should be within the existing ceiling for the heading.

The institutions will examine the scope for offsetting any raising of the ceiling for one heading by the lowering of the ceiling for another.

Any revision of the compulsory expenditure in the financial framework must not lead to a reduction in the amount available for non-compulsory expenditure.

Any revision must maintain an appropriate relationship between commitments and payments.

D. Consequences of the absence of a joint decision on the adjustment or revision of the financial framework

24. If the European Parliament and the Council fail to agree on any adjustment or revision of the financial framework proposed by the Commission, the amounts set previously will, after the annual technical adjustment, continue to apply as the expenditure ceilings for the year in question.

E. Emergency Aid Reserve

25. The Emergency Aid Reserve is intended to allow a rapid response to the specific aid requirements of third countries following events which could not be foreseen when the budget was established, first and foremost for humanitarian operations, but also for civil crisis management and protection where circumstances so require. The annual amount of the Reserve is fixed at EUR 221 million for the duration of the financial framework, in constant prices.

The Reserve is entered in the general budget of the European Union as a provision. The corresponding commitment appropriations will be entered in the budget, if necessary, over and above the ceilings laid down in Annex I.

414 EUROPEAN UNION PUBLIC FINANCE

When the Commission considers that the Reserve needs to be called on, it will present to the two arms of the budgetary authority a proposal for a transfer from the Reserve to the corresponding budgetary lines.

Any Commission proposal for a transfer to draw on the Reserve must, however, be preceded by an examination of the scope for reallocating appropriations.

At the same time as it presents its proposal for a transfer, the Commission will initiate a trilogue procedure, if necessary in a simplified form, to secure agreement of the two arms of the budgetary authority on the need to use the Reserve and on the amount required. The transfers will be made in accordance with Article 26 of the Financial Regulation.

F. European Union Solidarity Fund

26. The European Union Solidarity Fund is intended to allow rapid financial assistance in the event of major disasters occurring on the territory of a Member State or of a candidate country, as defined in the relevant basic act. There will be a ceiling on the annual amount available for the Fund of EUR 1 billion (current prices). On 1 October each year, at least one quarter of the annual amount will remain available in order to cover needs arising until the end of the year. The portion of the annual amount not entered in the budget may not be rolled over in the following years.

In exceptional cases and if the remaining financial resources available in the Fund in the year of occurrence of the disaster, as defined in the relevant basic act, are not sufficient to cover the amount of assistance considered necessary by the budgetary authority, the Commission may propose that the difference be financed through the annual amounts available for the following year. The annual amount of the Fund to be budgeted in each year may not, under any circumstances, exceed EUR 1 billion.

When the conditions for mobilising the Fund as set out in the relevant basic act are met, the Commission will make a proposal to deploy it. Where there is scope for reallocating appropriations under the heading requiring additional expenditure, the Commission shall take this into account when making the necessary proposal, in accordance with the Financial Regulation, by means of the appropriate budgetary instrument. The decision to deploy the Fund will be taken jointly by the two arms of the budgetary authority in accordance with Point 3.

The corresponding commitment appropriations will be entered in the budget, if necessary, over and above the ceilings of the relevant headings laid down in Annex I.

At the same time as it presents its proposal for a decision to deploy the Fund, the Commission will initiate a trilogue procedure, if necessary in a simplified form, to secure

agreement of the two arms of the budgetary authority on the need to use the Fund and on the amount required.

G. Flexibility Instrument

27. The Flexibility Instrument with an annual ceiling of EUR 200 million (current prices) is intended to allow the financing, for a given financial year and up to the amount indicated, of clearly identified expenditure which could not be financed within the limits of the ceilings available for one or more other headings.

The portion of the annual amount which is not used may be carried over up to year n+2. If the Flexibility Instrument is mobilised, any carryovers will be drawn on first, in order of age. The portion of the annual amount from year n which is not used in year n+2 will lapse.

The Commission will make a proposal for the Flexibility Instrument to be used after it has examined all possibilities for re-allocating appropriations under the heading requiring additional expenditure.

The proposal will concern the principle of making use of the Flexibility Instrument and will identify the needs to be covered and the amount. It may be presented, for any given financial year, during the budgetary procedure. The Commission proposal will be included in the preliminary draft budget or accompanied, in accordance with the Financial Regulation, by the appropriate budgetary instrument.

The decision to deploy the Flexibility Instrument will be taken jointly by the two arms of the budgetary authority in accordance with Point 3. Agreement will be reached by means of the conciliation procedure provided for in Annex II, Part C.

H. European Globalisation Adjustment Fund

28. The European Globalisation Adjustment Fund is intended to provide additional support for workers who suffer from the consequences of major structural changes in world trade patterns, to assist them with their reintegration into the labour market.

The Fund may not exceed a maximum annual amount of EUR 500 million (current prices) which can be drawn from any margin existing under the global expenditure ceiling of the previous year, and/or from cancelled commitment appropriations from the previous two years, excluding those related to heading 1B of the financial framework.

The appropriations will be entered in the general budget of the European Union as a provision through the normal budgetary procedure as soon as the Commission has identified the sufficient margins and/or cancelled commitments, in accordance with the second paragraph.

When the conditions for mobilising the Fund, as set out in the relevant basic act, are met, the Commission will make a proposal to deploy it. The decision to deploy the Fund will be taken jointly by the two arms of the budgetary authority in accordance with Point 3.

At the same time as it presents its proposal for a decision to deploy the Fund, the Commission will initiate a trilogue procedure, if necessary in a simplified form, to secure agreement of the two arms of the budgetary authority on the need to use the Fund and on the amount required, and will present to the two arms of the budgetary authority a proposal for a transfer to the relevant budgetary lines.

Transfers related to the Fund will be made in accordance with Article 24(4) of the Financial Regulation.

The corresponding commitment appropriations will be entered in the budget under the relevant heading, if necessary over and above the ceilings laid down in Annex I.

I. Adjustment of the financial framework to cater for enlargement

29. If new Member States accede to the European Union during the period covered by the financial framework, the European Parliament and the Council, acting on a proposal from the Commission and in accordance with Point 3, will jointly adjust the financial framework to take account of the expenditure requirements resulting from the outcome of the accession negotiations.

J. Duration of the financial framework and consequences of the absence of a financial framework

30. Before 1 July 2011, the Commission will present proposals for a new medium-term financial framework.

Should the two arms of the budgetary authority fail to agree on a new financial framework, and unless the existing financial framework is expressly terminated by one of the institutions, the ceilings for the last year covered by the existing financial framework will be adjusted in accordance with Point 16 so that the 2013 ceilings are maintained in constant prices. If new Member States accede to the European Union after 2013, and if deemed necessary, the extended financial framework will be adjusted in order to take into account the results of accession negotiations.

PART II

IMPROVEMENT OF INTERINSTITUTIONAL COLLABORATION DURING THE BUDGETARY PROCEDURE

A. The interinstitutional collaboration procedure

31. The institutions agree to set up a procedure for interinstitutional collaboration in budgetary matters. The details of this collaboration are set out in Annex II.

B. Establishment of the budget

32. The Commission will present each year a preliminary draft budget showing the Community's actual financing requirements.

It will take into account:

(a) forecasts in relation to the Structural Funds provided by the Member States,

(b) the capacity for utilising appropriations, endeavouring to maintain a strict relationship between appropriations for commitments and appropriations for payments,

(c) the possibilities for starting up new policies through pilot projects and/or new preparatory actions or continuing multiannual actions which are coming to an end, after assessing whether it will be possible to secure a basic act, within the meaning of Article 49 of the Financial Regulation (definition of a basic act, necessity of a basic act for implementation and exceptions),

(d) the need to ensure that any change in expenditure in relation to the previous year is in accordance with the constraints of budgetary discipline.

The preliminary draft budget will be accompanied by Activity Statements including such information as required under Article 27(3) and Article 33(2)(d) of the Financial Regulation (objectives, indicators and evaluation information).

33. The institutions will, as far as possible, avoid entering items in the budget involving insignificant amounts of expenditure on operations.

The two arms of the budgetary authority also undertake to bear in mind the assessment of the possibilities for implementing the budget made by the Commission in its preliminary drafts and in connection with implementation of the current budget.

Before the Council's second reading, the Commission will send a letter to the Chairman of the European Parliament's Committee on Budgets, with a copy to the other arm of the budgetary authority, containing its comments on the executability of the amendments to the draft budget adopted by the European Parliament at first reading.

The two arms of the budgetary authority will take those comments into account in the context of the conciliation procedure provided for in Annex II, Part C.

In the interest of sound financial management and owing to the effect of major changes in the budget nomenclature in the titles and chapters on the management reporting responsibilities of Commission departments, the two arms of the budgetary authority undertake to discuss any such major changes with the Commission during the conciliation procedure.

C 139/6   EN   Official Journal of the European Union   14.6.2006

C. Classification of expenditure

34. The institutions consider compulsory expenditure to be expenditure necessarily resulting from the Treaties or from acts adopted in accordance therewith.

35. The preliminary draft budget is to contain a proposal for the classification of each new budget item and of each budget item with an amended legal base.

If they do not accept the classification proposed in the preliminary draft budget, the European Parliament and the Council will examine the classification of the budget item concerned on the basis of Annex III. Agreement will be sought by means of the conciliation procedure provided for in Annex II, Part C.

D. Maximum rate of increase of non-compulsory expenditure in the absence of a financial framework

36. Without prejudice to the first paragraph of Point 13, the institutions agree on the following provisions:

(a) the European Parliament's autonomous margin for manoeuvre for the purposes of the fourth subparagraph of Article 272(9) of the EC Treaty — which is to be half the maximum rate — applies as from the establishment of the draft budget by the Council at first reading, including any letters of amendment.

The maximum rate is to be observed in respect of the annual budget, including amending budgets. Without prejudice to the setting of a new rate, any portion of the maximum rate which has not been utilised will remain available for use and may be used when draft amending budgets are considered;

(b) without prejudice to paragraph (a), if it appears in the course of the budgetary procedure that completion of the procedure might require agreement on the setting of a new rate of increase for non-compulsory expenditure to apply to appropriations for payments and/or a new rate to apply to appropriations for commitments (the latter rate may be at a level different from the former), the institutions will endeavour to secure agreement between the two arms of the budgetary authority by means of the conciliation procedure provided for in Annex II, Part C.

E. Incorporation of financial provisions in legislative acts

37. Each legislative act concerning a multiannual programme adopted under the codecision procedure will contain a provision in which the legislative authority lays down the financial envelope for the programme.

That amount will constitute the prime reference for the budgetary authority during the annual budgetary procedure.

The budgetary authority and the Commission, when it draws up the preliminary draft budget, undertake not to depart by more than 5 % from that amount for the entire duration of the programme concerned, unless new, objective, long-term circumstances arise for which explicit and precise reasons are given, with account being taken of the results obtained from implementing the programme, in particular on the basis of assessments. Any increase resulting from such variation must remain within the existing ceiling for the heading concerned, without prejudice to the use of instruments mentioned in this Agreement.

This Point does not apply to appropriations for cohesion adopted under the codecision procedure and pre-allocated by Member States which contain a financial envelope for the entire duration of the programme.

38. Legislative acts concerning multiannual programmes not subject to the codecision procedure will not contain an 'amount deemed necessary'.

Should the Council wish to include a financial reference, this will be taken as illustrating the will of the legislative authority and will not affect the powers of the budgetary authority as defined by the EC Treaty. This provision will be mentioned in all legislative acts which include such a financial reference.

If the amount concerned has been the subject of an agreement pursuant to the conciliation procedure provided for in the Joint Declaration of the European Parliament, the Council and the Commission of 4 March 1975 [1], it will be considered a reference amount within the meaning of Point 37 of this Agreement.

39. The financial statement provided for in Article 28 of the Financial Regulation will reflect in financial terms the objectives of the proposed programme and include a schedule covering the duration of the programme. It will be revised, where necessary, when the preliminary draft budget is drawn up, taking account of the extent of implementation of the programme. The revised statement will be forwarded to the budgetary authority when the preliminary draft budget is presented and after the budget is adopted.

40. Within the maximum rates of increase for non-compulsory expenditure specified in the first paragraph of Point 13, the two arms of the budgetary authority undertake to respect the allocations of commitment appropriations provided for in the relevant basic acts for structural operations, rural development and the European Fund for fisheries.

F. Expenditure relating to fisheries agreements

41. The institutions agree to finance expenditure on fisheries agreements in accordance with the arrangements set out in Annex IV.

---

[1] OJ C 89, 22.4.1975, p. 1.

G. Financing of the common foreign and security policy (CFSP)

42. As regards CFSP expenditure which is charged to the general budget of the European Communities in accordance with Article 28 of the Treaty on European Union, the institutions will endeavour, in the conciliation procedure provided for in Annex II, Part C, and on the basis of the preliminary draft budget established by the Commission, to secure agreement each year on the amount of the operating expenditure to be charged to the Community budget and on the distribution of this amount between the articles of the CFSP budget chapter suggested in the fourth paragraph of this Point. In the absence of agreement, it is understood that the European Parliament and the Council will enter in the budget the amount contained in the previous budget or the amount proposed in the preliminary draft budget, whichever is the lower.

The total amount of operating CFSP expenditure will be entered entirely in one budget chapter (CFSP) and distributed between the articles of that chapter as suggested in the fourth paragraph of this Point. That amount is to cover the real predictable needs, assessed in the framework of the establishment of the preliminary draft budget, on the basis of forecasts drawn up annually by the Council, and a reasonable margin for unforeseen actions. No funds will be entered in a reserve. Each article will cover instruments already adopted, instruments which are foreseen but not yet adopted and all future — that is unforeseen — instruments to be adopted by the Council during the financial year concerned.

Since, under the Financial Regulation, the Commission has the authority to transfer appropriations autonomously between articles within the CFSP budget chapter, the flexibility deemed necessary for speedy implementation of CFSP actions will accordingly be assured. In the event of the amount of the CFSP budget chapter during the financial year being insufficient to cover the necessary expenses, the European Parliament and the Council will seek a solution as a matter of urgency, on a proposal from the Commission, taking into account Point 25.

Within the CFSP budget chapter, the articles into which the CFSP actions are to be entered could read along the following lines:

— crisis management operations, conflict prevention, resolution and stabilisation, monitoring and implementation of peace and security processes,

— non-proliferation and disarmament,

— emergency measures,

— preparatory and follow-up measures,

— European Union Special Representatives.

The institutions agree that at least EUR 1 740 million will be available for the CFSP over the period 2007-2013 and that the amount for measures entered under the article

mentioned in the third indent may not exceed 20 % of the overall amount of the CFSP budget chapter.

43. Each year, the Council Presidency will consult the European Parliament on a forward-looking Council document, which will be transmitted by June 15 for the year in question, setting out the main aspects and basic choices of the CFSP, including the financial implications for the general budget of the European Union and an evaluation of the measures launched in the year n-1. Furthermore, the Council Presidency will keep the European Parliament informed by holding joint consultation meetings at least five times a year, in the framework of the regular political dialogue on the CFSP, to be agreed at the latest at the conciliation meeting to be held before the Council's second reading. Participation in these meetings shall be as follows:

— European Parliament: the bureaux of the two Committees concerned,

— Council: Ambassador (Chairman of the Political and Security Committee),

— The Commission will be associated and participate at these meetings.

Whenever it adopts a decision in the field of the CFSP entailing expenditure, the Council will immediately, and in any event no later than five working days following the final decision, send the European Parliament an estimate of the costs envisaged ('financial statement'), in particular those regarding time-frame, staff employed, use of premises and other infrastructure, transport facilities, training requirements and security arrangements.

Once a quarter the Commission will inform the budgetary authority about the implementation of CFSP actions and the financial forecasts for the remaining period of the year.

PART III

SOUND FINANCIAL MANAGEMENT OF EU FUNDS

A. Ensuring effective and integrated internal control of Community funds

44. The institutions agree on the importance of strengthening internal control without adding to the administrative burden for which the simplification of the underlying legislation is a prerequisite. In this context, priority will be given to sound financial management aiming at a positive Statement of Assurance, for funds under shared management. Provisions to this end could be laid down, as appropriate, in the basic legislative acts concerned. As part of their enhanced responsibilities for structural funds and in accordance with national constitutional requirements, the relevant audit authorities in Member States will produce an assessment concerning the compliance of management and control systems with the regulations of the Community.

C 139/8   EN   Official Journal of the European Union   14.6.2006

Member States therefore undertake to produce an annual summary at the appropriate national level of the available audits and declarations.

B. Financial Regulation

45. The institutions agree that this Agreement and the budget will be implemented in a context of sound financial management based on the principles of economy, efficiency, effectiveness, protection of financial interests, proportionality of administrative costs, and user-friendly procedures. The institutions will take appropriate measures, in particular in the Financial Regulation, that should be adopted in accordance with the conciliation procedure established by the Joint Declaration of the European Parliament, the Council and the Commission of 4 March 1975, in the spirit which enabled agreement in 2002.

C. Financial Programming

46. The Commission will submit twice a year, the first time in May/June (together with the documents accompanying the preliminary draft budget) and the second time in December/January (after the adoption of the budget), a complete financial programming for Headings 1A, 2 (for environment and fisheries), 3A, 3B and 4 of the financial framework. This document, structured by heading, policy area and budget line, should identify:

(a) the legislation in force, with a distinction being drawn between multiannual programmes and annual actions:

— for multiannual programmes the Commission should indicate the procedure under which they were adopted (codecision and consultation), their duration, the reference amounts, the share allocated to administrative expenditure;

— for annual actions (pilot projects, preparatory actions, Agencies) and actions financed under the prerogatives of the Commission, the Commission should provide multiannual estimates and (for pilot projects and preparatory actions) the margins left under the authorised ceilings fixed in Annex II, Part D;

(b) pending legislative proposals: ongoing Commission proposals referenced by budget line (lower level), chapter and policy area. A mechanism should be found to update the tables each time a new proposal is adopted in order to evaluate the financial consequences.

The Commission should consider ways of cross-referencing the financial programming with its legislative programming to provide more precise and reliable forecasts. For each legislative proposal, the Commission should indicate whether or not it is included in the May-December programme. The budgetary authority should in particular be informed of:

(a) all new legislative acts adopted but not included in the May-December document (with the corresponding amounts);

(b) all pending legislative proposals presented but not included in the May-December document (with the corresponding amounts);

(c) legislation foreseen in the Commission's annual legislative work programme with an indication of actions likely to have a financial impact (yes/no).

Whenever necessary, the Commission should indicate the reprogramming entailed by new legislative proposals.

On the basis of the data supplied by the Commission, stocktaking should be carried out at each trilogue as provided for in this Agreement.

D. Agencies and European Schools

47. When drawing up its proposal for the creation of any new agency, the Commission will assess the budgetary implications for the expenditure heading concerned. On the basis of that information and without prejudice to the legislative procedures governing the setting up of the agency, the two arms of the budgetary authority commit themselves, in the framework of budgetary cooperation, to arrive at a timely agreement on the financing of the agency.

A similar procedure is to be applied when the creation of a new European school is envisaged.

E. Adjustment of Structural Funds, Cohesion Fund, Rural Development and the European Fund for Fisheries in the light of the circumstances of their implementation

48. In the event of the adoption after 1 January 2007 of new rules or programmes governing the Structural Funds, the Cohesion Fund, Rural Development and the European Fund for Fisheries, the two arms of the budgetary authority undertake to authorise, on a proposal from the Commission, the transfer to subsequent years, in excess of the corresponding expenditure ceilings, of allocations not used in 2007.

The European Parliament and the Council will take decisions on Commission proposals concerning the transfer of unused allocations for the year 2007 before 1 May 2008, in accordance with Point 3.

F. New financial instruments

49. The institutions agree that the introduction of co-financing mechanisms is necessary to reinforce the leverage effect of the European Union budget by increasing the funding incentive.

They agree to encourage the development of appropriate multiannual financial instruments acting as catalysts for public and private investors.

When presenting the preliminary draft budget, the Commission will report to the budgetary authority on the activities financed by the European Investment Bank, the European Investment Fund and the European Bank for Reconstruction and Development to support investment in research and development, trans-European networks and small and medium-sized enterprises.

Done at Strasbourg, 17 May 2006.

For the European Parliament	*For the Council*	*For the Commission*
The President	*The President*	D. GRYBAUSKAITĖ
J. BORRELL FONTELLES	W. SCHÜSSEL	*Member of the Commission*

———

C 139/10   EN   Official Journal of the European Union   14.6.2006

ANNEX I

Financial Framework 2007-2013

(EUR million — 2004 prices)

Commitment appropriations	2007	2008	2009	2010	2011	2012	2013	Total 2007-2013
1. **Sustainable Growth**	**51 267**	**52 415**	**53 616**	**54 294**	**55 368**	**56 876**	**58 303**	**382 139**
1a Competitiveness for Growth and Employment	8 404	9 097	9 754	10 434	11 295	12 153	12 961	74 098
1b Cohesion for Growth and Employment	42 863	43 318	43 862	43 860	44 073	44 723	45 342	308 041
2. **Preservation and Management of Natural Resources**	**54 985**	**54 322**	**53 666**	**53 035**	**52 400**	**51 775**	**51 161**	**371 344**
of which: market related expenditure and direct payments	43 120	42 697	42 279	41 864	41 453	41 047	40 645	293 105
3. **Citizenship, freedom, security and justice**	**1 199**	**1 258**	**1 380**	**1 503**	**1 645**	**1 797**	**1 988**	**10 770**
3a. Freedom, Security and Justice	600	690	790	910	1 050	1 200	1 390	6 630
3b. Citizenship	599	568	590	593	595	597	598	4 140
4. **EU as a global player**	**6 199**	**6 469**	**6 739**	**7 009**	**7 339**	**7 679**	**8 029**	**49 463**
5. **Administration** (¹)	**6 633**	**6 818**	**6 973**	**7 111**	**7 255**	**7 400**	**7 610**	**49 800**
6. **Compensations**	**419**	**191**	**190**					**800**
Total commitment appropriations	**120 702**	**121 473**	**122 564**	**122 952**	**124 007**	**125 527**	**127 091**	**864 316**
as a percentage of GNI	1,10 %	1,08 %	1,07 %	1,04 %	1,03 %	1,02 %	1,01 %	1,048 %
Total payment appropriations	**116 650**	**119 620**	**111 990**	**118 280**	**115 860**	**119 410**	**118 970**	**820 780**
as a percentage of GNI	1,06 %	1,06 %	0,97 %	1,00 %	0,96 %	0,97 %	0,94 %	1,00 %
Margin available	0,18 %	0,18 %	0,27 %	0,24 %	0,28 %	0,27 %	0,30 %	0,24 %
Own Resources Ceiling as a percentage of GNI	1,24 %	1,24 %	1,24 %	1,24 %	1,24 %	1,24 %	1,24 %	1,24 %

(¹) The expenditure on pensions included under the ceiling for this heading is calculated net of the staff contributions to the relevant scheme, within the limit of EUR 500 million at 2004 prices for the period 2007-2013.

14.6.2006   EN   Official Journal of the European Union   C 139/11

ANNEX II

Interinstitutional collaboration in the budgetary sector

A. After the technical adjustment of the financial framework for the forthcoming financial year, taking into account the Annual Policy Strategy presented by the Commission and prior to its decision on the preliminary draft budget, a meeting of the trilogue will be convened to discuss the possible priorities for the budget of that year. Due account will be taken of the institutions' powers as well as the foreseeable development of the needs for the financial year to come and for the following years covered by the financial framework. Account will also be taken of new elements which have arisen since the establishment of the initial financial framework and which are likely to have a significant and lasting financial impact on the budget of the European Union.

B. As regards compulsory expenditure, the Commission, in presenting its preliminary draft budget, will identify:

(a) appropriations connected with new or planned legislation;

(b) appropriations arising from the application of legislation existing when the previous budget was adopted.

The Commission will make a careful estimate of the financial implications of the Community's obligations based on the rules. If necessary, it will update its estimates in the course of the budgetary procedure. It will supply the budgetary authority with all the duly justified reasons it may require.

If it considers it necessary, the Commission may present to the two arms of the budgetary authority an ad hoc letter of amendment to update the figures underlying the estimate of agricultural expenditure in the preliminary draft budget and/or to correct, on the basis of the most recent information available concerning fisheries agreements in force on 1 January of the financial year concerned, the amounts and their breakdown between the appropriations entered in the operational items for international fisheries agreements and those entered in reserve.

That letter of amendment must be sent to the budgetary authority before the end of October.

If it is presented to the Council less than one month before the European Parliament's first reading, the Council will, as a rule, consider the ad hoc letter of amendment when giving the draft budget its second reading.

As a consequence, before the Council's second reading of the budget, the two arms of the budgetary authority will try to meet the conditions necessary for the letter of amendment to be adopted on a single reading by each of the institutions concerned.

C. 1. A conciliation procedure is set up for all expenditure.

2. The purpose of the conciliation procedure is to:

(a) continue discussions on the general trend of expenditure and, in this framework, on the broad lines of the budget for the coming year in the light of the Commission's preliminary draft budget;

(b) secure agreement between the two arms of the budgetary authority on:

— the appropriations referred to in Points (a) and (b) of Part B, including those proposed in the ad hoc letter of amendment referred to that Part,

— the amounts to be entered in the budget for non-compulsory expenditure, in accordance with Point 40 of this Agreement, and

— in particular, matters for which reference to this procedure is made in this Agreement.

3. The procedure will begin with a trilogue meeting convened in time to allow the institutions to seek an agreement by no later than the date set by the Council for establishing its draft budget.

There will be conciliation on the results of this trilogue between the Council and a European Parliament delegation, with the Commission also taking part.

Unless decided otherwise during the trilogue, the conciliation meeting will be held at the traditional meeting between the same participants on the date set by the Council for establishing the draft budget.

4. If necessary, a new trilogue meeting could be held before the European Parliament's first reading on a written proposal by the Commission or a written request by either the chairman of the European Parliament's Committee on Budgets or the President of the Council (Budgets). The decision whether to hold this trilogue will be agreed between the institutions after the adoption of the Council draft budget and prior to the vote on the amendments at first reading by the European Parliament's Committee on Budgets.

C 139/12   EN   Official Journal of the European Union   14.6.2006

5. The institutions will continue the conciliation after the first reading of the budget by each of the two arms of the budgetary authority in order to secure agreement on compulsory and non-compulsory expenditure and, in particular, to discuss the ad hoc letter of amendment referred to in Part B.

A trilogue meeting will be held for this purpose after the European Parliament's first reading.

The results of the trilogue will be discussed at a second conciliation meeting to be held on the day of the Council's second reading.

If necessary, the institutions will continue their discussions on non-compulsory expenditure after the Council's second reading.

6. At those trilogue meetings, the institutions' delegations will be led by the President of the Council (Budgets), the Chairman of the European Parliament Committee's on Budgets and the Member of the Commission responsible for the budget.

7. Each arm of the budgetary authority will take whatever steps are required to ensure that the results which may be secured in the conciliation process are respected throughout the budgetary procedure.

D. In order for the Commission to be able to assess in due time the implementability of amendments envisaged by the budgetary authority which create new preparatory actions/pilot projects or prolong existing ones, both arms of the budgetary authority will inform the Commission by mid-June of their intentions in this regard, so that a first discussion may already take place at the conciliation meeting of the Council's first reading. The next steps of the conciliation procedure provided for in Part C will also apply, as well as the provisions on implementability mentioned in Point 36 of this Agreement.

Furthermore, the institutions agree to limit the total amount of appropriations for pilot schemes to EUR 40 million in any budget year. They also agree to limit to EUR 50 million the total amount of appropriations for new preparatory actions in any budget year, and to EUR 100 million the total amount of appropriations actually committed for preparatory actions.

———

14.6.2006 [EN] Official Journal of the European Union C 139/13

ANNEX III

Classification of expenditure

HEADING 1	Sustainable growth	
1A	Competitiveness for growth and employment	Non-compulsory expenditure (NCE)
1B	Cohesion for growth and employment	NCE
HEADING 2	Preservation and management of natural resources	NCE
	Except:	
	— Expenditure of the common agricultural policy concerning market measures and direct aids, including market measures for fisheries and fisheries agreements concluded with third parties	Compulsory expenditure (CE)
HEADING 3	Citizenship, freedom, security and justice	NCE
3A	Freedom, Security and Justice	NCE
3B	Citizenship	NCE
HEADING 4	EU as a global player	NCE
	Except:	
	— Expenditure resulting from international agreements which the European Union concluded with third parties	CE
	— Contributions to international organisations or institutions	CE
	— Contributions provisioning the loan guarantee fund	CE
HEADING 5	Administration	NCE
	Except:	
	— Pensions and severance grants	CE
	— Allowances and miscellaneous contributions on termination of service	CE
	— Legal expenses	CE
	— Damages	CE
HEADING 6	Compensations	CE

C 139/14   EN   Official Journal of the European Union   14.6.2006

ANNEX IV

Financing of expenditure deriving from fisheries agreements

A. Expenditure relating to fisheries agreements is financed by two items belonging to the 'fisheries' policy area (by reference to the activity based budget nomenclature):

(a) international fisheries agreements (11 03 01);

(b) contributions to international organisations (11 03 02).

All the amounts relating to agreements and protocols which are in force on 1 January of the year in question will be entered under heading 11 03 01. Amounts relating to all new or renewable agreements which come into force after 1 January of the year in question will be assigned to heading 40 02 41 02 — Reserves/Differentiated appropriations (compulsory expenditure).

B. In the conciliation procedure provided for in Annex II, Part C, the European Parliament and the Council will seek to agree on the amount to be entered in the budget headings and in the reserve on the basis of the proposal made by the Commission.

C. The Commission undertakes to keep the European Parliament regularly informed about the preparation and conduct of the negotiations, including the budgetary implications.

In the course of the legislative process relating to fisheries agreements, the institutions undertake to make every effort to ensure that all procedures are carried out as quickly as possible.

If appropriations relating to fisheries agreements (including the reserve) prove insufficient, the Commission will provide the budgetary authority with the necessary information for an exchange of views in the form of a trilogue, possibly simplified, on the causes of the situation, and on the measures which might be adopted under established procedures. Where necessary, the Commission will propose appropriate measures.

Each quarter the Commission will present to the budgetary authority detailed information about the implementation of agreements in force and financial forecasts for the remainder of the year.

DECLARATIONS

1. DECLARATION OF THE COMMISSION ON THE ASSESSMENT OF THE FUNCTIONING OF THE INTERINSTITU-TIONAL AGREEMENT

In relation to Point 7 of the Interinstitutional Agreement, the Commission will prepare a report on the functioning of the Interinstitutional Agreement by the end of 2009 accompanied, if necessary, by relevant proposals.

2. DECLARATION ON POINT 27 OF THE INTERINSTITUTIONAL AGREEMENT

Within the framework of the annual budgetary procedure, the Commission will inform the budgetary authority of the amount available for the Flexibility Instrument referred to in Point 27 of the Interinstitutional Agreement.

Any decision to mobilise the Flexibility Instrument for an amount exceeding EUR 200 million will imply a carry-forward decision.

3. DECLARATION ON THE REVIEW OF THE FINANCIAL FRAMEWORK

1. In accordance with the conclusions of the European Council, the Commission has been invited to undertake a full, wide-ranging review covering all aspects of EU spending, including the Common Agricultural Policy, and of resources, including the United Kingdom rebate, and to report in 2008/2009. That review should be accompanied by an assessment of the functioning of the Interinstitutional Agreement. The European Parliament will be associated with the review at all stages of the procedure on the basis of the following provisions:

— during the examination phase following the presentation of the review by the Commission, it will be ensured that appropriate discussions take place with the European Parliament on the basis of the normal political dialogue between the institutions and that the positions of the European Parliament are duly taken into account,

— in accordance with its conclusions of December 2005, the European Council 'can take decisions on all the subjects covered by the review'. The European Parliament will be part of any formal follow-up steps, in accordance with the relevant procedures and in full respect of its established rights.

2. The Commission undertakes, as part of the process of consultation and reflection leading up to the establishment of the review, to draw on the in-depth exchange of views it will conduct with European Parliament when analysing the situation. The Commission also takes note of the European Parliament's intention to call for a conference involving the European Parliament and the national parliaments to review the own-resources system. It will consider the outcome of any such conference as a contribution in the framework of that consultation process. It is understood that the Commission's proposals will be put forward entirely under its own responsibility.

4. DECLARATION ON DEMOCRATIC SCRUTINY AND COHERENCE OF EXTERNAL ACTIONS

The European Parliament, the Council and the Commission acknowledge the need for rationalisation of the various instruments for external actions. They agree that such rationalisation of instruments, while enhancing the coherence and the responsiveness of European Union action, should not affect the powers of either the legislative authority –notably in its political control of strategic choices — or the budgetary authority. The text of the relevant regulations should reflect those principles and include where appropriate the necessary policy content and an indicative breakdown of resources and, where necessary, a review clause aiming at evaluating the implementation of the regulation, after three years at the latest.

Under the basic legislative acts adopted under the codecision procedure, the Commission will systematically inform and consult the European Parliament and the Council by sending draft country, regional and thematic strategy papers.

Where the Council decides on the transition of potential candidates to pre-accession status during the period covered by the Interinstitutional Agreement, the Commission will revise and communicate to the European Parliament and the Council an indicative multi-annual framework according to Article 4 of the Regulation establishing an Instrument for Pre-Accession Assistance (IPA) to take account of the expenditure requirements resulting from such a transition.

C 139/16   EN   Official Journal of the European Union   14.6.2006

The Commission will provide in the preliminary draft budget a nomenclature which ensures the prerogatives of the budgetary authority for external actions.

5. DECLARATION OF THE COMMISSION ON THE DEMOCRATIC SCRUTINY AND COHERENCE OF EXTERNAL ACTIONS

The Commission undertakes to enter into a regular dialogue with the European Parliament on the content of the draft country, regional and thematic strategy papers and to take due account of the position of the European Parliament when implementing the strategies.

That dialogue will include a discussion on the transition of potential candidates to pre-accession status during the period covered by the Interinstitutional Agreement.

6. DECLARATION ON THE REVISION OF THE FINANCIAL REGULATION

Within the framework of the revision of the Financial Regulation the institutions commit themselves to improve implementation of the budget and increase the visibility and the benefit of Community funding towards the citizens without calling in question the progress achieved in the 2002 recasting of the Financial Regulation. They will also seek, as far as possible, during the final stage of the negotiations on the revision of the Financial Regulation and its Implementing Rules, the right balance between the protection of financial interests, the principle of proportionality of administrative costs, and user-friendly procedures.

The revision of the Financial Regulation will be carried out on the basis of a modified proposal from the Commission in accordance with the conciliation procedure established by the Joint Declaration of the European Parliament, the Council and the Commission of 4 March 1975, in the spirit which enabled agreement in 2002. The institutions will also seek close and constructive interinstitutional cooperation for the swift adoption of the Implementing Rules in order to simplify procedures for funding whilst ensuring a high level of protection of the Community's financial interests.

The European Parliament and the Council are firmly committed to concluding the negotiations on the Financial Regulation so as to allow its entry into force, if possible, on 1 January 2007.

7. DECLARATION OF THE COMMISSION ON THE REVISION OF THE FINANCIAL REGULATION

Within the framework of revision of the Financial Regulation, the Commission commits itself:

— to inform the European Parliament and the Council if, in a proposal for a legal act, it considers it necessary to depart from the provisions of the Financial Regulation, and to state the specific reasons for it;

— to ensure that regular legislative impact assessments, having due regard to the principles of subsidiarity and proportionality, are conducted on important legislative proposals and any substantive amendments thereof.

8. DECLARATION ON NEW FINANCIAL INSTRUMENTS

The European Parliament and the Council invite the Commission and the European Investment Bank (EIB), in their respective spheres of competence, to make proposals:

— in accordance with the conclusions of the European Council of December 2005, to increase the EIB's capacity for research and development loans and guarantees up to EUR 10 billion in the period 2007-2013, with an EIB contribution of up to EUR 1 billion from reserves for risk-sharing financing;

— to reinforce the instruments in favour of Trans-European Networks (TENs) and Small and Medium-sized Enterprises up to an approximate amount of loans and guarantees of EUR 20 billion and EUR 30 billion, respectively, with an EIB contribution of up to EUR 0,5 billion from reserves (TENs) and up to EUR 1 billion (Competitiveness and Innovation) respectively.

14.6.2006   [EN]   Official Journal of the European Union   C 139/17

9. DECLARATION OF THE EUROPEAN PARLIAMENT ON VOLUNTARY MODULATION

The European Parliament takes note of the conclusions of the European Council of December 2005 concerning voluntary modulation from market-related expenditure and direct payments of the Common Agricultural Policy to rural development up to a maximum of 20 % and the reductions for market-related expenditure. When the modalities of this modulation are laid down in the relevant legal acts, the European Parliament will evaluate the feasibility of these provisions in respect of EU principles, such as competition rules and others; the European Parliament currently reserves its position on the outcome of the procedure. It considers it would be useful to assess the issue of co-financing of agriculture in the context of the 2008-09 review.

10. DECLARATION OF THE COMMISSION ON VOLUNTARY MODULATION

The Commission takes note of Point 62 of the conclusions of the European Council of December 2005 whereby Member States may transfer additional sums from market-related expenditure and direct payments of the Common Agricultural Policy to Rural Development up to a maximum of 20 % of the amounts that accrue to them from market-related expenditure and direct payments.

When laying down the modalities of this modulation in the relevant legal acts, the Commission will endeavour to make voluntary modulation possible whilst making all efforts to ensure that such a mechanism reflects as closely as possible the basic rules governing the rural development policy.

11. DECLARATION OF THE EUROPEAN PARLIAMENT ON NATURA 2000

The European Parliament expresses its concern about the conclusions of the European Council of December 2005 relating to the reduction of the market-related expenditure and direct payments of the Common Agricultural Policy and its consequences on Community co-financing of Natura 2000. It invites the Commission to evaluate the consequences of these provisions before making new proposals. It considers that appropriate priority should be given to the integration of Natura 2000 in Structural Funds and Rural Development. As part of the legislative authority, it currently reserves it position on the outcome of the procedure.

12. DECLARATION OF THE EUROPEAN PARLIAMENT ON PRIVATE CO-FINANCING AND VAT FOR COHESION FOR GROWTH AND EMPLOYMENT

The European Parliament takes note of the conclusion of the European Council of December 2005 on the application of the N+3 automatic decommitment rule on a transitional basis; the European Parliament invites the Commission, when the latter lays down in the relevant legal acts the modalities for the application of this rule, to ensure common rules for private co-financing and VAT for cohesion for growth and employment.

13. DECLARATION OF THE EUROPEAN PARLIAMENT ON FINANCING THE AREA OF FREEDOM, SECURITY AND JUSTICE

The European Parliament considers that when presenting the preliminary draft budget the Commission should give a careful estimate of planned activities for Freedom, Security and Justice, and that the financing of these activities should be discussed in the framework of the procedures provided for in Annex II to the Interinstitutional Agreement.

European Commission

European Union Public Finance — Fourth edition

Luxembourg: Office for Official Publications of the European Communities

2008 — 427 pp. — 14.8 X 21 cm

ISBN 978-92-79-06937-6

Price (excluding VAT) in Luxembourg: EUR 30